JOHN CORNELIUS

His Life and Adventures

Hugh Walpole

Sir Hugh Seymour Walpole, CBE was an English novelist. He was the son of an Anglican clergyman, intended for a career in the church but drawn instead to writing. Among those who encouraged him were the authors Henry James and Arnold Bennett.

Born: March 13, 1884, Auckland, New Zealand

Died: June 1, 1941, Keswick, United Kingdom

Description:

"John Cornelius: His Life and Adventures" by Hugh Walpole. Published by Good Press. Good Press publishes a wide range of titles that encompasses every genre. From well-known classics & literary fiction and non-fiction to forgotten–or yet undiscovered gems–of world literature, we issue the books that need to be read. ...

Originally published: 1937

Content:

PART I: SEA AND LAND

CHAPTER I

At the Age of Five His Adventures Were Numerous; There Were

the Ducklings; Also His Father and Mother

His mother was the daughter of William Baring, proprietor of the White Horse Inn at Caerlyn Sands. Baring, from all I ever heard, must have been a grand, boasting, foolish character, famous locally and known even in distant parts of Glebeshire.

I have seen a brown faded daguerreotype of himself and his wife, she a small mean-faced woman with a tight mouth and with a locket almost as large as her face hanging on her meagre bosom. He greatly took my eye, big as an ox and dressed, for the occasion of the photograph, in awkward Sunday clothes, but his eyes were open and frank, his mouth strong and smiling. He carried in his hand one of those old top-hats with a broad and curling brim. Across his great spreading waistcoat was a vast gold watch-chain and against his trouser a fine swaggering fob.

He looked as though he could swallow his mean little wife at a mouthful, but of course it wasn't so. She swallowed him. For a time things went well with him. He made the 'White Horse' pay and was the best wrestler and boxer in North Glebeshire; a good cricketer too, I believe. Then horses were too much for him. He went to the races at Drymouth, drank more than he should, neglected his home (I should fancy out of distaste for Mrs. Baring).

He was killed in a drunken fight in Drymouth, and his widow, with her four children, went to Polchester to live with a sister. They ran a small dressmaking business there and did fairly well with it. Of the two boys, Cornelius' uncles, one went to sea, the other died in the South of Spain somewhere.

Daisy Baring, Cornelius' mother, must have been a most beautiful girl. In a faded photograph of her she is standing straight up, in her ridiculous ugly

clothes, her head proudly erect, looking out into the world with an eagerness that seemed to expect, even to demand, anything and everything of it. Her eyes remind me of her son's, filled with expectation, almost merry anticipation.

She is tall and of fine carriage in this picture of her, strong- boned, firm-

flanked, peasant stock, radiant with health. Soon she was stout and, later on, grossly fat. Laughing. Courageous. Hardworking. Stupid. Yes, I am sure that that was Daisy Cornelius.

As a little girl she hated Polchester where, after her father's death, she lived with her mother, her aunt and her brothers and sister. They lived in a poky little house beside the river at the bottom of Orange Street. She told John again and again of the Cathedral bells, the mist rising from the river, the cows lowing and the sheep bleating on market-days and the fluffy pieces of cloth and calico lying about from the dressmaking.

She was always a country girl; she hated the town and her aunt; she would long passionately for her grand, broad-chested, brave, horse- riding father.

She quarrelled with her aunt although she was really so good-tempered and warm-hearted, but her aunt was mean and meagre like her mother. So she went into the country to work on a farm, and there she met John's father who was a gentleman and owned Penny Hall, an ironic name because he and his little bow-legged father hadn't a farthing between them.

John never saw Penny Hall where his grandfather lived. When he was grown-up and went to look for it it was gone; nothing left of it, only the rooks' nests in the trees and the smell of dog-roses and, very faintly, the echo behind echo of the sea like a woman sighing or, when the wind was right, an old man heavily snoring.

All the same, although John never saw Penny Hall, it was there as part of his life until he died. The Cornelius family had lived in it for hundreds and hundreds of years, ever since Hans Cornelius, the Dane, built it in thirteen hundred and something. He was a Danish sailor wrecked on the coast in a storm. He made money breeding horses and married a Glebeshire girl and built that little house in the middle of the thick trees with the rooks cawing and the echo of the sea that had tried to drown him coming across the road

like an old man's snore just as it did hundreds of years later.

There they stayed, the Corneliuses, and turned into gentlemen, and one was killed at Bosworth Field and another served at Court in Henry VII's time and one went with Raleigh on the sea, and one was killed at Sedgemoor and one was a poet in Queen Anne's days.

At last all that they were was the little bow-legged man, John's grandfather, who was always a bit queer in the head but, all the same, never found what he wanted in life.

They sold Penny Hall and lost what they got from it through unwise speculation and a scoundrelly lawyer. John's grandfather lost his wits altogether and went to the Asylum at Port Merlin, and John's grandmother lived in a cottage near the Asylum so that she might be close to him. John's father and mother also lived in Port Merlin, where John's mother did laundry-

work and John's father painted pictures and made seashell boxes and toys which he sold when he was lucky enough. Daisy Cornelius' mother, now a shrivelled bitter little piece of needle and thread, died in Polchester, which was a good thing for everybody.

Port Merlin was, in those days in the 'eighties, a very interesting little town; everything that John had and was and afterwards did came from that place.

He talked of it so often to myself and everyone else that I can only see it with his eyes; it is of no use to say that the Port Merlin I now write of is not the Port Merlin that anyone can go to to-day in a train or motor-car. Of course it is not: John's Port Merlin will never be seen by anyone again.

Once upon a time—a phrase that will rightly recur often in Cornelius' story—

Merlin was one of the two principal seaports of Glebeshire, Drymouth being the other one. It supplied ships and men for Elizabeth's navy, and even in Nelson's time shipbuilding still had its place there. After the Reform Bill it sank into an undisturbed domestic peace, but, throughout the nineteenth century, it kept many of its old features, the Town Hall with the clock that has the brass figures playing the drum and fife, the Theatre with the red and gold decorations and the famous paintings of Venus and Adonis, the Penitentiary outside whose grey wall the old women on sunny days would sit

and sew, the Church of St. Mark and St. Luke with the Wrecked Mariners'

Pulpit, the stocks in the Market-place, and Seamen's Row, perhaps the oldest line of tumble-down cottages in England.

Some of these things are still there, but as with Treliss and other little Glebeshire and Cornish towns modern advertisement, modern tourists, modern traffic, have covered over the old loveliness with a new bustling life and trade, whether for final loss or profit who will be able to say until the Last Trump shall sound?

But the beautiful Theatre, the mother and father of Cornelius' art, is gone, the old houses of Seamen's Row where Mother Propit the witch once lived and the ghost of John Curley, the Demon Sailor, haunted are replaced with red-

brick villas, there is a car park where the stocks once stood, and the old women sew no longer outside the Penitentiary.

But it must have been very much as it had been for three hundred years on May 12th, 1884, the sunny morning when John Cornelius was born. Two sounds he remembers as beating concurrently and consistently on his ears from the very first—the swish and roll of the sea only a step or two away, and the wind singing through the wallpaper....

Then as now the sea dominated the town; not time nor the constant inventions of restless man can affect that. From the very beginning John was carried and settled in the sheltered corner of the sea-wall where he could be out of the way, and his twinkling, lively, humorous, expectant eyes would look out to the Lion Rock— shaped like a lioness, her three cubs nestled at her side—

where seals often were and on stormy days you could see the white tongues of the sea rise and fall through the mist and spume. In good weather he would gather into his very soul the deep purple shadows streaked with ebony, and the green glassy fields of clear water and the long line of mother-of-pearl created by the sun from the wet sand.

From the very beginning John, like every other Port Merlin child, breathed the sea, in all its moods and habits, into his very soul, and that is why so many of the stories—The Mermaid who lost her Comb, The Crab with the Broken Claw, The Big Seal and the Little

Seal, The Fisherman and his Three Sons—have the very sound and smell of the sea in every line of them.

But John Cornelius, from the start, had an endless curiosity and wonder about his fellow human beings so that the town was very soon as important to him as the sea. It must have been from very very early years that his father began to take him about with him everywhere. There was but very little room for him in the small overcrowded cottage.

His mother never had any of the gifts of tidiness or natural arrangement of things, nor, I fear, had she a passion for cleanliness. The three rooms all smelt alike of steaming clothes, and always Daisy Cornelius was behindhand with her laundry and meals were not prepared, beds not made, nothing brushed or put away. Daisy Cornelius did not mind the confusion, and stout, red-faced, perspiring, would be always in a bustle, always despairing because things were not done, always amazed at the muddle of life, always cheerful except when she had drunk a drop too much and then her temper was uncertain.

It was natural enough then that John's father should be most of his time out of doors and, as soon as he could walk, little John would be with him. Even before that, father Cornelius (who was a small man) would carry the child to some safe and warm place and then, sitting there, would paint his pictures or the lids of his shell-boxes or read aloud from Shakespeare or chat with neighbours or talk to his son about Penny Hall and the old days when he was a gentleman and went to dances in the family carriage.

John was a very ugly baby and soon grew into a yet more ugly boy. He developed almost at once that long and gawky body that would one day be well known. I have seen a cheap bad photograph of him when he was five or so, standing with his hand on a plush-covered table, a large white pillar and a storm-rolling sea in the background. He is wearing a sailor suit far too small for him so that his bony wrists project awkwardly from the sleeves, and his lanky legs with the thin ankles have little to say to the trousers that cover them. On his head is a ridiculous kind of jockey-cap, a prophecy of the curious hats that in later years so uncertainly failed to cover his head. There is here his sharp bony nose, his loose large mouth, here too his beautiful, lively eyes and the expression of sweetness and friendliness to all the world that led him into so many friendships, so many errors, so many misunderstandings.

'What a hideous, attractive child!' you might say, looking at this photograph.

'I am fortunate,' he once said to me, 'to have had so many friends in my life,

being, I suppose, the ugliest man in the world.' And then his impossibly childlike vanity would, of course, come in. 'But what a charming ugliness!'

Merlin in those days was a kind of family affair, everyone knew everyone else. Snobbish it was, as all small English towns were and are and always will be. Merlin's snobbishness was of a very special variety, for the great family of the West-Darlings still made it their headquarters. There was the Great House on the hill above the town, and Sir George West-Darling in his carriage with the two white horses, and Lady West-

Darling, very like Queen Victoria both in regal dignity and homely maternal care for those whom she called her 'people.'

One of John's very first public appearances was on the occasion when he was all but run over by the West–Darling carriage. He remembers the metal of the harness flashing in the sun and one great white horse rearing. He had run out into the middle of the street to see the man strike the drum on the Town Hall clock. The hour was three, and as the bell sounded the sea rushed in from the edge of the sky, the great white legs of the horse were raised, there was a cry and a shout. He fell on his face. But he was not hurt. That surely was a miracle and showed him, even if nothing else did, that he was destined for wonderful things.

Covered in dirt he was held in his father's arms while the pseudo– Queen Victoria leant graciously from the carriage and said that it was not the coachman's fault, but nevertheless ...

She was, I am sure, greatly surprised by the strange little boy who, face muddy and chin bleeding, looked at her full of excitement. 'You're a brave little fellow,' she said, and gave him half a crown. Then she drove on. That was the first time that he had held any coin larger than sixpence in his hand.

He gave it at once to his father. Neither then nor ever could he hold on to money. He gave it away as soon as he got it. And his father threw it into the road. He was trembling with rage; it might be the reaction of that moment of horror, of terror when he thought his son was killed.

But he felt that he had been patronized. He saw Penny Hall, the dining–room with the dark-brown panelling, with the sound of the sea and the smell of the

roses and the whirr of the haymaking machine coming in through the window on a fine summer day. I know just how he felt. 'I'm as good as she is. Every bit as good.'

But Johnny didn't care. He never gave the half–crown a thought. He was happy because he had been the centre of attraction. A small crowd had collected, morbidly hoping that there had been a bad accident, but the ugly boy stood there, his clothes and face very dirty, laughing and ready, for twopence, to recite the poem his grandmother had taught him—'Little Nell and the Caged Bird.'

However, his father hurried him away. He was taken home and washed; that evening his father talked and talked—about Penny Hall, the grand family of Cornelius, and the ancestor who had written poetry in the reign of Queen Anne....

For John, Port Merlin was, all his life, a town blazing with colour. When, as a grown man, he returned to it he must have found that it was not so, for all the houses in Glebeshire are grey.

Nevertheless he insisted. The Theatre was red and gold, there were the coloured windows in the Church, there were the booths brilliant with flowers on market-days, there was the shining metal of the clock on the Town Hall.

Perhaps he was right. What we believe to be true is true if we believe it hard enough. About the Theatre especially there could not be colour enough. The playbills were bright yellow with red lettering: sometimes he would see scenery being carried in through the big side door—blue mountains, red houses, and once a Chinese temple....

In his own home there were many bright things. For the first ten years of his life he slept in the front room which served as kitchen, dining-room and laundry. The windows had flowered calico curtains, red roses and green leaves. On his little bed was a rag counterpane, fragments of every possible colour worked into a crazy quilt. The room was steamy with heat; there were pots of mignonette in the windows and the floor was gritty with the sand that people brought in on their boots and shoes from the seashore. On a little table near one window stood the toys and boxes that his father was making, and these were always brilliant in colour, toy soldiers shining with red paint, dolls

with orange skirts and green jackets with silver beads. The boxes were painted crimson and very bright blue, and on to their brilliance the shells, silver and rose- pink and white like snow, were stuck with glue; you could smell the glue, the paint, the mignonette, the sea-sand, the humid damp from the drying clothes. He smelt it, he told me, all his life.

There were two yellow canary birds in a cage hanging in front of one of the windows between the calico curtains and they sang all day long. They had been given to his father once, instead of payment, for some work done.

Although these pleasant friendly things were around him, nevertheless when the candle was blown out and the room was dark save for the ruby glow of the dying fire he would, night after night, lie there fighting his fears. He could hear through the thin door the murmur of the voices of his father and mother, but soon they would die away. He was terrified of the dark and with good reason, for he knew, so very much better than most, of all the strange and fearful inhabitants of the dark. The old women who sewed in the sun outside the Penitentiary, they had many tales to tell him—of the man with one eye who, on a dark night, comes up from the sea across the sand; he has teeth like a dog and sometimes he drops on all-fours and crawls; he scratches on the window-pane with his long nails. Then there is the old woman with a face as black as jet and the white cat on her shoulder. You wake up and see her sitting at the end of the bed, she rolls the whites of her eyes. Her cat stretches itself and then slowly begins to walk across the bed towards you. Also there is the very old man who eats little children. He is shrivelled like a monkey and you can hear him crunching bones with his teeth. There is the policeman, seven feet high, who carries a lantern. He snatches little boys, takes them under his arm and locks them into a prison cell, quite dark, water dripping from the walls and toads crawling across the floor.

Then there were other nightmare figures of whom Cornelius told me; these are all I remember. There were, of course, the good fairies, the kind old woman with a basket full of gold and silver, the mermaids who sang such beautiful songs, the prince who carried you for a ride on his great white charger, the dear old lady with the spinning-wheel, and many more, but these good creatures never came in the dark. Only when there was a moon did they come out and enjoy the fun.

But although he was afraid of the dark all his life long he was not a coward.

He could not help his fear, but he could help surrendering to it. He would lie there, his eyes wide open, his heart hammering, and repeat to himself the prayer that his grandmother had taught him:

'Now I lay me down to sleep,

I give my soul to Christ to keep.

Wake I now or wake I never,

I give my soul to Christ for ever.'

He loved his grandmother, and with justice. She must have been a very sweet old lady. She was small of body, neat and fragile. She liked bright colours, and although she had white hair and was sixty- nine years of age when John was five she seemed always youthful and had great zest and vitality.

She must have been dreadfully poor and often, I suspect, had not enough to eat, because she was too proud to let John's parents know.

She lived in two rooms at the top of the town close to the Asylum. She paid visits to the Asylum twice a day, at ten o'clock in the morning and six in the evening. Whatever her health or the state of the weather she paid her visits just the same. The pathetic thing was that the old man never recognized her as his wife but thought that he was King Solomon and she the Queen of Sheba. He called her always 'Your Majesty' and bowed to her a great deal.

Sometimes his grandmother took John with her on these visits. It did not seem to the little boy, who already lived so much in the world of his imagination, strange to play this game of his grandfather being a mighty king.

The old man, who had a grizzled untidy beard, wore a black skull-cap and a long faded tail-coat, sat in his corner by the fireplace in the long room where the harmless lunatics read books, played games and indulged their fancies.

'Welcome, welcome, Your Majesty,' the old man would cry, his eyes shining with pleasure, and, after a most beautiful curtesy, John's grandmother would sit down close to her husband and tell him all that she had been doing, how that she had picked three primroses in the wood beyond Penrhyn, or that her cat Isabel had caught a baby rabbit, or that she had baked a gingerbread cake and here it was in her basket. It did not seem to the old man at all strange that

the Queen of Sheba should do these things, and he would tell her in return, in a quick whispering voice, of his multitudes of black slaves and the room with the pillars of silver, and how very shortly they would enjoy their meal of roasted peacock and lark's tongues and cakes made of honey and cinnamon.

At the same time he would stretch his old skinny hand towards the gingerbread, but she would not allow him to have it yet because if she did he would eat it all up at once, which would be very bad for his digestion.

He must have been a very dear old man, much more agreeable than the real King Solomon. He had not an evil thought against anyone in the world and was always perfectly happy. They loved him in the Asylum.

John's grandmother was filled with stories and she had the best faculty of a story-teller, that she believed in them all profoundly herself.

'Did that really happen?' John would ask her, his big mouth open, his eyes wide.

'Of course it did,' she would say, nodding her head. 'Don't you believe people when they say things couldn't happen. It's only stupid people who say that.'

'Mother says there aren't such things as unicorns.'

'How does she know?' says John's grandmother scornfully. 'Has she been everywhere? Has she been to Africa?'

'No. She hasn't,' says John.

'Well, then. As a matter of fact she's never been out of England.'

The truth must have been that old Mrs. Cornelius did not get on any too well with her daughter-in-law, and I cannot but feel a certain sympathy for John's mother who had no imagination and was compelled to live with people who suffered perhaps from too much.

Sure enough it is that it was John's mother who had to make a living for all of them because her husband earned but little with his pictures and his shell-

boxes. She was cheerful enough though, and never could grow out of a

feeling of intense gratitude because her husband, being a gentleman, had condescended to marry a simple farm-girl.

She was very garrulous, saying the same thing over and over again and always with the hope that THIS time she would make her meaning plain.

'Oh dear, oh dear, I told him that it was a shilling more that he owed us—yes, a shilling on the two shirts, the one with the blue stripes and the white one with the holes in the sleeves. Two shirts, one with the blue stripes ... '

So she talked on and no one listened, which is the sad lot of all garrulous people.

At the age of five he could not venture by himself, but, his hand in his father's, or trotting along a short way behind him or running ahead and looking back like a little dog to see whether his father were there, he would be always on the move.

He must have had, from the very beginning, that inexhaustible physical energy afterwards so characteristic of him. He was never tired, he told me. To the end of his life he did not know what physical weariness was.

Scenes remained in his mind in bright isolated pictures. And he would say to me: 'The street was so crowded that I'd hold on to father like a monkey. The lights just coming out in the shops, and suddenly as though a door opened you'd get a tang from the sea. The cliffs were at the end of the High Street then. I'd hear the sea and there'd be a musical-box in the shop-window. I remember it quite vividly. It had a shepherd and a shepherdess on the lid. It said "Old Musical-Box: Ten and sixpence" on the card. How I longed to go in and ask the shopman to play it! But what was the use? ... Father and I were obviously unable to pay for it. That was the time' he went on, laughing,

'when I used to steal things. Oh yes, and for years after—I couldn't see what was wrong in it. I'd give anyone anything of mine if they wanted it. Then I discovered you were punished if they caught you. I suppose the game suddenly didn't seem worth the candle. But I've never seen anything very wrong in it.'

A picture that he had most clearly in his mind was a day when there was a

sudden fall of snow. Snow doesn't fall very often in Glebeshire, but on this occasion it was, he fancies, a few days before Christmas.

He'd been longing for the snow to come because Santa Claus preferred reindeer and a sleigh. 'I don't know how old I was before I was finally persuaded that Santa Claus was only a myth. I don't know that I'm really persuaded even now. After all, can't you see every hair in his white beard, track every kindly wrinkle in his red cheeks? Don't you know more ABOUT

him than about many of your close friends? You'd trust him anywhere, wouldn't you? Don't you think of him as a marvellously WISE old bird who, in spite of his good heart, knows a wonderful lot about the people he visits?

Don't you feel that he knows you yourself a great deal better than most of your friends do, forgives your weaknesses and wishes you luck?'

In any case on this afternoon the snow fell, and at first the sun was shining.

The snow fell like silver threepenny-bits and, for a rarity, it lay. The roofs, the window-sills were white. He knelt up in the front window between the gay curtains and prayed to God (in whom he always believed as a child does.

How exasperating he could be about religion! It seemed to mean to him at once so much and so little) to make the snow last until Christmas Day. He was called out by some other children and they began to build a snow man.

But of course by the morning all the snow was gone. Rain fell. He would have cried with disappointment had there not been, as there always was with him, some new excitement to take the beautiful snow's place.

But the excitement of all excitements for him was centred round the Theatre, the beloved Theatre Royal of Port Merlin. This was created in him in the first place undoubtedly by his father, to whom the Theatre was always a palace of miracle and wonder. John was more than five years old when he saw his first real play; the stage-door keeper was a rather grand, condescending friend of his father's.

As this old man was one of the most important people, as it turned out, in John Cornelius' life, he is worth a description. But John could never describe him very well except that he was a little man with a squint who took snuff.

He thought, it seems, that he was about the most important man in Port Merlin, and to strangers he could be very haughty and unpleasant indeed. He would address the actors and actresses as they passed through into the

Theatre with a great deal of dignity. He was called 'Mr. Darlington.'

'Any letters, Mr. Darlington?'

'No, Miss Feather.'

'Oh dear, I did think ... Are you quite sure?'

'Quite sure, Miss Feather.'

John's father was a gentleman, as everyone knew, and Mr. Darlington was a snob. Moreover, Cornelius senior made him a present one day of one of his shell-boxes.

He often had tickets to dispose of when the piece wasn't going very well, and in this way Cornelius often went to a play, taking his wife or his mother or a crony of his. He would tell John afterwards and thus the boy knew all about The Bells, Colleen Bawn, Lord Lytton's Money, Caste, and many another almost before he could talk.

Everyone in the town, of course, knew the ugly, long-legged, excited little boy, and he was afraid of no one. Until he went to his first day-school no one was unkind to him or ill-treated him, so that he had complete confidence in everyone. Even before his sixth year he would go up to anyone and recite one of his little pieces to them. Afterwards when we come to the play-writing and singing time ... !

At home no one ever quarrelled. His mother would be often in despair—'Oh, Lordy, Lordy! ... Better I was dead. Better for everyone.'

That would be when a garment was lost in the laundry or she hadn't had time to cook a proper meal or her back was aching. John's father was marvellous at consoling her. A comic sight it must have been for a cynical observer to see that little man take that very large woman and hug her and pat her broad back and pinch her cheeks. But the Cornelius family did not think it comic, and soon Mrs. Cornelius would be wiping her eyes, young John dancing like a grasshopper on his long legs, and Cornelius Papa sitting down to the little table to stick shells on to his boxes. They were a very devoted, feckless, untidy, good-natured family.

The one real trouble at this time—and it became very much worse later on—

was that Mrs. Cornelius was a little too fond of the bottle. John's father, a very sober man, was afraid of this as of nothing else in life, and his son grew to be afraid of it too. From very early days they were conspirators together in this affair.

It was in his sixth year that John was first made aware of the unkindness that there is in the world. That moment, small in itself, big in its consequences, may well be counted the first real event in his history, the first moment of fear of his fellow-man. He had known before this, as I have already said, what fear is in dreams. Now he was to know what it is in the world of fact.

He was five years old and some four months. It was a quiet, sunny autumn afternoon and the sea coming in like a whisper and a promise, gulls flying and settling and screaming over some piece of dead fish or whatever, while the thump of the mining-stamps tramped like the tread of men from over the brow of the moor.

John often told of it with that eager egotism that took it for granted that anything happening to himself must be interesting to everybody even to its smallest detail.

'It was on one of those very still days with ivory cumuli of cloud resting on the horizon. I'd wandered off by myself and to that part of the beach where a fresh-water stream comes down through the sand to meet the sea. Before it reached the sand this stream was bordered with tall grasses. There were irises there in their proper season. A duck and half a dozen ducklings had come down to the stream and the ducklings were swimming about. They were irresistibly lovely to me and I seemed to know just what they were thinking and feeling and saying to one another. One duckling was less venturesome than the others and stayed close to its mother, but with a rather self-satisfied air like the child in the family who won't take risks and puts its money in the money-box very carefully. You think I'm inventing all this just to amuse you? I assure you I'm not. It happened just as I'm telling you—' (Cornelius would often break into his stories like this, throwing his head up, frowning, challenging anyone to disbelieve him)—'I was watching them, kneeling by the stream, and I heard people shouting. I looked up and saw a crowd of men

and boys coming over the sand-dune. And then, ahead of them, appearing from nowhere, outlined for a moment against the sky, an old crazy man whom I knew well, "Old Laces" they called him. Everyone knew "Laces." He was one of the harmless lunatics who lived in the Asylum but was allowed to roam about as he pleased. They called him "Laces" because he went about with a box slung over his shoulder in which were some odds and ends, shoe-

laces and reels of cotton and such things. He never tried to sell anything, but the box gave him pleasure, made him feel important perhaps. He was a quite harmless, good-natured old man and everyone liked him. But today they had set on him and were driving him down to the sea. They were shouting and laughing and cried out that they were going to give him a bath. He ran down the sand-bank and came right to where I was. He didn't recognize me. He was by far too terrified for that. I'd never seen fear in a human face before.

He had a grey straggly beard like my grandfather and was dressed in an old ragged black coat, and his trousers were torn. His cheek was bleeding where a stone had struck him. But it was his eyes! His eyes! They were staring with insanity and fear. His breath came in desperate little gasps. Another stone struck him just as he reached me and he fell on his knees. He gave one dreadful choking cry and rolled over. I remember that I saw the duck and her brood scurrying into the grasses. I couldn't move. I stared and stared and stared. The white cumuli of cloud rolled up over the sea making a noise like drums. It was exactly like one of the worst of my nightmares. The men and boys came up and were silent because "Old Laces" was dead.

'Silly, unintentional, like most cruelty.'

On that day, Cornelius always said, his life really began.

CHAPTER II

The Great Shell-box; and How Juliet Spoke From the Balcony

From the age of five years to eight John Cornelius must have led a quiet, domestic and very happy existence. During those years only two events of major importance occurred; it is with these that this chapter deals. He may be seen, a small restless enquiring figure, growing in vitality if not in beauty, moving up and down, in and out, talking to anybody, for ever asking questions, afraid of no one (although ALERT now against circumstance after the death of 'Old Laces').

About him, around him, lie the town and the sea, the fishing–boats sailing out silently against the morning sun, the gulls rising and falling like fragments of snow-breasted wave flung sky-high, the bells ringing softly the hour, the country carts creaking up the hill to the top of the moor, the never-ceasing murmur and scurry and roar of the sea, the Market with the flowers, the fruit, the vegetables, the cows and sheep in the pens, the long tranquil silence of the night, and the old watchman still calling out as he shook his scolding rattle—'One o'clock and a stormy sky.'

At the age of six John went for the first time to school—Mrs. Biggar's Kindergarten in Fall Street. He did not remain there long, only two days in fact.

Mrs. Cornelius, dressed in her best and panting with the heat of her unaccustomed garments, accompanied John. Mrs. Biggar, whom John remembered as a small woman with a sharp black eye, promised Mrs.

Cornelius that her little boy should not suffer corporal punishment.

On the second day, however, because she considered John impertinent (as very likely he was), she gave him several sharp taps on the back of his hand with a ruler. John gave her one look in return and walked straight home.

When he told his mother what had occurred she was in complete agreement with him. The woman had broken her word and that was enough. He did not go to a school again until he was seven, but before that his father had taught him to read and write. Arithmetic and everything to do with it he never could abide.

He loved his father and grandmother dearly, but his feeling for his mother was one of passionate devotion and remained so in spite of all her shortcomings. It was perhaps BECAUSE of her shortcomings that he loved her. He inherited from her her lack of orderliness and incapacity for arranging things. But most of all he felt that she needed care and protection in a way that the others did not. As her inebriety grew upon her he felt ever more strongly this protectiveness. He had throughout his life an especial care for and understanding of drunkards, although he was himself most abstemious all his days—and that too was perhaps because of his mother.

He adopted towards her from very early days a paternal attitude, chaffing her, telling her funny stories, helping her with her work (although in this he generally did more harm than good), cheering her depressed spirits. It was, I suppose, her constant bewildered despair at the muddle she was in that tempted her to the drink. She invented, like many a similar victim before and after her, a wonderfully alert system of lies, subterfuges and stratagems.

However, during those early years of John's the complaint was not severe.

When she was not troubled with too much work, too little money, before she became so corpulent, there were many hours when the two of them were as happy as two people could be.

He would sing his little songs, recite his poems, tell his stories, while she sat in the rocking–chair, her large red hands planted on her knees, staring at him as though he were an elf–visitor from another world. She might well have thought so, for with his extreme thinness, his long bony face, his brilliant searching eyes he looked little like any child of hers. He remembered that once he came in crying because some woman, exasperated with his determination to tell her a story, had cried out: 'Take your ugly face away. I can't abide the sight of it.'

'You AREN'T ugly! You AREN'T ugly!' his mother had passionately cried, taking him to her capacious bosom. 'I'll give her ugly!'

But he was ugly all the same and well he knew it.

Another bond that they had was their religion. Mrs. Cornelius, although she seldom entered a church, believed in God as though He might at any moment come in and inspect the laundry. So did John.

Now John's father was an atheist and that for the simple and to himself convincing reason of there being so much misery in the world. He but rarely spoke on these subjects, but Mrs. Cornelius, admiring him and feeling an eternal gratitude to him as she did, suffered great unhappiness and much bewilderment at his opinions. How could so fine and generous a gentleman as her husband think such dreadful things? But, worst of all, must he not suffer fearful punishment one day? And at the thought of this she would stare at him as he worked at his shell-boxes, and her eyes would fill with tears and she would long to take the little man in her arms and defend him from the Powers of Darkness.

The other great trouble that she had at this time was in the matter of John's

'lies.' She knew that all small children told lies, but John's were grander and more challenging than any others.

He would come in and tell her that he had seen an old dwarf with a bag of gold on his shoulder down by Lelant Rock looking in the pools for jellyfish.

He would assure her that he had taken some of the gold pieces and allowed them to trickle between his fingers. Why hadn't he brought any of them home then? Oh, well, they didn't belong to HIM! And the dwarf had turned surly because his fingers had been stung by a jelly-fish.

Of course children do make up stories which no one expects you to believe, and Johnny in especial had a marvellous imagination. So the dwarf with the jelly-fish might be forgiven—but what of it when Johnny comes in, stops at the door and says: 'The Queen of England has just arrived in the town, mother.' (He used to talk like an old man sometimes, even at the age of six.)

'I've seen her white horses and she's wearing a crown.' In a case like this Mrs.

Cornelius simply didn't know what to do and would consult her friends and neighbours, Mrs. Garriman and Mrs. Hoskin, to see whether they had any advice to offer. John remembered Mrs. Garriman and Mrs. Hoskin very well.

Mrs. Garriman was a tall, gaunt woman who believed in ghosts, spirits,

table-turning, and telling the cards. Mrs. Hoskin was a little sparrow of a woman with a suspicion of a light beard on the end of her chin. Neither Mrs.

Hoskin nor Mrs. Garriman liked Johnny, who bored them with his recitations and his refusal to take them as seriously as he took himself. This last characteristic was, as he never sufficiently realized, a great drawback to him in later life.

Mrs. Garriman terrified Mrs. Cornelius with her card-telling and table-

turning. Since she was already sufficiently superstitious, Mrs. Garriman's lugubrious voice saying: 'It's a Death in the House. That can mean nothink but a Death—and a bloody one too if I'm not mistaken,' would disturb Mrs.

Cornelius all the night long. She recognized, however, that Mrs. Hoskin was the more dangerous of the two. When Maggie Hoskin, in a gathering of friends, told many destructive little stories of OTHER friends—well, what would happen to yourself as soon as your back was turned?

Both ladies assured Mrs. Cornelius that her boy must end in gaol or even worse. Such lies! Why, only last week he had told Mrs. Hoskin that he'd seen a mermaid sitting on a rock and combing her hair!

'It's only his fun,' said Mrs. Cornelius weakly.

His fun! And the child not yet seven years of age! His fun! Mermaids indeed!

Nevertheless they did like to hear the child sing. By the time he was seven he could sing like a bird. There can have been none of the angel-boy treble about him, and Charlie Christian has told me of the way John looked, standing with his long skinny neck stretched, his big mouth immensely wide, and his funny thin fingers beating the time as he gave his audience 'Oft in the Stilly Night,' 'The Young May Moon is Beaming, Love,' 'The Harp that Once.' He was about seven and a half when Charlie first heard him; he knew all those songs then and many more.

The trouble about him was that once he had started nothing could stop him.

There were none of the shy affectations of the professional singer about him.

Nor did he need an accompaniment. He could sing anywhere, at any time, to anybody.

At seven years of age he went to school again, to Rush's Day School.

Rush's had been a famous town school in its day, but in the late 'eighties and early 'nineties a more practical Board School type of education destroyed it.

Anything but practical it must have been according to all that I have heard of it, but it did two fine things for John: gave him Mr. Bartholomew for an inspiring influence and introduced him to the two most faithful and devoted friends of all his life. Mr. Bartholomew was one of those little old men whom you meet in the books of Dickens and Borrow, in 'drab- coloured pantaloons and a nankeen waistcoat.' He was a deliberate and theatrical survival from an age that seemed to him the only real and beautiful one.

But he had a passion for books—not for your moderns, of course, and John well remembered his disgust when at a later stage he caught him with Cometh Up as a Flower in his hand. He would have nothing to say to Swinburne or 'Festus' Bailey or Rossetti. They were all too recent for him.

But Beddoes and the early Tennyson and Clough and Charles Auchester and the real Classics behind these— Pope and Gray and Boswell and Cowper ...

the eighteenth century was his passion ... Dr. Johnson his god ... he would read Rasselas to his slumbering pupils, pushing snuff up his nostrils, tickling the scanty grey hair on his head with the end of a ruler, suddenly breaking into Pope's Iliad, dancing about in ecstasy, discovering a boy, his head on his desk, fast in slumber, bringing the ruler down with a little scream of anger on the urchin's head ... how often John acted him to us, how we laughed and felt as though we ourselves had known him intimately ... but he was a blessing and a wonder to John all the same.

Anne and Charlie he met both on the same day when he had been a week or so at Rush's.

He was turning down the hill out of the High Street and had reached the little square patch of ground known as the Rock. She was standing, her satchel of school-books in her hand, laughing and sticking her tongue out at some boys who had been teasing her. She must have been a big girl for her age (she was two years older than John), rosy-cheeked and tallow-haired, freckled and untidy, broad in the beam, laughing and fearless and careless then as always.

I don't know whether Anne is the heroine of this book or no. There was, before the Great War, a fashion among novelists for free-and- easy and jolly

and give-you-a-blow-or-a-kiss kind of heroines. They couldn't, poor dears, survive the cynical post-War intellectual spirit. They had in fact very few brains but a lot of heart; the post-War heroines were exactly the opposite.

Anne was, I am afraid, something of a pre-War heroine in physique, courage, and good temper, but she had plenty of brains and a sort of healthy irony when she liked. The boys, shouting and laughing at her, vanished, and she threw some pebbles after them. When she saw John she stared as people very often did on first seeing him.

She spoke to him, and as they were going the same way they started off together. They liked one another very much at once. John told her that his mother did laundry and his father made boxes and painted pictures. Anne said that her name was Anne Swinnerton, that her father was dead and that she lived with her mother in a little house above Carp Cove. She went to school at Miss Bensatt's Academy. She liked everything—sailing, fishing, swimming, dancing. Reading? No, she hadn't any time for reading. They agreed to meet on the following day.

On that same morning John, running, had collided with a small, broad-

shouldered, sturdy boy who had simply said: 'Look out, you!' John was so thin and his legs so unsteady that the sturdy boy had held him up and waited until his breath came back. John grinned and the boy grinned. They stayed there talking; at least John talked as he always did, saying everything that came into his head. The sturdy boy looked at him with his quiet, observant blue eyes and said almost nothing. It did finally appear that the boy's name was Charlie Christian and that his father owned a fishing-smack with his two brothers, was a prominent member of the Port Merlin lifeboat and an important Methodist. It was Charlie's characteristic then and always to observe rather than communicate. His suspicions of his fellow human beings were as deep as the sea; he trusted no one until he had good sound reason.

However, the one person in all his life whom he did trust from the very beginning was John Cornelius; he trusted him and saw that, because of his simple impetuosities, he needed protection. From that very first day he made protecting John his business. He had no idea then, of course, what a life business it was going to be. John had no especial thought either that on this important day he had made the two best friendships he was ever to make. I am not sure whether he was ever to recognize it. We are always slightly indulgent towards those who show us that, without reservation, they love us and believe in us. John was always, without intending it, a little patronizing towards Anne and Charlie. Not that they minded. They stood a great deal from him before the end. Their reasons for loving him, though, were real and solid ones. On the whole he deserved that devotion.

And so we come to the Great Shell-box affair. John always considered this the beginning of all his real troubles—his and his family's. 'If ever I write my own life,' he would say to me, 'that business shall be shown to be the root of the matter.'

He recalled every detail of it, acted it for us over and over again. He had been one half-holiday with his grandmother to visit his grandfather in the Asylum.

The old man hadn't been so very well, complaining of pains in the head, and the little grandmother was distressed. You couldn't do anything for him when he was ill. He just sat there rocking himself like a sick monkey and altogether forgetting that he was King Solomon. He looked so pathetic, so helpless, clung to his wife's hand so passionately, begging her not to leave him, that the visit was truly upsetting.

They had, however, scarcely been in John's home for ten minutes before John's father came in like a conquering hero. He had suffered for many years, I am sure, from an appalling sense of failure. He made the best of it, but he knew that this was not where he ought to be, allowing his poor wife to work her heart out for their sustenance. There was some strain of weakness somewhere, a fear of himself (perhaps because of his father's insanity); he was an artist whose talents had led him nowhere, a gentleman married to a washerwoman (although that he never for a moment regretted), ineffectual, with ideas of form and colour that he could never make marketable. He must have become shyer and shyer, ever more reserved, ever more secretly unhappy as the years went on. Why didn't he try some more practical and profitable occupation? Well, he did later, as you shall hear.

John, I fancy, was his one cherished companion, his one pride and delight. To see little Mr. Cornelius, Charlie said, sitting in his chair, his legs crossed under him Turk-wise, while John sang, THAT was a pleasant sight. Yes, it must have been.

Melancholy or no, on this particular afternoon he came in radiant. Mrs.

Cornelius was getting out the tea-things, her mother-in-law half asleep in the rocking-chair (for she was a considerably old lady), John kneeling on the rough wooden seat in the window looking at an illustrated volume of Hans Andersen that Mr. Bartholomew had given him. 'I remember as though it were yesterday. I was reading "The Clogs of Fortune" and I can quote you the opening words: "Every author has something peculiar in his style of writing, and those who are unfriendly to him quickly fasten upon this peculiarity, shrug their shoulders and say, 'There he is again!' And I remember that I was thinking "When I come to write I hope I WILL have something peculiar!"'

The birds were singing in their cage and the warm sun coming in through the open window off the sea in a rhythm of heat like the rhythm of the waves. 'I remember,' John used to tell us, 'looking up and thinking at once: "Why, what's happened to father?" I'd never seen him look so triumphant before.

There he stood, a parcel in his hand, beaming on us all. I loved him so dearly that it was as though we were one person, and at once I too was bursting with happiness and there was the scent of the sun and the mignonette in the window and the hot cakes that mother had been baking. How happy we all were even before we knew any reason! Father went to his wife and kissed her, then he kissed his mother, then he kissed his son.

'"Mother—all of you," he said. "Our fortune's made!" Then he undid the parcel and showed us a red leather box studded with gold nails. The lid was a plain and shiny wood. A very handsome box indeed.

'"This belongs to Lady Mary Madox," he said quite reverentially.

'"And who may she be?" asked my mother.' (John imitated all their voices so that you could see them living and moving in front of you.)

'"She lives in London. She's staying here for her health with Mr. Carmichael who's a cousin of hers. He showed her one of my boxes and she's delighted and has sent this box, which she values more than anything she has, for me to paint a picture on the lid and decorate the sides with the best of my shells.

She'll pay handsomely for it.'

'"How much?" asked my mother.

'"And take it back to London and then there'll be more orders, many orders

—"

'"How much is she paying for it?" my mother asked again, rubbing her red hot hands on her apron.

'"Ten pounds if she likes it," said my father.

'"And if she doesn't like it?" asked my mother.

'"Of course she'll like it, darling," my father said, going up and kissing her.

"I'll paint such a beautiful picture—"

'"This!" I cried, rushing at him. "This! This! This!" and I showed him the picture in the Hans Andersen of the Wild Swans flying past the window.

'"Yes, yes!" he cried, as excited as I was. "That will do beautifully."

'It seemed as though our chance had truly come at last. We had always profoundly believed in my father's talent, and indeed I still think that for delicacy and a certain romantic charm the pictures that he painted are very delightful. They were, of course, in the fashion of their time—I mean the Royal Academy fashion, not at all the kind of things that a young man called Aubrey Beardsley was just then beginning to be famous for. They were frankly pretty rather than anything else—but he had imagination, father had, and the picture of the Wild Swans on Lady Mary Madox's box was the finest thing he ever did.

'Yes, how excited we all were! We were quite certain that our fortunes were made for ever!

'My father was a changed man, a new energy seemed to possess him. He could hardly wait to begin his work on the box. He described the old lady who had sent for him and shown great astonishment that he should be a gentleman. He described her to us, a funny old woman with a moustache on her upper lip, one shoulder higher than the other, a voice like a man's, and leaning on a cane—"like one of those old ladies in Thackeray's novels," said father, although that meant nothing to any of us.

'She had been inclined to patronize him and he'd been inclined to be angry. It was clear that she thought herself a very grand old lady indeed. I drank in every word of his description and saw the whole scene as though I had been present, my father, so small in body, so great in soul, very quiet, telling her a little about himself and not very much, and the old lady, feeling herself a grand patroness, delighted with herself for doing this small thing. Little I realized that one fine day I should know the old lady so well!'

They sat up ever so late talking about it and building, of course, tremendous castles in Spain. All that John's father had ever wanted, he explained to them gently, was some kind of a Chance. That Chance had, for one reason or another, always been denied him. This old lady—Lady Max her friends called her—had tremendous influence in London. She was very rich and to her house everyone of importance went. If she liked the box when it was finished she would have it in her drawing-room and all the grand people in London would see it. There would then come Orders and Orders and Orders

...

John's father, sitting beside his wife, her hand in his, explained that he had always had so many ideas in his head—wonderful unique ideas—but had been discouraged because there was no one in this little town who understood them.

It might be—it was in fact very likely—that they must go to London to live.

At this John's mother looked frightened and dismayed. What would they say in London to a fat red-faced washerwoman?

But at the word 'London' John's heart beat fast. London was to him the centre of all glory and splendour, where theatres abounded and the Tower of London and Westminster Abbey and Madame Tussaud's. Of this last he had read in an illustrated pamphlet lent to him at school. What a place! Where Kings, Queens, Soldiers lived in close proximity to hundreds of murderers!

That quiet sentence of his father did something to him—it made London not only a possibility but also a necessity.

In the early hours of the morning John woke to find his father seated at the little table working on the box. With his long, skinny, naked legs he jumped

out of bed and ran across the room. He watched breathlessly. 'I was frozen with cold. The candle jumped up and down. Neither of us cared. London and fortune were looking in at us through the window.'

Unfortunately Mrs. Cornelius couldn't hold her tongue, and she must tell Mrs.

Garriman and Mrs. Hoskin all about it. Mrs. Garriman 'did' the cards and said that a piece of good fortune, a journey and a man with dark hair were all in store for the Cornelius family.

Mrs. Hoskin was really the dangerous one. She was very vain, self- centred, and never forgot a slight or an injury. Bitterness, jealousy, vanity, these were her masters, so it was natural enough that good prospects for the Cornelius family should upset her very badly.

John remembered her, a small dark woman with her hair done up on the top of her head in a bun, looking in through the door, her ugly monkey-face furrowed with smiles.

'Any news? Oh, I do 'ope it's good. I do indeed.... 'Asn't 'e finished it yet?

Takes time of course. Anythink good always does.' She made a great impression on John. He never forgot her and, later, when some reviewer stung him for a moment with some hostile remarks, he'd say: 'That's Mrs.

Hoskin speaking.' He took the Witch in The Wood-Cutter's Green Clothes from her, I am sure.

Cornelius had promised that the box should be finished within ten days. That was wild wintry weather and the rain beat on the window- panes and the sea boomed on the beach so that you had to shout to make yourself heard. John remembered that the weather was important because of the shells. Cornelius found most of the shells himself, but he would buy them sometimes from an old man who knew just where to go for the largest and most beautiful.

The old man was tied to his bed with rheumatism, so that Cornelius did not have this time shells as perfect in their colour-gradations as he might have wished.

Those that he had he did marvels with. I've seen the box, so I know. Any close friend of John's has seen the box. Shell-boxes are considered things of

cheap and vulgar taste, but THIS box had a quality all its own. The picture on the lid must seem now old- fashioned. In any case Cornelius was not a great painter. The swans are flying through the evening sky while a young girl, kneeling beside her window, watches them. The swans are very white, the evening sky very blue, the girl's face very pink—and yet there is a freshness here, a simplicity of vision, a sincerity of faith that make it not altogether absurd to sustain Cornelius as a humble companion of William Blake. That good man would have discovered the spirit behind the workmanship of this old shell-box and welcomed it. John, whose imagination so often ran ahead of fact, allowed himself full liberty while the shell-box was making.

Although he was, as yet, only seven years of age, he had already fully determined to be a famous writer—a writer of many things but especially of plays. There was nothing very odd about that because fifty years ago many children dreamt of being writers; to-day it is airmen or motor-racers they'll be! But I think it can be said here that John Cornelius never, from his eighth year onwards, had the faintest doubts about his future destiny. There were to be many occasions when everyone doubted but he. He was, at one and the same time, the vainest and most humble of God's creatures, and that is true, perhaps, of many who are certain of their destinies.

During the whole of that week he was as bad as his mother and went strutting about the town and the school telling everyone that the Cornelius family was shortly departing for London and that his father was going to be the Court Painter.

'But your father wasn't going to be the Court Painter,' I would interrupt at this point. 'To begin with, there ISN'T a Court Painter. That was a downright lie.'

'It didn't seem to me a lie,' John would answer. 'I simply saw the whole scene

—father, mother, myself, grandmother, all marching down the London streets to a band between admiring crowds, the Palace gates swinging open, the Queen there in her crown, stepping forward, welcoming my father, and all of us having high tea in the Palace drawing-room.'

Myself: 'You were only seven, of course.'

Cornelius: 'When I imagine things they seem to me truer than what people call reality.'

Myself: 'Yes. That's why some people think you such a terrible liar.'

The opinion of both the town and the school was, I imagine, pretty equally divided about him. He had his warm friends and defenders who, even at this early time, felt that there was something special and peculiar about him, recognized also his courage, his independence and his passionate fidelity. To many others, even when he was little more than a baby, he was exasperating and irritating with his egotism, his insistence on his own importance, his physical oddities, and his constant certainty that he was right.

His schoolfellows were, I expect, considerably impressed by this approaching glory of his. They didn't know, as yet, that he was a liar. Port Merlin was, in those days, a long way from London, and to the children at the school such things might happen as taking tea with the Queen at Buckingham Palace.

Why not? The Queen had to have tea some time!

But it was after the Shell-box affair that John felt that he simply HAD to go to London: he had, in the face of the world, given his word and, in the face of the world, he must redeem it.

Well, the shell-box was finished at last and within the appointed time. The family had never seen anything so beautiful.

It was years later that John's mother told him of the awful temptation under which she suffered on this night when the shell- box, completed, stood on the little table ready to be delivered up to the old lady on the following day.

The temptation was to destroy the shell-box. She woke up, just as the clock was striking two, and, as she described it to her son, the Devil leapt at her and had her by the throat. She sat up in bed and, in the moonlight, saw her husband fast asleep beside her.

There was the box, brought from the other room, all the red and crimson and faint-pink shells coloured by the moon to a delicate and iridescent beauty.

The box in her eyes looked so lovely that she could not doubt but that it would make her husband famous in the world for ever. That fame would mean that she would lose him. She had, ever since she married him, been

afraid that this should one day occur. He was so fine a gentleman, so greatly superior to her in every way, the only thing that she could do for him was to work. Now others would do the work, and he and the boy would be carried where she could not follow them. Very easily she could tear the lid off the box and throw it into the fire that still showed some glowing embers.

The Devil had so powerful an influence that she told her son she could see him bending over her, dressed in black tights, with a red feather in his hair.

She might—who knows?—have yielded, but at that moment her little husband, in his sleep, turned towards her, and with the sigh of a child, rested his head on her ample breast. So, lying down, she put her arms around him and defied the Devil.

Mrs. Hoskin came in to see the finished box and paid it many a compliment.

'Never did I see anythink more beautiful. They birds are flying as natural as natural. 'Owever you can do it, Mr. Cornelius, I CAN'T think!'

Nevertheless young John caught the wicked malice in her eye. She remained for him, his life through, the principle of evil as the 'Bird-Man' was the opposite. Whether there ever WAS a Bird-Man no one will ever know, and I expect that Mrs. Hoskin herself was never anything but a little ill-natured, overworked woman who kept a grubby little shop with sweets, tobacco and penny novelettes. She scarcely deserved the grand rôle that Cornelius gave her.

On the following afternoon Mr. Cornelius went up the town with his treasure.

It happened to be a half-holiday, and young John sat with Charlie Christian on the sand-dunes looking out to sea. So it was, strangely enough, that Christian had his share in this early adventure of Cornelius' as he was to have his share in many later ones.

The two little boys sat looking solemnly out to sea and, so John affirms, for the best part of the time said nothing whatever. In any case Charlie was the one human being with whom John could always be silent—with anyone else he must talk his mind and imagination out, although he had, rather unexpectedly, the gift of being a good listener.

Since, in 1920, Boles' malicious portrait of him was published in Uncivil

Sketches the impression of him as a kind of long-legged, gyrating eel from whose wide mouth egoistic vapourings ceaselessly flowed has never quite died out in America, a country where Boles is rated more highly than he is in England.

Anyone who knew Cornelius saw at once the falsity of this caricature in many, many particulars, but Boles was clever enough (and honest enough from his point of view) to emphasize as well some real weaknesses of John's.

Not that it matters now. John had his enemies and detractors after his success like everyone else. Quite a number of them in fact. All his life he pretended not to mind that people should not like him. As a matter of fact he hated to be disliked unless he detested the disliker. The trouble was that he could never detest anyone for more than half an hour: the result of this was that so many people could hurt him—and did.

He remembered that on that afternoon the sun began to sink, a round red ball in waves of grey cloud. Slowly spears of bronze started up from the floor of the shell-cold sea, and as the waves of grey caught that red sun the spears cleft the heavens and stood like an approaching army on the world's rim.

At last Charlie said: 'You'll be seeing none of the boys after you go to London.'

'I'll ask you to London,' John remembered saying.

But Charlie shook his head.

'I like fishing,' he said.

He must have felt the drama of John's approaching fate because he did something very unlike his undemonstrative self. He felt in his pocket and produced a large, stained jack-knife.

'I don't want it,' he said. 'I've got another.'

John hated knives, guns, ropes, whips—anything that could possibly hurt either man or animal. But he took Charlie's present and thanked him.

'I expect father will be back,' he said, and they went to the cottage.

I had two accounts of the scene that followed, two very excellent ones: one from Charlie, the other from John himself. Charlie had two very marked characteristics: he never forgot ANYTHING, and he had not many words in his vocabulary. His account of anything was limited strictly to fact, a police report, and behind the facts you must build the picture.

He had scarcely seen Mrs. Cornelius before, and when he was introduced to the big, floppy, red-faced woman sitting on the bed, when he realized, without, of course, analysing it, her distress, anxiety, intense agitation, he felt at once that he was intruding; he had always beautiful, courtly manners.

But John wouldn't let him go. His sense of the dramatic wanted Charlie to be there to share in the triumph. Mrs. Cornelius really didn't notice him but sat there on the bed, crushing someone's damp chemise between her hands, murmuring over and over again: 'Oh, Lordy! ... Lordy! Why doesn't he come? What's keeping him?'

So the two boys just stood there, Charlie rubbing his hand up and down against the sympathetic corduroy of his little trousers while the birds sang in their cage and the room darkened.

The door opened just after Mrs. Cornelius had lit the gas over the mantelpiece, and Cornelius came in.

There was scarcely a need, Charlie told me, for Cornelius to say anything.

'Come to think of it, I don't know that I've ever seen a man's face more tragic than his was. It may have been the gaslight but he looked tragic all right.'

He went to the table without a word to anyone. With fumbling hands he undid the parcel he was carrying and he placed the shell-box on the table where it had stood until an hour or two ago. Then, looking straight at his wife, he told her.

The old woman had received him uncivilly in the first place. She had been in a temper about something before he arrived. She had told him to leave the box, but he wanted to see her look of surprised pleasure when he showed it

her. So he showed it her.

Surprised pleasure had NOT been her reaction, for she had held the box scornfully to the light, glanced at the painting, screamed out: 'What do you say those things are? Birds?' and had thrown the box on to the floor with such violence that many of the shells were broken. She had rated him like a cheated fishwife, told him that he had misunderstood her intentions completely, that his picture was a miserable daub, his shells ridiculous.

Moreover, he had ruined her beautiful box. It was ruined for ever. He could pick the thing up and take it away with him. She never wanted to see either him or it again. So he picked the thing up and came away.

He sat down at the table and began, fumblingly, to straighten some of the shells. Mrs. Cornelius got up from the bed, came over to him, put her arms round him and kissed him. Charlie slipped away out of the room without anyone noticing.

John was exceedingly sharp for his years and he realized at once that it was only his father who needed any consoling. 'I don't know how it could have been with anyone as young as I was, but I knew instantly that this was the end of everything for father. A little thing, an absurd thing—but you can say all the same that my father was killed by a shell-box, one of those absurd cheap things that you see in little shops in watering-places. Killed,' he would say, his face all working, dramatically pointing with his long fingers, 'by that box on the table there.'

He wasn't killed at once. People seldom are. There was no melodrama. Very little was said. Everything went on apparently the same—only Mrs. Cornelius drank a little more. Mrs. Garriman and Mrs. Hoskin were in the house more often, and John began to grow up.

He must have been a funny-looking boy round his eighth year. It's a fact, I believe, that many people in the town thought him a bit 'off his head' like King Solomon, his grandfather.

He was pretty popular at school. He was clever, he learned by heart with extraordinary facility, but often enough in class he would sit staring at the large coarsely-coloured Bible pictures on the wall, making up stories in his

head about them when he should have been working.

He was such an odd-looking boy, with his big nose and his small bright eyes and his untidy mop of hair, his long thin legs and arms in grey jacket and trousers far too small for him. Everyone— masters and boys alike—must have felt both the egotism and the sweetness of his nature. Often the children would tease him, especially if Charlie were not near. He would insist on telling them stories, and of these stories he was always the hero. To tease him was easy, however—one allusion to madness and the story would die on his lips and he would turn, walk away, his head forward, his long arms swinging.

This, even in those early days, was his one haunting fear. Beyond this he hated to be laughed at, not because he was vain (although if to consider yourself a completely exceptional person is vanity he WAS vain) but because he always thought the unkind jeerer MIGHT be right!

Although he had friends at the school—and especially Mr. Bartholomew for whom he always bought a bunch of flowers on his birthday and laid it on his desk—and, among the children, Anne and Charlie, he cared most for the company of mature people. He had, by now, friends all over the town, the two night-watchmen who called the hours, the old woman who went round with her barrow selling handkerchiefs and laces, the old women knitting along the wall, many of the fishermen, including by now Charlie's splendid father, Anne's mother, who was a little flighty, giggling, pretty lady greatly interested in gentlemen, and above all, two old ladies, the widow and virgin sister of a clergyman, who lived in a cottage near the Cornelius family. These two old ladies, Mrs.

Gordon and Miss Gracie, soon became more exciting to him than any others because they wrote poetry—religious verse which was frequently published in the Glebeshire Sentinel.

And now John had himself written a play! It was founded on Shakespeare's Winter's Tale, which the two old ladies had read to him, taking parts alternately. A good deal of it John did not understand, but the main point was abundantly clear—that the King Leontes had been unjustly jealous of his lovely wife Hermione, so she pretended to be dead, and then, many years after, when Leontes had bitterly repented his jealousy, she pretended to be a statue, slowly came to life, stepped from her pedestal and threw her arms foolishly about her silly husband's neck. What a scene this must have been!—

the two old ladies in their small cottage room, crowded with bric-à-brac, very hot and smelling of tea and plum-cake, read with trembling voices the great closing scenes of this wonderful play.

Myself: 'You were all very excited?'

Cornelius: 'Excited! That's not the word. When Miss Gracie came to Leontes'

cry, "Oh! She's warm. If this be magic, let it be an art Lawful as eating"—and the gentlemen near at hand make enthusiastic comments, "She embraces him"; "She hangs about his neck"—I could stand it no longer but jumped up from my chair and waved my arms and cried:

'"Oh, good, good, good!"

'And then I embraced Miss Gracie as though she was responsible for the whole thing, and we all cried a little.'

John saw no harm in cribbing from Shakespeare, and although he situated his play in London rather than in Sicilia the affair of the statue was common to both Shakespeare and Cornelius. But then Shakespeare himself had borrowed it from somewhere, so what matter?

The only trouble with John's play was that it was too short—six pages, in a very large infantile hand, of an exercise-book. On the other side this brevity made it quick in the reading, and that was fortunate because he insisted on reading it to everyone. He was so brimful himself of enchanted happiness that he should be a creator of this kind, that (now as always) he was certain that everyone must wish to share in his own joy.

He was beginning now to read ferociously. He was afraid of no one when it came to book-borrowing. He was passing a house one evening and he could see into the sitting-room, the blind not being drawn. The wall opposite the window was lined with books. He rang the bell, and a white-haired, bespectacled, severe-eyebrowed lady opened the door.

'I beg your pardon,' John said, 'but I passed your window and saw the books you have. Wouldn't you lend me one or two, ma'am? I'd take the greatest care of them.'

'Certainly not,' said the lady very indignantly. 'I never heard of such a thing,'

and she tried to close the door.

John slipped inside and looking at her very beseechingly cried: 'Oh, please, ma'am, do! Please do! If you will, I'll read you a play I've written—I will indeed.'

The lady told him afterwards that she was greatly astonished and that he looked unlike anything she'd ever seen before—and then the idea of a child like that writing a play! But it was his little deep-set burning eyes that conquered her. Before she knew it she was with him in the sitting-room and he, in a frenzy of excitement, was pulling out one book after another.

It was on her shelves that he first found Lavengro and Romany Rye, Kinglake's Crimea, Macaulay's History of England, Feats on the Fiord, and Charles Kingsley's Heroes. They became great friends, the lady and he. She was a widow and her name was Mrs. Winchester.

Now it happened that he knew very well old Jimmy Lipscombe who was the bill-poster of the town. Jimmy had a wooden leg and a shaggy black mongrel of a dog as constant companions. He went stumping about, talking to himself and the dog. He was one of the people in the town who loved to hear John recite and sing. He never could have enough of it. In return he would often give John a spare poster which John would tack on to the front-room chimney-piece at home. They were always coloured yellow, with red lettering.

One morning Jimmy was going about everywhere posting up: GREAT SENSATION!

THEATRE ROYAL

PORT MERLIN

——

SHAKESPEARE'S

ROMEO AND JULIET

——

MISS ADA MONTGOMERY

as

JULIET

Three Performances Only

THURSDAY, FRIDAY and SATURDAY

July 7, 8, 9, at 8 p.m.

Doors Open 7.30 p.m.

I must confess that there are certain episodes in John's early life that follow along very conventional lines. I don't know how many novels in my youth contained the episode of the young stage aspirant who, adoring the beautiful leading lady, is graciously kissed by her on the forehead!

Thackeray made good use of it once. But the differences here are that in the first place Johnny, unlike Mr. Pendennis, was only eight years old when he spoke for the first time to his Miss Fotheringay, and secondly he was thinking more of himself, I am afraid, than of the great artist. Of himself and Shakespeare, I might perhaps venture.

As soon as he read Jimmy's announcement he made love to Mr. Darlington.

Mr. Darlington sat inside his stuffy little box like a squirrel in a cage. Pasted on to the faded wallpaper behind him were photographs signed 'Yours in the Pink, Wal. Peach,' or 'Yours very sincerely, Flossie Armstrong,' or (as John remembers especially well because she was so lovely a lady) 'Yours, dear Mr.

Darlington, ever sincerely, Connie May.'

'Do you think,' he asked Mr. Darlington, 'Ada Montgomery is as beautiful as Connie May?'

'A bit long in the tooth she must be. Long time since she was here.'

'Juliet was only fourteen,' John remembered that he priggishly remarked, and Mr. Darlington wisely replied: 'That's the whole trouble with Juliet if you ask me—all the Juliets I've ever seen. If they're fourteen or thereabouts they can't act, and if they can act, they're a damned sight more than fourteen.'

He let himself go with John, dropped his dignity and sense of class importance. In fact, as he told him, he was always forgetting that John was only eight years old. This irritated him. It always annoyed him that John should think so much of himself.

'Life'll teach yer! Life'll teach yer!' he would remark gloomily.

'I want it to,' said John—and yet he could be a child too when he liked, as for instance when at a moment's notice he would leave Shakespeare and Mr.

Darlington and run down the street after the fire-engine, waving his long arms and running so wildly that you'd think he'd crack his thin knees at any moment.

He was determined to get into the Theatre for the first performance of Romeo and Juliet. It wasn't easy. There were no free tickets this time and Mr.

Darlington was quite honest and straightforward.

'It's no use you hanging around THIS time, Johnny. Ada Montgomery's got a sort of world celebrity. She's acted in America. Last time she was here the house was sold right out. It'll be the same this time.... No, it will be of no use your reading your play to me. You've done that once already. And I'm not so mighty set on plays. I'm like the girl in the sweet-shop. Too much of it around all the time. No, I tell you it's no good.'

John says he remembers that he promised to pick Mr. Darlington a large bunch of flowers. But that didn't move him.

'Now it's no use your going on. I tell you there won't be a empty seat.'

Every day, as soon as school was over, John hung around the Theatre. There was a lot of bustle, scenery going in and out, actors and actresses coming and going for rehearsal.

So it was that John discovered Mr. Beakin. Dear Mr. Beakin!

'I suppose,' John would continue, 'I owe everything, if you look into it, to Sam Beakin. I don't see any other way that I'd have got into that Theatre, and if I hadn't, why, then I wouldn't ... but listen and I'll tell you.' Then he'd throw his head back, wink with his left eye at myself who'd heard the story so very often before, and regale the flattered third party with the whole affair.

'No one remembers Sam Beakin nowadays of course. No one perhaps in the whole world but myself. Just after this tour with Ada Montgomery he was with Irving at the Lyceum. After that again with Tree at His Majesty's. Then he became too fat and, I'm afraid, too fond of the bottle. He dropped out of engagements and of friends. I found him in wretched rooms in Bloomsbury, and ... but that's another story.

'What happened now was that I was standing (eight years and a bit I was at the time) outside the Theatre Royal, Port Merlin, waiting for some kind of miracle. I believed in miracles then, I believe in them now. Sam Beakin comes along, traditional actor of the time, coat with velvet collar, cane with gold top, hat hitched on one side of his head. But he was a fine-looking man in those days, not so fat, broad-chested, holding his head up, full of confidence and childlike vanity and self-absorption. Even then, I expect, much too fond of drink and women.

'Well, he was striding along to the stage-door, swinging his cane, and he saw me. He was to play Mercutio and he was reciting some of the Queen Mab speech aloud, and as he got up to me I continued it for him. I was only eight but my father had first read the play to me when I was three, I should think.

And I'd read it again and again since the announcement of its performance.

'I always had complete confidence in the friendliness of everybody and I looked up at him grinning. I expect I danced a little on both feet. It's a habit I still have. We were almost inside the stage-door, and Mr. Darlington, within his little box, was being dignified, fussy, self-important.

'"What the devil's this, Darlington?" Beakin said, and Mr. Darlington answered very solemnly, "It's a boy I know, Mr. Beakin, sir. He's mad about the theatre."

'It was a piece of luck for me, of course, that Beakin was there at all. Often enough the company wouldn't arrive at the town where they were performing until the actual day. But on this occasion the first part of the week had been empty. During the preceding week they'd been at Weymouth. So Sam was free of care, a little inebriated perhaps, full of charity.

'"He's pestering me," Mr. Darlington said, "to get him in to the performance to-morrow night. I tell him it can't be done."

'"Want to see me as Mercutio, do you?" says Sam Beakin grinning.

'I answered fervently something or another, and it was then he really noticed me. Beakin told me years later that he thought I was the ugliest boy he'd ever seen in his life. All the same striking. That's the way I used to hit people, you know,' Cornelius would add, throwing his untidy hair back from his forehead.

To cut John's reminiscences short, what happened was that Sam Beakin promised to get him into the Theatre. And he kept his promise.

John wanted to bring his father in too. He assured him that it would be all right, that Mr. Beakin would do anything for him and that he'd promised to listen to his play. But something had happened to John's father. He seemed to have no enterprise any longer. He sat there, looking through the window at the cobble- path, the shoulder of the sand-dune and the tangled cup of the sea....

So John went alone, with a clean white collar and the grey trousers that were so much too short and tight for him. He carried a bunch of flowers that he intended to give to Miss Montgomery. He was quite confident that he would speak to her.

When he reached the stage-door there was a tremendous bustle, and for a little while he was afraid that he would never be able to reach Mr. Darlington.

This was agonizing.

The crowd around him was cheerful and humorous, consisting very largely of members of the orchestra, scene-shifters, friends of the company. Many of them knew Johnny.

'Hullo, young Cock o' the Walk. Where are you going to?'

'I've been asked to come—Mr. Beakin asked me. Please will you— would you mind? Mr. Darlington wants me.'

John, when he wished, had very beautiful manners which he inherited from the Ancient Scandinavian, who was, so tradition said, always charming to ladies before he assaulted them. Some big man handed him through to Mr.

Darlington, who was by far too officially busy to pay any attention to him.

But it happened that someone pushed an arm through the swinging door with the words 'Mr. Beakin's drink there yet?' and a big pewter pot was handed over. John caught the arm and, with the drink, was pulled to the other side of the door.

'I'm the boy—' Johnny began, clutching his flowers in one hand and holding on to the hairy arm with the other.

'Oh, 'e said something about a boy.'

At least that's how John told the story. He said that he was never so passionately excited again. That isn't true, of course, because he was so frequently and so easily excited.

'You won't find any theatre like that ever any more. It was one of the curious things about Merlin, as I remember it, that you were conscious of the sea everywhere. The "Royal" was right in the middle of the town and yet, quite easily, if you went in the interval to the front of the Theatre for a breath of air, you could hear, if there was any sea on, the echo of the waves pounding on the beach. It must have been a kind of echo— it was like the musical rhythm in a sea-shell held up to the ear.

'But INSIDE the Theatre that night there was the smell of gas, of wet paint, of beer, of sweating human bodies. It was a little, compact eighteenth-century building and they'd had the good sense, or perhaps simply the carelessness, to leave the old red and gold on the pillars and the exteriors of the boxes. The ceiling was painted with a fine, now faded, representation of Venus and Adonis, considered by many Merlin citizens indecent because of the general nudity.

'On this present occasion they had been repainting the doors and walls of the lobby. That smell of new paint, which somehow had salt in it because I was always thinking of the sea, I shall have in my nostrils till my dying day.'

The man with the hairy arms led John to a corner behind the stage and whispered to him fiercely that he was to stay exactly there and not move for the rest of the evening.

Exactly there he stayed with a wing of scenery stretching forward to the right of him, a ladder against the wall on his left, and in front of him a straight pattern of light and colour holding a strip of stage, a piece of scenery painted with ancient buildings, and a large papier-mâché tree with a big hole in it.

So, and thus, he saw his first Shakespearian play, standing there without moving a limb even in the intermission, shivering with cold (for there was a terrible draught), excitement, pleasure, anticipation. For on this night he knew for the first time that this was where he ought to be. It was to be his fate to know that always and yet never to translate that knowledge into fact. From the night of Romeo and Juliet he was to be a frustrated human being.

He shivered so that his teeth chattered, for, as the evening went on, he was convinced that it was he who had written the play and not Shakespeare. He had even created Ada Montgomery. He did not see her with any critical eye, for he was responsible for her. When she stood on the balcony and it trembled ominously she flashed a side-look to the wings so fierce and angry that Johnny wondered how anyone could survive it. And yet a moment later in a deep melodious tone she was ravishing the elderly and pigeon-breasted Romeo:

'O gentle Romeo!

If thou dost love, pronounce it faithfully;

Or if thou think'st I am too quickly won,

I'll frown and be perverse and say thee nay,

So thou wilt woo; but else, not for the world.

In truth, fair Montague, I am too fond,

And therefore thou mayst think my 'haviour light....'

To which the elderly Romeo, in a voice sadly feminine and shrill, replied:

'Lady, by yonder blessed moon I swear

That tips with silver all these fruit-tree tops ... '

'That tips with silver ... ' Had not Johnny known that exactly? Not the fruit-

trees, but the dunes with their rough dark grasses, the fresh-water stream running into the sand, and the moon first stretching its long finger over the thin ridge of the dark sea, then spreading until it marbled the wet shore to mother-of-pearl, then flashing all the running stream into a glitter and sparkle of silver?

He had seen his friend Mercutio, now handsome indeed in doublet, hose and feathered hat. Johnny's heart beat with ancient friendship, for he felt as though he had known Mr. Beakin for ever and ever!

'He was an old, old friend, you know, and the finest thing in physical splendour I'd ever seen, pushing up his stomach into his chest and shaking his black curly wig under his broad-brimmed hat:

"She is the fairies' midwife and she comes, In shape no bigger than an agate-stone

On the forefinger of an alderman,

Drawn with a team of little atomies

Athwart men's noses as they lie asleep ... "

'I tell you I could repeat every word of it when I was five. There was a bright baby for you!

'Anyway on this occasion when the scene changed to Capulet's house and Beakin strode off, brushing right past me, I didn't attempt to stop him, for it was still Mercutio, MY Mercutio, who was dancing in my brain.'

Then the moment came.

Ada Montgomery had cried:

'O, look! Methinks I see my cousin's ghost

Seeking out Romeo, that did spit his body Upon a rapier's point. Stay, Tybalt, stay!

Romeo, I come! This do I drink to thee!'

At once, after the curtain fell, John remembered, Ada Montgomery sat up in her nightdress and gave vent to a terrific sneeze. She was a large-faced, large-bosomed lady and her sneeze was like a thunderclap.

'Just kept it in, by God!' she cried and strode to the wings.

Fate decided that she should run straight into Johnny, nearly fall, fold her arms about him to steady herself, so that he found himself enwrapped in rolls of white cotton, his hands pressed against steel corsets, and savour of peppermint, lily of the valley and good honest beer.

'What the hell—' cried the lady (or so John always insisted). Then: 'Body of God, it's a boy!'

She stood staring at him, then she laughed.

John, so soon as he could get his breath, was entirely at his ease and presented his bunch of flowers, now, alas, crushed and faded.

He explained that he was a friend of Mr. Beakin's who had permitted him—

that he worshipped Ada Montgomery—Shakespeare also—that he had gathered these flowers for her.

She sat down on an upturned box, spread her legs and scratched her thigh while the scene-shifters pushed the shabby scenery apart.

'And you want to be an actor? ... Well, you could be a comic with a mouth like that. How old are you? Eight? And you know this damned play by heart?

What do you think of me? A bit more than fourteen, eh? Christ! Should think I was! Want to come to London?'

'Yes, if you don't mind,' said John.

' *I* mind! A lot of bloody good MY minding anything does. There I am, swearing in front of a kid. Here! I must go and change! Lord, if you aren't the oddest ... '

Johnny then asked if he might come and see her in London.

See her? Of course he could.

Where did she live?

She called to a scene-shifter and got the back of an envelope and the stub of a pencil. In a childish hand she wrote:

Ada Montgomery,

11 Dickens Mansions,

Taggart Street,

Portland Place.

'There! Come and see me!'

If he'd been a prettier little boy she'd have kissed him. As it was, she nodded in a friendly manner and went off, taking the bunch of flowers. But Johnny, stepping out to see where she went to, observed that round the corner and mounting the crooked little staircase to her dressing-room, she dropped the withered bunch.

He was practically-minded. He had the address. So he stood, heart, soul filled with ambition and an eight-year-old conquest of the world, to watch the rest of the performance.

CHAPTER III

Death of His Father

Reverently he put Ada Montgomery's address away in the little shell- box that his father had given him two years before for Christmas; he then proceeded on the solemn business of growing older.

Shortly after his ninth birthday his grandfather died. The old man's end was very peaceful. During the last week of his reign he was dispensing offices to his friends in the Asylum, making one Lord High Chancellor, another General of his Eastern Forces. He made some excellent laws too in those last days, as, for instance, the caging of birds was an offence deserving of two years in gaol, everyone with more than one hundred pounds a year must have a rose- garden, and anyone chaining a dog for more than six hours at a time was himself to be chained for a like duration. He very solemnly nominated Johnny as heir to the throne. He died with a smile on his lips, in all probability the happiest man in England.

John's grandmother did not long survive him. It had been so great a part of her life that she should care for her husband that she naturally followed him with the hope that he would still be needing her care. She was also greatly distressed by the unhappiness of her son, John's father. After her husband's death she spent most of the day in the Cornelius' cottage, looking at her son with the loving anxiety of a mother, which, when there is no way of appeasing it, can be very irritating. Little Mr. Cornelius sat at his table, pretending to work, while his mother in a voice of tremulous brightness asked him, once every half-hour, whether there wasn't anything she could do for him.

Poor Daisy Cornelius went on with her washing and felt no loving- kindness towards her mother-in-law. And then one day the little woman gave a cry and fell back on to John's patchwork quilt. Her son, whose arms were round her, suddenly realized that one of the last supports left to him in life was

dying. She looked into his eyes and, with the realization that he loved her, contentedly died.

One of the things that had happened to John by this time was that his voice had developed into one of the finest ever heard in Glebeshire. I have not only his word for it; Anne, Charlie and other later acquaintances testified quite sufficiently. He might, I don't doubt, had he known the right people, have won a singing scholarship in one of the Cathedrals—and what would have been his fate then?

However, there was no one in Port Merlin to advise him, and his audiences consisted principally of washerwomen, fishermen, boys and girls who laughed at him, Mr. Bartholomew, Mr. Darlington, Mrs. Winchester, Jimmy Lipscombe—and, for a brief while, the congregation at St. Peter's Church.

This last episode was characteristic of much that happened to him through life. It seems that the Rector of St. Peter's, Mr. Dunlop was his name, heard of John's voice and invited him to sing to him, which he very readily did. He was then asked to sing in St. Peter's choir. John enquired—what benefits were there? Well, there was a Choir Treat in the summer and a jolly Party at Christmas-time. John said that he would see how he liked it.

Mr. Dunlop was, I understand, the 'motherly' kind of clergyman. All his choir-boys were his children and, of course, like many mothers, he had his favourite child. John used to imitate him very well—his cherubic smile, his chuckle, his kindly pressure on the lucky boy's shoulder. 'But I was never one of the lucky boys. I was far too ugly and my clothes were too shabby.

Besides, I was always upsetting the other boys, telling them stories in church, generally misbehaving. As a matter of fact I could not bear Mr. Dunlop touching me. I've been always like that. I hate to be touched by the wrong person. So I shrank away when his fat fingers caught my arm.'

The unhappy climax came when on a gala day, Easter Sunday perhaps it was, Mr. Dunlop's favourite child was to sing as solo in the anthem 'O for the Wings of a Dove.'

The little singer was the favourite child of the Dunlop family just then and he had, John always asserted, a voice like a pencil on a slate.

In any case, he had but just started on his song when John could endure it no longer and started also. He knew the music perfectly, his voice was strong, pure, resonant, and very soon he was the only singer. Nothing very romantic occurred. Charlie Christian was in the congregation, but John's beautiful eyes, as his voice soared higher and higher, did NOT meet, over the heads of the people, Charlie's beautiful eyes. John simply occupied himself with his business, which was not, alas, his business at all. The congregation was unaware of anything save that its soul was being given the most delectable bread and treacle.

Afterwards in the vestry Mr. Dunlop had a great deal to say. He was, most rightly, indignant. John simply remarked that his voice could lick any other boy's voice in England and he could read music at sight, which was more than Mr. Dunlop could. He ceased, from that moment, to be a member of St.

Peter's choir, and Charlie ceased to be a member of its congregation, which he had joined only as John's supporter.

The friendship between the two boys was now something of real importance.

The deeper I look into it, the more surely I discover its essential character, the more I recall to mind the Lama and Kim, two noble gentlemen not, at this time of which I am writing, yet created. Charlie was physically like the Lama as little as may be, neither in brains nor in character had he any resemblance to him. He was looking neither for an Arrow nor a River and the only Wheel of which he was conscious was the wheel of mechanics.

Moreover it was he who protected John and it was Kim who protected the Lama. Nevertheless the resemblance is there. Charlie had, I fancy, the kind of influence over John that the Lama had over Kim. Charlie was quiet, still, reflective. John had the Lama's naïveté and the Lama's wisdom, but he had the mischievousness and the charming arrogance of Kim. I am thinking, perhaps, when all is said, of the Lama's quiet and beautiful fidelity, his unswerving insistence on the final values; Charlie had that more than any man I have ever known.

Charlie's mind was entirely of a mechanical character and it was through machines that he came to a perception of human beings. His ambition was to be an engineer and it often worried him that John should tell lies and believe so many things that were clearly untrue. He liked then and always to argue

and he was one of the most obstinate of God's creatures. Argument with Charlie meant repeating the same thing over and over again.

'There bain't no mermaids.'

'How do you know there aren't?'

'Everyone knows there's not.'

'How do you know what's under the sea?'

'There bain't no mermaids, I tell you. It's silly to talk so soft.'

'I'll tell you what's under the sea. There are trees of coral, pink coral, and the sun shines down through the green water and touches the tips of the coral trees, while a little swarm of fish, fish all mouths with scales of gold—'

'There bain't no mermaids. 'Tis silly—'

'How do you know? Have you ever been to the bottom of the sea?'

'Of course not. But there bain't—'

Charlie would sit, his fingers active, whittling a stick, sharpening a pencil, mending a box. He could do anything with his hands.

At the age of six he swam like a fish, whereas John was never a good swimmer. But he liked to be IN the water, and Charlie would swim out ahead of him tempting him further and further, and then, as John sank, he would feel Charlie's muscular arm around him. He was afraid of nothing if Charlie were near.

Anne Swinnerton was altogether a different problem. The critical moment of Anne's life arrived when, at the age of eleven and a little over, she was informed by a girl to whom she had been impertinent (or as she herself would call it, independent) exactly and precisely how her mother earned a living.

Anne, being no fool, had from a very early age realized that a considerable number of gentlemen called upon her mother and appeared to like her very much. Mrs. Swinnerton was pretty, gay and lively. She also had, as Anne

knew, a heady temper and moods of extreme misery and despair. Anne often described to me that queer life in that queer house on the cliff. Where Mr.

Swinnerton was she never knew.

Not only did she never see her father in the flesh, she never even saw a photograph of him. She never knew whether she were legitimate or no; she suspected she was not.

When she was six she was given a bedroom in the little house on the ground floor looking over the cliff to the sea. The only other person in the house beside a weekly char was a grim young woman called Miss Merkle who came straight out of the pages of Dickens, where her name was Rosa Dartle.

This lady was fierce-tempered and gave little Anne many a slap and a shaking. She had a sort of unkind, vexed angry love for Anne's mother. She cooked very well and looked after the house. She never spoke to any of Mrs.

Swinnerton's gentlemen friends. If she encountered one she passed him as though he were not.

Mrs. Swinnerton's friends came sometimes from a distance, sometimes from near at hand. Often they stayed all night. Some of them little Anne came to know quite well. There was Uncle George, who was large, burly, red-faced, with side-whiskers. Often she saw Uncle George in his nightshirt—once she saw him in the sitting- room and her mother was sitting on his knee. There was Mr. Saunders, who was a little shy man, regarding her with eyes of terror, why she couldn't imagine. Then there was a young, gay, very pleasant gentleman with the odd name of Uncle Percy Garden. Perhaps because of his name, perhaps because of the strong scent that he used, she always connected him with flowers.

It sometimes seemed to her unusual that it should be always gentlemen who visited their house and never ladies. Between her mother and herself an undoubted affection existed, but it was of a kind that checked in Anne any sort of demonstrativeness—for when her mother showed affection she was so VERY demonstrative that Anne felt a little sick, and when her mother didn't need affection she disliked even to be touched. This early training was greatly responsible for Anne's own dislike of demonstrations in later life.

It was an untidy little house with the smell of cigarette-smoke, bon-bons,

Miss Merkle's cooking, and the salt sea air all over it. But Anne was quite happy in that life until the girl at school informed her plainly that Anne's mother slept with all these different gentlemen and that they paid her mother money for the pleasure of doing so. Even then Anne understood very little of it; she could see no reason why the gentlemen should pay her mother money for so very slight a pleasure. She herself disliked extremely to sleep with her mother.

What she did understand was that, in some mysterious fashion, it was disgraceful that this should occur, and that she and her mother were 'bad'

because of it. Shortly after this she was taken away from the school and sent to a boarding-school at Truro in Cornwall. This interrupted her friendship with John for five whole years. The result of this crisis was to make her outwardly proud, reserved, defiant, unfriendly. Her warmth of heart, her loyalty of spirit, were hidden.

She did not, in these years in Truro, forget John. She has told me how strange it was that she should remember him and think of him more than of any other human being. He also remembered her. He wrote to her funny letters and little pieces of very bad poetry. All these she kept.

One was:

DEAR ANNE—I'm thinking of going fishing with Charlie not that I ever catch anything but it's a half-holiday. I cheeked Mrs. Hoskin last night and stood behind a door when she didn't know and made her jump like anything.

I'm beginning to write a play about Robin Hood. It's in twelve acts and the first act is in the greenwood and the second act is King Richard landing from Palestine. I've written a poem. Here it is:

When I was at the glassy sea

Two crabs said to me

There's the wind blowing

Over the rocks

And the mermaids

Will hide

Under the Tide

Tearfully.

I'm very clever I think, not like others, and I am going to write some of the finest books there have ever been. I am seeing after father because he is not very well.

Your loving friend,

John Cornelius.

At a very early age his writing was excellently clear and his spelling remarkably good. This letter, on a kind of pink rough paper in which you pack meat or vegetables, is before me on my table now.

Those words about his father were true enough. He had now become his father's guard, guide, friend and general cheerer-up. His mind at the mature age of nine was entirely divided between his father and his career!

Myself: 'Your career?'

John: 'Well—what would you call it? Writing plays, telling people stories, singing songs to anyone who would listen.'

Myself: 'You must have had many rebuffs.'

John: 'I did. I didn't care in the least. It wasn't until the Bicycle Factory ... '

In any case poor Mrs. Cornelius was quite incapable of looking after her husband. That fear of him, the sense of inferiority that she had always had, was now very much stronger, for he had withdrawn himself from her into the world of his own griefs. Then he earned no more with his toys and his boxes, for the capacity for work seemed entirely to have deserted him, and he would sit, hour by hour, staring out at the sea and doing nothing. So she must earn more, and the stronger this necessity was upon her the more desperate was her disorder and flurry and unpunctuality.

She was, I understand, a really good laundress, a laundress by nature—but that nature was also entirely without discipline or technique and she would go about wringing her hands and crying: 'Oh, Lordy! Lordy! Whatever are we going to do now?'

John at this moment, although he loved her so dearly, had little time to spend on her; his care was all for his father.

It was the son who took the father out for walks now, rather than the father the son. John would hurry home from school, would find his father seated at the table, toys and boxes unfinished before him, his hands folded.

'Come on now,' John would cry, and Cornelius would get up, as though moving out of a dream, and nod his head. They very seldom went into the town now; more and more they chose the same course, the rough sea-path that ran between the wiry spear-shaped grass and the nodding sea-pinks at the edge of the dunes above the shore in the direction of St. Gertrude Head.

There St. Gertrude sat like a fat old market-woman, her skirts drawn up to her knees, paddling in the level metallic sea.

While the gulls cried and the wind tugged at the grass and the sea tramped, murmured, and tramped again below them, the two of them would walk quietly forward, as though they had a serious destination. John would talk, thinking of everything that might cheer his father. But his father would not be cheered. He would be silent for a long while, simply pounding along, looking sometimes out to sea, his lips moving once and again as though he were going to speak. Then, quite precipitately, he would exclaim:

'It's unbelievable, John, how cruel life is. Yes, whichever way you look at it.

Nobody's happy. They may have been once but they aren't any more. Human beings have lost the way of running the world and, mark me, the more they learn the more bewildered they'll get. Bewildered! That's the word. Why, what a comment on the present world when you can say that my poor old father, who was a lunatic in the paupers' Asylum, was happier than anyone else in this town. Isn't that a shameful thing, John? But it's true.'

And John told me that he would stand up for life as though he had been appointed life's especial defender. He would cry, pouring out floods of words to the gulls, and the rose-coloured evening sky, and the long white lines that threaded the purple sea, that it wasn't true. That there were many happy

people—Miss Gracie and Mrs. Winchester and Mr. Bartholomew and Mr.

Dunlop (although he didn't like him) and Charlie Christian ... they were all happy.

Well, then—and John's father's voice would fall low and tremble with emotion—wasn't it unfair that for no fault of their own some people should be chosen to be unhappy and failures—such failures that they were unable even to earn enough to keep wife and child and the wife must kill herself with working to keep the family?

'If there's a God, John, He's cruel. He is there only to torture us; it amuses Him. There's nothing new about that. You know that, don't you? Men have been finding that to be true for thousands of years but they can't bear to admit it. They cheat themselves deliberately.' And then his father would burst out:

'But there isn't a God. We are like these weeds, the gulls there. We are born like them, millions of us, and are lost and forgotten as quickly. We suffer, they suffer. We torture ourselves and one another and the sea advances and retreats not caring. Nothing cares.'

And then he'd remember that John was a boy, only nine years old, and he'd say he was ashamed to talk with such despair. Perhaps he was wrong—

maybe he was wrong.

John would do everything he could to comfort him. He would put his arm through his father's (he was already almost as tall) and tell him that of course he was wrong and that any time now someone would come along and make him famous, and that he wasn't to be unhappy because that horrible old woman ...

'I would say that it didn't seem to me to matter very much whether people admired what you did or not if what you made was beautiful. A bit priggish, do you think? If it was, I was punished later on for saying such a thing: I was to be taught just that lesson. And then I would talk about God and say that I didn't believe there could be so much beauty in the world if it was only accident. If it was all accident, I would say, why, then the world would be ugly— tin cans and garbage-heaps—fish and birds would be colourless and flowers have no scent ... A bit priggish? I don't think so. I had tried to think these things out. I was so much with older people and of course I talked too

much. In any case I was doing everything I could to comfort my father. Now when he was unhappy he seemed to me younger than myself and more helpless.'

But nothing would rouse him. The two old women, Mrs. Hoskin and Mrs.

Garriman, would come in and see him sitting there and mutter that it was a shame for poor Mrs. Cornelius, her having so much to do, working her poor fingers to the bone, and they'd drive him crazy....

So one afternoon John comes back from school and finds his mother crying her heart out and his father gone. While Mrs. Cornelius was away, seeing about some laundry, he had seized his chance and gone, leaving a note behind him. The note said that he was off to try and get some work. Perhaps in Drymouth. That he couldn't endure any longer to sit there idle while Daisy worked her hands to the bone to keep him. As soon as he had found work he would let them know. In any case she would have now only two mouths to feed rather than three.

The emptiness caused by his departure was terrible. They both loved him so much. Mrs. Cornelius could not believe that he was really gone. She would start up every five minutes or so with a cry: 'There he is! He's come back! I knew he would!' She could not sleep but tossed from side to side all night long. And of course her work suffered. She began to be sadly behindhand with it— neither eating nor sleeping, looking out of window to see whether he were returning ...

Mrs. Hoskin and Mrs. Garriman were for ever poking their heads round the door. They must have been women who really rejoiced in the misfortunes of others, who revelled in unkindness, who were as conceited as they were unkind. They brooded like two untidy slightly-inebriated crows over the scene. Their arrogance was their trouble. They could not endure the success or happiness of others because the failure of their own lives, neither too successful nor too happy, was thus emphasized. They knew that they would never achieve anything in the world but would be always peevish, destructive commentators on the achievements of others.

'They were so ugly,' John said, 'that they hurt you to look at them. Mrs.

Hoskin was small and dirty, and if she had been a man would have been bald.

Her complexion was pallid, muddy; her nose hooked. Mrs. Garriman was tall and thin and, it seemed, suffered from dyspepsia. She had a green slanting eye. She was the more conceited of the two, the less harmful, for Mrs. Hoskin suffered from an inferiority complex, which made her savage with anyone who had any luck.

'She saw everyone as the American sometimes sees the Englishman—

pompous, self-satisfied, complacent, affected, self-centred. That was the outside world to Mrs. Hoskin, who was a widow and had a little shop with sweets, tobacco, some indecent postcards in a drawer. She was pimp, procuress, moneylender to the sailors, fishermen and others who got into her clutches. She had a high- pitched eager voice:

'"Oh, 'e'll come back, never you be afraid. You cheer up, Daisy— as many fish in the sea as ... What about a drop? Cheer you up. Come on. Never bother what the kid says." She hated me,' John would go on, 'and I hated her.

She's been a symbol to me all my life of the self-satisfied destroyer, the evil that there is in the world, the eternal mischief-maker.'

That is the kind of exaggerated romanticism John indulged in. As I have said already, Mrs. Hoskin was nothing ... and no doubt, poor dear, she had her own troubles....

In any case matters were now serious. John must begin to earn something.

Little Mr. Bartholomew got him into a bicycle factory.

This, I fancy, was so small an affair that it was absurd perhaps to dignify it with the name of factory. In 1893 bicycles were beginning to be all the rage in England and little branches of hopeful new enterprises were to be found everywhere.

In Port Merlin there was for a decade or so Bennett's Bicycle Manufactory.

Mr. Bartholomew, who was by this time greatly attached to John, knew a Mr.

Roper who was manager of the place. John was, of course, too young to be allowed to leave school and earn his living in any serious way, but it was arranged that from five to seven he should fetch and carry for Mr. Roper and should receive so many shillings a week from Mr. Roper's own personal pocket. The incident that ended this affair was to have an effect on John for

many years to come. By this time he was very tall for his age, and his ugliness of feature was not less marked. At the same time, because of the brightness of his watching eye, because his hair was inclined to be long, because of a certain softness of cheek and gentleness of voice, because, too, of his singing abilities, his story-telling, the awkwardness with which he ran, because finally of his general unlikeness to all other boys whatever, there was something feminine about him. He had in his nature, like all true artists, a mingling of the masculine and feminine....

When he had been obliging fat, fussy, breathless little Mr. Roper for a week or so some of the rougher hands about the place waylaid him. Laughing, not, in any real intention, brutal, they dragged him to a deserted corner and there informed him that they were certain that he was a sweet little girl in disguise, that they had bets on the matter and must make sure.

'At that moment for the first time for many a day all the nightmares of my earlier childhood returned on me. A horror, a disgust, a despair far greater than the situation deserved, leapt on me. The man with the jagged teeth, the man with the taloned hands ... As they caught hold of me I uttered a cry of passionate despair. They had pulled my trousers down ... with much laughter their hands were about my body. I began to cry so desperately, so forlornly, that their rough sense of fun was itself surprised. They hadn't intended anything so tragic. They slunk away, pretending to mock my defencelessness; I, weeping bitterly, dragged up my trousers and went home. That was the end of Bennett's Bicycles....'

It was then that he began his serious resolve to go to London. He did not know how it could be done and at present at least he could not leave his mother, but, in one way or another, he must be in London. Once there he was as confident of his abilities, as vain of his talents as though someone had whispered in his ear....

It was at this time of great distress and apprehension that he said he first met the Bird-Man.

Myself: 'No one has ever seen the Bird-Man but yourself.'

John: 'What of that? No one has ever met YOU but myself—the YOU that I

meet, I mean. Do you suppose that anyone else sees you as I see you, any one else alive or dead? We all of us meet one another uniquely and that meeting is only a shadow of the only real meeting we have—our meeting with ourselves. If you'd met the Bird-Man he would have seemed to you in all probability a tramp walking from Exeter to Truro. You would probably never have noticed the birds at all.'

Myself: 'This is all very tiresome. People in these days hate this kind of vague fantasy....'

John (paying no attention): 'He looked like a tramp, or perhaps like a tree turned into a tramp by some evil magician. He had that kind of regretful remembering look. When I first saw him he was sitting with his back to a hummock on Gunbarrow Moor. It was a grand day and the moor glittered with sun, the sea expanse beyond it in a trembling white haze. He was in rags

—you could see his bare brown thigh. He wore an old black bishop's hat on his head, the tags still on it. He had a long fleshy fat nose and a ragged beard.

On his finger was a fine bishop's ring, a fat, fussy robin—'

Myself: 'I don't believe it.'

John: 'That doesn't matter in the least. Do you suppose your believing or not believing anything makes any difference to the facts? That's what's the matter with critics, religious sects, bankers and politicians. He was there all right and very nice too. I sat down beside him and he said I was the first boy who hadn't driven the birds away. I asked him why they stayed with him so quietly and he said because they trusted him, because they knew he wouldn't break his word to them. Also he had a very special bird-seed, which he showed me. He carried a coloured bag made of leather. It was full of grey seed. He scattered a little of this on the ground, but the birds wouldn't touch it. He said they knew it wasn't their meal-time. I asked him where he lived and he said he could be faithful to any place. He used the word "faithful" a great many times.'

Myself: 'The trouble with being faithful is that your mind doesn't grow.'

John: 'Well, considering the little that anyone's mind grows anyway, perhaps fidelity is more important.'

Myself: 'You will irritate many serious-minded people with all this pretty-

pretty nonsense about bird-men—'

John: 'That doesn't matter in the least. It isn't my business to consider whether I irritate people—'

All the same, after John left Mr. Roper's service, things became very serious.

He had suddenly to wrestle with a number of problems for which he was much too young.

Those two old devils, Mrs. Hoskin and Mrs. Garriman, were now for ever persuading his poor mother to take a 'drop.' One of the hardest things for John was the way in which his mother appeared now humble and self-accusing in front of him. She would always appear to be working her hardest on his return from school and she would look at him rather like a dog who expects to be scolded. She would chatter to him with a heightened eagerness and would want to hear about all that had happened to him. Then, when he began to tell her, her interest would droop, her eyes wander. She would listen as though for footsteps. She would begin to work with a feverish energy, ironing and scrubbing, sighing as she worked. He would wake in the night and hear her crying. Once or twice he saw her standing, in her nightdress, by the table, handling the toy soldiers, the two or three little unfinished boxes.

They were very definitely hungry most of the time or would have been had not Charlie Christian shared his lunch with John at school. John was too proud to allow anyone else to know. He brought things home for his mother, however. He stole food on several easy occasions.

Then one night, when it was raining in a frenzy and John was reading Lavengro to his mother, who didn't understand a word of it, the door was pushed open and Mr. Cornelius stood there. He looked at them, opened his mouth to speak, then stumbled to the ground.

They took off his wet clothes and put him to bed. They could see that he was very ill and they sent for a doctor. Yes, he was very ill. He had not had enough to eat; had caught a bad chill, had a very serious fever. He needed many things—medicine, special food. But there was no money in the house.

Well, then, he must go to the hospital.

But Mr. Cornelius refused to go to the hospital. Physically weak though he was he resisted with surprising energy. In a feeble trembling whisper, his fingers shaking against the sheet, he told them that he had come home to die and in his own home his death should be.

John, as soon as he saw the desire in his father's eyes, pleaded with them also.

He would look after his father, he would see that he had everything. Where was the money? Oh, he'd get the money somehow.

'I was quite prepared to steal it. I didn't care where from. It seemed to me monstrous that father should be dying for want of a pound or two and that other people should have more than they could use. Not an original idea! ...

But if you had seen my mother apologizing to that little sharp ferrety-eyed doctor, rubbing her red hands one against another and murmuring: "It isn't my fault, doctor, really it is not.... I work as well as I am able ... indeed I do." And my father, so white and thin and small now that he looked like a child lying there, with his mouth set obstinately, summoning all his strength to resist anyone who tried to remove him. Over and over again, moistening his lips with his tongue, he murmured: "I've come back ... to die."'

They were saved by a most unexpected person. Anne Swinnerton's mother.

She appeared on the morning after Cornelius' return. The doctor was saying:

'There's nothing for it but the hospital.'

Mrs. Swinnerton—wearing, John remembered, a large girlish floppy summer hat with masses of paper roses—stepped forward and said:

'Oh, why need he go to the hospital?'

It seems that Mrs. Swinnerton had helped him the night before to reach his house. She had been shy of entering with him but, through the night, had been disturbed by her conscience. Poor man! He had looked so dreadfully ill.... Frightened out of her life at her interference, she had come to enquire....

She was a chattering, giggling, face-painted little woman but exceedingly capable. If Mrs. Cornelius knew of her immoral reputation it did not worry her in the least: nor did either herself or John hesitate to take anything that

Mrs. Swinnerton might have to offer. The situation had become too real for fantasies about morals or property.

Mrs. Swinnerton established herself in the Cornelius' cottage and became quite a domineering person. Even Mrs. Garriman and Mrs. Hoskin did not venture to obtrude their heads.

But John was concentrated on his father. That passionate love always in his heart poured out now as never before. He thought that if he cared intensely enough, if he put everything that he had into saving his father, he WOULD

save him.

The little man was really dying of exhaustion, of starvation. He had succeeded in reaching Polchester and with good fortune he found a job with a haberdasher. His gentlemanly appearance and voice suggested to his employer that he would be a good salesman. And so for a while he was, but his strength could not sustain the long unbroken hours on his feet. He found, too, that he had a hunger for his wife and child. His loneliness was appalling.

He would listen to the Cathedral bells chiming the hours at night and would cry—too weak, too weary to check his tears. Then he fell ill, lost his job, started back for Port Merlin. A friendly waggoner helped him part of the way.

A lady driving a trap took him ten miles. He walked the rest. He knew that he was dying and for the last part of his journey he was accompanied, he thought, by a fellow-traveller, who assured him again and again that death was nothing to be disturbed about....

If he had not been so sure that he was going to die he might have lived. He had everything that he needed. Little Mrs. Swinnerton's kindness was astonishing. 'Now, now, don't thank me. Your boy and my girl are friends.' ...

'Now you lie down and get a sleep, Mrs. Cornelius—do now.' She sat, with her skirt turned up to her knees, a lot of bad jewellery about her neck, powdering her nose. But there was no duty too menial for her to perform.

'Bless your soul, *I* don't mind.... There's nothing about men *I* don't know.'

'Poor dears, poor dears! ... Poor dears, that's what men are!'

During the last two days Mr. Cornelius lay there, saying nothing, thinking only of his wife and his son. He held John's hand, stared into his face as though he were searching for something.

He died without saying a word—only looking, looking for an assurance, a comfort, a purpose that all his life he had not found.

CHAPTER IV

As Country Heroes Always Do, John Leaves for London, After

Meeting Mr. Lipper

For the next eighteen months John and his mother succeeded in existing.

When John was nearly eleven years of age, had a good sentimental education but no sort of a practical one, had still Ada Montgomery's address in his shell-box but was not a step nearer London, enter Mr. Lipper, the God out of the Machine, the spider in the wash-tub.

He had been, it seems, in the town for a considerable time already, earning a living as a tailor's cutter and assistant. He entered the private lives of John and his mother on a certain sunny day when he sat down beside them on a bench looking out to the sea and proceeded to eat, like the King in Alice, a large sandwich out of a paper bag.

John liked in after days to talk about Mr. Lipper—and well he might, for Mr.

Lipper was important. He spoke of him so often that I feel now that I must myself have known him. Perhaps I did—and better than many of my friends.

'Joe Lipper,' John would say. 'White and heavy, like dough. Very fair semi-

reddish hair. The eyebrows faintly red and an untidy, drooping, very pale moustache. His skin was so white and so dead and so loose that you felt you could take lumps of it in your hand. Later, when he lived with us, I would see him washing himself, a great expanse of dead white skin and this faintly red, faintly gleaming hair on his chest. Of course he was fat and out of condition.

And lazy. I never knew so lazy a man.

'He wore a faded black suit, always very dusty. His real trade was cadging on people. He was a master at it. He had a kind of charm. Impossible to deny that he had. I felt it myself. He was gentle, had a soft voice like a woman's, a most amiable temper. He adored to eat and to sleep. How many many hours I've seen him lying on my mother's bed, stripped to the waist, his eyes closed,

his mouth open, and the long hairs of his moustache lifting and falling with his gentle breathing. If it didn't put him out he would oblige anybody—and he had an extraordinary fascination for women, perhaps because he was at heart indifferent to their charms. He would grant them favours simply because it was too much trouble to deny them. He would smile and look at them between half-closed eyes and press their hands very gently and drive them quite crazy with anticipation and desire. He was never upset, never angry, never rude.

'He fascinated and charmed my mother at once. I had realized a great change in her since my father's death. It was as though she were relieved of a great burden. She had loved him dearly (she was full of heart, my poor mother) but her conviction that, because he was a gentleman, he had condescended in marrying her had always weighed upon her, made her self-conscious. She had also been oppressed by her mother-in-law. Now she could let herself go; she was growing stouter but, at this time, had a blooming, fresh look— her last touch of youth before she surrendered to inevitable decay. She was wearing that day, I remember, a crisp print dress; it was summer, the sea gleamed and glittered; even Joe Lipper had a sort of fleshy allure. They soon began to talk. Lipper could talk to women. He knew how to make them feel important, how to arouse their maternal care. Very quickly my mother felt that he needed looking after, and although, poor soul, she was in reality incapable of looking after anyone, her heart went readily out to anyone in need.

'They were a fine stout pair sitting on the bench looking out to the sea. I didn't dislike Joe. I never disliked him. He seemed to me like a faded descendant of the Jolly Miller I so often read about in fairy-stories.

'I remember that after a while I left them and they didn't even notice that I had gone....'

It was now that his mother and himself tried to have serious conversations on his future prospects. It was certainly time, for he was getting on for eleven years of age and it was right that he should earn something. None of his mother's suggestions were of any practical value. He wanted to go to London and be an actor. He would write plays and act in them himself.

In the town he was beginning to be both a nuisance and a joke. He was here, there and everywhere, no respecter of persons, always poking his nose in where he wasn't wanted. He couldn't bear to see anything or anyone ill-

treated. Any kind of cruelty roused him to a sort of madness. On one occasion he saw a group of boys throwing stones at a cat with a broken leg.

He rushed into the middle of them, screaming in a high treble, hitting with his long thin arms to right and left. They mauled him, threw him down, sat on him, tore his clothes off his back. At another time he saw a big carter going up the road out of town lashing a horse that had too heavy a load. He jumped on the cart and caught the driver round the neck. He was thrown off and lashed with the carter's whip. He gave away anything that he had—he was the most generous boy in the school. He never, of course, had very much.

On the other hand his vanity and arrogance made him an easy mark for the mockers. He thought that he knew more than anyone else in the town, and yet he would be ignorant of many simple things. He was always telling children stories that were obviously quite untrue. He said, for instance, that there was a Chinese City under the sea near Fortress Rock. He said that, on calm days, he had seen it and he would describe the temples with their bells and the rose–red walls of the palaces. He would recite his poems, in his high shrill voice, to anyone who would listen. He would act characters from plays that he had read, looking ridiculous in his ill–fitting clothes, with his large nose and mouth and ears, his whimbley–shambley body....

Only they would, any of them, listen when he sang. He was not ridiculous then.

But his unpopularity grew and it happened one day that a band of boys chased him along the High Street and down the hill, calling out: 'Who's a playwriter? Where's the playwriter?' and throwing stones after him. He minded this terribly but was too proud to complain. He wished to be loved by everybody, but possibly he was never to learn the important lesson that people not only like you for what you are but also for your individual attitude to THEM. No, he was never to learn this. He would always be too sincerely himself.

Then he came home one day and found his mother sitting in a chair and crying. He tried to comfort her by making her laugh. When he imitated

people like Mr. Bartholomew or the butcher up the road or (not unkindly) Mrs. Swinnerton she always laughed and forgot her troubles. But not to–day.

Half an hour before she had promised to marry Mr. Lipper. On the whole Johnny was glad and for one reason especially. His mother was often damp and chilled with the laundry- work. Mrs. Garriman had told by the cards that she would die of a consumption. She had yielded increasingly to nips of whisky and gin. John thought that Joe Lipper would keep her sober. Joe was sober himself. He enjoyed eating much more than drinking.

But she was greatly disturbed. She pulled John to her and hugged him and fondled his untidy hair and kissed his eyes.

'Oh, Lordy, Lordy, I don't know, I'm sure. I'm sure I don't know. It may be for the best, dearie, and Joe says he'll work, and what's more he says he'll have you taught the tailoring, Johnny, but here am I getting married again and there'll be a man in the house.... You like Joe, don't you, Johnny? Gertie Garriman says the cards spell trouble, but I'm sure I don't know. It's trouble anyway whichever way you look at it. What's life for but troubles?'

'I'm not going to be a tailor, mother,' John said.

'Oh, but why not, Johnny? Why in heaven's name not? It's a good trade and Joe will see you through it. Everyone says he's a good worker if he wants to be.'

'I'm not going to be a tailor, mother.'

'Oh, Lordy, Lordy.... What ARE you going to be?'

'I'm going to London to make a name. I'm going to be famous. First you suffer the most AWFUL things and THEN you get to be famous.'

John used to tell me that after saying this he was aware suddenly of a kind of illumination. He KNEW that it would be so. He would suffer terrible things and be famous....

Myself: 'I wonder how many small boys have known the same kind of illumination. And then what has it come to?'

John: 'Oh, I daresay ... but what I didn't know then, and know now, is that being famous isn't the point. Anyone can be famous if they want to hard enough. The point is—to find—what? I don't know. The thing that gives you tranquillity. The Peace of God perhaps. My little fish found it in the great floating piece of seaweed ... the BEST, most shining piece of seaweed, where the little fish could lose himself as the light pierced it and the warmth came from the sun.... I think I never loved my mother more than at that moment when she told me that she was going to marry Joe Lipper. I realized that our lives parted there—at that exact point. That now we would always be separated. I was handing her over to somebody else. I had a tremendous proprietary feeling towards her, and when the boys chased me through the street throwing stones at me it was she whom I felt they were hurting. And now, poor mother, she would be in Joe Lipper's hands. I wasn't at all sure that he would be able to look after her. I knew how lazy and selfish he was. But it was those two old women, Garriman and Hoskin, I was chiefly afraid of.

When I was about, although I was only a boy, they had a kind of fear of me. I could be in a rage sometimes and say things that really got into their thick salty unwashen hides.

'But gradually, bit by bit, they were invading our cottage more and more.

Mother liked a gossip and a warming drink and Mrs. Garriman's fortune-

telling and Mrs. Hoskin's stories. How they hated me, those two! And it showed how deep and strong was my mother's love for me that she would never hear a word against me from either of them. But they could hurt her through me—when they told her how the town laughed at me, and the boys shouted after me and the rest.

'She'd nod her head and say: "You wait, Gertie. You just wait. He'll be famous one day, you see!"

'But they'd mock at my wanting to be an actor. An actor with that face and figure!

'I thought that possibly they would not be in the cottage so much when Joe had married mother. And I would be gone of course. Now that mother was going to marry again London for me was a certainty!'

The point for him now was how to get there. There was an old clay pig-faced

money-box that he had, and into this from time to time he had put pennies, sixpences and even shillings.

Now he burst it open and discovered that in all it amounted to some twelve shillings and odd pence—not enough to go to London with!

There were people—Mr. Bartholomew, Miss Gracie and others—whom he could ask to lend him something. But there oddly enough he denied himself.

He had never hesitated to ask anyone for anything that he needed, but now some sort of superstition stopped him—he wanted to EARN his way to London.

So he thought of the Theatre. He was always thinking of it. Mr. Darlington, alas! had died in the last year of a chill that had turned to pneumonia. There now sat in his place a big bull-faced man who 'knew not Joseph.' His great merit, however, was that he was often asleep. The Theatre in fact was fast slipping downhill. No one seemed to trouble any more as to the standard of acting or plays. The house was now never more than half full.

It was quite easy now for John to slip through the door, and then he would swim, like a fish, in and out among the chairs in the darkened empty theatre or sit somewhere hidden in the dusky corners listening to rehearsals or overhearing two or three very shabby Thespians discussing their unsuccessful fates.

On this special occasion he intended business and pushed his way on to the stage. A very tenth-rate company held the boards that week, and their programme changed easily and lightly from Fair Rosamond to The Private Secretary, from The Private Secretary to The Lyons Mail.

It was Fair Rosamond that they were rehearsing when John found his way into the middle of them, and a stout, blowzy lady in the exaggerated puffed sleeves and the small waist of the period was reclining in a very rickety bower discussing with a thin unshaven out-at-elbows friend some topic of the social world.

It can be imagined that they stared when John appeared, gave a low bow and asked for their assistance. He explained at once what he wanted and, I

suppose, with that intensity he always gave to any discussion of his own affairs. He intended to go to London; he hadn't money enough; he thought they might help him. But, he explained, he expected to work for his fee.

No other of the episodes of his childhood did John enjoy to describe so greatly as this, his first public appearance in any theatre. For it began by their gathering round and wondering what on earth this strange-looking boy was doing there.

'At that time I used to wear a pair of long thick fisherman's trousers that Charlie had found for me somewhere—these and a short, very short-in-the-

sleeves, brown norfolk jacket that Miss Gracie had given me. I didn't mind how ridiculous I looked, then or ever. But I WAS worried by the clumsiness of my movements. Never was a boy so awkward as I. I really seemed to have no control over my limbs at all, and when I was excited, as I so often was, I would crack my fingers and jerk my knees as though I had St. Vitus' dance.

And this for someone who wanted to be an actor and a dancer was very unfortunate.

'On this occasion I was so desperately in earnest that I didn't care what I did. I told them that I had to go up to London to earn my living and that I MUST

have the means to get there. So they laughed and asked me what my plans were. So I said I had twelve shillings in my money-box but that wasn't enough and they must provide the rest.

'So then they laughed a lot more and asked me what I could do. I strode to the front of the stage and out into the darkness spouted some of my pieces:

"Friends, Romans, countrymen," "When Death on the plain appears" and

"Annabel Lee." When, with my hand on my stomach, my voice trembling with emotion, I cried:

'"Tell me, my heart, can this be love?"

they all shouted with laughter. I was not in the least disturbed and suggested that I should sing. So, turning my back on the empty stalls and facing the funny, rather forlorn little group of actors, I gave them "Oft in the stilly night," "Gone were but the winter cold" and "Weep you no more, sad fountains." After these they laughed no longer. I knew what is dearest of all

things to the actor's and singer's heart, that silence of absorption, of emotional fulfilment. And what followed was quite marvellous. There was a moment, it seemed, in Fair Rosamond, when a minstrel sings beneath her bower. On the following evening, dressed in red tights with a feather in my cap and a property lute in my hand, I should step forward and sing to the bower "Weep you no more, sad fountains." Little Jimmy Despard, who always played the flute in the four-piece Theatre orchestra, was found (he was easily discovered in "The Hare and Hound" next door) and I rehearsed the song to his accompaniment, and everyone was ravished. I was to be paid. I was, in fact, for one night at least, to be a real professional actor.'

It was not from John but from Charlie Christian that I learnt how John ran all over the town that day telling everyone of the marvellous thing that was to happen on the following evening. And the town—or rather the lower portions of it—nobly responded.

The cheaper parts of the house were filled that next evening and everyone was expecting to have an excellent joke.

'I was desperately serious about it,' John would say, 'as in fact I always have been about anything I've had to do. I could see no joke in the matter although the red tights were so much too large for my skinny legs and the red saucer-

shaped cap with the dirty white feather in it must have looked comic enough.

'Do you remember the picture of Smike dressed up in Nicholas Nickleby?

The very image of myself that night. It was a horribly cold smelly little room that we dressed in, and I prepared ages before it was necessary, sat there shivering in my tights, clearing my throat to make sure of my voice and hearing through the thin boards the ridiculous dialogue of Fair Rosamond.

And how I loved it! Cold, shaking with nervousness, hungry (for I had eaten nothing all day), I was yet burning with pride and joy. My first professional appearance—and not, I was sure, my last! The rest of the company, when not occupied, came and cheered me up. How I love actors! How brave and comradely and bold-spirited they are! It has always been said of them that they are self-occupied, one- idea'd, jealous and the rest. Their profession compels them, for they live on a tight-rope. A piece of good luck for a little while and then perhaps months of sickening anxiety. But how good they are to one another in distress, how understanding of the REALITIES of life, the

actual! "Where is my bed, my meal? If I fall ill to- day I am a ruined man....

This won't last. In a few weeks I shall be on the road again...." Love actors?

They are the only real unstandardized human beings anywhere in the world to-day. The poets are gone, the painters are gone, the cooks are gone, the prophets and priests and saints are gone....' (This is the way that Johnny would ramble. Actors were always his passion.)

'In any case one fat old boy in a large dirty ruff gave me a drink that made my eyes water, and a young woman with a cast in her eye stood and looked at me and laughed until I thought that she would have died—all in the friendliest manner.

'My moment came. I had no words to speak, but when the King cried,

"Where is my Page? Ho, Page, a song for my lady!", I was to step forward with my lute and sing my song.

'I stepped forward and paused for a moment at the flickering gas footlights. I paused, also, because of the roar that greeted me. I stood there, blinking, not knowing what to do. There were shouts and screams from all over the house, shouts, as I remember, of "Playwriter! Playwriter!" "Where DID you get those clothes?" "How's the washing? Does your mother know you're out?" It was not the first time I had been mocked nor would it be the last. I stared up at the red blowzy face of Fair Rosamond who was leaning out of the rickety little window of the bower and looking at me with great anxiety. They were afraid, they told me afterwards, that someone would start to throw things.

And so, I expect, it would have been. The King hissed in my ear, "Get off, you brat!" The noise was so deafening that I could with difficulty hear him.

But I didn't get off. Anger, as it was often to do, came to my rescue.

Throwing my property lute on to the floor I went to the footlights, held up my hand, and for a wonder they were quiet. I told them that it was cowardly to interrupt players who were doing their best for them and that whether they liked it or not I would sing. So I sang—some of the most beautiful words in the world.

'"Weep you no more, sad fountains;

What need you flow so fast?

Look how the snowy mountains

Heaven's sun doth gently waste!

But my Sun's heavenly eyes

View not your weeping,

That now lies sleeping

Softly, now softly lies

Sleeping.

Sleep is a reconciling,

A rest that peace begets;

Doth not the sun rise smiling

When fair at even he sets?

Rest you then, rest, sad eyes!

Melt not in weeping,

While she lies sleeping

Softly, now softly lies

Sleeping."'

Johnny, who was to sing for so short a time longer, always said that this

'Weep you no more' was of all his songs the loveliest and that he sang it like an angel.

He may have done. Men have denied him many things, but none who heard him sing as a boy has ever forgotten its loveliness. His audience, on this night, was altogether conquered. Charlie, who was in the audience and on the edge of a terrific fight with two lads near him, says that the instant change from derision to ecstasy was a remarkable thing—his own nature being by far too well controlled for those extremes. They demanded song after song. John gave them 'Drink to me only,' 'I have a mistress for perfections rare,' and 'The lark now leaves his watery nest.' It was these old songs that especially saved him. He delayed Fair Rosamond for half an hour. They engaged him to sing on the remaining two nights. They even invited him to travel with the company. He had greater, more magnificent ambitions. But he had attained his object. He had enough money now to make his London adventure a certainty.

It was now that his aunt, his mother's sister, came into view. Mrs. Hunnable

was her name. John had barely heard her name before this, but now that it was settled that John was to go, Daisy Cornelius' mind, generally steamed into stupor by soap-suds and hot water, stirred itself. She had had a line from Maggie a year or more ago. Where was it? Last February come a year Maggie had written to say that she was married again. Where was the letter?

It was searched for and, by a miracle, found. Here was the address— 15

Broadman Street, Pimlico.

'She's very religious,' John's mother told him. 'Not religious like any ordinary person. It's a sect that believes there'll be another Flood that will destroy the earth. They know the date and everything. This new marriage she's made—

well, it ain't new any longer, I suppose—year and a half—but he's one of them. "To William Hunnable, First Preacher of the Church Expectant"—

that's what he called himself on the card.'

John could wonderfully re-create his mother for us—her large mild eyes full of love and bewilderment, her soft, rather sleepy voice, her fair untidy hair, locks of it often tickling her forehead, her big stout body now, alas, beginning to be gross, her damp warmth and fluttering hands, the movement as, impatiently, she pushed her hair back....

'But it must be all right. Maggie has a whole house. She lets rooms to religious lodgers. There must be room for you.'

So John helped his mother to write a letter, and soon a very warm and affectionate reply was received saying how welcome 'little John' would be for a visit.

At last it was really settled! Mrs. Garriman and Mrs. Hoskin had plenty to say

—behind John's back of course. Words they were never at a loss for.

The sad thing now was that Joe Lipper encouraged them rather than prevented them! All laziness, and a sort of vanity that made him ready to please any woman. They amused him. He would lie on the bed and laugh at Mrs. Hoskin by the hour.

They gave poor Daisy Cornelius a terrible time about her son. The absurdity of allowing that boy to go to London at his age all by himself! He was

already on the way to ruin, singing and making a fool of himself before the whole town—but now! ... and everyone knew that he would steal and lay his hands on anything that wasn't his—a London gaol was the first place he'd find himself. They didn't say the really bad things in front of Daisy herself; they said plenty to Joe Lipper, though, and he, lazy as he was, began to fancy that the boy was no good and that he'd be better gone.

John, at this particular crisis in his affairs, had very few friends in the world.

There were at any rate two.

Here is the letter that he wrote to Anne Swinnerton, now at school in Truro: DEAR ANNE—I'm going to London next week. I shall stay with my aunt, Mrs. Hunnable, as a beginning. Her address is 15 Broadman Street, Pimlico, London.

I shall not be there very long of course because I am going into the theatre—

Miss Montgomery will start me I expect. I told you last time about my singing in Fair Rosamond. They say it's the best singing the town ever heard and they'll say the same in London. I'll write from London and tell you how it all is—I expect I'll see the Queen. I wish you were coming, Anne, but as that cannot be I have written you a poem instead.

Dear Anne

In the train

When houses run and the fields jump

Like a camel with a hump—

In Truro

You're so

Quiet—

But, when I'm famous

I'll be the same

To you, Anne.

I don't like it at home much now because Joe Lipper is a fat fat pig and there isn't much room any more so I go out with Charlie. He is very strong now and wrestled with a policeman who knows his father and got the policeman who

is as fat as Joe Lipper in the stomach so that he was winded and had to lie down. I like Charlie better than anyone in the world except mother and you.

Well good–bye now, Anne. I shall tell you all about London and the success I have. My aunt I'm going to is very religious and believes there will be a Flood again—very soon they say. So look out in Truro. I shall let you know before the Flood comes.

Good–bye Anne. I shall write you another Poem very soon. I have thought of a story about three beetles. One beetle is blind.

Your loving friend,

JOHN CORNELIUS.

Anne kept all his letters. They are before me now in several packets, each packet bound with pink tape.

And here, in Anne's neat small sharply defined writing, is her letter to him in answer:

DEAR JOHN—I am writing this under Miss Trefusis' eye when I ought to be doing geography so it may be interrupted at any minute. I wish I were coming to London with you. I could stick pins into all the old dears because I have to stay here and do nothing— only play hockey and learn French.

Be careful in London and don't think you can do everything everyone else can. It was nice of you, John, to write a poem for me and say you will be the same to me when you're famous but how do you know you ever will be? You must have looked funny in red tights didn't you? Dear John I'm only teasing

—(I've just said 'Yes, Miss Trefusis, I'm reading about Morocco'). Give that awful old woman Hoskin a pinch from me before you go.

Write to me from London as soon as you get there, and tell me all about the Flood!

Your loving, loving,

ANNE.

Everything being settled there remained Charlie.

Charlie's fidelity both to things and to people was fanatical and, if he had been an orphan at this time, he would have gone, I am sure, to London with John. Meanwhile he settled his problem, as he was always to settle his problems, silently within himself. In some way or another he would do his duty towards his father and mother; at the same time he would look after John. There was something almost mystical here, although to talk about mysticism in connection with a strong exclusively matter-of-fact small boy may seem an affectation, but the fact was that Charlie always knew far more about what John was doing and thinking than did anyone else in this world.

Later on, Charlie told me many things, dropping, as it were, his caution because he knew that at last there was no reason to preserve it. One of the interesting things was that his account of this talk that he had with John before he went to London is exactly, allowing for differences in temperament, in agreement with John's account—both of them given to me so many years later. To both men it was one of the epochal things of their lives— and yet so little was said. John, now that he was going away for the first time in his life, quite suddenly realized that Charlie wouldn't be at his side any more.

Then, as was his way, he threw himself into a panic. The two boys sat on the low rocks at the end of Mackerel Beach and watched the warm sun bathe the little pools that swayed so lazily with the tide— little pools coloured now saffron and silver, the seaweed blood-red against the pale-bone-under-water stones. Over the wide sea itself it must have been hazy, for Charlie once when we were crossing fields in a honey-coloured mist said to me, 'It was this way over the sea the day before John first went to London.'

I know how it can be on those Glebeshire March days when the weather is kind. The sun can be Sahara-warm and the air glows almost with apricot scent. The sea faintly heaves in the sunny mist and the gulls' cry is spectral.

Above the spring fields beyond the cliffs larks rise, primroses are pale in the hedges, cottages and farms seem to burn in smoke and flame through the mist.

On such a day John and Charlie sat close side by side on the rock watching

the little swaying pools.

John talked a great deal, Charlie said scarcely a word. John was full of himself, of all that he would do, of how remarkable he was, of what the world would think of him. And then (as Charlie remembered but John didn't) he put his arm around Charlie's thick neck and told him that he liked him better than anyone in the world except his mother and Anne Swinnerton and that when he'd made his name Charlie should come to London and John should introduce him.

There Charlie interrupted.

'I'm not waiting for you to make no name,' he said. 'I'll manage pretty, all by myself. No man ain't going to have to run ME.'

John remembered this part of it and that he suddenly realized what life would be without Charlie and how London might be cold, the world unable to see that he was remarkable. A kind of vision of some of the things that were to happen to him. As so often, he was humble in the middle of his conceit.

'We'll swear friendship,' he said, 'for ever and ever.' They plucked strands of seaweed from the bottom of a pool, held a strand between them and tore it in half.

'I John Cornelius swear I'll be the true friend of Charles Christian so long as I live, so help me God.'

'I Charles Christian swear I'll be the true friend of John Cornelius so long as I live, so help me God.'

They stood on the rock, arms around one another's necks, looking out to sea while white streaks like serpent's trails struck the water and the sea began to rise, the little pools lapping over the rock-edge.

John, as usual, was a little unsteady on his long legs, so Charlie held him firmly, held him as though defending him against the whole world. And so he was.

There was more sentiment on that last evening in the Cornelius' home. There occurred also what must have been an unpleasant little scene. Anyone who is something of an oddity and no fool will often laugh at his own oddness. This was the way of Oliver Goldsmith. Sometimes an oddity will be amazed at the things he says and does, but will sit back from them as it were, will amuse others but refuse himself to join in the fun. This last was the way of White Mallison, who from his aesthetic rooms in Bunbury Street with their Manets and Renoirs would emphasize in beautiful prose to his readers how VERY

odd he was; he would do this coldly, with a kind of chill amorality.

But John Cornelius was of the former kind: in fact he was like Goldsmith in many things. He shared in all the jokes about himself, but with that he longed to be impressive, to win applause, and, more than applause, affection and love. But he was always a child in his inability to decide between the things he could do and the things he couldn't.

There were occasions, however, when he was serious, when he forgot altogether whether he were an oddity or no. His heat of indignation, when it was stirred, had a white light of intensity, at its centre. On such occasions he lost altogether his childishness and naïveté; he was mature and strong and unflinching.

He was packing his few possessions, his mother helping, while Joe Lipper lay stretched on the bed watching.

The door opened and Mrs. Hoskin came in.

Myself: 'Even now, after all these years, when you speak of her your voice shakes.'

John: 'Yes, because I've never been able to get rid of her, her black bonnet, the black bugles shaking on her shabby jacket, her hooked nose and thin upper lip, her little beard, her dim red– lidded eyes that seemed to have a film over them (although in fact she saw sharply enough), and her voice, strident, just off the note. There was my story about the Musical–Box and the Nutmeg– Grater—do you remember? And the Nutmeg–Grater waits till the Musical–Box is asleep and then she tries to steal the little tune and all that she does is to ruin it so that the world will never hear that music again. Mrs.

Hoskin pokes her head in at the door and croaks: 'What about havin' a drop at my place, Daisy?' Then she sees me. She hadn't known that I was going so soon, perhaps.... She was angry at my going although she hated me. She liked to have me there that she might torture my mother about me, might watch for mistakes that I made or report quarrels that I was in.... She was a little woman, squat, bow–legged, and her head made a perpetual trembling.

She stood there, looking at me.

'"So the son and heir's goin' all by hisself to London?"

'Joe Lipper laughed. "Get out of here, you old bitch," he said.

'She wasn't afraid of him in the least. Her relationship seemed, at that moment, to be entirely with me. She came further forward into the room. She looked at me as though she were delivering maledictions.

'"Good luck," she said. "All the best."

'I turned round on her so fiercely that they all looked at me with surprise. I was tall for my age, you know, and so thin that I looked taller.

'"No, you don't," I said. "You don't wish me luck. But I don't care what you wish me. You can't do ME any harm. But you leave my mother alone. You leave her alone, do you hear?"

'It was like a battle there between the two of us—as though we were alone on a windy heath with no one near us—physical, tearing one another's hair out.

'She looked at me with those faded red eyes, her black bonnet nodding, and said: "You'll come to no good, you won't. You're a thief and a braggart; that's what you are—and a liar. Lord, what a liar! Your poor dear mother, she's the sufferin' one, she is...." And so on, and so on.

'But then she did something. The shell-box that my father had given me (I kept my most precious things in it, Ada Montgomery's address for instance) was on the little table waiting to be packed. Mrs. Hoskin put her hand out and took it. I don't know what she meant to do with it—nothing perhaps—but that was too much for me. I snatched it from her, caught her by the shoulders, and

then there followed, as I remember it, the most ludicrous struggle. I was only eleven years of age and she was a strong old woman, but I pushed her, and her bonnet fell off, and she tried to scratch my face, and my mother screamed, and Joe Lipper laughed until his big stomach ached, and the woman fell over a chair, and I pushed her, with all the strength I had, out of the door.... It was as though I were, in actual fact, fighting the Powers of Darkness.

'Later on my mother and I sat, our arms around one another's necks, as though we were alone in the world. Joe Lipper didn't exist for either of us. I told her again and again that I was going to London to make a fortune for us both and that we should have a grand house and she should want for nothing.

And I implored her not to drink, not to let anybody tempt her, and she, hugging me and crying, swore that she would never touch a drop, that she would never touch a drop....

'I told her that I would write to her all the time, and that she must answer my letters however difficult it might be, and she swore that she would.

'Then we heard Joe Lipper snoring and looked at him lying there with his mouth open, and I, under a sudden impulse, begged her to come up to London with me. I said that Joe was no good and would only live on her earnings and that I could make enough for us both. I, God forgive me, such a child, so sure of myself. It's good that we can't see what's coming to us. It was good that we could neither of us see into the future that night.

'Mother shook her head. She wouldn't be happy in London. Joe wasn't such a bad sort when you knew him....

'And, as we sat there, I forgot even my mother in my wondering amazed anticipation of all my future glories!'

CHAPTER V

Road to Hunnable's; What Hunnable's is Like When You Get

There

John differed from all the other children who have, in so many romances, gone penniless to London in that no one ill-treated, abused, mocked, satirized, starved, robbed, beat or lectured him. Every living soul on this momentous journey behaved to him kindly.

In those days there was a VERY local, halt-when-you-like, blow-my-

whistle-when-I'm-happy-and-the-sun's-shining kind of little train running from Merlin to Polchester and stopping, of course, at every little once-a-

minute station. Very different from these present days when the London express, taking the Glebeshire coastline, makes Merlin one of its principal destinations.

The little station had a real country air then, the platform open to the sea and smelling of seaweed and hot sand, the station-master proud of his flower-

beds, and the moors, spacious, windswept, looking benevolently down from their higher kingdom.

Daisy Cornelius, Joe Lipper, Charlie and little Mr. Bartholomew all came to see John off. He felt of exceeding importance and when he was important he showed it by strutting about like a hen, kicking his legs out in front of him, snapping his fingers.

He was very happy and very miserable too. He never could abide to leave people he was fond of; it always seemed to him that he was leaving them for ever. And Daisy Cornelius was in floods of tears— indeed justly, for the only person in all the world who really and truly loved her was leaving her.

Perhaps she knew as she looked down the sunny platform and sniffed the fresh salt tang of the sea that all good times for her were over.

As she looked up and saw Joe Lipper yawning there was, maybe, a frantic impulse suddenly to cry: 'I'm going with Johnny! I'm going with Johnny!

Don't try to stop me.'

But Daisy Cornelius was not like that. She was never able to come to a decision about anything and the way of least resistance was the way that she always chose.

So she said nothing but soaked her handkerchief with tears, and smiled vacantly at anyone near to her.

Mr. Bartholomew gave John a copy of Religio Medici and some words of advice; these last John always afterwards remembered but, of course, never acted upon. 'Old Mr. Bartholomew,' John remembered, 'thought three things important—keeping the bowels open, keeping the body clean, keeping your word. The first included the exercises he did every morning, philosophic meditation and spiritual calm. The second included his charming fresh complexion, his amber-coloured velvet coat, his fresh sparkling white collars and cuffs, and everything that has to do with STYLE. Style in living, in reading, in writing—aesthetics and old silver, Sir Thomas Browne and the best spring-mattress. "Style is yourself," he would say (a platitude of course),

"yourself at the highest denominator." As to keeping your word integrity was his vice. Very boring he would be about it, as all fanatical people can be.

Giving your word was as though you were pledging your faith before a multitude of unseen witnesses. As a child I used to see the air thronged with them, and the first time I heard Mrs. Hoskin tell my mother a lie with a wink at me I expected the sky to fall in. And yet I was always telling lies myself.'

I have in my mind a picture of little Mr. Bartholomew, with his rosy cheeks, his amber velvet jacket, a flower in his button-hole, presenting John with the Religio Medici, sniffing the sea air, rubbing his hands, skipping on his little legs.... The official voice ushering John into the world.... Not a bad one either....

John didn't cry. He clutched his green bag that had the old stiff metal clasp (a family heirloom from Penny Hall), he hugged his Thomas Browne, kissed his mother, shook Joe Lipper's soft hand, was kissed on the brow by Mr.

Bartholomew ... the train steamed out.

He didn't feel so badly about it until they reached Polchester. The third-class carriage was empty save for two women who knew the boy and were greatly interested in his adventure. So he talked to them all the time—about the marvellous things he was going to do, the actor, singer, dancer he was going to be, the plays he was going to write. The two women, I expect, believed every word of it.

But once in Polchester it was quite another matter. Here was a big noisy station with porters pushing barrows and shouting to you to get out of the way, engines hooting, puffing, exulting, complaining, sneering and whispering. But worst of all were the strange, hostile faces. He realized now that he was nothing, nobody. He would get over this—his restless egotism would soon assert itself again, but for the moment he was so badly frightened that he was ready to burst into tears. The sound of the Cathedral bells, chiming the hour, came across the roofs to him, and he could look through the station entrance and see the town, the Rock, the winding Pol and, in the distance, on its hill, the Cathedral soft and gentle in the smoky, hazy morning light.

He hadn't, however, much time to consider the town (although he was never to forget that vision of it), for the London express was steaming in, having gathered self-importance all the way from Penzance. He jumped into a third-class carriage, determined to get a seat by the window, and secured one. Then the carriage filled. The people he remembered as his travelling companions were a woman with two little girls, a stout old clergyman and a lady who looked round on everyone else as though no one had any right to be alive but herself.

It was then, as the train slowly heaved itself out of the station, that misery and terror took possession of him. What was he doing, thrusting himself all alone into the world like this? Merlin and everyone in it, his mother's house, his beloved mother herself, even Mrs. Garriman and Mrs. Hoskin, appeared as part of himself, part of his flesh and bones, his body torn into pieces. How defenceless he was! His little tricks—his singing, his story- telling—now seemed to him worthless nonsense. Often in his life he was to have this consciousness of a simultaneous self-distrust and self-confidence.

But now he wanted to be loved, he wanted someone to be kind to him. He

rubbed his knuckles in his eyes, he gulped down his sobs. He said his nightly prayer: 'Now I lay me down to sleep.' He opened the Religio Medici and found that he didn't understand a word of it....

In those days the seats of third-class carriages were very hard and space was limited. It was a fresh spring morning and of course the windows mustn't be opened. The two little girls cried that they wanted to 'see,' so they came to the window and one of them stood on John's toes and the other laid her podgy fingers confidently on the old clergyman's knee.

'You mustn't permit your children to annoy other passengers,' the clergyman said to the anxious harassed mother. Then he turned and beamed on John.

John was sitting nursing his green bag on his knees, staring, his large mouth a little open, his hair falling untidily over his forehead. So the clergyman could not help but smile. 'And where are you making for?' he asked. 'London?'

But John didn't answer, for the train, now running towards Exeter, was throwing into John's lap a confusion of shape and colour. It wasn't that he had not known shape and colour at Merlin, but this was his first journey in a train, and the speed of change, the rhythm behind the speed, excited almost to a frenzy all his imagination and wonder. That spring morning must have been fresh and sweet, and he realized perhaps for the first time the England that was to be at the heart of all his stories, the England to which he was to be unflinchingly faithful as his only adored mistress. This was never a loose, sentimental emotion with him. He could criticize his country and his countrymen as acutely as any foreigner—often more bitterly—but he knew that certain things here were incomparable in the world—kippers and soles, primroses in a deep Glebeshire lane, theatre lights through a thin London fog on a November evening, the early morning sun on Grasmere, the slope of a Wiltshire down, leather shops in St. James's Street, old carved pews of a country church on a summer evening with the door open and the bells creaking their final notes, boats dancing on the Mersey in storm, a sheep-dog trial and the thin appealing note of the farmer's call, coming out of the National Gallery and looking across the lions to Westminster, the lovely lift of the Yorkshire moor above Haworth, the creamy white of the Cotswold stone.... Oh, these and many, many more, he and I and patient exiles at the earth's end know to be our good fortune and pride and heritage whatever

history or the whole host of vandals may do! And Johnny, catching first a stream, then a gently-heaving hill, then the light on a winding silent road, could only stare and stare as though now at last he had made the discovery of a lifetime. The green bag dropped from his knees. The book fell after it. The old clergyman, who must, from John's description of him, have been a mixture of Sterne and his Uncle Toby (for he was both sharp and sarcastic and plumply beneficent) stooped and picked them up, one after the other.

'There! You'd better put the bag on the rack above your head.'

John did so and everyone must have seen how short and light his jacket was, how long and ill-fitting his trousers.

'And what is the book? Dear me! Religio Medici....' He read a few words:

'"Those that hold, the sanctity of their souls doth leave behind a tincture and sacred faculty on their bodies, speak naturally of miracles, and do not salve the doubt. Now one reason I tender so little devotion unto relics is, I think, the slender and doubtful respect I have always held unto antiquities. For that, indeed, which I admire is far before antiquity, that is, Eternity; and that is, God Himself."'

I have no assurance whatever that this was the piece of Religio Medici that the old clergyman read, but John always said that it was about miracles and it is a favourite passage of mine, so let it stand.

'Do you understand a word of it, my boy?' asked the old clergyman, pushing his spectacles back on to his forehead.

'It's something to do with miracles.'

'And what are miracles?'

'Things that happen when you least expect them.'

'I remember that answer I gave him,' John said, 'because at that moment a small white dog crept out from under the seat, yawned and scratched its ear—

a most unexpected event.

'The old clergyman was dreadfully embarrassed and explained to us that it wasn't that he was trying to cheat the Company—he had a ticket for the dog

—but that he couldn't bear the thought of the dog being alone in the guard's van all the way to London. He thought that he would be permitted to keep it in the carriage if no fellow-traveller objected to it. He looked beseechingly about him. Did anyone object? Only the grand lady, who had diamond rings on her fingers, I remember, smelt of violets and wore puffed sleeves almost up to her ears, said in a little thin voice that she didn't like dogs, thought them messy and unclean, and that it had been a great mistake on her part to travel third-class and that she'd only done it to show up the Railway Company who charged so scandalously for first-class privileges, but if she had known—'

And so on and so on and all in a thin papery voice while silver chains rose and fell on her black-silk-protected bosom and her diamond rings flashed....

I remember the lady so vividly because she was the first of a kind I was to meet so frequently in after years.

'The little clergyman, looking now like Sterne rather than Uncle Toby, asked sharply whether she did object to the white dog or no, and the lady, suddenly nervous, said that she supposed she didn't.'

The white dog broke the ice for everybody. It was, I suppose, enchanted with its sudden freedom and, without being a nuisance, simply told everyone that this was a glorious world and everyone was lucky to be alive in it. Dogs are no respecters of persons; that is, they advance, with the same gay trust, upon those who dislike them as upon their warm admirers. The little white dog considered the grand lady as his dearest friend, and I suppose she was flattered, for John said she was quite humanly amiable during the rest of the journey.

After Exeter they ran out to sea. When John saw the red cliffs, and the pale-

green water faintly heaving in that fresh morning light, some epoch of discovery began for him. In Little Bill and the Sea-King there is this paragraph:

'Climbing on the table and then lifting himself on to the window- sill Little Bill could see across the field to the rocks that closed in the Bay. To his great surprise and delight these rocks were coloured red, the colour of the breast of a robin. He was so greatly astonished that he almost fell back on to the table.

Then he heard the voice of the farmer's wife and, still holding the tin box tightly in his hand, he climbed down on to the floor again. But in his bed that night he saw the red rocks and he dreamt of them in his dreams.'

Like Herman Melville, whose books he was afterwards to love so dearly, these red rocks were as the first vision of the South Seas. This world was indeed a marvellous place when it could contain such wonders.

As he gazed the clergyman asked him questions:

'So you're going to London?'

'Yes, I am.'

'Are you going to school there?'

'Oh no.' (Scornfully.) 'I'm finished with school.' (How could he doubt it, staring out to that sea where, as he always remembered, the clouds piled up on the horizon in an intense purity of whiteness?)

'You're very young to be finished with school.'

'I'm going to be an actor.'

'An actor?'

'I've been one already. I was in Fair Rosamond. I can sing and dance.' For now they were moving inland from the sea again, but the revelation that those red rocks had been to him gave him a new courage. With such beauty in the world as this he had the hardihood to challenge anything or anybody. So now everything poured out of him, and to everyone in the carriage he told all his achievements. He even, with very little hesitation, lifted up his voice and sang, to the rattle and jerking of the train, a verse or two of 'Sad Fountains.'

He would have danced one of his funny little grotesque dances had there been room enough. Certainly no one in the carriage had met so queer a boy before, and the grand lady, who smelt of violets, must for weeks after have amused her friends with this account of how she had travelled with a white dog and a dancing, singing boy all the way to London. Oh yes, he was going to stay

with an aunt in London, but not for long—only until he had secured an engagement at one of the London theatres.

'It isn't very easy to get an engagement at the London theatres,' said the clergyman. 'So many people want one.'

'Then I remember,' John would say, 'that I burst into a marvellous self-

confident prophecy of the wonders I was going to accomplish. It wasn't conceit exactly but rather a perfect assumption of my coming destiny as though I had seen in those red rocks, that green glassy sea, those cumuli of white cloud, a picture of fame and glory. Isn't it ironical that that mantle of splendour should be snatched from us in those later years when we need it so badly?

'I've no doubt I jerked my legs and swung my arms and told them of how easy it would be for me to have the world at my feet! Thomas Browne on the floor, the green bag on the rack, they must have smiled in their own private and age–old hearts. Down at Penny Hall the green bag had heard just such prophecies and seen them fade into the flickering candle–light of the panelled dining–room and the sough of the trees of the wood beyond the windows.'

In any case John's self–enthusiasms were brought to a halt, as his romantic imaginations were so often to be, by what Vernon Whiteley has called

'stomachic realities.' It was time to eat; everyone was producing paper packages. The grand lady had a beautiful leather case wherein lay little white parcels as snug and symmetrical as eggs in a grocer's box. The two little girls cried, like young birds in a nest, for food; the stout clergyman brought out sandwiches, plum cake, an apple and a pear. He had also a bottle of red wine, and John remembered it well, for this was the first wine that ever passed his lips.

Himself he had no food and he was ravenously hungry.

'How hungry I was, for I had had a piece of ham and bread and dripping at six that same morning and nothing since. But here my pride came in. No one had remembered to supply me with food for the journey. It was so like my dear mother that she should have altogether forgotten so obvious a necessity.

And I! Travelling into the world for the first time, what did I need but the

nectar and ambrosia of my own imagination?

'But now how hungry I was! How horribly hungry! But was I, who had just been proclaiming my unique greatness, to throw longing looks on ham and bread and plum cake? Not I. I took up Sir Thomas Browne and plunged into his decorated vitals, my eyes on the book, my intelligence fastened on unsatisfied hunger.'

It was the clergyman who saved him by holding out a sandwich and begging him, of charity, to save an already over-ripe figure. 'I'm too fat, you know, but my cook won't listen.... And this piece of plum cake. You're young, but for MY digestion it's altogether too rich....' And finally, out of a small pocket-tumbler, two swills at the red wine.

John took everything that was offered, as he always did, but, again as always, wanted to give everyone everything in return.

It was now, as the pale, softly clouded afternoon closed in about the carriage, that he noticed the elder of the two little girls. She was a thin little girl in a bright-green frock that ill became her. She was sitting beside her mother, looking straight in front of her, very miserable. Quite suddenly she was violently sick.

She was hurried to the window, her head held out of it. Everyone was greatly disgusted and the grand lady scolded the poor mother: 'You should know the strength of your child's stomach by now. I saw that you gave her two large ham sandwiches....'

But the mother only sat there, her arm around her little girl who, with eyes closed, leaned against her mother's breast.

John was moved by an urgent desire to help. He had suddenly fallen in love with the little girl in the green dress, but only because of her misfortunes. He would have offered her anything he had, gone anywhere for her, sacrificed himself for her in any way. He suggested to the mother that she should take his corner seat, then, when she, with a tired sad smile, refused that, he said very politely to the clergyman that perhaps the little girl would feel better if she were sitting on the other side—wouldn't the clergyman perhaps like to

change with her? In fact his desire to help quickly became a nuisance to everybody. The clergyman, with the white dog crooked asleep in the hollow of his arm, was perfectly happy reading his book and had no intention of being disturbed.

'I was being a nuisance and I suddenly perceived it. I had another shiver of that awful consciousness of loneliness—this new strange world that didn't want me, that I could offend so easily without knowing why.

'I always moved so quickly from the heights to the depths, and I sat there, staring out of the window, wondering where the beauty had gone, whither my red rocks had vanished. For now the early spring day must have been closing in and a thin vapour dimmed the sun, made fields and houses spectral and sent a chill through the world. I wanted desperately to help the little girl in the green dress and yet I did not wish to be a nuisance to the people in the carriage either, for only a short time before they had seemed to like me very much and had given me part of their lunch.

'Then a pleasant thing happened. The mother's arm grew tired and she placed the little girl on the other side of her, so that now both little girls were sitting next to me. The smaller girl plainly wished to look out of the window, so I gave her my place and now I was sitting between them. After a while I asked them in a whisper (for the clergyman and the grand lady were sleeping) whether they would like me to tell them a story, and they said that they would. So we sat, all three of us, close together, and the child in the green dress put her hand in mine. I seemed to move away into my country of imagination, for the whole world was now dimly lit with a muted sun, the fields without contours, and the English scene bathed in that especial sleep of history, timeless and indifferent to the present.

'Even when we came to a big station we were not disturbed but, all together, shared an intimacy that perhaps—who knows?—none of us was ever to find again. I began to tell them the story of a wonderful old room that was filled with beautiful old things. There was a splendid oak chest covered with fine carving of flowers and beasts and birds. Inside the deep drawers of the chest lay many old things, long forgotten. There were dolls in gone-by fashions, dressed in red and blue silks, figures of porcelain, white and gold, some of them with broken arms and legs, Chinese mandarins who still would nod

their heads if only they stood upright, toy soldiers and a fine musical-box. In the bottom drawer of the chest there was a Chinese Princess who had been trying for years to stand upright, because near her was the musical-box, its lid painted with flowers and birds, that once on a time she had stood beside in the drawing-room. She longed to hear the tunes again and thought that if she were on her feet she could persuade the musical-box to play its tunes once more. Then with those tunes all her beautiful old life would come back to her and she would escape from the chest—'

Myself: 'That's the story of The Chinese Princess and the Musical- Box.'

John: 'Yes—to be written years after. I have sometimes wondered whether the little girl in the green dress lived to be a woman and whether she read the story and remembered. It was never finished on that train journey, for the air became dark and I looked up and there was London crowding in upon us.

Everyone in the carriage woke up and people shook themselves and straightened their clothes, and once again I was frightened and lonely, wondering what my Aunt Hunnable would be like and what should I do if she didn't care for me.

'But what a station that was! What dirt, what noise, what space, what smoky indifference to the sufferings of poor lonely boys! I stood there not knowing what the next step was to be. I had worried as to what I would do if my aunt did not care for me, but the question now was—What should I do if she wasn't here to meet me? I had the address; I could travel on an omnibus, I supposed, but the vast sweep of that station with its glass roof, the sudden shriek of an engine at my ear, the sharp indifferent faces seemed to take all courage from me. It was a foretaste, that arrival at Paddington, of so many things that I was to experience! But my aunt was there all right. Oh, certainly!

Aunt Hunnable never missed an appointment, forgot a duty or made a mistake in time. She came bustling up, a stout masculine-looking woman in a black bonnet and black costume with white cuffs. She always looked like an official of some institution, as indeed she was—the institution of the Second Coming of Christ.

'She knew me at once. "You're John! Don't tell me you're not. For of course you are."

'We stared at one another, she, I suppose, astonished to see such an ugly, shabby slip of a boy, and myself really surprised that she could be so different from my mother. There were no Women Police in those days, but if there had been she would have been taken for one. As it was, I thought of the Salvation Army, who figured in my mind as a drum and trumpet making a deal of noise in an empty space on a still-born Sunday.

'She was a good soul, Aunt Hunnable, but had she not been so methodical and accurate would have closely resembled Mrs. Jellaby. The Cause was more to her than any individual, very much including my uncle, William Hunnable.

'However, she had come to meet me, which was kind of her, and she gathered me up very much as someone might discover a fragment belonging to a picture-puzzle and delightedly put it into place. Not that Aunt Hunnable ever showed delight about anything, nor aggravation either. Again like Mrs.

Jellaby she was never to be distracted from her main purpose by any outside human emotion.

'So now we were in the street, and what an adventure THAT was for me! You know, in the middle 'nineties London had still the aromas, the haphazard incongruities of a country town. Oddly enough it has them even now! It will perhaps never lose them. I remember that evening as a wonder and a miracle, London wrapped in a purple haze through which the lamps dimly bloomed.

The smell in my nostrils of hay and horse-dung, smoke and a kind of windy river-mud. And the smell of meat and flowers and human flesh and the breath of horses, and always this mild foggy exudation that seems to issue from the stones, the house-bricks, the grubby, uncleaned windows. And then the noises! In Merlin I had been brought up to isolated cries, the slide of the oar in the boat, the scream of a sea-gull, the rattle of a wheel on the road, the lonely clangour of a church-bell. But now the roar assaulted me as though it were directed personally against me. The motorcar was yet in its infancy, but bells, wheels, newspaper boys, screaming women, all together made ONE voice, one derisive, cheerful, threatening, indifferent challenge to my childishness, ignorance and obstinate ambition.

'We rode on the top of an omnibus just behind the driver—and was THAT an ecstasy and delight or wasn't it?

'There is no time. There is no space. I am riding at this precise moment on this precise bus—and so shall "for ever ride" like Browning's lover. I am sitting on the narrow bench, close against the thin bones of my Aunt Hunnable, I have taken my cap in my hand and the night breeze is blowing through my young and ardent hair; with my hand I clutch, as well as my cap, my green bag and my Religio Medici. The old driver, a cape over his shoulders, is leaning forward hunch-wise, while a thin elderly man in a bowler hat, sitting behind him, leans forward also and talks over his shoulder.

Their voices come quite clearly to me, sounding thin against the breeze but contented, satisfied. "Well, if it's a good night I'll be there, Mr.

Thomlinson...." "Not that I questioned the voting of the Committee, mind you. THAT wasn't what I was questioning...." Were those the words? Was Thomlinson the name? At this distance it seems to me to be so. In any case that was the first note of London that I caught and held—the quiet, cosy satisfaction, suggesting in those warm voices the homes to which so many were at this moment hurrying—the muffins, the dusky romantic light of the coal fire, the drawn curtains, the carpet- slippers—"Supper ready, father!"—

and all through the town the rumble of omnibuses, carts, carriages; the dark spaces of silent streets between the lights of lamps, the little trembling, trailing wisps of fog, the plane-trees, London's guardian angels, in spirit a trifle dusty, a tree suddenly lit by a neighbouring lamp changing its new spring leaves into a green that is almost music.

'And how I sat there staring! How the Town flew like an eager bird straight into my open mouth and has rested in my heart ever since! The steps of the grey churches, the glare of the butcher's stall, the flutter in the wind of the books in the twopenny boxes, instant flashes of a lighted room with a bust over the mantelpiece, houses running together as though in a panic, a break between the grey sooty stone into the bright green of a Square all lit now with the lamps of the Square—the Square lying in wait there, as we lumber past, its green eye meditatively curious....

'And the people! I am still receiving them—sailing on the top of my bus as they dance, sway, swerve, bend to my command. I had not known that there were so many people in the world, so many that knew not Merlin nor the sea-

gulls in line on the wet shore and the carts climbing the hill to the moor....

Faces, clothes, caps and boots, the high sleeves, the feet moving, falling,

rising, black, grey, white, here suddenly a red ribbon, a green feather, a yellow scarf ... and I am falling forward at the sudden jerk.... I hear the tortoise-like head from the shell of the black cape rumbling "Whoa! Whoaa!"

'"This is Pimlico," says my aunt. "Here we descend."

'Yes, this is Pimlico—and I seem at once, with those words, to be inserted, as a small corner of coloured wood is inserted as a fragment of a patterned table, into that tall, thin, coughing, sneezing house of a faint and faded red brick where passages are like the thin tubes of rubber used in operations—just that, smelling a little of gas, of sanitary wrappers, of dusk and the bubbles of water heated in a pan. For Hunnable's was both fanatically clean and passionately ugly. On that first evening I stood in my little room washing my face. On the wall was a text— simply "The Lord Cometh." My little bed was of iron painted white. From my window, now that the world was dark, I saw the roofs of London like the backs of thousands of recumbent animals, rhinoceroses packed into a vast sea, and above them a steadily glowing, incandescent sky.

'I began to cry. I could not help myself. I looked at my poor little green bag and cried the more. I longed for my mother, for my dead father, for Charlie, for Anne.... I prayed, frantically, desperately, as though I were a prisoner condemned in a few moments to die by the guillotine. The knife was about to fall. The backs of the rhinoceroses stirred to the menacing shiver of the traffic far below my window. Then a bell rang in the house. It was for supper. I wiped my eyes and went down. And there, in the long, grey-walled dining-

room, I saw, standing in their places behind their chairs, the motionless forms of those who expected, shortly, the Second Flood.

'Very sheepishly I took the place pointed out to me at the table. It seemed that they had been waiting for me.

'Uncle Hunnable, far away at the other end of the table, began: "O Lord, Who knowest that Thy servants ... "'

CHAPTER VI

Did You Know That Actresses Are Untidy?--john Sings for Fame

At the height of John's maturity he was given to declare, when anyone asked him, that his favourite writers were Shakespeare, Bacon, Marlowe, Oxford ('The Elizabethan Syndicate' John said was the author of the Plays), La Fontaine, Dickens, Cervantes, Hans Andersen, Herman Melville, Keats and Browning. (He always said that Browning was the uncle of all post-War poetry in England and America.) And among his contemporaries White Mallison, Anne Norwood, W. G. Byrne and Owen Roughwood (NOT to give them their proper names!).

His direct influences were, of course, Hans Andersen and Charles Dickens, but as Roughwood once cleverly said of him, 'In Cornelius' stories what Hans Andersen is doing with one hand Freud is doing with the other.' There was never anyone less Freudian than John, but there is truth in Roughwood's statement all the same. It was this deep instinctive knowledge of the springs of human nature that made John's stories possible for his generation.

However, in his own personal history, at least until his twenty- first birthday, it was the coloured–waistcoated, exuberant, noisy– restless–genius–twisted Charles Dickens who provided many of his scenes and characters for him.

For Andersen, Dickens, and Herman Melville he had a strong personal affection as though he had been well acquainted with all of them. He would assert that they were, all three, lonely men from first to last, haunted by a desire whose fulfilment was just out of their reach. 'They gave themselves away just as I have given myself away—and for nothing, uselessly. They meant well by their fellow-kind but were too simple-natured to conceal themselves. They had no armour. They were terribly easy to attack. They could, and did, make dreadful fools of themselves. I love them for that. And they love me. We are brothers in folly.'

Dickens himself would most certainly have enjoyed a visit to Hunnable's.

From John's many accounts of it two impressions remain with me. One is spectral, impersonal, scarcely defined, and in this the house is almost the only character in the story. John was not, on this first occasion, in it very long, but had he never seen it again after this first visit its impression would have indelibly been printed on his soul—its long thin body clothed in rusty red, venting at all times of day and night spiteful and irascible noises— the splutter of pipes, the cold querulous dripping of cisterns, the sudden angry outbreak of a water-closet plug, and on stormy nights the hiss and whine of wind through wallpaper. It was cold with the chill of a spiteful virgin, bare with the prudery of a village matron. It was filled too with the constant, almost silent coming and going of human beings. What they were all about John never, either now or later, really discovered.

The visitors and residents in Hunnable's seemed to him to have always the same aspect, a certain faint unwholesome colour as of men and women who had lived far too long out of sunlight, a pallor of almost cellar intensity.

That is one vision I have of Hunnable's. The other is more actual, for it contains figures. Certain names remain to me from John's concrete pictures.

If anyone ever seized his imagination strongly enough, that figure stayed with him for life. He never, for instance, shook off Mrs. Hoskin as most children would have done. She only died when he himself died.

Well, I know that Mr. Lacey, Mr. and Mrs. Mortimer, Mr. James Abel, Mr.

Humphries were Second Advent lodgers at Hunnable's when John was there.

And then there were, of course, Aunt and Uncle Hunnable themselves. Aunt Hunnable was the one figure, with an important exception, of energy in the Society. William Hunnable himself, who had been for many years a clerk in one of the Midland Banks, may, in that earlier period, have been a bright and active figure, but when Aunt Hunnable, assisted by the Reverend Mr.

Clement Mortimer and the gigantic James Abel, founded so successfully the Society of the Second Flood Adventists and the boarding-house that belonged to it, Will Hunnable left the Bank and became merely the silent and brooding assistant of the Triple Power. Aunt Hunnable was a most admirable policewoman of business. She kept the mechanics of the affair properly running. The Reverend Clement Mortimer, a tall, thin, pale-faced clergyman, very like a primrose in colour and quiet, clothed the mechanics gently in

spiritual garments. But the true genius of the Society was, of course, James Abel. Hunnable's was important to John Cornelius for two reasons—one was James Abel, the other was that it was at Hunnable's that he was to have his first meeting with Carstang.

James Abel must have been a sufficiently astonishing figure at first sight. He was, for one thing, some six feet seven inches in height. I have before me now a photograph taken at a much later period than this of John, Abel and Carstang, and a most remarkable trio they are. It was taken on the seashore at Merlin. John, clad only in bathing-drawers, is tall enough with his thin bony body, his hatchet face, his hair blowing low on his forehead as usual; he is laughing like a child. Carstang, too, with his breadth of shoulder, thick black eyebrows and scowling countenance (in the photograph he is stripped to his trousers and with his hair-covered chest and dark skin looks more foreign than any foreigner), is no unimposing figure. But both men are completely dwarfed by the gigantic Abel, who, also naked save for bathing-trunks, seems to tower to the heavens with his heavy, pale, flabby body, his bare German-cropped head, his big belly, his gigantic hands and feet. Abel, both at this earlier time of John's first visit and later, was known as the Prophet.

The description of John's Giant-Killer in Green Castle and Grey Hamlet is, I should imagine, an exact portrait of James Abel. It was Abel who was the real spiritual force behind the Second Flood Adventists. Whether he was charlatan or no who will ever tell? Mrs. Mortimer, the Reverend's wife, was a little, anxious, nervous woman. The coming of the Second Flood weighed on her morning, noon and night—and not selfishly. It was torture to her to know that, within a few years, all these helpless people, men, women, children, whom she saw in the streets, in shops, riding placidly on omnibuses, would inevitably be drowned and through, she could not help thinking, no fault of their own. It was Aunt Hunnable, John always thought, who hypnotized her.

She would look up at that severe, white-cuffed, uniformed-souled lady and sigh but utter no word. She suggested to John once that perhaps after all God might be more merciful than many people expected.

Mr. Lacey was a saint, and a madman. He was Aunt Hunnable's greatest problem, for he loved to rush out into the streets and preach wherever one or two might be gathered together. He warned them of the wrath to come—not of the Flood especially, for that seemed to him no very evil destiny—but rather of their spiritual and eternal damnation. He saw Hell's fires with a certainty that made the blaze crackle in your ear. Mr. Humphries, on the other hand, I always have seen as a stout practical man with side- whiskers and the air of a church sidesman.

He indeed supported Aunt Hunnable in the business necessities of the Adventists. His private life was, I understand, not above suspicion. He was believed to have been heard to say that when the Second Flood DID arrive it was the pretty girls who would be saved first if HE had anything to do with it.

Into this strange household young John was jumped. I have the evidence of Abel and Aunt Hunnable, both of whom I was one day to know, as to the effect he had upon everyone. They thought him the queerest creature. Aunt Hunnable, who had a kind heart beneath her officialdom, loved him from the first: I have always suspected that poor Aunt Hunnable should in reality have married a prosperous tradesman and had by him a very large family. She was caught up into the Second Flood Adventists more, I suspect, because they called to her business instincts than from any very spiritual belief or longings.

What appealed to her so strongly in Johnny's character was first his generosity and then his loyalty. She didn't think much of his artistic ambitions and for many years considered that he would be a lost soul if he didn't serve in a bank or behind a counter.

But she was his warm friend from the moment of meeting him at the station, and later she was to show it.

They all liked him and it was something of a novelty to them, on that first evening, to watch him go through his performance. He sang and acted and danced for them. Tears poured down Mrs. Mortimer's cheeks when he sang

'Sad Fountains.'

Nothing, on the other hand, seemed strange to John in Hunnable's. He expected things to be strange. It seemed to him quite normal that there should be a devastating flood in a few years' time—only he had so many things to do first. Hunnable's was simply a jumping- off ground for all the triumphs that he must bring off for himself. He made great friends with both James Abel and Mr. Lacey. He distinguished, young as he was, perfectly between them.

One was a Prophet by profession, the other a Saint by nature.

John: 'I used to say to Abel, "How do you make your prophecies, Mr. Abel?

What makes you so sure you know what's coming?" And he would stroke his belly and look at me from under his pale-coloured eyebrows and then slowly, without a word, lift me by the slack of my breeches and hold me dangling in mid-air. I can feel now the scent of his breath on my neck. It always smelt of sweets— peppermint, chocolate, raspberry. He was for ever eating them.

'In those first days at Hunnable's I was always trying to "catch somebody at it." What I mean was that both London and Hunnable's seemed to move entirely in mystery.

Pimlico wasn't in any case a very lively quarter. It was a decaying survival of one-time glories. Nothing seemed actually to happen there, but everything was hinted at. A cab would come cloppetty-clopping up the street, and I, from behind the window, would see a lady, veiled, get out of the cab, wait outside a door and quickly enter a house. Always in the distance, just out of reach, things would be happening—bells ringing, people shouting, horns hooting. Never under my nose. And in the house it would be the same. A door would open and I would see within the suddenly revealed room a number of people on their knees praying. Then the door would be hurriedly closed again. Or I would hear somewhere in the house a high shrill voice raised almost to a scream. But myself, I would never see more than this group of rather pallid people gathered together for their vegetarian meal, or, in the melancholy green drawing-room, filled with cheap nick-nacks, we would sit, and the ladies—Mrs. Mortimer, Miss Yellowly, Miss Forster—I remember, would say: "Well, little man, how are things with you?" and I would invent stories about Beerbohm Tree wanting to see me or of Ellen Terry having heard how beautifully I sang. They knew I was lying, I suspect, but they were all very good to me.'

It is, in fact, very clear that most of the people at Hunnable's very quickly came to love him. For one thing he had an original and undaunted courage.

He was afraid of no one, and more than that he took it for granted that everyone would be kind to him. His distress and surprise when someone betrayed or otherwise ill-treated him were, in spite of experience after experience, always extreme. No one ill-treated him at Hunnable's. He chattered to all and sundry, ran messages for anybody and everybody, read Lady Audley's Secret to Mrs. Mortimer when she had a severe cold, spent half a crown that Aunt Hunnable gave him entirely on a bunch of lilies-of-

the-valley for Miss Forster and admired the Prophet for his physique and supreme self-confidence.

They cannot have been at all a priggish or formally pious crowd, these Second Flood Adventists, for they enjoyed John's singing and little dances, talked about the theatre and read novels. Their real trouble, I suspect, was that, for the most part, they did not enjoy very good physical health. When the end of the world was to come so shortly the body was of small value; unless like side- whiskered Mr. Humphries you considered that because the time was short you must make the most of it. John never for a moment dropped his purpose of furthering his career. After a week or so at Hunnable's he set out in search of Miss Ada Montgomery.

There was a drizzle falling that afternoon and London was in that sulky, indifferent-spirited, I-don't-care-if-the-whole-lot-of-you- die kind of mood which is so especially depressing.

'I should have chosen quite another sort of day,' John would go on, 'but I simply could not wait any longer. For one thing my pride refused to allow me to be Aunt Hunnable's guest for ever without giving her some return. Then the money from my clay pig was almost exhausted and, once that was gone, I should not have a penny in the world. Get my living I must: I seemed to myself a man already. I thought I was clever enough for anything, and in that conceited spirit I set out.

'I was not conceited so much because of my own talents, I think, as for the certainty that God was with me. I rode on that omnibus that afternoon in sober truth like the Chosen of the Lord. I had received careful directions and I climbed up to sit just behind the driver so that I might feel that the omnibus belonged to me.

'I won't pretend but that I was frightfully excited. When I received permission to go to London, that had been something, entering the train at Polchester something more, arriving in London something further, but now I was in actual fact on my way to Miss Montgomery's. The event was at last, at last to be fulfilled! It never occurred to me that by this time she might have changed her address. I was sure that I would find the house at once and that, half an hour later, I would be engaged for a long term in some company with which

she was connected.

'Of course, I told the driver all about it, leaning forward and pushing my cold, damp nose against his cold, damp cape. I was on my way now to become one of England's greatest actors. I remember that he turned and looked at me although he still had his eye on his horses. In a husky voice that was full of coughs and whisky he observed that I was very young and when was I to learn my schooling? I told him that I'd learnt my schooling already. Could I do mathematics, he asked me, winking at my neighbour in the other seat, and, if I could, how much did it make when you were getting two bob a week and spending half a crown 'cause you'd got three kids and a wife and a mother–

in-law—especially the mother–in–law? That was mathematics, that was. We all laughed a great deal, I remember, and I told him that when I was a rich and successful actor I'd give a feast to his whole family. I meant it, too, for sitting up there on the omnibus with the drizzle soaking the umbrella that the Prophet had lent me I felt excitedly generous enough to give all the world a meal. I remember thinking that the Flood's arrival in a year or two did not seem too unlikely, for the rain was coming down now, changing from drizzle to torrents, in a way that swallowed man, beast, house and pavement.

'London became submerged and diluvian. We were back into primeval mud and only from the misty torrent lights shone out like marsh– fires....

'I liked the rain, the dusky grey, the sound of moving traffic, the lurch and rumble of the omnibus, the sense of a bustling life on every side of me, and when I came to the street where I was to descend I was the happiest small boy in the United Kingdom. Under my large umbrella I hunted about for the number of my house and soon I found it, dirty, grey-faced, soaked in rain, with a sodden newspaper lying on the steps. Up I marched and rang an echoing bell. After a while a woman opened the door and looked at me. I don't know what we said except that I was inside the narrow food– smelling hall in half a moment and demanded to see Miss Montgomery. I see now that it was a miracle that she hadn't moved in all those years. I didn't wonder at it then, taking everything altogether for granted. I said I had an appointment with Miss Montgomery, but the woman stoutly answered that I couldn't have, and by the way she looked at me I could tell that she thought me nothing but an impertinent little vagrant.

'I smiled my most winning smile but it had no effect at all. I then showed the dirty piece of paper with the address on it so long and lovingly cherished by me. That, too, had no effect. She opened the door and told me to go. So what did I do but run past her up the stairs and she after me, up the stairs and through a half-open door and into a room where a stout, red-nosed man with grey hair was sitting in his shirt and trousers reading a newspaper, and my dear Miss Montgomery herself lying on a sofa reading a book. I stopped in the doorway, the woman caught me by the shoulder, the man looked up and said, "My God!" and only Ada Montgomery, who was in a stained, pink dressing-gown and curl- papers, languidly said: "What is it, Agnes?"—or Sarah, or Mary, or Alice as the case may be.

'I began at once: "Some while ago you were acting in Port Merlin and I spoke to you and you wrote your address on a piece of paper and said I was to see you in London and here I am."

'To tell you the truth the room must have seemed quite as extraordinary to me as I did to them. I had never seen so untidy a place in all my life. Mess though my home in Merlin often had been, it never had had this kind of stale foulness. The room stank as though the grimy windows had not been opened for years, on the soiled tablecloth were the remains of a meal, a pair of trousers hung over the back of one of the chairs, and in the middle of the floor was a cracked bowl with the disgusting remains of a dog's meal.

'I stood there, I remember, with my heart hammering, and simply praying that I should make a success of it. I had pictured a lovely room, a beautiful lady

... but what did it matter? So I smiled bravely and bowed to the gentleman at the table. Miss Montgomery sat up with a bounce and stared; the gentleman looked over the top of his paper. I simply went on smiling.

'"Well, I'm damned!" said Miss Montgomery. "What's this?"

'"I'm the boy—" I began again.

'"My DEAR Ada—" said the gentleman in a voice of disgust and went back to his newspaper. I think now, on staring behind me, through all these years, that they had just been enjoying a violent quarrel.

'It never entered my head at the time of course—I didn't in fact regard the gentleman at all. I fixed my gaze, my heart and soul on Ada Montgomery and prayed—how passionately I prayed—for success.

'Another thing that I didn't know then was that she had been slipping downhill in her profession since I had last seen her. She would have the greatest difficulty in finding a career for herself much less for wandering young boys from the country. And a third thing that I didn't know was that she was quite a little drunk....

'I like to think now that, in very tiresome circumstances, she really did her best.

'"Why, of course, I remember you," she said. (Perhaps she did, perhaps she didn't.) "You're the funny little boy from Port Merlin. He's the boy from Port Merlin, Jim."

'She sat there kicking her heels. She was wearing soiled pink mules on her not-very-clean bare feet. I remember that I caught my breath, that panic suddenly did not seem very far away—for THIS, THIS was my only chance.

Ada Montgomery's writing on the soiled envelope was my only bridge to fame.

'"Please, Miss Montgomery," I said. (There IS no John. I am myself now standing up, heart beating frantically, speaking these words.) "You were very kind and you said that if I ever came to London I was to go and see you and you would get me an engagement in the theatre and I am—really I am—ever so much better than I was when I saw you there—"

'"Really, Ada," said the gentleman behind his newspaper. "WHAT a thing to promise anyone!"

'"But I didn't—" I can see Miss Montgomery now, scratching her head, yawning, kicking her heels. "I didn't do anything of the sort." I did then a desperate thing. I went right up to her, took her hand, held it, lifting it up and down as you lift the handle of a pump, imploring her, beseeching her to see what I could do.

'I felt, I imagine, that there was not a moment to be lost, that at any minute the horrible man behind the newspaper might pick her up and carry her headlong out of the room.

'"Let me show you! Let me show you!" I cried. "I can recite, dance, sing—"

'"Well, I'm damned—" she said again. Then the gentleman really did put his newspaper down and stared at me. And perhaps (I cannot tell, for I never saw him again and he is the merest shadow of a shade to me) he was touched, for in spite of my long trousers and my ridiculous, little stick-up collar (which I had put on to look like a man), I had the face and voice and body of a child.

But I had vivacity and energy and persistence, too.

'"Listen, please," I commanded, and I stood away from them both there in the window near the remains of the dog's dinner, and began the Queen Mab speech from Romeo and Juliet. The moment that was finished (for I did not intend to give them a chance of not hearing me) I rushed into some pathos from Caste. Then, waiting for half a minute to get my breath, I did some Harlequinade business, acting the Clown, the Policeman and the Dog with great fire and energy that found their climax in my doing two somersaults and standing on my head. This last was too much for my worn and slender braces.

They snapped. Nothing daunted, however, with one hand holding up my trousers, I sang (pretty well, too, I imagine) "Sad Fountains."

'There was a pause while I stood there, anxiously, almost beseechingly, looking into their faces. Had I brought it off? Had I convinced them? In my heart, I remember, was pride, as though I said to myself: "If I can do these things here in such difficult and odious circumstances *I* can do them anywhere." Then—and the horrid shock of it still remains with me—the gentleman at the table began to laugh, and he laughed and laughed and laughed.

'He laughed till the tears came, he laughed, his hands holding his bulging sides, he laughed, rocking in his chair, until he almost fell to the ground; he laughed so that you could name it hysteria and not be far wrong. Ada, trying for a moment to be grave, was caught into the turmoil and SHE laughed and she laughed and she laughed.

'They both together, rocking to and fro, laughed like hell. I stared, I looked at them beseechingly, and then I burst into tears. I turned round from them to the window and cried, with one hand across my face, the other holding up my trousers.

'No word was spoken. I don't know how long the scene continued. It was quite horrible and awful. I am ashamed now when I think of it.

'They noticed soon my tears, my dejection, my disappointment, and tried in their own way to be kind. Ada called me to her, she put her arm round my neck, she drew me close to her dirty and shabby pink peignoir. I stood there, sniffing, I suppose, and drawing those sad little sporadic gulps that are the after-grief of children.

'I think that she told me that I wasn't to be disappointed, that life was full of bitterness and agony—hadn't she herself found it so? I fancy—although of this I cannot be altogether sure—she talked about her own art, its greatness and splendour, and how disgracefully the world had ill-treated it. If she did not it was a wonder, for it is a thing we all do, under the slightest encouragement—talk passionately, I mean, of the way that life has disregarded our finest points! I especially with my many failures behind me....

'What I do very clearly remember is that the gentleman, with the idea, I suppose, that he would like to do something to help, asked me whether I wasn't hungry and wouldn't like a chop or something. I, with a shuddering look at the neglected table, said, oh no, thank you, I had had my dinner and was in need of nothing.

'With a sharp and almost poignant sensitiveness I now realized that the only thing for me to do was to vanish as quickly as possible. They on their side did not want me to go without proffering some kind of help (which would, they well knew, be perfectly useless). Had I been a pretty boy or even reasonably good-looking they might have made a real try to place me somewhere, but now, my cheeks mottled with tears, my hair untidy, my nose red, I must have been quite supremely unattractive. Their only thought can have been how to get rid of me quickly and at the same time to preserve their own self-esteem.

'Then Miss Montgomery thought of Mr. Schaaf. How strange, now when I look back, was that chain of persons—Mr. Darlington, the actor of Ada's company, Ada herself, Edward Schaaf, Lady Max.... And a chain for what?

Would I not be precisely here with my same record of much failure and little success had they not transferred me, like a chain-letter, from one to another?

A mingling of destiny and free-will, I suppose, like everything else. One thing at least— no one could ever accuse me of not snapping eagerly at my chance!

'Ada went into the next room, sat down at a little escritoire piled high with papers and unpleasant-looking documents and wrote her letter to Edward Schaaf. What she wrote in it I shall never know.

'Once the letter was written her great burning purpose was to be rid of me as soon as possible, and once I had received it MY burning purpose was to go!

'They almost bundled me away and my last memory of them is of a white dog with black spots crawling out from under the sofa and looking at me with such evil, red-rimmed eyes that I was at once reminded of Mrs. Hoskin. The gentleman threw him a bone from the table and the last sound I heard, as the door closed behind me, was the malevolent crushing of bones. I was now as riotously elated as five minutes before I had been most miserably depressed. I had no notion, of course, as to who Mr. Edward Schaaf might be. Miss Montgomery had told me that he was one of her oldest and dearest friends and that his power in the theatre was almost limitless. I do remember wondering why, if that were so, he hadn't been able to do more for Miss Montgomery. I remember too that now the rain had ceased. London's face was washed and over her head little clouds, like the angels in Reynolds'

picture, floated through the purest light and air. The smoke of all the chimneys went straight like plumes of feathers into the sky and the gold of the Indies glowed in the window-panes.

'In the heart of the Second Flood Adventists I found there was plenty to do.

Mrs. Mortimer had a terrible cold, and I shall, as long as life remains to me, connect Lady Audley's Secret with eucalyptus and peppermint, a bedroom of Sahara heat and Mrs. Mortimer's strange choking sniffles which were so purely animal as to be almost improper. Had I remained at Hunnable's I would most certainly have become the little fetch-and-carry boy of the place.

There was, I think, a sort of creeping laziness about all of them save my aunt and the Prophet. Those who sincerely believed in the Second Flood naturally felt their efforts a little superfluous when so soon they were to be washed away, and those who did not believe were, to some degree (and often to a large degree), parasitical. Myself, I was full of energy and love of my fellow human beings. Of the first of these only a few quietists will to-day disapprove; the second almost everyone will regard as a sentimental weakness. I don't know. It depends, I suppose, how you look at it. You pay your money and you take your choice.

'At Hunnable's, however, I HAD no choice. They were all so exceedingly kind to me. They were always pressing upon me shillings and half-crowns, apples and oranges, bulls'-eyes and toffee, garments, caps and stockings, braces and shoes. I may say at once that I took without any hesitation at all everything that I was given.

'During this present visit I had little share in the religious side of their life.

Most of the Hunnable lodgers worked hard during the day—there were bank-clerks, secretaries, shop-assistants, one actor and one commercial traveller.

There were some fifteen in all and it would have been difficult to accommodate them had it not been for a long attic-shaped room at the top of the house which was turned into a dormitory for six gentlemen—and I have never in my life seen anything colder or neater than the appearance of that room in the daytime with the six white beds, the six washing-basins and looking-glasses and the six night-shirts neatly folded on the six beds. It was almost like one of my own fairy stories. I believe that, for those who would suffer the company of the dormitory, lodging at Hunnable's was very cheap.

'At nine o'clock every evening there was a service in the dining- room, now cleared of its evening meal. Visitors from outside came to this and sometimes it was very crowded. The Prophet preached— wordy and eloquent, "sound and fury signifying nothing"—Mr. Mortimer, of course, gentle and persuasive, and on occasions Aunt Hunnable, for here there was no distinction between sexes.

'Both sexes alike would shortly suffer the Flood....

'I have no very vivid memory of the services save that there was a very

handsome, highly coloured painting of Noah's family and the animals moving into the Ark; this hung at the end of the drawing- room and under it was arranged a table with a pair of silver candlesticks as a kind of unpretentious altar.

'Noah, in fact, was the High Prophet of the company, and I was never, after my visit there, able quite to get him out of my head. He is the most real to me of all the Old Testament figures, and when, later on, I was to make the acquaintance of Frederick Austin Crabbe, he always seemed to me, in spite of his beard and vegetarianism, to have a lot of Father Noah in his composition; his common sense, his being always against the Government, his self-

confidence—these resembled the character of the Patriarch. He would not, however, have any dealings with doves as messengers!

'It was a week after my visit to Ada Montgomery that I set out to find Mr.

Schaaf. I waited, I fancy, chiefly because they all kept me so busy at Hunnable's that I had no chance of escape. Or it may have been that I was afraid to put this final all-important challenge to the test. However, at last I put on once again my stiff spiky collar and my over-tight trousers, soaked my rebellious hair in water and sallied forth. I had not the slightest notion as to who Mr. Edward Schaaf might be—I knew only that he was of immense importance and that he lived at 25 Berkeley Square. I was accustomed to omnibuses by this time and I rode very comfortably to Piccadilly Circus and then walked through a lovely spring afternoon up Piccadilly.

'I had never before seen the West End of London, and its splendour completely dazzled me. The constant procession of carriages and omnibuses; the brilliance of the shop-windows, so that I must stop every instant to admire a silk dressing-gown or a sporting print of gentlemen in pink coats on shining horses leaping ditches; or, best of all, the windows of the bookshop of Mr. Sotheran in which the new books in their fresh covers looked so dazzling as almost to blind the eye.

'"Oh, let me but come among you!" I thought. "Wait until I have written my novels and plays. There will be rows and rows of them there and people will be standing in line...." And I remember that almost next door there was a sweetshop with such miraculous piles of brown glistening toffee, of peppermint white as snow, of bar upon bar of pink coconut icing, that,

pressing my long nose against the window-pane, I almost swooned of desire.

'And so I passed into the quiet reticence and fresh spring beauty of Berkeley Square. That was still, in 1895, a place where anyone's caravan might have rested. Devonshire House still guarded it; no hordes of motor-cars herded together at its entrance like an army panting for the word of command. On the steps of one house stood a young footman taking the air; in the gardened enclosure were two nursemaids chatting beside their perambulators. Those figures, on this, perhaps the most important day of all my life, will be remembered by me for ever.... The new green leaves gently rustled in the sunshine somewhere; mellowed by distance a hurdy-gurdy played; a carriage or two magnificently rolled northward.

'I found No. 25, and outside it there were several carriages. I mounted the steps and rang the bell. The door was opened to me by the most elegant of footmen, who stared as though I were a naked, but decorated, native from Central Africa. So certain, however, was I of my destiny that I refused to be discouraged by any footman. I asked him whether Mr. Schaaf lived there and told him what I wanted.

'He said that Mr. Schaaf DID live there but was very busily engaged. I said that I had a letter for Mr. Schaaf. He said that he would deliver it. I said no—

I would deliver it myself.

'At that moment a superb gentleman, dressed in what I took to be evening-

clothes, appeared and asked what the trouble was. As with Miss Montgomery, so now— I walked straight past them into the hall.

'The old boy in the evening-clothes turned out in the end to be my Official Guardian Angel. He told me later that he had a little nephew just like me and added, "Poor little devil! He's that ugly everyone makes fun of him. That's why I've a kind of soft spot for him." Anyway Ralph, as I afterwards knew him, was one of the most important behind-the-scenes butlers in London at that time. A novel, almost as long as one of Simeon Rose's longest novels, might be written about Ralph and the social secrets that he kept with such imperturbable dignity. I little knew at that moment that he would so soon be inhabiting the same house as myself!

'In any case, there he stood with his splendid figure (he had the shoulders, chest and legs of a heavy-weight boxer in superb condition); his shining smartness, so that the black silk lapels of his coat shone against the glassy purity of his white shirt; his dark hair beautifully crowning his round, rosy, episcopal countenance; there he stood and looked at me as the Duke gazed benevolently on Sancho Panza. I could tell that there was a party, for I heard bursts of laughter, many voices, the tinkling of a piano.

'Apollo smiled.

'"And what can I do for you, young man?" he asked.

'"He says he has a letter for Mr. Schaaf, Mr. Lambert," said the footman.

"And I've told him—"

'Ralph and I looked at one another and were friends from that moment.

'"I must give the letter myself," I explained very seriously. "It's life and death to me," I added, quoting from one of my favourite romances but meaning it with the utmost literalness all the same.

'"Mr. Schaaf," said Apollo, "is entertaining a number of his friends to tea. I myself will see that he has the letter."

'"Oh, but that won't do," I said urgently. (I remember that, tall for my age as I was, I reached up to Ralph's magnificent middle only, and, try as I might, never seemed to advance further than his lowest waistcoat-button.) "I MUST

see him. It's a letter from one of his very best friends, a lady; he would be dreadfully upset if he didn't see me—"

'But he WAS to see me! For at that moment there appeared at the turn of the stair Mr. Edward Schaaf himself, conducting a perfect beauty with high puffed sleeves and a tiny tiny waist—yes, I remember—to the door.

'Poor Edward Schaaf! No one remembers him now or that he crossed the Channel at some time in 1900 very much more quickly than he wished, never to return to England again. He used to say wistfully when you lunched with him at Nice, where he finally resided, that in his exile he missed nothing but

the English policeman. As a fact, I think his heart was broken, and he died in 1903.

'Now, on my first view of him, he was like the most elegant pug dressed to the absolute Brummel perfection. He walked like a lady's maid who has just been entrusted with a most important secret by her mistress. He had a movement with the little finger of his right hand—raised, crooked, quivering

—which was somehow of a quite grave indecency. He knew more about eighteenth-century music and the French Impressionist painters than anyone then in London. He owned three of London's most important theatres. He painted his face, wore stays, would cry at almost anything, was kind to his friends, and had as malicious a tongue as Pope. He had a large hairy mole in the middle of his painted cheek.

'If I am unkind about him, God forgive me. He was certainly unkind about me.

'I think that the moment he saw me he perceived that here was an oddity for his party. An ugly small boy was of all things in the world the most unpleasant sight to him, offending as it must his deepest, most sensual intimacies. I was ugly enough, but I was also something of a clown, and that he was clever enough at once to seize.

'So soon as—bowing from the corseted waist, kissing the lady's glove—he had said farewell to his lovely visitor he turned and cast his little pointed eyes on me; he said to Ralph (and I remember how startled I was by the sharp shrill voice), "Who is it?"

'Ralph said that the boy had a letter, and I think, on looking back, that Ralph's warm benevolent eyes watched me already with a fatherly care (he knew, though, that *I* ran no possible risk).

'"This is Mr. Schaaf," Ralph said to me. So I presented the letter....

'Two minutes later I was in the drawing-room, that beautiful cream-

shadowed room with the Courbet "Seascape" over the mantelpiece, the Manet

"Breakfast Table," and—my especial delight as I looked at it later—the pale orange Chinese rug with the purple leopards and temple of rose red. Did I

think as I looked about me and saw that world of colour and scent and silk and amber dancing before me in the light of the crystal chandelier, did I think of the room in Merlin, dim in the steam of the laundry, the little table with my father's shell-boxes, the bed with the patched quilt, the murmur of the sea beyond the window? Yes, very, very shortly, within another half-hour, I was to think exactly of those things.

'I didn't realize at all, I fancy, that I was being made a show of. I knew nothing, of course, of the nature of a man like Schaaf. I stood there, blinking a little in the brilliant light, still holding my cap in my hands, smiling, looking at all the ladies and gentlemen with the friendliest gaze, quite confident, feeling that my great chance had at last come, ready for any miracle.... And indeed a miracle, a positive, actual miracle was shortly to occur!

'Schaaf's guests had been standing about, chatting, laughing, drinking tea, the women in enormous hats that seemed to turn the middle air into a brilliant variegated garden. Someone was playing at the piano.

'Schaaf, holding up his hand for silence, introduced me.

'I was an artist, he said, who had just come up from the country, recommended to him by a very old friend. I could do, he understood, every kind of thing—dance, sing, act. He begged their attention.

'I hadn't the slightest notion of his irony. I thought that he meant sincerely every word that he said. As I looked about me they seemed to me to have kind, indulgent faces. I didn't know that I was looking for the first time at the cruellest, unkindest, most brutally selfish, most callously vain group in the whole of England. I didn't know that I was being butchered for a Schaaf holiday; I was confident of their kindly good-nature. I loved them all at sight.

'So I stood, twisting my cap in my hands and smiling at them all inanely.

What should I do? "Anything you like," said Mr. Schaaf, purring at the unexpected God-sent piece of entertainment.

'What DID I do? I don't remember. Very much, I suppose, what I had done for Ada Montgomery. And I sang 'Sad Fountains.' There was silence. I suddenly, as suddenly as though someone had slapped my cheek, realized the

hostility. Someone tittered; someone began to talk. I saw faces, cold, ironic, inhuman. I realized far more vividly than I had done with Ada Montgomery that I was a complete, absolute, and total failure. But now I didn't cry as I had done there. My heart was too dry; my shame too deep. I would have turned and run from that horrible house, but then the first of two miracles occurred.

A thin, pale-faced young man rose from the piano at which he had been sitting.

'"What else do you sing?" he said. "I have a number of old English songs here."

'I stumbled, knocking my ugly knees together, through the lot of them to the young man's side. Had he commanded me I would have died for him. I trod on someone's gown. I nearly knocked over a small table. A Pekingese dog barked at me. I reached the young man, stood at his side, looked the song over. I sang "Fair Pledges of a Fruitful Tree", "Beauty Clear and Fair" and

"The Young May Moon." Yes, and more. They applauded. They were as kind as they had been brutal. I sang as though they did not exist. I sang as though with my friends in Merlin. I stopped, saw my cap had fallen to the ground, stooped to pick it up—and the second miracle occurred!

'For, on raising my body, I met the eyes—sharp, cruel, ironical but beautiful, and shining like ripe blackberries—of a very old lady. She was sitting in a chair of black wood and gold, a little before the rest, leaning forward on a black ebony cane with a carved silver bird topping it. She was wearing a huge hat; floppy, grey, and covered with a perfect garden of flowers—roses, poppies, bluebells, and I know not what. Her dress was of grey silk and very voluminous. Her face, under the garden hat, was rouged and seamed with a thousand wrinkles. Her fingers were crab-like and covered with rings. She had a moustache. One shoulder was higher than the other. She was the old harpy of all the English novelists from Thackeray to Simeon Rose. I was to discover that she ran not only to type. She was an individual in her own right....

'She sat there, leaning on her stick, looking at me. And at once I knew her.

How? Ah, that is the second miracle. Had I, subconsciously, heard someone name her? Did my father describe her on that tragic day so dramatically that he presented her to me? Or was it really one of those miracles with which, although we will not perceive it, we are so constantly confronted? I can't tell you. I explain nothing. I only know that as I straightened myself out it was as though myself and the old lady were quite alone in the world, and I, looking full in those blackberry eyes, said:

'"Your name is Lady Max—and you killed my father."

'That must have been something of a bombshell thrown into the middle of that company of lazy jesters. The very ugly little boy from the country saying such a thing to the venerable old witch of Endor who dealt so liberally in her own spells that she quite naturally scorned anyone else's!

'I might, of course, so easily have been wrong. It was a shot in the dark, if you like. Ever since my father's death I had dwelt persistently in my mind on this old murderess, as I thought her. The first ancient female grandee seen by me in London would probably raise that accusation out of me. The miracle was that I was right the very first time. It WAS Lady Max.

'She was frightened. I remember that very clearly indeed. She had killed, I don't doubt, a number of fathers in her time. She must have sat there, staring at me, and saying to herself, "WHICH father does the child mean?"

'"I AM Lady Max," she said, never taking her eyes off my face.

'Breathlessly I told her, seeing nothing now but my dear, dear father standing in the doorway of our room, the broken shell-box in his hand, the grind and crash of the sea on the evening shore coming through, carrying the fading light in its clatter. The broken shell-box! I told her everything, of our hopes, of how father had worked, of how his heart had been broken. I ended with a little gasp, staring at her as though I were bewitched.

'"The boy is quite right," she said. "But it wasn't a very good box, you know,"

she added to me, quite gently.

'"But it was, it was!" I cried. "The best he ever made"—and I burst into tears.

You'll think I was for ever crying. But it wasn't so. At Ada Montgomery's I cried for myself—now I cried for my father.

'People left us, I think, to ourselves. There was something here that they didn't quite understand. They began to say good-bye and Edward Schaaf stood at the door and hoped they'd enjoyed themselves. They had, really. And what a queer little boy!

'But Lady Max went further. "You must come home with me," she said.

"Perhaps we can make something of you."

'"Now?" I asked.

'"Yes, now.... I may forget all about it in half an hour if you don't. I owe you something."

'I went with her.

'Edward Schaaf watched us drive off.'

CHAPTER VII

House of Jade and Amethyst

And thus John's voice slowly vanished into the wind; its last echo on the words, 'No Time ... Time is not, but I am here,' almost persuades me as I write at my table, staring out on to this blue brittle autumn sky, the chrysanthemums like torn shreds of ragged paper, red-amber above the chiselled leaves. Yes, persuades me that he is here, bending from his thin, untidy height, his hair in his eyes so that he must brush it back with his lean hand, his spade-like shoulders bent, and that child-kindliness, dream-

oddity....

'It's right, old friend, as it is. Everything is right. Have faith in me.'

It was not that John, like one of those garrulous literary seafarers, talked for ever over beer-tankards while the clock ticked the twenty-four hours. Many places—the brine-stung beach at Merlin, the room in St. James's, Manchester, Bridgate in Yorkshire, St. Malo, the little hotel in the Rue du Bac, mid-way Atlantic—were backgrounds for that high eager voice, the long legs tumbling about the room, the gesture brushing back the hair, the eyes shining, the lifted tumbler, the short black pipe, the turn on the heel and the sudden phrase: 'She'd bark like a puppy, you know, half whine, half struggling effort at maturity. Then laugh, fall down and look up at me from under her tangled hair. When she was two and a bit.' I've strung many things together when he speaks at length, but always trying to give the rhythm, the tone, the gesture.... I've caught tone and gesture FROM him. His influence on me in those last years was emphatic.

He was carried off to Lady Max's like a new toy. He didn't know that. He was simply placed in the old-fashioned carriage like a parcel, and Lady Max sat upright beside him, speaking never a word.

She must have been an extraordinary old woman, by all accounts— not, I

repeat, one of those dominant old dowagers out of Simeon Rose, like the Duchess of Camelot who, between her Dragons, was alive as long as she didn't utter a word but betrayed her author sadly when she spoke. There was nothing artificial about Lady Max. She was the offspring of a mid-Victorian lion-huntress who lived in Pimlico somewhere and, on very humble means, entertained George Lewes, Wilkie Collins, Forster, and, when she was lucky, Dickens, and even once or twice Thackeray. The ugly little girl grew up, having to starve in order to shake hands with a celebrity. She was hideous and had no brilliance, but she managed to marry three wealthy husbands one after the other. She was born in the late 1820's, so that now, when John knew her, she was seventy odd. John used to say of her that her face was a map—of a country poisoned with malaria.

She was immensely rich, and mad in so far as she yielded always to the impulses of the moment, and these impulses changed with crazy jerkiness.

She was desperately restless and could be cruel, generous, sympathetic, cold, ill and perfectly well all within the same five minutes. For some weeks she would entertain madly; socially, she moved in and out of the Herries set. She was rather a friend of Ellis Herries, who was himself an eccentric; she considered his wife, Vanessa, stuck-up. At one time she warmly cultivated a younger member of the Herries clan, Cynthia Worcester, because Cynthia was aesthetic and knew Oscar Wilde, Dowson, Whistler. After the scandal of

'95, Lady Max was one of Wilde's supporters, sent him money and helped him later when he was in France and Naples.

She considered herself an aesthete because of her Collections. These were of the most extravagant kind and ranged from dolls of different periods and countries to Chinese jade, ivory and amethyst. She collected madly under the impulse of a particular mood and could be cheated by anybody. There were, therefore, many quite worthless things in each of her collections, but she would permit nothing to be thrown away.

She lived in a big hideous house in one of the smaller squares off Sloane Street. I have seen the house, which is now divided into flats, and it is big enough for a school or hospital. The rooms have now been cut up, but in her time they must have been vast indeed, and, because she was for ever changing her servants and had not, in any case, any real caretaker for her

treasures, the dirt and confusion must have been terrible.

John has told me that his first impression on entering that house was of dust.

He began to cough as soon as he was in the hall. Then, behind the dust, he caught glimpses of astonishing things—a sedan-chair of faded pink silk, a doll four feet high in a wedding- dress, two Chinese warriors on horses, a stuffed monkey, a glass cabinet with the colours of the rainbow inside it, his first view of jade and amethyst and ivory, a temple made of silver with multitudes of little silver bells, a great screen covered with theatre playbills (these at once caught his eye), pictures made of straw, two figures with dreadful dead wax faces holding sceptres in their waxen hands.

The living-rooms—the vast dining-room, the icy-cold drawing-room, were dead as mausoleums. He had himself a little attic bedroom on the top floor where the servants slept. The butler, before Ralph arrived, was always drunk and terrified John one night by coming into his room, stumbling half over his bed, and there stertorously snoring for the rest of the night. Meals were haphazard and casual unless there was a party, and then John would be lucky if he got anything to eat at all.

All the same, so far as I can understand it, at the beginning at least Lady Max took her duties to John very seriously. He, on his side, was grateful beyond all words and, at first, would have done anything she asked.

On the morning after his arrival he went over in the carriage to Hunnable's to fetch his few belongings. Aunt Hunnable and himself had a tender parting.

Aunt Hunnable had the anxiety that she might be handing her sister's child over to miscreants. He promised, though, that he would come to her immediately if there were any kind of trouble, and he almost made her believe what he so firmly believed himself; namely, that he was the child of destiny and that extraordinary things would be certain to happen to him.

'You are certainly unlike any other boy I've ever seen,' Aunt Hunnable agreed. 'That makes me the more anxious about you.'

'I can look after myself,' he assured her.

So he took his very few possessions over to Lady Max's.

For the first week or two he was, I imagine, in spite of the drunken butler, very happy indeed. He was a fresh addition to Lady Max's collection, and his eagerness, his determination to love everyone, his certainty of his future fame, his quaint appearance, the gestures he made, the stories he told, all made him, at first, an original excitement.

Lady Max liked him to come up to her bedroom in the morning and talk to her while she had her roll and coffee. That would have been a good picture for any painter, I should imagine. John said she looked exactly like an agitated, sad-eyed monkey, her yellow forehead wrinkled, sitting up in her Chinese bed that was all gilt and red-maned Chinese lions, a lace cap crooked on her head, her long-nailed fingers clutching her coffee-cup. Not that she was especially impressive, I imagine. Just a silly, spoilt, bad-

tempered old woman who never, in spite of her wealth, really got what she wanted.

At first she gave John full range and liberty. The room was filled with things; there were two dog-baskets containing two Pekingese who, at this time of day, yapped and snapped all over her bed, asking for food. Her sour-faced maid moved about the room fussing over garments which lay there, here, and under the bed. There was a great deal of noise. Lady Max screaming at the maid, the dogs barking and the inebriated butler suddenly pushing his nose in at the door with information or excuses or insulting comments.

In and out of all this John moved about, pouring forth all his ideas, imaginations, prophecies. Here at last it seemed to him that he had found the Fairy Godmother. With his passion for seizing at once on all the most glorious possibilities and crowning them as achieved facts, he saw himself marching to victory and flinging all his rewards into two laps—those of his mother and Lady Max. He was going to write plays, stories that would astonish the world. At the great dinner given to him by the Crowned Heads of Europe he would point to Lady Max sitting on his right hand and say: 'There is my benefactress. It is she to whom I owe everything.'

'Amy,' (or Abigail or Rebecca or whatever the maid was called), Lady Max would scream, 'where's my black bodice with the French lace? I haven't seen it for months. You've stolen it, I'm sure you have.'

'And then,' John would go on proclaiming, his eyes on fire, 'when I'm in Italy and staying with the King in Rome we'll have a festival at the theatre. I'll write three plays about Garibaldi. Do you know about Garibaldi?'

'Do I know about Garibaldi? My mother entertained Mazzini to dinner. Amy, take Tong. He's going to be sick.'

When she had time to listen she marvelled at all that the boy knew, at his fire and versatility. She talked of him everywhere just then—the prodigy that she had discovered, the son of a washerwoman in Glebeshire, and he could act, sing, dance, and was already writing marvellous plays. She gave, in fact, a party for him, but at this, as I understand it, John did not distinguish himself, having a sudden fit of not wishing to show off before all these people. It was his first suspicion perhaps that they were not all so friendly as they seemed.

He was beginning now in London to repeat his earlier Merlin experience (and he would repeat it again and again). He would start with complete trust and confidence only to discover the inevitable falsities, insincerities, mockeries.

This party was a failure and it was from then, I suspect, that Lady Max began to be tired of her prodigy....

He wrote to his mother, to Anne, to Charlie, and his letters are piled beside me on my table as I write. His handwriting is already acquiring the thick, stubby characters one day to be so familiar to the world. The letters are a boy's letters but sometimes astonishingly mature. I have selected two or three of the more vivid.

May 6, 1895.

MY DEAR MOTHER—You will be very surprised dear mother, that I am not any more living with Aunt Hunnable. I am in a very grand house for as long as I want to be and you can tell Mrs. Hoskin and the others that it is like what I always said. You can't keep me back because it's my Destiny to be famous, however Mrs. Hoskin and those like her try to hurt me they cannot really hurt me because it is my Destiny. Well dear mother I love you very much and I say my prayers every morning and evening but what do you think, it is the same old lady who killed father because she wouldn't take his shell box. I was at a party singing. I sang Sad Fountains and other songs, and they liked them very much and suddenly I saw the old lady and knew she was

the one that killed father. I don't know how I knew but I did and I was so angry that I told her in front of everybody and the old lady said it was true.

She said I must come and live with her right away so I went in her carriage without any clothes or anything. She lives in a house that's so big it's like the asylum where Grandfather was and it is so full of things that you always knock something over if you are not careful. There is a doll's house covered with lace curtains and there are Chinese precious stones and a screen with theatre papers. She likes me very much and says I will be a great man. I do everything to please her, I dance and sing my songs. I go up to her room every morning when she has her coffee and make her laugh. She has two dogs that bark on the bed. The food is fine and I like everything except Mr.

Coggins he is the Butler and one night he was drunk and slept on my bed.

Now dear mother I must stop for the present and please write a letter very soon because I am always your loving,

SON JOHN.

And here is one to Anne:

June 3, 1895.

MY DEAR ANNE—I had a letter from you yesterday and was very pleased because I think of you every day—you and mother and Charlie and I wish you were here all the time.

Sometimes Anne I am lonely because for three or four days I won't see anybody except Amy and Mr. Coggins when old Lady M. is ill and she has been now for more than a week and Amy says it's because she's eaten too much and her stomach is weak as water Amy says. Yesterday I thought I would run away to Aunt Hunnable's and I thought of you and Charlie and I must stay here because it is the only way I can get a job but for three days nobody spoke to me except when I was in the kitchen to get my meals but I can go over the whole house as I like and I could steal any fine thing I pleased but you told me stealing was wrong only how is it wrong if someone has something beautiful and does not know even she has it only you can feel very lonely going everywhere all day in a house as large as anything and things everywhere jewels from China only everything is dusty.

Dear Anne I would like to see you so very much because I could tell you more than I think of now but I will give you a secret. I am writing a book and it is called The Doom of Carne and it is dedicated to you and Charlie. I have put For Anne and Charlie from their loving admirer the Author don't you like that I do. It's funny about money because last week Lady Max gave me five pounds and I sent all except ten shillings to mother because she would need it and it would show her I was getting on grandly and teach that old beast Hoskin what I told her would happen but after that Lady Max hasn't given me anything and I haven't got a farthing now. Do you think, dear Anne, if you have some money you could give me a little. When my book is published I will pay you back or perhaps earlier if I have a job at a theatre but if you haven't got any it doesn't matter in the least.

Love from

John.

June 18, 1895.

MY DEAR MOTHER—Thank you for your letter only it didn't say much except about the money. Dear Mother I am sending you in this letter three pounds which Lady Max gave me yesterday at least she gave me four pounds but I must keep one pound because I don't know when I shall have another one. You say you're not at all well and you are very unhappy and I couldn't read some of the words because the words are so shakey. I wish you would be happy because you need not worry about me I am getting on very well and now I am writing a book called The Doom of Carne and I have done one chapter and a half. Lady Max is very kind to me when she is there but some of the days she isn't there at all only she is in her room or at parties and then I have to amuse myself. I haven't seen Aunt Hunnable nor been in London much because it costs money and I want to be there if Lady Max wants to see me because she said she will get me a grand job at one of the theatres and I must wait for the right moment.

You don't tell me anything about Merlin mother or how the weather is or what they have been acting at the theatre and don't you let Mrs. H. or Mrs. G.

give you medicines for your pain in the back because I wouldn't trust them to give you anything and I expect it's the damp from the laundry gives you

pains. I must stop now.

Your loving

SON JOHN.

June 28, 1895.

MY DEAR CHARLIE—I must thank you for sending me the pen for my birthday. I was eleven. I miss you very much Charlie, more than anything except mother. As I told you in my last I am still waiting for a job in the theatre and some days I haven't anything to do at all and then I begin to fancy things in the house because there are so many things. There are two figures with wax faces and wax hands and there is one place where she has all the Chinese carved things. Some are blue with smoke in it and that's amethyst and some are yellow and that's amber and there are two gods with long beards all carved in ivory and you can see their fingers and everything but if you touch anything it's covered with dust except the things in the cases.

There's one good thing and that is Mr. Coggins is gone and who do you think has come to be butler that is Ralph who I saw the first time at Mr. Schaaf's party and he is very kind I like him very much. He is so strong he can bend a poker and I sit in his room with him and he tells me about Kings and Queens he's been familiar with.

I am reading a fine book I found in one of the rooms, it is called Mobey Dick and it is all about Whale Hunting. There is a lot of words I don't understand but he is a wonderful man who tells it and in the first chapter he goes to sleep with a Cannibal who has a tomahawk with him and when he dresses puts on his hat before his trousers.

Dear Charlie I am getting on in the world but sometimes I am very lonely and I wish you were here so much and I tell Ralph all about you and what we did in Merlin and how you catch fish and everything. Lady Max doesn't listen so much now I expect she had heard all my stories.

Your loving friend,

JOHN CORNELIUS.

He was beginning in fact to be nervous and very considerably unhappy. He was always one who distrusted himself at once if the omens seemed to be against him, and then went up to heaven immediately with the slightest encouragement. The fact was that Lady Max very soon began to grow tired of him. Like many another benefactor she considered the novelty and immediate generosity of her benefaction more than the drudgery of it. Benefactions are like love—after the first selfish ecstasy there is always hard work.

All that Lady Max now found on her hands was an ugly lanky boy whose few tricks were already stale. Moreover, poor John had, although he was little aware of it, an enemy. Edward Schaaf could not endure ugly boys; they seemed to him a deep offence against nature. And especially he could not endure ugly boys with a good opinion of themselves. On one of the few occasions when Johnny met Mr. Schaaf at Lady Max's he, believing that the pink pouting gentleman was his most ardent patron, poured out his plans, prospects, and certainties of future greatness, even confiding to him the involved plot of The Doom of Carne.

This, quite naturally, disgusted Edward Schaaf, who must have everything handsome and aesthetic about him. Also, as with many selfish and self-

centred people, it was a real humiliation to be suspected of being weak and silly enough to be unselfish.

So he apologized profoundly to Lady Max for burdening her with this washerwoman's offspring and encouraged her to rid herself of him as quickly as possible. This she would probably have done at once had it not been for the amiable omniscient Ralph. Ralph left Mr. Schaaf's service after an incident which was too much even for HIS social tolerance. His worldly creed was perfectly clear: he did not mind what anyone did so long as the decencies were observed, and what the decencies were Ralph settled. He was himself such a bottomless repository of the social weakness of his period that nothing could possibly shock him—but something happened at Edward Schaaf's 'that no gentleman should be guilty of' and he transferred himself to Lady Max, who was wildly delighted to secure him.

His affection for Johnny was deep and real to the day of his death. He was himself now between fifty and sixty and had grown out of all sexual excesses. His tastes were for Stock Exchange adventures, a little racing and

society intrigues. The last had become a habit with him, and it is a thousand thousand pities that he kept no diary. He must have been by now very wealthy and he owned, I believe, considerable property in Surbiton and Ealing.

He had never married. In his earlier days he preferred casual intercourse as

'less involving'. He had an almost universal acquaintance amongst the ladies'

maids, cooks, housekeepers of Mayfair, but he used these persons as

'communicating officials' rather than as provokers of sentiment.

'The trouble about intercourse between the sexes,' he would tell John, 'is that the timing is all wrong.'

'The timing?' John would ask.

'Like two clocks always a little behind or before one another. They never strike the hour at the same second. I remember once,' he would go on (John could imitate his deep chuckling voice most admirably), 'it was on one of Her Majesty's earliest visits to Nice, Lord—we'll call him X—Lord X was deeply enamoured of a pretty young dancer at the Casino. Old Countess B had been keeping Lord X for a number of years. He never had a bean—and SHE could be a 'arpy when she pleased. Well, she found out one night where Lord X was making for, so what does she do but disguise herself as one of Prince Felipoff's coachmen—all dressed up with padded coats and things—and she drives a smart trap along to the Hotel des Vignes and when she gets there ... '

John listened to all Ralph's confidences with absorbed attention, for he felt that here was grist indeed for his all-devouring mill. Some of the romantic and (as the more realistic critics assert) tinsel glitter of his more elaborate novels may have had its origin in these Ralph stories.

According to Ralph's experience the one and only aim of any member of the upper classes was to be 'bedded' as soon as possible with some other member of the upper classes.

'Why?' asked John.

'I suppose it's because they haven't enough to do,' Ralph would answer. 'Not

enough to occupy their minds.'

This 'bedding' business had very little to do, in John's mind, with love. He had long ago learnt, of course, at the Merlin school all there was to learn about the physical facts of sex, but these were completely dissociated in his mind from love. He had always in his nature a purity that was neither censorious nor inquisitive. He was always to regard sexual offences as minor as compared with cruelty or spiritual meannesses. He loved his mother and Charlie and Anne and now Ralph, and he loved them with a warmth of heart and fidelity of spirit that could be called passionate. He did not conceive of these feelings as being in the same world of nature as the intrigues of Lord X

and Lady B.

Ralph's friendship could not prevent him now from feeling miserable and lonely. Lady Max no longer wished him to pay her early-morning visits. She very soon did not see him from the beginning of the day to the end. He spent hours in his bedroom writing The Doom of Carne. (His facility even then was as miraculous as it was dangerous).

Ralph was busy about his own affairs and, I fancy, found it no easy matter to turn that 'old woman's pig-sty,' as he used to call it, into something respectable.

So John was quite desperately alone.

'It was as though,' he told me, 'I had fallen quite suddenly, most unexpectedly into a well, a well that, from where I was at its very bottom, seemed full of green shifting lights, spiders' webs, beetles on the damp walls. I couldn't think why I was there and I hadn't any plan of escape.

'I would wander about that beastly house all day long. The room that I liked was the one with the Chinese jade and amethyst. They were in four large cabinets against the wall, such wonderful colours! I will never, all my life long, forget a carved-amethyst figure. When the light fell on it, it was like crushed blackberries seen through a cloud of silver—and an amber tear-

bottle, the stain of blood upon a gold as rich as a sunset—and two Tang horses, I remember, their riders sitting up as though they did indeed rule the world, and thought nothing of it. Their fine beards swung sideways on their

chests and the faint pinks, blues, greens were exquisitely shaded and softened by time—and a figure in white and green jade, a sort of "Una and the Lion," a most delicate Chinese lady standing with her hand on a lion with a noble green mane. These, and dozens more, all neglected there in that dusty room with a hideous Victorian wallpaper and a roll-top desk.... No one ever came there but myself.

'She didn't want to show the things to people once she had collected them.

Poor things! Forgotten! Clouded with dust! And Ralph used to say he never knew a house for dust like that house. Do what you would the dust was everywhere!'

The time came, of course, when the old woman had to do something about him. She had lost all interest, all belief in him. He was just a bore and a nuisance. The climax came when he broke a small rose quartz bowl right at her feet. It was a late afternoon and he was going through one of the rooms on the way up to his own place. He suddenly came upon her just in from her drive and wearing her most absurd hat bordered with roses and her heavy black velvet cape. He was so greatly startled that he brushed a table with his hand and the small bowl fell to the ground. She raised her gloved hand and slapped his cheek.

He said no word but stood there with his hands clasped together. She was repentant of her temper, perhaps, or was struck suddenly by his pallor or his shabby clothes or by his sharp burning eyes or his awkward look of helplessness or by all these things together.

She said abruptly: 'I'm sorry.'

He had picked up the fragments of the bowl and said huskily:

'This can be mended so that you won't see it.'

Then they stood looking at one another in that dim room with two large Chinese figures menacing them with their uplifted tapering fingers.

She tore her big hat off her head and said:

'The truth is I should never have brought you here. Another of my damned impulses.'

He didn't say a word but fancied that before his very eyes she was turning into Mrs. Hoskin.

'I have a responsibility,' she said. 'And I must fulfil it. You must go to school.'

Then she just said 'Damn! Damn! Damn!' and went stumping off up the staircase, her large rose–covered hat swinging in her hand.

He stood there looking at the broken pieces of rose quartz.

CHAPTER VIII

How John Got His First Sight of Salisbury Downs and the True

Nature of the Contemporary World Both at the Same Time

How little John realized at that moment when the old woman uttered the word 'School' that his fate was well and truly settled!

He did not, in fact, believe it credible that anyone at this time of day should think of sending him to school again. He did not look upon himself as a boy at all but rather as a mature man who had already been actor, writer, supporter of his mother and social entertainer. No, he could not contemplate such a catastrophe. What he was doing was waiting to secure a job in a London theatre!

It was Ralph who broke the news to him. Ralph sitting in shirt and trousers in the pantry reading the evening paper. John, who had been frightened of the dusk in the Chinese room, sought the pantry for safety.

'You know, Johnny,' Ralph said, looking over the top of his paper, 'you seem to have no gift for keeping yourself tidy. Look at the mess you're in. Come here!'

So John went over and stood between Ralph's broad knees and received the odour of shaving–soap and tobacco from Ralph's smooth and rubicund cheeks.

'For your age you're remarkable tall—AND skinny.' Ralph put his arm round him.

'You know, I've developed a kind of liking for you, so to speak.' John would imitate Ralph, who, he said, dealt out his words as though they were cards in an important card-game.

'I love YOU,' John said.

'Do you? That's most gratifying, but all the same I'd be careful of those words

—love and such words.'

'Why?' John asked.

'They're apt to lose their colour if they're used too often. As well as I remember, I've loved only three people in my life and I've known plenty—

my mother, my brother Bob, and a woman kept a lodging-house in Brighton.

But that was years ago ... years ago. I've noticed if you go around saying you love people they're apt to take advantage of you. There was that poor Mr.

Betterton I was valet to once, he was always telling people he loved them and DIDN'T they take advantage?

'Believe me, Johnny, there's only two sorts of love—one's sex, one's not. You can go bad in the head like poor Lady Lucy Beaminster did for that young Ricketts. And what good did it do her? Laughing-stock of London she was, poor young thing. All that madness for two minutes' excitement. When it's over they wonder why they were so crazy.

'Then there's the other sort of love, that's so quiet that you don't know it's there unless you look close.'

'That's the way I love you,' said John.

'Not you, Johnny. You can't. That's the sort only time can prove. It takes years, and then it may not be right after all.'

He gave John a push. 'There. You look a bit straighter now.'

He coughed, John said, and looked uncomfortable.

'You're going to school,' he said.

John had then a very important decision to make. He could go back to Aunt Hunnable and start all over again. But he hadn't now a penny in the world and to go back would seem like defeat. To return to Merlin was altogether impossible. Ralph told him that this was a fine school Lady Max was sending him to, that she wanted him to be educated so that he could take his place in

the world, and that it was a chance any boy would jump at. Ralph didn't know the Reverend Thomas Reiner, of course, but he DID know Lady Max. He knew that she was sick to death of the boy and must be rid of him. He thought, I am sure, that this was a fine chance for John.

This was a school near Salisbury, it seemed, for Gentlemen's Sons. John stared at Ralph bewildered. He didn't see what he could gain by going to school. The theatre, yes. There he had everything to learn. But school!

'I wish I'D been sent to a proper school and kept there,' Ralph said. 'There I was, all done up in livery, perched up at the back of Lord Pontacute's carriage and pair when I was eight year old AND sleeping in a cupboard under the staircase where the beetles was horrible. I never learnt a thing. LIFE taught me.' He pointed out to John that it was kind of Lady Max and he ought to be grateful.

Johnny was. He still didn't realize in the very least that what she wanted was to see the last of him and be rid for ever of the consequences of a silly impulse. He thought that he would return to her every holidays and he would thus be able to find his theatre job. His schooldays, he assured himself, would be brief.

She acted quite nobly at the last, fitting him out with clothes, giving him ten pounds for pocket-money. When he came to her bedroom to say good-bye she called him to her and kissed him. She found perhaps something touching in his implicit unstained faith in her, his belief that she was simply the kindest, most unselfish person in the world.

'Now you'll work hard and be a good boy and do all you're told,' she said, longing no doubt for the interview to be over.

'Indeed I will,' said John, 'and when I come back in the holidays I'll tell you everything. Perhaps I'll have finished my book then.'

She must have eyed him with many mixed emotions. If only he were not so ugly! If only he were more presentable! Already his black tie was up above his stiff white collar. Suppose, though, that he WERE a genius! He was absurdly old for his age and remarkable when you remembered that he was

the son of a washerwoman! On the other hand, there was something strangely irritating about him. He was always doing or saying something that made you feel awkward. She dismissed him and when he was gone sighed with relief.

She intended never to set eyes on him again.

And here John shall once again speak for himself. The first twenty- four hours at Reiner's, it is no exaggeration to say, were present with him to the day of his death.

So actual to him were they that in the worst hours, for him, of the War he thought: 'This isn't so bad as Reiner's.'

When, later, he knew Westcott they found curious parallels in their histories and nothing more startling in resemblance than Reiner's and Westcott's own horrible 'home from home.'

All the same Reiner's had some interesting features of its own....

'As usual I started off in the gayest fashion and filled with the brightest hopes.

Lady Max had given me two suits of clothes and ten pounds pocket-money and I'd stolen the small Chinese clay figure that you see on my table there now.'

Myself: 'You stole it? That's why you had the bad time at Reiner's.'

John: 'You think the punishment always fits the crime? I can assure you it doesn't. Besides it wasn't a crime. Yin (that's the State of Rest in Chinese philosophy) has been nothing but grateful to me ever since I rescued him.

That's what it was—a rescue, not a robbing. There he was, in his green jacket and round red scallop hat, riding his elephant in a dusty deserted corner of the Chinese room. No one had given him a glance for years. I restored him to usefulness. I love him and he loves me. But what I really marvel at is that he survived Reiner's. He did by some especial magic of his own. There he stood on the shelf above my bed and no one even touched him. And in some strange way I knew that he wouldn't be touched. I never had the slightest fear for him.

'Oh yes, and I had a light grey overcoat and a new brown bag and a new

playbox. Ralph had bought these things for me and left Lady Max to pay the bill. I don't suppose she ever noticed the items. And what do you think I did?

I gave Ralph, on parting, a Bible. Of all the things! Ralph, the repository of all the sins and vices of Society! It wasn't priggishness on my part and Lord knows it wasn't any desire to improve Ralph's morals. But he seemed to have everything in the world—only not a Bible. There was no sign of one in his bedroom—and myself I liked the Bible. I thought it exciting, moving, and full of beautiful words. And so it is—all those things. Ralph was greatly moved. He kissed me. He was one of the best and truest friends I've ever had.

'I went in the train to Salisbury and slipped through the English country on a lovely golden soft summer afternoon. I would be arriving at Reiner's in the middle of the summer term, although I didn't realize, of course, how that was going to add to my troubles. In the train I read Stevenson's Master of Ballantrae.

'At Salisbury there was an old gnarled man like one of Hoffman's dwarfs waiting for me. I don't know how he recognized me but he did and took me to one of the most ancient cabs in history.

Into it I got and we rattled along through one of the loveliest evenings of any summer anywhere. I am dealing in superlatives, but this, had I known it, was to be my last happy hour for a very long time. This was LAND to me as Merlin had been SEA. The two of them, with London in the middle, completed England for me—a completed, rounded, lovely, faithful England that I was never going to lose. I had seen the waves break over the small rocks into swirls of creaming spray. Now I saw the sun lie like the palest

Chinese amber over fields as ancient as time, and I heard a voice say: "You be faithful to me. I'll be faithful to you."

'I was bumped about on the old worn seat that was hard on my posterior as iron, and as I bumped England bumped with me. There came then that most wonderful moment of an English summer afternoon when the colours drain from sky and soil, everything is hushed to an expectant silence. I had never been INSIDE England before, RIGHT inside as Wonderland Alice would say. The small clusters of buildings, cream, grey, hawthorn-berry red, sleepily passive but wakefully watching too, the oaks so solid, dark, and this translucent whitening sky.

'There I was with my nose jumping up and down out of the window and, in a kind of curtain-raising–now-the-performance-is-beginning moment the Downs appeared.

'It was the right moment for them. They belong to quiet stillness, their repose is immortal, and I remember Simeon Rose telling me how once when he was walking on that cool springing turf a flight of aeroplanes—some dozen or more—came manoeuvring from a skyey distance. They roared as they approached, but as the Downs lay under their wings their engines seemed hushed, they were muffled and dim and their shadows swung through the sky.

'The Downs were very silent now, coloured shell-green, softly rounded against that white-green sky. I gazed and gazed. My heart beat triumphantly.

Nothing evil could happen to me when such beauty and such strength were so near!'

Myself: 'And you bounced into Reiner's expecting that world to share with you your enchantment.'

John: 'Did I not? I was almost bewildered, I suppose, by the beauty I had seen, and I had my bag, my playbox, my two suits, my ten pounds and Yin.

Yes, I walked into Reiner's a boy blinded by light. And this is what I saw.

The cab had driven up through a dark laurelled drive. I can smell the laurels in my nostrils now. And, simultaneously with the drawing up of the cab in front of the long window-lit gabled building, came a sound that I had never heard before—from inside the closed house a hundred boys shouting, laughing, screaming at the same moment. I drew back into the shelter of the musty cab. I was suddenly frightened. This was a boarding-school. I had some mysterious foreboding perhaps of what that building would do to me and how impossible it would be to escape from it.

'And so I came through the stone passage, hearing, as you do at once in every boarding-school, the rattle of crockery, the high- pitched servants' voices, and smelling the boarding-school aroma of damp towels, steam-pipes and mouse-trap. Then through a swinging green-baize door and so into the presence of Reiner. Mrs. Reiner was there too.

'Reiner ought to have a book all to himself. In these grimly realistic days he would make an admirable subject. In the old novels the characters were always divided into the sheep and the goats. You had only to look at the illustrations to see to which class a character belonged. Well, we laugh at it now, but the system had its advantages. Can't you see the soiled cuffs of Quilp's shirt, the long bending neck of Jonas Chuzzlewit? Aren't all the characters in clever novels to-day seen through an intellectual glass darkly?

'Reiner in the old novels would have been undoubtedly a Goat. I can just imagine how Phiz or Cruikshank would have caricatured him. In a novel to-

day he would be, I suppose, a kind of hero. There was something really strong, courageous about him. He was interesting in his Freudian complexes.

He was what H. B. Terence would have called "a dark antagonist." For me he was quite simply the Ogre of all my fairy-stories.

'He was standing in his hot, desperately-crowded drawing-room, and Mrs.

Reiner was sitting knitting. Every tiniest detail of my first twenty-four hours at that place do I remember! Even the dreams that I had that first night, the black coach trundling down the moonlit road and plunging over the cliff into the sea, the serpent uncoiling from my playbox, its scales shining like greased silk under the blaze of Lady Max's candelabra—but especially do I remember that drawing-room. The beastly red-plush curtains, the little tables laden with albums, that had covers like tombstones, photograph-frames on whose surfaces flowers and vines were painted, the heavy rug with the tiger-head in front of the fireplace. How often, how sadly often I was to visit that hot confusing room!

'Reiner stood there, his legs spread, his hands behind his back.

'He was a man of about forty, short of stature, bull-necked, thick- set, untidily dressed in clergyman's garments, wearing heavy black- rimmed spectacles, dusty-red hair going thin on the top. I am myself untidy as you know well, but have had always a passion for personal cleanliness. I noticed that the cuffs of his shirt were soiled, that there were spots of food on his waistcoat, and that his finger-nails were black. His cheeks had the stubbly hot appearance of one who was but half shaved. His body was sturdy and strong and his eyes, behind the glasses, fine, penetrating and intelligent.

'Mrs. Reiner was also a little dingy in a rather faded pink tea- gown, with a lot of lace and some strings unfastened. She was a plump rather affected-

looking little lady with what the Victorians used to call "languishing eyes."

'I suppose that, at the beginning at any rate, they intended to be impressed by me because I had been sent to them by Lady Max. Lady Mary Madox, niece of the Earl of Hardacre, cousin of the Duchess of Wrexe, that meant a good deal to the Reiners. But the very last thing that they can have expected to see was the lanky, uncouth boy who stood now grinning on their drawing-room carpet. I, of course, was determined to make them like me at once, and so as usual went all the wrong way about it, talking and laughing and holding the floor, telling them all about myself as Mrs. Reiner gave me some tea and a damp cold scone.

'"HOW old are you?" I remember Reiner asking me in a puzzled tone.

'I told him.

'"You're very tall for your years." There was something in the way he said that that frightened me. I suddenly longed for Ralph. I was near tears again, always my cursed disability when I was lonely or filled with self-pity. I stopped abruptly in the middle of my exuberant confession. I looked at them and they looked at me.

'Reiner asked me what sort of education I had had and I began to talk about Moby Dick.

'"Moby Dick? What's that?"

'I went on, but now confusedly, uncertain of my position, of my safety. I told them that I had written a book. They both stared at me in an ominous silence.

'I was like the starling—I wanted to get out.

'Reiner said in his rather rich plummy voice, the voice of a man who is accustomed to reading prayers in church, "Now you shall come and see your companions." I followed him.

'I doubt if there is any school like Reiner's nowadays. Westcott, you know, says the same of his place. They were alike, his and mine, in this, that although they were ostensibly Private Schools— that is, Reiner prepared his boys for Rugby, Winchester, Clifton and so on—yet there were some quite old boys there, boys of seventeen and eighteen, sons, I suppose, of parents who didn't want to be bothered with them. Fat loutish boys for the most part.

I remember the names of some of them—Paulton, Rowe, Clinton....

'English schools are supposedly immoral and I'll not say another word about that except that cruelty and meanness of spirit have always seemed to me so much worse than any kind of immorality anywhere. Reiner's had its immoral moments. They never touched myself and, looking back, it was Charlie Christian who helped me there, I fancy. All through my life Charlie and I have been together. But the cruelty and meanness touched me all right, touched me, stained me so that I was a maimed man, if you like, ever after.'

I remember that on the first occasion when John really told me about Reiner's I had not known him very long and he stopped there. He wouldn't tell me another word. His whole body was shivering, as he sat, his long legs stretched out in front of the fire.

'Dickens, Melville,' I remember his ending, 'were scorned in their time as romantic writers. Well, by God, that's the way romantic writers are made, by having your nose rubbed in the mud, by knowing what fear is, by loneliness, a small boy crying in his bed at night. If you don't see the glory of God after that you can't endure it—you cut your throat.'

One afternoon sitting on the sea-wall at Whitby watching the holiday-

makers driven off the sands by the encroaching tide, he told me the rest of it.

'A boy has a bad introduction if he goes to school for the first time in the middle of a term. He is the only novelty, the natural object for everyone's fun and amusement. I said nothing about my home, my achievements. I watched them, warily, as my enemies. I was uncouth in appearance and therefore a comic for them. I think too that I had annoyed Reiner in my first interview with him—by my innocent remark about Moby Dick perhaps—and he had given them to understand—boys are miserable little sycophants—that he would not interfere with anything that they chose to do.

'They did not, in fact, do anything very much on that first evening, but at once I encountered my torturer in chief. This was a boy called Stubbs. He must have been seventeen or eighteen years of age, was tall and stout, with thick heavy thighs and legs like young trees. I can still on occasion see him in my dreams. He developed, I don't doubt, into a worthy if heavy-minded citizen in later years. His crimes were stupidity and an inhibited sexual freedom. My thin legs and arms, ugly face, shambling gait, above all my ridiculous propensity to tears, these must have been very tempting to him. He yielded, I should imagine, to any temptation that came along.

'No, they didn't do very much to me on that first evening, but I realized at once that I was in the hands of my enemies as I had never yet in my life been, as I was never perhaps in my life to be again.

'Worst of all, the private integrity of my body was violated. I had been mocked by the boys in Merlin, even chased down the street, I had fought and bit the dust, but nearly always I, John Cornelius, had been myself, inviolate, myself by myself.

'Demonstrative to those I love, I have always hated to be touched by men in general. I loathe it in a crowd when I am pressed upon. Now I was at once handled as though I did not exist—pinched, kicked a little, my long nose pulled—not very much that first night, you understand, but enough....

'They crowded round me and asked every sort of insulting question. How it was I don't know, but I had the sense to keep my mother's occupation to myself, but, poor little defenceless idiot, I boasted, I think, about Lady Max and her grand house and Ralph—all with some dim hope of protecting myself. There were indecencies, too, but they meant nothing at all to me. I was, in some ways, already so much older than any of these children, had seen so much more of life as it really is. That old assault on me of the Merlin workmen was very much more than anything these boys could do now.

'No, what I dreadfully minded was their unkindness, their apparent loathing of me. They DIDN'T loathe me of course. Boys are cruel to those weaker than themselves as animals are cruel—Nature working as it used to work among grown men even a hundred years ago when lunatics were tied to the stake, crawling in their own filth, for the public to gaze on. Humanity not

improved? Read the old English law records and see.

'But I THOUGHT that they hated me and I'd never been hated like this before. There was no possibility of escape and I was terrified when I looked into face after face and saw only the hard, speculative gaze, the ironical lips.

No kindness anywhere and the walls closing me in.

'They let me go after all and I went and sat, I remember, on the seat of the water–closet with the door locked, refuge of many another terrified small boy although I did not know it.

'That night when we went to bed the old familiar public–school– story act was performed. I knelt down by my bed and said my prayers. I had always said my prayers morning and evening. I had not read Tom Brown or Eric or any of the Baines Reed masterpieces. I saw no reason whatever why I should not say my prayers. In my dormitory there were some twelve boys. Stubbs was captain of the dormitory.

'I knelt down. I prayed confusedly over and over again to be helped to escape from this horrible place. There was a deep silence while I was on my knees, I remember, and when I got on my feet again no one said a word. I was allowed to sleep undisturbed. In the morning at the clang of a foul bell we jumped up, washed in icily–cold water and hurried down, still, in spite of the water, half asleep, to a classroom. Here for an hour I stared at a book without consciousness. Followed a breakfast of bread and dripping and tea. Through all this not one word was spoken to me by a living soul. I moved in a world of ghostly bodies and screaming voices. But it was as though I had no existence. I spoke to no one. No one spoke to me.

'After breakfast I wandered where other boys were wandering into a stone courtyard, built in on three sides with plastered wall, open on the fourth side to the country. I turned and stared, for there, facing me as though they had a personal message for me, were the Downs washed with the morning sun, radiating light. I stared, my mouth open. I think I half expected to hear them say good–morning.

'But instead of THEIR voices there were others. I found I was surrounded. I heard, as though from a long way off, Stubbs' voice.

'"Go on. Kneel down and say your prayers as you did last night." And everyone shouted: "Say your prayers! Say your prayers! Say your prayers!"

'I was bewildered. I had no idea what they wanted. Stubbs showed me. He took my arms, twisted them, forced me to my knees. He rubbed my eyes with his knuckles, he twisted my ear, he kicked me, he hit me in the mouth so that I felt the warm trickle of blood on my chin.

'"Now pray!"

'"Say your prayers! Say your prayers!" The world danced with delight.

'They made me hold up my arms and fold my hands as though I were praying. Stubbs held my neck back.

'"Say 'Our Father.'"

'"Our Father."

'"Which art in Heaven."

'"Which art in Heaven."

'"Hallowed be Thy Name."

'"Hallowed be Thy Name."

'I went through the whole prayer and after every sentence I received a kick in the back.

'I knelt, my hands raised, staring at the Downs. I stared at them and they enfolded me. I did not cry, I scarcely breathed, I said the Lord's Prayer into the very heart of that green light.

'Something else happened to me, perhaps the most important thing in all my life until then. I was aware for the first time of my other personality, the other personality of all creative artists, bad and good. I was standing beside my kneeling self. I looked at the boys, the stone walls, the Downs. I felt the pain of my eyes, my cut lip, my arm, my wrists, my back, my knees. I felt it

atrociously. I felt the taunting, the cruelty, the savagery. I felt the loneliness, the imprisonment.... I felt my own wild helpless rage.

'But I was standing there beside my kneeling self, as completely, coldly detached as though I were my own enemy. I was the creative artist watching the suffering actor and wondering what he could make of it. "Here's a pretty incident, a dramatic scene, something to use, some experience here that will surely prove useful."

'I was the conscious artist for the first time. Also I fainted. I fell forward on the last words of the Lord's Prayer, sinking into the warm embrace of the shelving sunlit hill....

'"The Power and the Glory for ever and ever ... "

'I floated down, meeting the soil, kissing the short springing turf, finding it warm, sun-drenched....

PART II: THE BRIGHT-GREEN SHOES

CHAPTER I

Mr. Reiner's Shadow

How fortunate it was that John so little realized the captive that he was now to be, a captive of three years and a little bit!

He WAS a captive in all solemn fact, as he learned with a sort of sick dismay in the last week of that first summer term. He was NOT to return to London; he was to remain through the holidays as boarder with the Reiners. And after that? No one knew about after that.

His first thought was of flight and he might, I fancy, have attempted it (and very possibly have succeeded in it—he was good at escape) had it not been for the curious power that Reiner exercised over him from the first: the one thing in the world that he wanted now was Reiner's good opinion of him!

Three years he wanted that, three years he strove for it! Nothing is stranger, perhaps, in all John Cornelius' story than his striving to win the affection and admiration of Reiner. What was the fascination that Reiner had for him?

In the first place, perhaps, Reiner represented brute strength and egotistic will, two things that Cornelius always ardently admired.

Reiner was dirty in his person and, when angry, filthy in his language. On the other hand he had courage, believed himself a good clergyman and an upright man. He was not, like many bullies, weak of will and sycophantic. He bowed to no one and thought himself the finest schoolmaster in all England. He had his own troubles too, poor man, as a few words later about Mrs. Reiner will show. John says that he hated and feared him, but a kind word from him or any sort of praise brought an ecstasy of gratitude to his heart. In retrospect indeed he was not sure that he had not, in a kind of way, loved him. There was nothing in the world he would not have done for him. Reiner had his unbending moments. There were times when he relished a sort of horseplay,

and boys, invited to tea, would see him on all-fours, his broad back stretched, and he would enjoy a sort of tournament, carrying a boy on his back and charging two other boys. In these moods he would roar with laughter and play practical jokes, tweak boys' ears, pinch their legs. The boys, too, accepted these physical gestures with pride and pleasure.

But for the better part of the time he was morose and cantankerous.

John told me that never in after life did he experience so silent and awful an atmosphere of terror as that of the waiting class before Reiner made his entrance. There the class would sit, frozen into immobility, the tramp of the heavy feet would be heard down the passage, the thick brow-bending figure would enter, sit down behind the desk, survey them....

He did not in actual fact offer much physical violence in class; he would rap a boy's head with a ruler, throw a book, twist an ear. One odd fact about him was that he never beat a boy. The terror that he conveyed was all spiritual and mental. John said that there was nothing in the world more horrible than his close approach when he was angry.

His dirty nails seemed to grow, his tobacco-tainted breath to enclose you in a kind of miasmic fog, his sturdy legs would be planted square, and his thick neck would jerk forward, his round eyes protruding. Then he would touch you and your body would tremble, your heart quake, your knees quiver. His scrubby hair seemed to have some animal life of its own.

Johnny was, of course, the ideal boy for the satisfaction of his egotism.

Reiner must have had in him a great deal of the play-actor and here was a child who reacted instantly to any part that he chose to play.

Later he claimed that he had recognized at once how unusual a child John was, and John believed that that was so. Reiner had all the vanity that goes with strong physical egotism, and John on his side had the vanity that belongs to certain consciousness of exceptional power. Nothing that Reiner did in all these years to John ever shook John's belief in himself fundamentally. After Reiner had made some especial public fool of him he would suffer agonies of self-doubt and mistrust, as he always did when someone disliked or disapproved of him.

But back his deeper self-confidence would come. Cornelius was, I suppose, as little CONCEITED as any human being ever was; he never, his life long, thought himself fine or grand because of his gifts. They had been given to him and there they were. He felt that had he been himself nobler, finer, the gifts would have been expressed more nobly. That was perhaps why he wanted the love of his fellow-beings so desperately, because, when someone loved him, his gifts shone the more brightly.

But you must not long to be loved. Love is given to those who are aware, through unselfishness of spirit, of others more than of themselves. That is why genius is loved so rarely until the possessor of it is dead. John was unselfish in very truth but he could never forget himself.

The element of coarseness and good earthy vulgarity in Reiner made John's fastidious delicacy especially irritating to him. Reiner liked to make vulgar noises, while he was eating, in class, anywhere he pleased. By these he asserted his honest don't-give-a-damn personality. For the majority of the boys Reiner's habits had no significance whatever, but he knew on that first afternoon that John would be sensitive and alive to every sound and movement. He would probably be antagonized by John's unusualness. He looked on himself doubtless as unusual, secretly distinguished, exceptional.

That is perhaps true of all of us. Here was a boy who WAS unusual, in his thoughts, in the history that was being made in his subconscious, undefined darkness.

When John on his first day said of the sloping, fading Downs, seen from that overcrowded stuffy Reiner room: "They have thrown the sun away and are slipping under cover"—said it quite unselfconsciously and to himself—

Reiner knew that he had never had a boy in his school before who had seen them like that. In later years he would quote it, describe the lanky awkward boy standing in the middle of the room, the cup of tea in his hand threatening to pitch over at any moment, staring through the window, oblivious of everything, himself included. 'Catching up with the Downs,' he wrote to his mother, 'before they were gone.' He smiled with them perhaps all that night in that cold, snoring, desolate dormitory....

And then when John in his innocence said that he had written a book and quoted Moby Dick, Reiner's conceit was hurt. It would never do to have this boy in HIS school, showing off, talking to him like an equal. No, no, it would never do! So he started off from the very beginning to torment and torture and finally to subdue and capture the boy.

It was a kind of battle between them all the three years, Reiner pursuing like some clumsy satyr through the forest that hid them both, the forest that they both alone inhabited. John fled for his life—and escaped.

John was always able to make terms with his conditions rather as a prisoner in his cell makes a pet of mouse or spider. Externally he became, I imagine, very quickly the untidy, hurrying, half- frightened, half-bewildered schoolboy that so many schools breed. There is a kind of boy—sensitive, shy, apprehensive—who goes through the whole school world like an incompetent slave in some harsh master's service.

He gazes bewildered about him, he hurries because he is always late, he loses his property, his back is slightly bent because he is for ever expecting a blow, his sleep is broken and disturbed because of evil dreams, he catches every complaint and disease there is, he is nervously damaged for life. The boy of this sort is the marked victim of all the bright, healthy, normal boys who eat like fighting–cocks, whose bowels function perfectly, who have no imagination and therefore no apprehension, who are heartlessly, heedlessly cruel in a jolly, joyous, Britons–never–shall–be–slaves fashion. The masters are irritated, and rightly so, by the shambling, dirty, nervous children who invite sternness by their trembling fear, who never know their lessons, who gaze vacantly like little lunatics, who are sycophantic when they should be independent, who lie because they dread a beating. Together in their Common–Room the masters dismiss these dirty trembling creatures with gestures of contempt. If they ARE kicked and beaten by their contemporaries, do they not deserve a little roughness? Surely it will, with luck, make men of them, turn them into the Englishmen we wish them to be! These trembling children have at least this consolation—that never, in their after lives, no, not when poison–gas blinds and chokes them, not when their wives betray them, not when men scorn them and spit upon them, will they know again such terror, despair and loneliness as in the happy carefree schooldays of their youth.

John went half–way with all this. He became outwardly the untidy, harassed,

nervous outcast of that little society. Physically unclean he never was; he managed somehow to wash in that icy water and his once–a–week hot bath was the Paradise moment of the seven days. He did not have enough to eat, but that, except for the London days, he had never had. He was unfortunate in his height. He rose like a church–tower among his classmates.

He was, I imagine, neither popular nor unpopular. The boys realized his difference from themselves. They leapt avidly upon his story–telling gifts: THAT was his one great merit in their eyes. After a while they left him very much alone. It was as though they recognized that his true battle was with Reiner.

For himself after a while what he hated most was his sense of imprisonment.

He had always been able to go where he would; even in Lady Max's house he had been free. Now from seven-thirty until midday, with a brief interval for breakfast, from two-thirty until six except on half-holidays, from seven-

thirty until nine, he sat for the most part motionless on his wooden bench puzzling to attach to himself fragments of knowledge that seemed to have nothing to do with himself at all. There, too, he had formerly been free, learning with amazing speed and accuracy when his imagination was alive.

Of the mathematical world he never had the slightest conception. From the beginning to the end he could neither divide nor subtract. Greek and Latin he could grasp only when poetry was stirring behind the words. Greek accents, Latin verbs, were as dead for him as slain flies on the window-pane.

No one ever tried more desperately to do what was expected of him, but, even had the ability been there, one glance from Reiner's bulging eyes sent every thought flying.

During all these three years he never made a friend—the only period barren in THAT way. He depended desperately on Charlie Christian and Anne. He wrote to these two and his mother every week of the three years, something of a feat when one considers how small boys hate to write letters. John was the exception there, for he adored to write letters just as he adored to talk. Not that he talked a great deal at this place.

He talked to Yin when there was no one in the dormitory to overhear him. He says that life became so queer that it seemed to him certain that Yin answered

him back—a high-pitched rather shrill voice imparting fragments of Chinese philosophy.

The boys noticed that he talked to himself and that he was always lying. They decided that he was as mad as a hatter and they called him 'Looney.' A gentleman who would wish, I think, that his name should not be mentioned here was at school with him during his third year and remembers a few things.

'I recall Cornelius very well physically. He was very like then to the later well-known portraits. There's the one that everyone knows, painted by Stirling—the one where he's walking across the room, his long thin head with the lock of hair over his forehead, the long thin hands, the shambling half-

jointed legs. He is looking in Stirling's picture as though someone had just said something that MIGHT be the answer to the question he's always asking.

Well, he was just like that at Reiner's. He would stop, throw up his head, jerk out "What's that?" But he never got his answer, of course. I was a lot junior—

two years means a great deal at school—and, by the time I arrived, he was well up in the school. A big fat white-faced brute, who must have been nearly twenty by that time, bullied him—Stubbs, do you say his name was?

Yes, that's right. This fellow hated Cornelius and spent hours in thinking out ways to torment him. I don't think he DID torment him much, though. Two things I remember the boys liked Cornelius for: one was his capacity for telling stories. I never knew anyone like him for that. He could go on and on and make you see everything he was describing; in fact, after a while HIS

world became more real than your own. That is where his lies came in, because when he wasn't telling us stories that were confessedly made up, he was asserting as gospel truth things that couldn't be true.

'I recollect that he used to talk about a Bird–Man who was to be found, he said, in the lanes and on the Downs. He described him minutely and I remember the description still, a thin ragged man with birds perching on his hat, his shoulders, his hands. And he would scatter bird–seed out of the bag on the ground. Quite a lot of boys went out to look for him, but of course nobody ever saw him. There was a matter–of–fact small boy, I remember, who tried to tie Cornelius down. Was he really there, this man with the birds?

"Yes," said Cornelius. "Well, if he's there, why can't anyone else see him?" "I

don't care whether anyone else sees him or not," Cornelius said, "if *I* see him.

That's all I'VE got to bother about." It was natural enough that the boys should call him "Looney." The other thing that they liked about him besides his story–telling was his kindly nature. He would always be ready to do anything for anybody and he would give everything he had away. Everything except a Chinese clay figure on an elephant which he kept above his bed in the dormitory. The boys had a funny superstitious feeling about that figure.

None of them would touch it for anything. He got a little money sent him sometimes and he would spend it at once in the tuck–shop and all on other boys. There was no sense that he was kind and generous in order to win good opinions. He did it as naturally as he breathed.

'The other thing that I remember was that he was very touchy, very sensitive.

He could fly into the most fearful tempers and, when he did, all his body seemed to jump about as though it moved on wires. It used to be one of the favourite games—"Let's make Looney lose his hair." He was often terribly unhappy, I think. I remember that he was one of the boys who didn't go home in the holidays. His parents were very poor, I believe, somewhere in the South of England, and some woman in London paid for his keep. But it must have been hateful for him in the holidays, because Reiner was always shouting at him, nagging him. I remember that I asked him once why he didn't go home for the holidays, and he told me he wasn't going home until he was famous. That seemed to me very comic. How could a schoolboy be famous? He should have been good at games because he could run like the wind, but he was too clumsy. He seemed to be quite unable to control his body. In the rugby football games boys would get him in the scrum and pull his ears and do other things to him. I've seen him with the tears pouring down his face but never uttering a sound. Boys are brutal, aren't they? And yet, although he was often miserable, I wouldn't say that my memory of him is really of an unhappy boy. He was too active in mind and body and when he did enjoy things he enjoyed them so tremendously.'

There are a number of thick exercise-books in black covers. These books are half-empty, but scattered about them are ideas for stories, fragments of poetry, and, more than anything else, personal appeals to God.

'God, don't make me distrust You. I trust You always. You are my Father, the

only one I have. Please when I move into the Upper Fourth next term help me with my Latin grammar because it was You helped me to make my move and now I'm frightened because Reiner teaches Latin and You know I can never remember anything when he asks me questions.'

And again: 'God, when Stubbs twists my arms next time help me to go away in my mind even more than last time because if I go far enough I don't feel what he is doing and, please, God, show me how to make Reiner like me a little. He almost does sometimes. He waits and I think he's going to but I annoy him.'

And here is an idea for a story. 'It will be called Clara Hopkins and will be a long story with lots of people in it, but Clara Hopkins isn't there at all. People hear of her everywhere and are always just going to meet her but they never do. Everyone thinks when they do meet her they will be perfectly happy.'

And here is part of a letter to Charlie:

'...It is a shame to ask you, Charlie, but I can't ask my mother nor Aunt Hunnable and I don't know where Ralph is now. He has left Lady Max. You see, Lady Max only sends Reiner enough for my keep and she won't answer my letters. I have no money except Anne sends me some sometimes. I know I ought to run away from here and earn my own living, but I think if I can be DISTINGUISHED here I can start better after. I feel older than anyone in the school.' (He was fourteen and a half when he wrote this.) 'So if you could manage it, send me a pair of boots. The pair I have is all in pieces. They let in water although they have been mended. It's difficult to ask you, Charlie, and I know it's better never to ask anyone for anything, but when I'm rich, as I shall be one day, you shall share everything I have. I'll make you proud of me one day, really I will. I'm in the Upper Fourth now and would do well but Reiner teaches Latin and he frightens me so I forget everything. Also if you have a coat you don't use send it me. Never mind how rough it is. I can wear it out of doors when it's cold and wet.

'Don't be angry and if you can't send me anything I'll understand exactly.

Don't think I'm unhappy here. I AM on the outside and if it were only what one does, like games and lessons and the beastly food and Reiner, I couldn't bear it, Charlie, really I couldn't. But you've only got to think hard and you're

somewhere else. Stubbs is a beast. I think he must be Mrs. Hoskin's son. You will go and see mother, won't you?

'She wrote me a letter last week which said she had been ill. The school beat Longleat at football last week ten points to nothing and we all went to Longleat for the day. It is a wonderful place and belongs to the Marquis of Bath. There is a gallery with pictures and they are all dark with rich colours but the faces are as alive as yours or mine. There are peacocks on the lawn.

Some of the house is so old that the stone is like ivory. Lady Max had a big box the same colour. Reiner took the Upper School into Salisbury one evening to see Charley's Aunt. We drove in waggonettes and coming back the moon was quite red. I told a story all the way back.'

Nevertheless, as I have said, the whole importance of John's life during these three years lay in his relationship with Reiner and Reiner's with him.

They must have been a queer couple, the Reiners. Mrs. Reiner was, as I have described her, a fluffy pink-faced short little woman, overdressed, rather vulgar, but apparently kind-hearted and amiable. It was not until towards the end of his third year there that John discovered her true character. He developed at this time too quickly for his years. Life made him learn some things too soon, while there were other things about which he would be a child always. He learnt about Mrs. Reiner because one day, in the summer holidays, when she was alone in the house with him, she called him a dear little boy and embraced him too warmly for his comfort. She longed, in fact, poor Mrs. Reiner, to be loved, and many people in the neighbourhood knew this to be so. In short, she had been a public scandal for years. The older boys at the school must have known this, of course, and much of Reiner's ill-

temper and malignancy came, I suspect, from this unhappy marital state.

They were, I am sure, a tortured pair. John was the only inhabitant of that house who gave Reiner a sense that he was aware of all that went on. He was aware of nothing until just towards the end, but, child though he was, his alert vitality made everyone conscious of him in any place where he was. He had an affection for Mrs. Reiner because she was kind, and had they been living in a boarding-house in London she might have confided to him all her amorous troubles and he would have tried to help her. But here the dark shadow of Reiner lay over him at every minute of the day. They were

abnormally conscious of one another. Reiner, I fancy, suffered from a torturing loneliness and self-disappointment. It was to be fifteen years later than this that he committed suicide by jumping off a Cornish cliff; behind all his brutality and coarseness this final self-destructive act was lurking.

The account of the climax of the Reiner affair had better, as nearly as possible, be given in John's own words. On this occasion, unlike others, John told me the story in one long sweep, the two of us together in the bedroom of the Scarborough hotel on an afternoon of unceasing rain; we looked down from a height to the long grey stretch of sea and sand, while the lances of rain broke into bubbles, spluttering on the window-pane.

Some woman in the dining-room downstairs had reminded him of Mrs.

Reiner. He stood, looking out, spiritually on one leg like a stork in one of his own fairy-tales. Then he would turn about from wall to wall, his hands behind his back, his head on one side....

I wrote it down that same evening as nearly as possible in his own words.

Later as the sky darkened and the rain came down torrentially we turned on the electric light. Over the bed there was a coloured picture of a little girl riding triumphantly beside Father Christmas on his sleigh. On the bed were John's drab woollen pyjamas. He was famous by that time. While we were there someone telephoned asking whether there might be an interview for the local paper.

'Mr. Cornelius isn't here,' I answered. 'And I don't know where he is.' I DID

know, of course. He was with the Reiners, body and soul. After a little while I was there too.

'It happened at last one fine afternoon early in the summer holidays. You can have no idea how truly beastly that house was in the holidays—beastly and tantalizing. For just beyond it was the loveliest country in the world. But I couldn't get to it because of my consciousness of Reiner. By this time I was physically his slave. I fetched and carried for him like a little dog and what I wanted was for him to approve of me. We were tied up together in the most extraordinary way.

'He hated me, had done from the first, and looking back now I don't blame

him; to have an ugly scraggy untidy boy always there, always staring at you, sycophantic, ready to run messages, do anything, but at the same time a kind of spy on you, knowing more about you than anybody else knows. I think I really did in some extraordinary way. I knew that he was unhappy, disappointed, angry with himself as well as with everyone else.

'He didn't want to lose me, I suppose, because of the money I brought. The school never paid, I fancy, and every penny meant a lot to them. But I think towards the end, just before the row, he would have thanked his stars if I'd just wandered away and been lost.

'Meanwhile he became my entire obsession. There's nothing I wouldn't have done for him. Not because I liked him—who could?— but because I hated to be disliked so much by anybody. It made me wonder for hours at night in bed what there was about me that made me so awful.

'Remember I was quite alone at that school—I hadn't a friend. I used to say to myself over and over: "Charlie loves me. Charlie believes in me. Charlie and Anne believe in me." I wasn't, you see, a fool. I knew that and everyone knew it. I was well up in the school although I was bad at Greek and Latin and hopeless at mathematics. Had I been a little more attractive and a little less obsessed by him, Reiner might have tried to make me his "spot" boy, worked at me for a grand Oxford or Cambridge scholarship or something. As it was, the very sight of me annoyed him.

'There were only two other holiday boarders at that time, twins whose parents were in India. They went about together always. I don't even remember their names.

'After breakfast I was free to do as I liked. I would start off sometimes meaning to be on the Downs all day, but I hadn't got far before I'd feel that Reiner would want me for something. I could see his red hair shining in the sun. And I would hurry back. We'd have conversations something like this:

'"What are you staring at me for?"

'"I didn't know I was."

'"Well, you are. Have you done your Latin exercise?"

'"Yes, sir."

'"All right. Go off and don't let me see your face till supper."

'"Yes, sir."

'"Here, come back!"

'I would come back and then he would catch my arm and hold it as though he would break it. He'd stare me in the face and I'd see the red stubble on his chin, each separate hair alive.

'"What's that old woman going to do for you in London?"

'"I don't know, sir."

'"She never writes to you, does she?"

'"No, sir."

'"Everybody's forgotten you. She just gave orders to her lawyer three years ago to pay me on such-and-such a date and he's gone on doing it. Everyone's forgotten you."

'"Yes, sir."

'"Do you still think you're a genius?"

'"No, sir."

'"You did when you came here. But you're not, you know. You're a lazy, good-for-nothing waster. What do you stare at me like that for?"

'"I don't know, sir."

'"Well, don't do it. It gets on my nerves."

'He'd shake me then as though he'd rattle my teeth out of my head. We achieved at these times a dreadful sort of intimacy, as though, behind all our words, we knew one another better than we knew anyone else in the world.

'He caught me once or twice writing a story or a poem. Then he was really furious. This truly maddened him. He would tear the stuff to shreds and I would look at the torn pieces in a kind of bitter despair.

'The end of it all came in this way.

'As time went on Mrs. Reiner took increasingly to the bottle. Poor lady, she must have been most unhappy. What she wanted, I think, was to be comforted and consoled by some male; after a while, I fear, ANY male. She wasn't sensual so much as sentimental. She wanted someone to kiss her tenderly, to stroke her hair, to tell her that she was the only one in the world.

'Because she was known by this time in the neighbourhood she went further and further afield. She invented friends in Salisbury. They may, for all I know, have been genuine. During the holidays she would be away for a day or two at a time. Awful stories began to go round—that she had been seen in low Salisbury haunts and so on. Through all this Reiner never gave a sign, never spoke a word, and, in public at least, he behaved to her exactly as he had always done.

'I was by this time nearly six-foot in height and she and I were often alone together, so that we formed, almost against our will, a kind of friendship. She was now always nervous, apprehensive, very restless.

'You've no idea how desolate that house could be! One fine summer afternoon I was sitting on my bed in the empty dormitory—often so cheerless and cold, but on this day the summer sun was pouring in— trying to write something or other while Yin stared benevolently at me under his little cockle-shaped hat. There was a step. I looked up and there was Mrs. Reiner.

'She was wearing, I vividly remember, a shabby green dress. She stood staring at me and I stared back at her. I realized at once that something was wrong and, with that realization, all I wanted was to get up and run for my life. I looked through the dusty sunny windows at the blazing triumphant

Downs. I got up and with a nervous smile tried to pass her. I knew as I came close to her that she was a little drunk. She caught my hand, murmured something, then threw her arms around me and began to kiss me. At that same moment I was aware that Reiner was standing in the doorway.

'"Priscilla!" he said. (She was called Priscilla. Priscilla Reiner. Isn't there something incredibly silly and pathetic about that?)

'At the sound of his voice she gave a little cry, stood away from me, then sat down on one of the beds and stared at him with her mouth open.

'He came up to me and we stood staring at one another. It seems to me now, looking back, that we stood there without a word for an eternity of ages. It can't, in actual fact, have been for more than a moment, but I'll swear that the sun left the room, it was suddenly cool and early evening. It may be that, at that exact moment, the sun fell behind the Downs.

'Mrs. Reiner began to cry. She said some absurd things, that I was a poor, homeless boy, so lonely, my mother so far away....

'He looked at me with loathing and with such an intentness of malice that I really thought that he would kill me then and there. I remember thinking

"Perhaps he will strangle me and bury me under the cellar, and I don't want to die." But he never touched me. He told her to get up and go, and she went.

'All he said to me was: "I'll have something to say to you later."

'To which I, trembling all over, answered: "Yes, sir."

'When I was alone I had only one thought, and that was to get away as soon as possible. To get away, to get away!'

Myself: 'You should have done that long before.'

John: 'Yes, but I had always had the thought that to run away meant confessing my failure. Here I was, fifteen years of age, and worse off than when I had come to the place. If only I could hang on long enough to win a scholarship or FORCE Reiner to admire me and help me to some work in

London!

'But now I knew that he would never forgive me, never, never, and that to stay meant, in literal fact, ruin of body and soul. Besides—NOW, after this—

I felt SICK. I couldn't endure that room where I must sleep or the sound of Mrs. Reiner's voice.

'As I stood there, thinking, there was a sound of a tap dripping in the passage and I HATED that tap, almost with a frenzy.

'By good luck Anne had sent me two pounds only a fortnight before. I had enough to get to London with and I decided to walk to Salisbury. My bag was in the lock-up room; my playbox was under my bed, but that was too heavy to take. All I did was to wrap Yin in a piece of paper. Then I opened the window, caught the water-pipe with one arm and shinned down into the garden. You must remember that I had been down that pipe, often enough, on forced night forays.

'Not a soul saw me, and a moment later I was on the road to Salisbury.

Salisbury was ten miles. I had a divine walk. The hour slipped into the summer evening peace when the scents of the hay, the grass, of the hedges seemed to come from the heart of the white luminous summer sky.

'A stream ran singing by the road. A fellow in a cart picked me up and gave me a lift. I was suddenly so happy that I lifted my head and sang in my ugly cracked voice (it had broken nearly a year before) and the young carter sang too. A round moon, faintly cherry-coloured, I remember, scent of hay and roses, and such peace, such stillness....

'I caught the night train to London.'

CHAPTER II

The Tower and the Wash-house

John arrived in London and found it hot and dusty. He went straight away to Lady Max's house, very tired (for he had not slept), very hungry (for he had not eaten).

He knew that he would not find Ralph there, but nevertheless was discomforted by the chill pomposity with which the tall fish-like butler informed him that Lady Max was in the country. No, he did not know when she would return. A letter to her town address would, of course, be forwarded.

So that evening, under Ralph's roof, John sat down and wrote a letter, thanking her for all her goodness, regretting that he had had an argument with Mr. Reiner compelling his departure, and telling her that he was on his way to pay a visit to his mother before taking up a very important appointment in London. On his return to London he would pay his respects, and he hoped, before long, to prove to her that her efforts had not been in vain. Very stilted, very 'aged' for a boy of fifteen, very sincere.

She never answered it. He never saw nor heard from her again.

As the train approached London, he had discovered that he COULD not go to Aunt Hunnable's. He was a failure. When he had written to her from Reiner's he had told her that he was a success. He loved her and would not ask her for charity. He loved Ralph too, but Ralph was different. Ralph, when he had written to John telling him that he had purchased "The Boar's Head" in Winchester Street, Knightsbridge, and that there was a room there for John whenever he needed it, had written as man to man. It was of no use for John to pretend to Ralph that he was a success. Ralph knew different. Only three months earlier Ralph had sent him a box of toffee, a cake and a photograph of himself, marking the occasion of John's birthday, and, in his brief letter, had

said that John was always welcome, so to the 'Boar's Head' in Knightsbridge, after being turned away from Lady Max's door, Yin his only worldly possession, John had gone.

He found Ralph, in his shirt-sleeves, talking politics with a policeman, a soldier, and a nondescript. When he saw John standing in the doorway he was as calmly delighted as though John were his own son—and I think perhaps that John was nearer his own son than anyone else alive. Ralph was stouter.

There was otherwise no change. He was as shining and spick and span, as royally distinguished in manner, as courteous, as dignified, as diplomatic as ever he had been.

I suspect, though, that he was sometimes lonely in spirit, although, except when he was in bed, never alone. For he made an exaggerated fuss of John.

They were as happy that summer afternoon and evening as any two people in the United Kingdom. In the afternoon Ralph left his 'public' under the command of a pale earnest-looking man whom he called Julius Caesar. Why Julius Caesar? Because he was divided into four parts, one more than Gaul:

'There's his Head and his Tail—that's two—his Hands and his Indigestion—

that's two more. And they don't have anything to do with one another. His hands move independently of his head— that's why he breaks so many things

—and his indigestion is so independent you can almost see it walking about the pub. That's like old Lord Pestrel's used to be. He suffered terribly, he did.

So does Julius Caesar, and he talks to his stomach as though it's a dog or cat or something WILL follow him around.'

They took a walk in the Park in the afternoon and John told him all about Reiner's. Ralph, who had a wonderful understanding of human nature, had a great sympathy for Mrs. Reiner.

'It isn't viciousness drives people wrong, nine times out of ten, and it isn't all this clever stuff foreigners write about either. It's just wanting someone to make a fuss of you. When you get over thirty a bit you wake up and discover that you aren't going to be something wonderful after all—as you thought you were at twenty. So you want to find SOMEBODY you can cheat into thinking you ARE wonderful. Women especially. They MUST be made a fuss of by somebody. They're more urgent about it than men are. I like women. After all, what's a kiss? The cheapest thing in the market.'

That evening John sat in the Bar Parlour and listened to a great deal of mixed conversation. There were Guardsmen from the Knightsbridge Barracks, some lady tipplers, some betting men, and one gentleman with untidy white hair and a red nose who, Ralph told John, was a 'tumbledown author.'

'There was a day,' Ralph said, 'when that old boy there was the talk of the town. Early in the 'nineties he wrote a story about marriage, what a mistake it was, and how women were ill-treated and all that. He went everywhere for a bit. I remember him at Lady Victoria Manchester's luncheon-parties. But success went to his head, he took to the bottle and—look at him. No, Mr.

Meaker, afraid not.... Yes, I know ... you've told me that story before.'

John says that he stared at Mr. Meaker, quite fascinated. This was a REAL author, the first REAL one he'd ever seen. If he'd had any money he'd have given him as many drinks as he wanted.

He slept in Ralph's room that night, in Ralph's double bed in one of Ralph's enormous nightshirts. John remembers that just before they went to sleep Ralph patted his head and said that he wished John was his son. He was a bit lonely at times. Then he turned over and was asleep in a tick of the rather noisy clock on the chair by the bedside.

In the morning he gave John a pound and a large packet of sandwiches and two bottles of ginger-ale. At the last, although he was now as tall as his friend, John threw his arms around Ralph's neck and kissed him.

John, from the top of the Knightsbridge omnibus, looked back to Ralph standing bare-headed in the morning sun and saw him through a mist of tears.

If that was sentimental the journey down to Merlin was stern reality.

'I didn't send a telegram or anything,' John said. 'In fact when I was in the train I had a strong impulse to get out at some small station and bury myself somewhere. With the remains of Anne's gift and Ralph's pound I should have sufficient for my fare to Merlin, but I should arrive there, no doubt at all, poorer than I had left it. I had Yin and the clothes I wore, but no bag, no Religio Medici, no plans for conquering the world. I had failed dismally and

completely.

'Why hadn't I stayed in London, lodging with Ralph?

'I had to see my mother and Charlie. I had been for so long without affection, and that battle with Reiner that had gone on for three whole years had had something mysteriously horrible about it. I was going back to Merlin with no illusions about human nature, young as I was. But then I had no illusions on the other side either. While such a soul as Charlie Christian's lived in the world, I knew that fidelity, beauty, courage were positively actual ... after all, ONE friend is enough....

'But I was frightened of returning. It was a dreadful blow to my pride. I didn't realize at all that I was only fifteen; I seemed to myself to be fifty, with all my life behind me.

'I remember, by the way, that it was on that journey that I first heard the name, or perhaps I should say, encountered the personality of Owen Roughwood. I bought for sixpence at Paddington Station a paper-covered copy of The World Invaded. And how, in the train, I devoured it, how my hair stood on end at the description of the Martian emerging from his shell on the Hampstead heights, how incredible but how exciting to me that picture of London's destruction from the sky, and how little I realized that I would, one day, with my own eyes see that very thing!'

After changing trains at Polchester, he moved slowly into a white clinging mist. He was alone in his hard-seated stuffy little carriage and he says that he felt, when he saw that vaporous white rolling in from the sea, swallowing up, like smoke from a cold fire, hedges, woods and trees, a great exaltation and happiness. This was coming home.

There had been fogs in London and wet clinging vapours on the Downs, but this thick fog-horned blanket that smelt, even in his carriage, of salt and snails and wet woollen stockings, was his, his own, his life's, his timeless cloak. Entering it he left all strangers behind him.

The town was like a buried town under it. With the paper-parcelled Yin under his arm he walked from the station to his home, without seeing a soul.

He heard steps, rumble of carts, and, at certain turnings, quite unmistakably, the fog-horn from Lankin Lighthouse. He found his way unerringly. It was

exactly as though he had never left the place.

Once, he said, the sea-mist broke and he saw houses as men walking. It was as you sometimes behold in the theatre when the curtain rises too early and walls and trees are still shifting into their places. And everything was shining with a white sun, as it so often is at the heart of a summer mist. He stood in that dazzling light and heard clearly the waves breaking on the shore—a purr, a snarl, a purr again. How happy he was at that sound!

And he went on from there:

'When I turned the little cobbled path, stepped on to the ragged bit of turf that led to our fence and little patch of garden, I couldn't believe, you know, that it had changed so little. Changed! It hadn't changed at all. There was the pump, at the corner turning towards the sea, still dripping water with the choking chuckle it had always had. The mist had cleared enough for me to see the immediate surroundings. The sea sounded very near and very friendly. I opened the door and went in. I don't know why it is that I have enjoyed so much lately recalling all these early scenes in such detail. Perhaps it is because they are so real to me and my present life is, as you know, so unreal.

I suppose it is only the past that is real to anybody. It isn't time that crystallizes events but thought. You don't know what thought is working on, how it selects and retains and emphasizes. You are a good listener, you know.

You LOOK, anyway, as though you are interested.... Nothing that has ever happened to me is more actual and present than that moment when I went into our old cottage, with Yin under my arm, and stood in the doorway and saw my mother leaning back in the shabby armchair with her eyes half-

closed and heard Mrs. Hoskin say: "'E'll 'ave to pay up or I'll know the reason. 'E thinks 'e's clever...." Those were her words or as near as not to matter. It was, in fact, a séance of the Three Witches. There WAS a third one now, an immensely fat woman with untidy white hair and a goitre. I discovered later that HER name was Mrs. Hankinson. I was able to look at them for a respectable time before they realized me. Mrs. Hoskin and Mrs.

Garriman had aged, Mrs. Hoskin was smaller, I thought, than she had been, smaller and sharper with a projecting tooth, and a faded green bonnet on her head. Mrs. Garriman was thin and erect as she had always been, still with that air of a foreboding prophetess. Even now there was a pack of dirty playing–

cards on the table in front of her.

'Mrs. Hoskin turned and saw me. She gave a little cry and her projecting tooth seemed to shoot out like a snake's tongue. How she did hate me, that old woman! I was as tall now, you must remember, as a grown man although I had the face and hands of a boy.

'At her cry my mother looked up, and a moment later we were in one another's arms. It mattered nothing that the Three Witches were present. We forgot them entirely.

'You know, I'd never experienced such happiness in all my life before as at that moment: not when poor father was commissioned to make the shell–box, not when I drove with Lady Max to her house, not when I sang my first song on any stage to a delighted public....

'I had never known such happiness with my mother before. I had been a child then, filled with my own idea of what I was going to do in the world. Now I had learnt this one lesson at least—that man is always an exile, catching only in rare and often unexpected moments a glimpse of the country that is truly his own. This was such a moment for me. I knew, as I knelt on the floor, and put my arms around her and kissed her and felt her soft damp hand on my forehead, that here, in my love for her and hers for me, was an actual radiant positive joy that no misgivings or philosophies or idle tales could make untrue. She cried, of course. I felt her tears on my cheeks. She cried, very easily, poor mother. We stayed there, cheek to cheek, our hearts beating together as though in one body.

'Then I got up and looked about me. I saw that my home was still a wash–

house. Above the fireplace clothes were hanging up. In the room was the old familiar damp, steamy smell. Only it was all now on a small scale. Not a laundry now, but an intimate, family wash– house!

'Where, I asked, was Mr. Lipper? At that the Three Witches all made separate and individual noises. Mr. Lipper, my mother explained, drying her eyes, laughing confusedly, staring at me as though she couldn't believe it, Mr.

Lipper had gone away. Oh, long ago. He had just slipped off one fine afternoon and never come back. There had never been a word from him

since.

'"If it 'adn't been for 'er friends," Mrs. Hoskin hinted darkly. Meaning, of course, that her wretched, good–for–nothing son had been away enjoying himself.

'"You've sent me money, Johnny darling, haven't you?" said my mother.

"Time and time. And what a fine boy you've grown! If only your father ... "

'"Come back with a fortune, I don't doubt," said Mrs. Hoskin.

'But I didn't care for Mrs. Hoskin now. I was too happy for HER to touch me.

'"Now out you go," I said to the Witches. "All three of you. Mother and I have things to talk over."

'They got up and went. Mrs. Hoskin had her parting shot at the door.

'"Been actin' before Royalty, 'aven't yer?" she said.

'Alone with my mother I realized that she had grown old, had reached that sad state of not caring, of indifference, of surrendering to the enemy.

'She tried to make a show of it. She told me that the laundry wasn't so bad, she still did her bit of work, kept the wolf from the door ... but soon she was crying again, and this time in a real abandonment of desolation. She had been lonely, lonely, lonely. She clung to me then, as though, unless she held me, I'd be gone. And I promised her that we should never be parted again. I lied to her, of course, about my successes, told her that I was a figure in London now, talked of Lady Max as though she were my greatest friend. But my mother was not deceived. She knew that I was lonely too, a failure too, that I needed her quite as sorely as she needed me....

He obtained work within a week of his arrival—a strange job that he was to hold during all the six years of his life in Merlin.

On the first day after his arrival he encountered a tall, broad- shouldered, big-bellied, red-faced man called Henry Bottislaw— known in the Conservative Club and other homes of Merlin wits as 'Bluff King Hal.'

Johnny encountered him because he ran into him. Johnny was walking, his head in the air, sniffing the sea-salt and the melting tar on the road and the breeze from the moor on that sunny morning; discovering his home again, in fact, seeing it still in the sky rather than on the Glebeshire soil. So he tumbled straight into King Hal's stomach. Mr. Bottislaw had a school, and a very unusual one.

It was unusual in the first place because of its location. The Tower had been in former days an old fortified place high on Sale Head, prepared with at least one cannon against England's enemies. Sir Francis Merlin had built it and for two centuries the Merlins had inhabited it. The family had died out, leaving two ghosts and a skeleton found in the cellar to posterity. In the eighteenth century and part of the nineteenth the Tower ruins had been built on and transformed into a farm. About 1850 it had again been desolate, tumbled into ruin. About 1880 Mr. Bottislaw senior, a Drymouth lawyer, had on retirement bought the ruin and, building with comfortable and ugly Victorian taste, had made a country manor of it. Henry Bottislaw, only son, after a sporting career at Cambridge, masterships in various parts of England, had inherited the Tower, married, settled down there and opened a small school for 'backward and difficult' boys. This little school, in this year 1899, was quite a flourishing affair. The ruined Tower still stood, a little apart from the Victorian manor, in the middle of a grass field, looking out to sea, a landmark for fishing vessels, a tradition, a symbol and a warning.

Mr. Bottislaw decided to have a school for backward boys because of his own exuberant optimistic energy. Like Mark Tapley he wanted a job that would do his nature credit. He was as conscious of his splendid exuberance as Dickens was of Tapley's. He was a good generous fellow but so thoroughly aware of it that he was perpetual showman to his own exhibition.

This self-consciousness, however, suited his job exactly, for his backward pupils were as conscious of their backwardness as he was of his vitality.

Master and pupils were perfectly suited to one another. His pupils said to him in effect: 'You allow us to exhibit our drawbacks, inhibitions, melancholies, and oddities as much as we please, and WE will allow YOU to be as exuberant, hearty, and health-giving as you wish.' So everyone was satisfied.

Now Johnny, on his first morning in Merlin, had dressed himself to look like

a grown man as much as was possible. He had seen at once that he must make a living for his mother and himself. That, for a boy of fifteen, was not an easy thing to do. But he had grown to six-foot; people in Merlin would have forgotten how old he was. Charlie gave me one day an old yellow-faded photograph of himself and John standing rather sheepishly under an umbrella.

This was taken for them by an itinerant at a Fair. Charlie, short and square, his hair ruffled, looks no beauty but hard to move. Johnny is a hop-pole with trousers too short and too tight and the funniest sharp-pointed stick-up collar you ever saw! His bow-tie is clearly a made-up one. Cuffs hang down almost covering his fingers. The whole outfit was a hired one from Mr.

Morris in the High Street.

It doesn't, of course, make him look like a man; he is a boy out on Guy Fawkes Night or playing a part in very amateur theatricals. In the photograph he looks serious but happy. Under the umbrella, with them, is a marble-

topped table and behind them a pillar, a rolling sea and a stormy, cloud-

racked sky.

It was not the grown-up clothes that clinched the deal with Henry Bottislaw.

It was rather the ghost of little Mr. Bartholomew, now pursuing form in the Elysian fields, for, years ago, Mr. Bartholomew had told Bottislaw of the brilliant young genius developing under his care. Bottislaw had not forgotten.

'You are Johnny Cornelius,' he said, holding Johnny with one strong hand lest he should tumble.

'Yes, I am,' said Johnny, breathing hard.

'Where have you been all this time?'

John told him, colouring his adventures a trifle as he was inclined on occasion.

'What are you going to do now?'

John explained that he would be shortly returning to London to take up a superb job now awaiting him. He was for the moment on holiday.

The end of it was that John was engaged to serve, for a week or two, at the Tower as assistant pedagogue for two pounds a week and his luncheon. As I have said, he remained there for six years.

John was very happy at the Tower, but it was a funny business. He understood children as perhaps no other writer, save Hans Andersen, has ever understood them, and that was partly because he was always so much of a child himself.

But he understood these twenty children as no one else, not even Andersen, could have understood them. He had exactly their desire for personal drama, their passion for exhibitionism. They had been encouraged, ever since they could observe or listen at all, to consider themselves as odd. They had been sighed over, discussed, been excused and defended as he had not been, for they came from careful and considerate homes; but when, on his first morning at the Tower, a small plump-faced boy said to him very seriously:

'If I suddenly begin to cry, please don't take any notice. I often cry in the middle of the morning,' he understood exactly the mixture of self-

dramatization and real apprehension that was responsible. He knew himself well enough to realize that the healthy normal schoolmaster's advice—'Boys like that want their bottoms smacked'— wouldn't, in these cases, work at all.

So he felt tenderness and compassion for these children—also comradeship.

And he was happy because his heart was engaged without anyone laughing at him.

Bluff King Hal and his nervous, myopic, novel-reading wife certainly didn't laugh at him. They quickly discovered that Cornelius was able to do things with the children that no one else could do. The children concluded at once that he was one of themselves, but as they permitted everyone his or her favourite dramatic illusion, so they permitted Cornelius his pretence that he was a grown man and their schoolmaster. They were a queer lot. Cornelius often dramatized them for me. I remember especially three. A big, tall, lanky, white-cheeked boy who could not bear that anyone should touch him.

Cornelius called him 'Moon-calf.' He would shamble about, talking to himself, cracking his fingers just as Cornelius used to crack his. He had a genius for mathematics. He grew up, I believe, to be perfectly sensible and became a leading Professor in an Australian university. There was an immensely fat boy (there always is, at such places) who had an unpleasant fancy for torturing animals—flies, beetles, frogs, dogs, cats. This was, of all things, the most appalling to Cornelius. He told me that he would watch the Fat Boy tracking down a fly with a horror and a repulsion that turned his bowels to water. But it was the Fat Boy who was his most successful cure, because he told him stories that made animals so human and attractive that the Fat Boy ultimately became a naturalist of a most intelligent and moral order. That sounds like one of the Cautionary Tales by the Misses Taylor. I can't help that. It's true, all the same.

The third child, I remember, was a frail, golden-haired, blue-eyed little boy who was the perfect mischief-maker. This child had an uncanny genius for knowing where trouble could be engendered, fostered, and brought to a dramatic crisis. His own idiosyncrasy was that he liked to take his clothes off and enter the Bottislaw sitting-room with nothing on. He certainly, as Mrs.

Bottislaw said, looked an angel from heaven thus innocently bare, but visitors from Merlin were shocked and distressed. With this child, Cornelius could do nothing. He hated him from the beginning to the end, as he hated Mrs.

Hoskin, Reiner, and one or two more. He was quite as faithful in his hatreds as in his affections.

He became very fond indeed of Henry Bottislaw, whom he looked upon as a child with the rest. Bottislaw would enter a class-room of the morning, beating his stomach, waving his arms and crying: 'Fine! Fine! Glorious day!

All well and hearty'—upon which several children instantly burst into tears.

This was expected of them, and it was then expected of Bottislaw that he should show his good heart by laughing and calling out and lifting a child by the slack of his breeches, handing out sweets and bowling an imaginary ball at an imaginary bat. All this concluded, everyone would settle down and the business of the day begin.

John really loved his boys, all except the little mischief-maker, who was a sort of serpent in the simple Eden. There was one other master besides Johnny. Of him I know nothing, not even his name.

Besides the boys there was the place. I myself have seen the Tower; indeed, it still stands, and Bottislaw's manor is once again a farm. It is wonderfully sea-

conscious here. The fields run to the cliff, and the cliff falls sheer to the sea.

Standing by the Tower, the wind stirring the grass, the sea wave-wrinkled, there is no limit of time or space. The Tower itself is a little bent, like a man listening for a message. Its stone is broken with weed but rises at the last to a pearl-grey orange-tinted pallor. When the white sun strikes it this pallor is illumined as though with an inside fire.

Birds haunt it, and at times the wind, blowing through its ivy, seems to play a tune.

For John this Tower was a personal possession. He felt as though, while it lasted, he had a certain reassurance about the things that he wanted to be true.

His days very soon fell into a regular routine. Although the laundry business was as dead as nearly not to matter, he wished his mother to cherish the illusion that she was supporting the household. Every week he brought her thirty shillings. Ten shillings he kept for himself. On this they lived with the addition of the few shillings that she earned from the one or two families who still trusted her. He had breakfast with his mother and was at the Tower by nine. On every day save Sunday he was there until five. On Wednesdays and Saturdays there were half- holidays and the boys played ridiculous travesties of football and cricket, Bottislaw rushing about, shouting and waving his arms. John, who had a poor idea of games, would stop and consider the Tower and the sea or console a crying child or reproach a bullying one.

With all this school life he had also his friends and his life in the town.

Charlie and Anne both lived at Merlin throughout these six years. Anne's mother had died and Anne became secretary and companion to an elderly woman called Miss Malton.

Miss Malton Anne used to describe as the 'Prince Regent of Suburbia.' She was apparently a rich, immensely stout, bawdy woman, dressed in stiff collars and waistcoats, with a kind of Court of relatives who waited around for benefices. Anne liked her and detested the relations. Anne herself was growing into a big- boned, tall, clear-eyed girl who had no illusions about life. There was never any nonsense about Anne, unless it was her love for Cornelius, which sprang to life at her first meeting with him and only ceased with her death, if indeed it ceased then.

Johnny was always so completely the reason and object of her living that everything else was secondary to it. She possessed to the full that fearless, self-forgetful fidelity that is one of woman's grandest superiorities to man.

But she was not too solemn about it. 'I was always dedicated to Johnny,' she said. 'Dedicated people are tiresome, so I never mention it.'

She was aware that he had genius, but she thought him no paragon. She knew always that he would never love her as she understood love. She had an exceedingly generous nature; she could not endure not to give anything anyone wanted if it was in her power. That is why, afterwards, she was considered scandalous by many people. And, when your soul and spirit is dedicated to something, what happens to your body is not very important.

During these years in Merlin she was considered, I imagine, a jolly, sporting, good-natured girl, an easy companion, trustworthy, good fun. Everyone knew that her mother had been a lady prostitute.

Charlie, during this time, was at school for a while and then worked at Steele and Parington's, learning to be an engineer. He was a boy of few words, lived to himself, had no close friend but Johnny. He must, at sixteen and seventeen, have been very like the grown man he became. He was an astute judge of character, although inclined to discover faults rather than virtues. He was exceedingly obstinate, soft-hearted and generous, but not at all romantic, and believed only in what he saw with his physical eyes. He was fearless and of great physical strength, a fine swimmer, excellent at any ball games, always determined to win, sometimes sulky when he lost. Like Anne and Cornelius he was almost blindly faithful to the things and persons in which he believed.

In appearance he was short, broad-shouldered, thick-chested, with fair hair and light blue eyes. He had a great contempt for anyone who wasn't English, but could criticize his own country as often as he read his morning newspaper. He was as warm-hearted and tender of nature as he was silent and obstinate.

Of these two friends, his mother, and the life at the Tower, Cornelius made his world.

But it was his life with his mother that was the central motive of these years; it might, I should imagine, make a finely sufficient book of itself. It demands some space, for what happened in the course of it was the strongest formative

influence of his life. During it he grew from boy to man; it proved also to be the chief surrender of his life to any other person.

John himself saw it, I am sure, as the very simplest thing—his determination to make his mother happy. It was, in reality, very much more than that, for, although he never knew it, this was a battle between his mother and himself, a battle which his mother ultimately won.

John, I fancy, never knew the whole truth of it. He was a boy when this business started, but he took up the responsibilities of a man without a moment's hesitation. He forgot, however, that he had been away from his mother for four years and that during this time her character had disintegrated. It was his work to pull her together again, to make her the fine woman she had never been but always might have become. He loved her so dearly that he believed anything was possible. He might have saved her had it not been that he was absent from her during the most of the day, for he had, it seems, a curious and touching influence over her. She loved him quite as truly as he loved her, but she loved also the bottle, was bone-lazy, and had always the Three Witches at her elbow. She had also now a regular weekly income to spend.

This last was the first thing that he discovered: that the larger part of the thirty shillings went in drink. After that discovery he did the housekeeping himself. Child though he looked in his stiff collar and grown-up suit, he obtained a strong authority over her. Charlie says she was deeply afraid of him. And she was not the only one. As he grew he developed authority. There was a good deal of the fanatic about him: if he loved you, you could do almost everything with him except shake his fidelity. He could become, when aroused, quite terrifying, as though he were giving you a glimpse into some world that you had never believed in the existence of. The old witch in Hansel and Gretel is more real and of a deeper significance than most of the figures in history—that is, if facts seem unimportant to you in comparison with the truth. It was just this genius that Cornelius had, both in his books and in his life, for showing you glimpses of the truth, that gave him his authority.

However, facts count, and it was the facts here—the facts of the Three Witches, drink, his mother's laziness, his own busy life, that defeated him.

The Three Witches were his real antagonists, and they were the more dangerous in that he never saw them. They very soon learnt the hours of his coming in and his going out. When he hurried back from the Tower there was his mother, sitting, slack and placid, waiting for him. As soon as he appeared she would wake to a kind of energy and they would share a very happy hour preparing a kind of 'high tea'—eggs and bacon, or fish, or meat-pie with tea and toast and jam. Charlie, from whom much of this account is derived, often joined them.

He himself liked the poor lady. She thought him one of the funniest of men, which was odd, because, whatever Charlie was, he was very seldom funny.

He enjoyed a joke quietly when he saw it and, for some reason or other, he was never a bore, but Mrs. Cornelius apparently had only to see him to go into fits of laughter.

If she had been drinking during the day she hid it quite successfully when Johnny came home, but I am afraid that she often lied to him as she had, in the old days, lied to his father. Johnny, all his life, believed almost anything that anybody said to him, which was, once and again, a pity.

They would have great jokes, the three of them, over this evening meal. No one ever told stories better than Johnny and he would delight them with the happenings at the Tower during the day, the antics of Mr. Bottislaw, the scenes and hysterias of the pupils, his own actions and absurdities.

Because he never saw Mrs. Hoskin he began to forget her. He didn't wonder enough as to what his mother was doing all day, and when he asked her she replied with some innocent plausible account. She soon, then, began to lead a double life.

One evening, when Johnny was between seventeen and eighteen, he returned from the Tower to find his mother stretched dead-drunk on the floor. He had arranged, it seems, for Charlie to come and fetch him for a walk. So Charlie arrived to find John kneeling beside his mother. The two boys lifted her up with great difficulty and laid her on the bed, where she stayed, her mouth open, snoring. She had cut her forehead, her grey hair lay loosely about her face, but Charlie says that he remembers that the worst thing about it was a look of loose insanity around the mouth. She was like an idiot woman.

They did all they could for her, locked the door, and walked out along the sea-path and sat down on a sand-dune as they had often done before.

Johnny's face had been very white, his mouth set, but Charlie says that until they sat down side by side he showed no emotion. Then, quite suddenly, he burst into tears, hiding his head in his hands as though he were deeply ashamed.

John's account of the scene was that it was memorable to him because it was the first time that he realized how deep and strong Charlie's love for him was.

Charlie put his arms around him, held him close to him.

'You know, Johnny, I don't say much—I'm not that sort. It makes me uncomfortable; but you'll never be alone while I'm around, Johnny. You don't ever need to be afraid of nobody. I love you like I'll never love another, woman or no. I don't know why. It's something born inside of me when I was born. I'll always be there when you want me. I'll come across the whole world if you want me to.'

Charlie's own account of it is that John seemed, at that moment, in a kind of despair. If he failed with his mother he failed with everything. He had failed with himself, anyway. Here he was, seventeen years of age, and he'd accomplished nothing.

'I told him,' Charlie said, 'that seventeen was no kind of age. Most boys at seventeen were still at school and there he was earning his living and teaching other boys. And I told him that he was going to be a great writer one day, and all the world wonder at him. At that he sat straight up and stared out to sea and said in a sort of whisper: "I believe I am, Charlie," and then, after thinking a bit, he said: "But suppose I am and then it seems nothing after all?"

'I told him,' Charlie ended, 'not to be looking ahead too much. "You imagine things before they happen," I told him, "and then, if they don't happen after all, you've wasted all that energy."'

It was after this affair that Anne lent a hand. She never, I think, liked John's mother. She thought her selfish and weak and that she took everything from John without giving him anything in return. But after a while she did realize

that the woman loved her son.

'It was a curious thing,' she said to me once, 'the panic that Mrs. Cornelius would be in if John didn't arrive at the proper hour. It was as though she were always expecting him to disappear, as though she were not quite sure that he was mortal. He always returned from the Tower about five-thirty. After that time, if he wasn't there she began to be excitedly restless. If I was reading something to her she wouldn't hear a word. If I was talking she wasn't listening. She was a very stout woman and very untidy. She would pad about the room in her soft slippers saying to herself: "Oh, Lordy, Lordy—where can he be? WHERE can he be? What's keeping him?"

'And I'd say: "It's all right, Mrs. Cornelius. Don't be anxious. He always comes."

'And she'd answer: "You don't know. You don't know. He's not like other boys. One day he won't come. Oh dear, oh dear! Whatever shall I do?"'

Anne told me that she herself used to get anxious, as though Mrs. Cornelius convinced her in some way. Then would come the lift of the latch and Johnny would rush in, grinning all over his face, and throw his books on the bed and the two of them would rush into one another's arms and hug one another as though they hadn't met for weeks.

And one evening he really did disappear. He didn't return until the next morning, wouldn't tell anyone where he had been, and, grinning, said something about the Bird–

Man. He seemed very happy. But they had all been quite frantic, especially Charlie, who had been out all night with a lantern, searching everywhere.

Anne told me, though, that Charlie never said a word when John did return.

Only sat down and started whittling a stick with a knife.

Of John's life in the town during those years I know very little. He was too busy at the Tower to be in the town very much. He was no longer the queer odd-fish child, so old and so young for his years, running everywhere, talking to everybody. The Tower and his mother were his whole life.

He read a vast deal during this time and one very important thing happened to him: he discovered the so-called minor works of Herman Melville in an old collection of books at the Tower, a collection made by Henry Bottislaw's grandfather. He found Pierre, Israel Potter, White Jacket, Redburn and Mardi.

He had, from the first reading of Moby Dick, known a strange intimacy with that melancholy, mystical, black-bearded hero. But now Pierre, White Jacket and Mardi seemed to give him Melville as though the man had come to him, laid his hand on his shoulder and said: 'Friend, we march together, side by side, from now on.' Melville's life was a search and so was John's. Melville was a romantic, if to believe in a world beyond physical sight and touch is to be a romantic—and so was John. John was happy with a great capacity for unhappiness; Melville was unhappy with a great capacity for happiness. Both men longed to love their fellow-men, to help them and be helped by them.

Both were children in naïveté, in generosity, in response to affection. Both men were lonely. Both men believed in the life of the spirit. Both men were easy to mock, easy to ostracize, easy to patronize. Melville has written: 'The subterranean miner that works in us all, how can one tell whither leads his shaft by the ever-shifting, muffled sound of his pick? Who does not feel the irresistible arm drag? What skiff in tow of a seventy-four can stand still? For one, I gave myself up to the abandonment of the time and the place; but while all a-rush to encounter the whale, could see naught in that brute but the deadliest ill.'

Are not those who are conscious of that subterranean miner marked off from their fellow-men? So was Cornelius from birth to death conscious.

In any case he marked November 13th, 1902, as one of the days of his life.

On that day, with every succeeding year, he drank a glass of wine to Melville, for that was the date of his finishing that absurd, ridiculous, fantastic, astonishing work Pierre, and always said he was a changed man from that day on.

I would only add that Campion in The Three Beggar-Men is unquestionably Melville, and it is an ironic fact perhaps that this, the most neglected and forgotten of Cornelius' works, is possibly his most powerful. From this Merlin period Melville was more real, more close, more living to him than most of God's men who still trod the earth.

And now I must say what I can of the Hoskin affair. I have already recorded that during the first years of his return—when he grew from fifteen to eighteen—he scarcely saw the old woman. She must by now have become really aged and considerably insane. Charlie and Anne remember her as an old creature, doubled up, with a sort of a hump now to her back, thick white eyebrows, a projecting tooth, a jutting chin, limping a little in her walk, wearing always a rusty green bonnet and a faded shapeless black costume.

She drank incessantly, but drink had little power over her. She still had her small shop with tobacco, sweets, and indecent postcards. She could also act as procuress on occasion, and did quite a profitable business as moneylender of small sums for immense profits.

So it might have continued to the end had not a group of boys and children in the neighbourhood decided to tease and persecute her. Superstition of a quite mediaeval kind still lingers in the obscurer parts of Britain, and Mrs. Hoskin looked witch enough to be named that, and to be made to run, on occasion, before a shower of stones and dirt. The children would come and call outside her cottage window.

Maybe this persecution really turned her insane. She had always been a person of small wits, jealous of those above her, tormenting when she dared.

Now she fancied that John stirred up the children to pursue her. Her hatred of him became fanatical....

One other event before I describe the climax of Cornelius' life in Merlin, the end of his youth.

On March 3rd, 1905, a month or two before his twenty-first birthday, John began to write his first real book, The Walk from Merlin to St. Ladd.

The first page of the manuscript is a rough dark-blue paper. On the right-

hand corner there is the drawing of a ship and a mermaid looking up at it out of the sea. On the left corner there is a drawing of two shoes.

The title runs:

THE WALK FROM MERLIN TO ST. LADD

A Journey

by

JOHN CORNELIUS

CHAPTER III

Over the House the Last Seagull Cries

I find in my Cornelius note-book this entry:

October 3, 1912.

This evening after dining at the Basque Restaurant in Dover Street we came back to my rooms, and Cornelius, in his old, open, excited manner, which he hasn't shown me for a long while, told me about the inception of The Walk from Merlin to St. Ladd.

These are, as nearly as possible, his own words:

'I remember that I hadn't written anything for a long while. For one thing, I was now tremendously busy—at the Tower all day, with my mother in the evening. And then I had one intense constant preoccupation—to make my mother happy. I had been back in Merlin now for over five years and the thing was becoming an obsession. I fancy we were both an obsession to one another, my mother and I. We loved each other so much and seemed to be able to do so little for one another. I didn't even then realize, although I had been at home for so long, that as soon as my back was turned my poor mother became another person, dominated by those old women. It was partly my fault, for I left her for most of the day with nothing to do. I cheated myself into thinking that she was at work although in my heart I knew that she wasn't.

'Anne promised me that she would go in and see her when she could, but she had her own work with Miss Malton, and my mother and Anne never understood one another until the end.

'Then also I had, after all this time, become intensely absorbed by the boys at the school—at any rate while I was with them. I can't tell you how strange that life up there was: apparently so artificial and yet at heart so tragically

real. Nearly all the children appeared to be play-acting, but I, who all my life have loved to act, understood how, behind the acting, life, even for a child, is intensely real. They knew that they weren't like other children, and, when they were very young, that seemed to be something to be proud of, but as they grew older and recognized that they wouldn't be at the Tower for ever, they began to be frightened. I recognized that moment of realization and understood it. They knew that I understood them as no one else did.

'So that I had plenty to occupy me. I had my friends too. I was very happy most of the time and, besides Charlie and Anne, there were plenty of people in the town who were kind to me.

'But of course if you have something you HAVE to write, you HAVE to write it!

'Some write quickly and some slowly, some correct a lot, others don't change a line. None of that matters at all, you know. Once you can express yourself, after that all that matters is what YOU are. Are you someone by yourself, original, first-hand? Flaubert agonized for a week over a sentence, didn't he?

And Dostoeffsky poured himself out on to paper without a pause. Which is the greater? Who knows? Who cares? If you've a bit of Dostoeffsky in you then it's Dostoeffsky. Or perhaps you have a bit of both men. Don't give a damn. Enjoy what's for you....

'And there I stood by the Tower that day—the lunch-hour. Quite alone, not a soul stirring, but some cows at the end of the field, munching, their heads down; the scent of wet grass in the air, and it had been raining, and my hand was on the old, rough, pitted stone of the Tower while the clouds raced overhead, and the whole waste of the sea was broken with grey pits and furrows that danced into flashes of dazzling white as the sun came and went like a lighthouse lantern turning.

'Oh, how well I remember it, the smell of the sea, the wind, the hard, cold, friendly stone and the sudden ecstasy of creation! THAT is the compensation, isn't it, for the failures, the jealousies, the bitterness, the obliterating flight of time! That first possession when you have your notion, as good as Shakespeare's notion or Dante's or Goethe's. My murder, still uncommitted, is as devastating as Macbeth's, my problem as baffling as Hamlet's, my villain

as passionless as Iago! All that is needed is the great transmitter.... Once again the middle man will fail, but as yet you are not assured of that failure.

Perhaps THIS time ... this time ...

'And this time was really my FIRST time, remember! Standing there, I saw it all—the walk from Merlin to St. Ladd. Leaving the house with my pack on my shoulder, very early, the beach still invisible, only the white line of the surf on the shore and the first, faint, deathly pale break in the sky, rose suggested not formed against the grey....

'And then the adventures. Everything small, real, ordinary, but exciting and English. English! That above all, as I stood there, was what I meant to make my book.

'Staring out to sea I repeated to myself the names and titles of the places that would mark my pilgrimage—Merlin Shore, St. Battocks, the Gimble Rock, Little St. Joseph, Crocket House, Daisy Reach, St. Forrest, the Vailing Valley, High Vailing, Garna Cove, Eustace Hill and Eustace Church, Morven, Cable Point, Great Cable and Little Cable, Gryn Moor and, at last, St. Ladd. I saw them all as a chain of beauties all smelling of England. The English sounds, the lowing of cows, the quick breaking through the lope of the hill of the crash of wave on shingle, the roaring of the wind through my hair as I stood on Cable Point, digging my feet into the ground as cliff after cliff stretched to right and left of me, old rocky giants leaning their wrinkled knees into the wet splash and comfort of the waves.

'And the colours! The sudden purple shadow of the valleyed wood in Vailing, the high marbled stretch of soil above Cable Point running to Little Cable village where the old Norman church has a tower white as bleached bone.

The delicate shades of the sea-pink, the red earth of a ploughed field, and, with a quick flash of sun, the sand of Garna Cove as yellow as honey.

'Into this book I thought that I would put everything: my philosophy of life, my belief in God and confidence in His wisdom, my misgiving about myself and pride in myself, too, the cats and the dogs, the ghost of Eustace Church and the bulls'-eyes of the little shop in Morven, famous all Glebeshire over, the retired pugilist of St. Forrest and how he kept chickens, the history of Gryn House and the smugglers of Little Cable.

'And if perhaps then, at the very heart of my ecstasy, there came the thought (as such thoughts will always come), "Well—and what of it? Who, at the last, will read all this? How soon must it be forgotten and lost and its pages blown to the wind?" Well, there came the dark-bearded, grave figure of Melville to console me, for had I not that very morning in bed at home finished the last pages of White Jacket, that most noble of all warship chronicles? Had not that same masterpiece been all these years neglected and forgotten so that over the length and breadth of Great Britain only in an old library or two, or on some dust-covered shelf, a copy or so yet lingered? Had it, shame to the publishers of two continents, never in all these years been once reprinted?

And yet as I sat up in my bed that morning was not my soul on fire with the reality and poetry and bravery of that picture, was I not keeping company with noble Jack Chase and timber-shanks Surgeon Cuticle and Mad Jack and Captain Clant? Had I not been present at poor Shenley's funeral and rebelled at the great Massacre of the Beards and fallen with Melville himself from yard-arm to the deep waters, saved only by the shedding of that White Jacket that marked him off, as Melville was always marked off, from all other living men?

'Say that, in all its fifty and odd years, White Jacket had raised that glory and exultation and confidence that life was meant to be a glorious thing in one boy's heart only (and he nothing to boast about), was that not of itself justification for Melville's labour and frustration and final tragedy?

'My book was to be no White Jacket; even then, in that moment of glorious expectancy, I knew it—but in its own manner it, too, would be justified, as have all the honest and independent books under the sun! Honest and independent it was to be! Honest and independent it was. That at least I can say of it....'

I am sorry that I never knew Johnny's mother, Mrs. Cornelius. It is at this point in his story that she assumes especial importance— now, just before she leaves it. I have had to build her up for myself from three very different accounts—Johnny's, Charlie's and Anne's. Johnny loved her, Charlie thought of her as John's mother, Anne never really liked her. I fancy that the true Daisy Cornelius was someone very different from any of their portraits of her.

For one thing I am sure that she loved John so deeply that she was conscious, all these six years, that she had betrayed him. Or perhaps it was that she thought that HE had betrayed HER! For, since his baby years, she had been quite certain that he was to be a great man, to conquer the world with his genius, and now here he was, almost a grown man, in his own little town, a schoolmaster at a small school. He had done this, she supposed, for her sake, but although she loved him, how greatly she would have preferred to find him famous in London and neighbours looking in at her door to congratulate her on a photograph or a paragraph in the London paper!

When that rich old lady had taken him up and given him a gentleman's education she had supposed that this fame of which he himself had always spoken would shortly blaze forth. But nothing had come of it. He had returned home poorer than he had left it and now was apparently ready to sit down for the rest of his days teaching poor idiot boys for two pounds a week.

She loved him, of course, almost worshipped him, thought him so complete a marvel that she was often afraid of him, but oh! why wasn't he ... WHY

wasn't he—the genius that he had promised that he would be?

Every account of Daisy Cornelius is agreed that she was the laziest creature alive. She would wait, almost in an agony, for John's return from the Tower at the appointed time, but I can imagine that during the day she liked nothing better than to lie back in her chair sipping at something out of a bottle and listening to Mrs. Hoskin's evil tongue, or the goitred one's murder stories, or Mrs. Garriman's prophecies and astrological forebodings.

Of one thing I am sure: that she was often bored with Anne and even resented her. There was something honest, downright and energetic about Anne that often irritated the lazy and indifferent. Not that Anne ever preached, not that she wasn't the most generous and forgiving soul alive. It may be that Mrs.

Cornelius was jealous of John's affection for Anne. She was never jealous of Charlie, whom John loved more than anyone else on earth. But then Charlie made her laugh and I think that physically he pleased her because he was so clean and so strong and growing into a proper man. Then she wasn't afraid of Charlie, because he was of her own class and talked ungrammatically sometimes and there was no nonsense about him.

The Three Witches, I'm sure, never left her alone about Johnny. They hated and feared him, and now they could taunt the poor woman with his failure and the silly figure he'd cut in London, and here he was, teaching little idiots for twopence a week. I expect that they were clever about it. Mrs. Hoskin had her subtleties. Anyway she never forgave anyone who showed her, as John showed her, what a wretched old creature she was.

And now John was writing every night after he came home. They would have their high tea together as they had always done, but after that was over John would sit down at the little table in the window where his father had made his shell-boxes, draw out his paper and get on with his book. He would not tell his mother what he was writing nor read any of it to her. That was a grievance, but if he had read it to her she would not have appreciated it but would have asked him what was the use in writing about things that happened every day, about places that everyone knew. He realized that, and she would sit watching him, pursing up her lips, rocking her body discontentedly, muttering 'Hum!' and 'Ha!'

'There he sits,' she would complain to the Three Witches, 'writing and writing and he won't tell me a word about it.'

She complained in this way to Anne, and Anne tried to explain to her that authors were like that; it was bad luck to read things aloud before they were finished.

'He's always told me everything,' she would murmur. 'Always until now.'

Perhaps she was jealous of her son's writing just as once she had been jealous of her husband's beautiful shell-box.

Finally there is a description by White Mallison in his essay on Ingres and Corot that always makes me think of Mrs. Cornelius—and I can't tell you why. He is describing a picture of Monet.

'This picture is in his most radiant manner. A line of snow- enchanted architecture passes through the picture—only poor houses with a single square church-tower, but they are beautiful as Greek temples in the supernatural whiteness of the great immaculate snow. Below the village, but not quite in the foreground, a few yellow bushes bare and crippled by the

frost, and around and above a marvellous glitter in pale blue and pale rose tints.'

The queer thing is that there is a landscape of Derain that I have seen in Simeon Rose's house exactly the opposite of this: a hot Southern France landscape, a burning blue sky, thick-tufted, thunder-green trees, a falling field dry and sunburnt, a red-amber barn, a hidden gold-sanded path, all dry, languorous, burning. In the foreground of either of these I can see Mrs.

Cornelius sitting, stout, heavy, lazy, her large soft hand on her lap, her haunches spreading out over her chair, her dewlapped, dairymaid face with the smooth pale forehead, the eyes that still are beautiful, the double chin—

Mrs. Cornelius, whether in the 'marvellous glitter of pale blue and pale rose'

or in the dry gritty foreground pale against Derain's blue sky.... Is it perhaps that both of these landscapes belong to her son's fairy-stories, the pale snow-

shine of The Princess's Spinning-Wheel, the heat and breathlessness of The Bright-Green Shoes? In any case there Mrs. Cornelius sits for ever for me in front of one of her son's fairy-stories....

Her crisis, poor lady, when it came was no fairy-story but macabre, a little out of normal drawing like so many of the crises in John's life. A month or two before John's twenty-first birthday, Mrs. Cornelius began to feel unwell.

She didn't know what was the matter with her. She complained to Anne of indigestion, of pain under her heart, of breathlessness, and none of this was unexpected because she was now very stout and took no exercise whatever.

Into her mild dairymaid's eyes there came now a look of great determination.

Johnny was to know nothing of this whatever; both Anne and Charlie swore that he should not. The apprehension that she now had of something terrible about to happen concentrated all her emotion on her son.

She didn't know what was going to happen, but something, she was sure, and that soon. She told Anne that the only thing she cared for now was to make Johnny happy and they had jokes and games together as they had never had before. Johnny was always a marvel for inventing games and acting stories.

When he was happy he was terribly happy, like a child going to a Christmas party. He liked to be happy and when there was a chance of it he would seize it and extract the very last drop of juice out of it. He didn't at first realize that there was anything the matter with his mother. She was always pale and grey

beneath the eyes. So they had games and fun now in the evenings.

But the other Witches knew all about it and they crowded in upon her, ghoul-

like, licking their lips over the details of her discomforts, frightening her with their prophecies. Charlie discovered when it was too late that Mrs. Garriman produced some kind of a magical brew, made of herbs and birds' eggs and seaweed and God knows what, and poor Mrs. Cornelius drank it. Mrs.

Hoskin now would look out of her little window (just like one of John's witches) and so soon as she had seen him go off to the Tower of a morning she would skip along and find Mrs. Cornelius in bed and sit beside her and watch from under her shaggy eyebrows and say: 'There go the birds over the roof—one, two, three....'

And Mrs. Cornelius would murmur: 'There it is—just under the heart—as though someone was pinching.'

Charlie and Anne were busy of a morning; they didn't know of these visits for a long time. They found then that she was seriously ill. They sent for a doctor and they told John.

When John knew that his mother was seriously ill he became absolutely part of her as she was of him.

The doctor said that it was nothing very serious, and Johnny, who was always eager to accept anything pleasant that anyone told him, believed this.

Nevertheless, Mr. Bottislaw allowed him to leave school earlier of an afternoon, and on half-holidays he would come home at midday. He read The Walk to her now and would sit beside her chair, holding her hand and reading to her, and she would murmur: 'How you can think of such things, Johnny!' and 'You see everything just as though you were there!'

There came one of those spring days, so lovely in Glebeshire, when with a shout of almost derisive joy everything—waves and trees, pebbles on the road, sheets of daffodils, lambs furiously butting their impatient mothers, the only shirt of the solitary tramp hung on a bush to dry and the church ladies decorating the pulpit for Easter— everything cheats Death's jest-book.

Three of these spring days, Charlie said there were. Mrs. Cornelius died on the second of them.

Charlie called in to take Johnny to the theatre—to Romeo and Juliet played by a touring company. It wasn't that Johnny left his mother of an evening, but there was to be something especial about this, a new Juliet or a handsome Romeo. They and Mr. Bottislaw were to have supper together afterwards.

Charlie came in to find Mrs. Cornelius crying and Johnny comforting her.

Mrs. Cornelius had dreamed of Death, who had taken her for a walk, and his touch had been so cold on her arm that she was shivering still. He had had the body of a skeleton—she heard the bones rattle under his black suit—and his face had been pale, with small sleepy eyes. He had been courteous and kind, the perfect gentleman, she said. His feet had made no sound when he walked and the sea-gulls had fled away at sight of him (Cornelius used this description of Death later in Nostradamus).

Johnny held her hand, rubbing it between his to make it warm.

'You are not going to die, mother. You know how much I love you. I'll keep you well. Besides, there's my birthday coming, five weeks from now—'

'Yes, there's your birthday,' she murmured.

'You know what we're going to do that day. We're going over to Crale and take our lunch. I'm to be allowed a holiday that day. You and I and Charlie.

Charlie and I will bathe. It will be as warm as toast. The sand will be so hot you won't be able to sit on it hardly. After lunch you'll have a nap. You know how it is in May there. You can smell the flowers in the valley and there's no beach anywhere where the sea comes in so gently. And there are the shells. It was Crale where father always found his best ones.'

'I'm so cold,' Mrs. Cornelius said. 'My knees don't feel they belong to me.'

They sent for the doctor and he said there was nothing much to worry about.

She would be up again in a day or two. She was too fat, that was the trouble.

She was sleeping in the morning and Johnny went to the Tower as usual. But at the midday break he was suddenly disturbed and anxious. Some small boy

ran across the field, fell down and began to howl. Johnny picked him up and then, straightening himself, looked at the Tower which was shining away in the spring sun like a Botticelli painting.

'I looked at it and I knew at once that something terrible was happening.

'I ran home as though I was afraid I wouldn't be in time.

'Well, it seems that Mrs. Hoskin, seeing the coast was clear, had crept in—

crept in with a bottle.'

She sat beside the bed and after a nip or two we can imagine that Mrs.

Cornelius felt better. It may be, too, that Mrs. Hoskin lost control a little, for John arrived to find her dancing about the room holding up her skirts with one hand and a pile of his manuscript in the other.

'Diddle–de–dee ... diddle–de–dee, the cow jumped over the moon.... You just see me tear this up, dearie!' And Mrs. Cornelius, sitting up in bed, naked to the waist, sipping gin out of a tumbler, nodded stupidly.

At sight of Johnny both women, I suppose, were sobered, for he says that his mother dropped the bottle, which fell on the floor with a crash, and Mrs.

Hoskin dropped the sheets of manuscript, which lay everywhere.

He went to his mother, covered her over, laid her down; she began to cry and kissed his hand.

When he turned, Mrs. Hoskin stood there as though a little pillar of black salt.

Her bonnet quivering with a life of its own, he remembered, she said over and over: 'Don't you touch me, now. Don't you touch me!'

There was something terrible about Johnny when he was angry. He was so long and thin, his nose was so bony, his eyes so penetrating; he meant his rage so utterly. He says that he went to Mrs. Hoskin and seized her by the shoulders and when he held her she was nothing—two spiky shoulder–blades smelling of gin and liquorice–powder. When he seized her she screamed out:

'Don't kill me! Don't kill me!' and through the open window there came the shrill derisive cry of a floating, hesitating sea–gull. Every detail he

remembered: how, when he shook her, a little shower of dust fell from her bonnet, from her seedy clothing. Her false teeth fell out. He shook her and she crumpled to the floor, on to her knees. He shook her and her bonnet fell on to her neck. She didn't say a word, but knelt there on the floor staring at him in terror, for she was certain that he was going to kill her. He even remembers that as he stared down at her he could read some of his own sentences from a page of his manuscript.

So they stared at one another, the most ancient enemies in the world—the all–venturing, foolish, exploring creator and the stupid, worthless, cumbering destroyer. Mrs. Hoskin bit her thumb and sat back on her hams.

He told her to get up. She did, and he followed her out of the door into the spring sunshine.

'You're never coming in here again,' he said. 'Never. You've been a filthy nuisance all my life long. I'll know if you set foot in there. I'll know—and I think I WILL kill you next time. It's more than likely.'

He says that he was trembling with rage, shaking all over. Then a funny thing happened. The children who hung around the cottages and liked to persecute Mrs. Hoskin had arrived on the scene and suddenly began to call dirty words and throw stones. She couldn't move. She stood there, her grey hair over her face, her toothless upper jaw working, her eyes wide with terror.

'They'll kill me! ... The children ... the horrible children!'

He shouted at the children and, his arm around her for protection, almost carried her to her cottage. The children followed at a distance.

At her door the old woman fell in a heap and the children shouted. He told them to be off, and they shouted back she was a witch.

'A witch! A witch! A witch!'

He carried her in and dumped her on her bed. He got some water from a pitcher and revived her, and she caught his hand and besought him not to leave her. The children would get her....

But he couldn't stay. He had forgotten Mrs. Hoskin. His mind was all on his mother, and it was, too, as though when he carried her into her cottage he had conquered her for ever. She would never bother him again. Her successors might, but she never....

He left her there and hurried back. When he came to his mother's bedside he saw that she was dying.

'The room seemed to have a peace it had never had before. So many things had happened in it but nothing like this. The sun was shining in through the open window; the noise of the sea was very soft and gentle. The sun was warm on my shoulder. They say you don't notice such things at such a crisis.

But I did. They were all part of my mother's dying. She lay there, not drunken, nor stupid—clear-headed and happy. The broken bottle was on the floor and I could smell the hateful gin. That didn't matter either. I lay down beside her and put my arm round her. I whispered that I loved her and wouldn't lose her, and she—she said she was tired and that she had done wrong so often in her life but never through wickedness—through weakness, through weakness ...

'That she loved my father and me. It had been good of him to marry a farm-

girl. He had always been so good.

'Then one thing seemed to possess her. She caught my hand, held it and said again and again: "Be a great man, Johnny, be a great man. I've wanted that more than anything—more than anything. Be a great man, be a great man."

'Just before she closed her eyes she stared at the ceiling and said that she saw a light there—a light burning. She said something about the laundry; that no one was better at washing shirts and starching them if only she could take the trouble.

'I remember a sea-gull cried, long, poignantly, rising above the house, crying

... the only sound.

'And she died in my arms.'

CHAPTER IV

The Adventures of the Ark That Wasn't Needed and the Man

With the Green Ink

A few months after Mrs. Cornelius' funeral Charlie came to John and told him that he had a chance of a job in London, to work at a shop as apprentice, the owner a friend of a cousin of his father. He would also have the opportunity of studying at the Polytechnic. He would have, with what his father allowed him and one thing and another, some two pounds a week—

plenty for anybody. He had had this offer but he would not leave John, neither now nor ever ... 'not if you don't want me to.'

'You won't leave me,' said John, 'because I'm going to London, too.'

His ambition had never died; it had only been that through these years one resolve had swallowed up all the others—to help his mother. Now she was gone. Meanwhile there was The Walk. It was more than half finished. He was so sure that it was a work of genius; all that was needed was to finish it. After that, the world would be at his feet. So why not go to London?

He had not a penny but he was as certain now of finding a job immediately as he had been ten years ago. And he was a man now. He was twenty-one.

They had been bathing and now were in Johnny's room sluicing the salt water off them. They made a contrast to be sure. Johnny's skin was as soft and white as a woman's; there was not a hair on his chest. He was so thin that he was, as he said, like an umbrella-stick. His legs and arms were as long as windmills. His ribs stood out like hoops of a cask.

He remembered how deeply at that moment he envied Charlie's broad shoulders and deep chest. He looked in the glass by the bed and hated himself. Charlie was bending down drying with an unconscious natural grace and symmetry of movement.

'Lord! I'm ugly! Look at my nose, my knees, my toes! My mouth is as large as a gate.'

'You're all right,' said Charlie, rubbing his chest. He added with an unusual burst of sentiment: ' *I* like you better than anyone. You know that. And I'm no fool about people.'

Yet John remembered that, as he drew his shirt over his head, the deep self-

distress, self-suspicion, that always followed his magnificent self-assurances hit him. 'What is the use of writing works of genius if you're so ugly? Who will ever want me around— such a scarecrow? ... Charlie does, Anne does.

Poor Charlie, poor Anne! What do they know of the world? Anyway they've seen me all my life and are used to me.'

But by the time he was dressed he had looked at the pages of The Walk piled there on the table and was reassured again.

He remembered that and he remembered a last talk that he had with Anne.

All was ready now for departure as soon as the term at the Tower was over.

Bottislaw was very sorry to lose him but understood that he must go to London; understood but secretly thought it absurd, as did also Mrs. Bottislaw, that Cornelius should think himself a genius. Didn't we all, in our youth, think ourselves so? Cornelius was a nice lad and wonderfully good with the little boys: Bottislaw would never find anyone again who understood them so well— but a GENIUS? Did Cornelius understand at all the rivalry that he would face in London? Why, there were thousands upon thousands of writers there, all very brilliant and clever! And what had Cornelius done to justify his hopes? He was writing a book about a walk from Merlin to St. Ladd? Did Cornelius really suppose that anyone in London cared what happened in Merlin?

And what did Cornelius intend to live on?

He said very tactfully some of these things to John, and John answered him:

'If every writer had always thought like that there wouldn't have been any writers. Shakespeare came up to London and held horses for gentlemen outside the theatre....'

'Oh, well ... Shakespeare ... ' said Bottislaw.

The boys were dreadfully distressed when they heard that John was leaving them and most of them cried and cried. But they had become so readily accustomed to tragic crises that this was a kind of game, in a way.

However, they clubbed together and gave him a travelling-bag with his initials in gold on the outside. One of them—a very melodramatic little boy—

said he would throw himself from the top of the Tower, but all he did was to go there, look mournfully about him and come down again.

And then John said good-bye to Anne.

This conversation—possibly one of the real crises in Anne's life— Cornelius remembered but wouldn't describe, Anne remembered and told every word of.

Once Cornelius was talking about the morning of his and Charlie's departure from Merlin, how bright and silent it was, blue and crystal and so still that you could hear the thud-thud of the mining-stamps miles away at Borlock, you could hear them there on the station-platform.

'It was,' Johnny said, 'like when you've been bathing and come up out of the water, look about you, clear your salt-blurred eyes, and there are the sky, the rocks, as fresh and brightly coloured as though they had just been painted.'

'Didn't you,' I asked, 'have a very important conversation with Anne the night before you went away?'

He shifted his long legs, looked out of window.

'I behaved very badly. I've never forgiven myself. Anne wanted to come to London with Charlie and me and I didn't wish her to. She didn't say so, mind you. That wouldn't be Anne if she had. But I knew and she knew that I knew.'

'Why didn't you wish her to?' I asked.

'Oh, I don't know.... I had an idea I wouldn't be free. I thought she'd want to run me. Dear Anne! ... Why does one always see everything too late? If she'd

come with us, perhaps everything for both of us ... ' He wouldn't say any more. He knew and I knew that too many things were involved....

Anne told me everything and because it was important I wrote it all down immediately after. This is HER memory of what they said, translated into my own style of things. All the same, I believe that it is fundamentally true.

She told me one evening in those, to myself, horrid rooms of hers behind Dean's Yard, Westminster. She told me everything except that she had come that long-ago evening with the intention of asking Johnny to take her up to London with them—the thing that she never did ask him. It was the night before she went off on that final and most disastrous of all her generous adventures. I didn't know, of course, what she was going to do, but SHE must have known, and that knowledge gave her, as I look back on her, a certain brilliance, the trappings and dignity with which you clothe some hero just before his departure on some forlorn hope.

She was always sporting, merry, gay. She never, her life through, gave in to anything.

'I came to say good-bye. Almost everything in the cottage had been sold, but the bed hadn't been removed, so we sat side by side on that.

'"Well, good-bye, Johnny," I said. "You'll write, won't you?"

'"Of course I will. Every week."

'And then I was possessed of a devil. Why? Perhaps I know. In any case there was something about Johnny's certainty that he would have the world at his feet that always irritated me. Poor Johnny! He was the least arrogant man in the world. I was far more arrogant than he was and with no reason at all.

'But I couldn't resist lecturing him. So many people did, are still doing....

'"I hope you'll be happy, Johnny, and don't be disappointed if everything doesn't come your way at once."

'He laughed and kicked his long legs.

'"Why should I? Nothing's come my way yet."

'"No, but you are quite sure it will. What are you going to live on?"

'"Oh, all sorts of things."

'I waited. He didn't say anything and I got angry. It was the last thing in the world I wanted to be, angry. Why had I always cared for him so much, always, always? Why had I always felt that he was my especial property for me to look after and protect and guide? That's an awful thing in women, that longing to possess someone, to make them do exactly what you want them to.

Well, I've got what I deserved.

'I was angry, so I said:

'"I don't want you to be disappointed, Johnny. So many people think that they have great talent and that everyone will recognize it. And it hardly ever comes off. Hardly ever."

'"Doesn't it?" he said. And he looked at me humorously with that charming smile as though he knew everything that was in my mind.

'"I'll tell you one thing, Anne," he said, "that if you think you're going to do a thing you can't help thinking it whatever people say to you. It's like believing in God. If you are faithful to that belief you'll never be lonely—even if God doesn't exist after all."

'"Then you're pledging yourself to a lie," I cried.

'"I said 'believe,'" he answered. "But anyway, DEAR Anne, don't let's quarrel.

We're friends for ever and ever, and if I fail in everything we're still friends.

And if I DO fail in everything I shall still believe in myself."

'He kissed me just as though I were his brother and then he went on packing.

He talked and laughed and told me stories and I sat there without saying a word. I suppose my whole life changed in those minutes.

'Anyway I was ashamed of myself and I jumped up and helped him, laughing and telling stories. Then we said good-bye and I went home and cried myself sick....'

She sat, I remember, leaning forward in that ugly faded purple armchair of hers, puffing at a cigarette. She threw the cigarette away and said, as though to herself: 'I've often thought of that since: "If you believe in God you can't be lonely—even though He doesn't exist," and then, when I called him a liar, his repeating: "I said 'believe.' ... "'

She threw up her head, looking at me with a challenge.

'I don't know. That's one of Johnny's sayings that would seem to Bertrand

"the brayings of an intolerable ass." But who can tell? There are a hell of a lot of things Bertrand doesn't know.'

Johnny and Charlie arrived in London on one of those dry dusty August evenings when the place seems an utterly dead town. At least John remembered 'a bright blue evening sky without a speck, no one in sight but a policeman; a smell of saltpetre, wisps of straw clinging to a lamppost, fields and fields of crooked chimneys.'

The Hunnable bell was rung and an old woman unknown to Johnny opened the door. When she heard their names she said they could come in, but 'they'

(jerking her skinny fingers) were at prayers.

It must, I think, have been a startling sight for the matter-of-fact Charlie to look in the room where the picture of Noah and the Ark was, and to see the Society seated while Abel preached, whirling his arms like a windmill. John was always very clever in his imitation of Abel, for he also had long swinging arms, and in a high shrill voice he would go on:

'Because others are blind, is it any reason why YOU should be blind?

Because YOU have been chosen to receive the good news, should you not receive it? Do you think that Noah would have been saved had he not been warned? When the rains began, who noticed them? And have not in our own day the rains already ... ' and so on, and so on.

It may not have been so odd to Charlie after all, for he was accustomed to Methodist services in his own Merlin, but Abel must have astonished him, so

large, so long in the face and leg, so shrill, so spiritually self-satisfied!

The thing that struck Cornelius was that the Society had so woefully declined since his last sight of them. There were not more than a dozen now in all.

He recognized at once, of course, his aunt and poor William sitting beside her, but neither Mr. nor Mrs. Mortimer was there.

As soon as the service was over, Aunt Hunnable came and kissed him.

William shook him warmly by the hand and Abel pressed him to his bosom as though he were his long-lost and despaired-of prodigal son.

Charlie was introduced and greeted everyone in turn with that slight blush and slow suspicious stare, as though he said: 'I'm not much myself, although I'm quite all right. You MAY be all right, but on the other hand you may be a crook or forger or put broken glass in your wife's coffee.' Charlie, on meeting someone for the first time, was always polite and courteous but metaphorically set his shoulders back and closed his fist, watching and waiting, as the boxer does, for the bell to go. He must have been very cautious on this occasion, for it was all so very new to him.

Aunt Hunnable explained to Johnny a little later: 'You see, my dear boy, the date arrived and nothing at all happened. At least, there WAS a wind that morning and all the sitting-room fires smoked most horribly, but beyond that nothing.' (Had she, Johnny thought, looking at her, ever really believed in it?)

'There'd been no rain for weeks and it was January when there are generally the Thames floods, but this time there weren't even those. We stayed in prayer, waiting all the day through and all the night too, but the morning after was the sunniest you ever did see, cold and frosty but not a cloud in the sky.

So there it was clear enough: in some way we'd got the date wrong. It's set now for March the thirteenth, nineteen hundred and nine, but of course when you've once been disappointed it's never quite the same again. Many fell away and went to live elsewhere, so your Uncle William has been forced to take in lodgers who have nothing to do with the Society— there's Mr.

Carstang, for instance, Miss Peters, and now you and your friend, Mr.

Christian.'

Johnny remembered that dear Aunt Hunnable, who had grown more haggard

and austere of feature in these hard years, looked at him with a loving glance that was almost beseeching, as much as to say: 'Please don't leave us this time, dear Johnny. Last time you went away almost directly after coming here.'

John felt that he must explain:

'I'll tell you frankly, Aunt, that I haven't at present a penny in the world. No, but I've written more than half a book that, when it's published, will be a terrific success. It can't help but be, and then we'll go out and dine at the swellest restaurants and—'

'When do you think you'll finish it, dear boy?' Aunt Hunnable asked him.

'Oh, in a week or two now. And this room will do beautifully for Charlie and me to sleep in, and I can write in the little room next to it. Charlie will be out all day. Did you say a Mr. Carstang?' he remembered asking abruptly.

'Oh yes,' said Aunt Hunnable with pride. 'He's a writer too.'

'I know his name,' Johnny said. 'He wrote The Count of Solferino.'

'Did he? Maybe. He's a very strange gentleman indeed and has a terrible temper. He hasn't paid his rent for weeks, but he will. He always does in the end. I'm sure he's a genius. You should see his room. You never dreamt of such things as he has, and he won't let anyone touch anything, to dust I mean.

I never thought I'd have TWO authors in a house of mine!

Something of the kind Aunt Hunnable said, and so Johnny heard for the first time in detail about Mr. Philip Crawford Carstang.

He was to meet him some three or four days later, and this moment was to present also my own first meeting with Cornelius. For it happened that I brought a friend of mine, Peter Westcott, to tea with Carstang on that same afternoon when Aunt Hunnable brought Cornelius in to call on Carstang.

So there quite suddenly we all four were: Carstang, Westcott, Cornelius and myself—all of us destined to a long bond of friendship, in the course of

which many strange things would occur. On this day in the summer of 1905

Carstang was thirty. I was twenty-five, Westcott was thirty-five and Cornelius twenty-one.

Westcott was a man of somewhat tragical history. He was from this moment to the end a true friend of Cornelius, but the most interesting thing about Westcott in this connection was that his story was in many ways parallel to Johnny's. He was born in a small Cornish seaside resort, Treliss, came up to London with a friend after a hard and stern childhood, starved in London, and then wrote a popular novel, Reuben Hallard, long since forgotten. For a while he was fêted and indulged: he married, published two novels, The Stone House and Mortimer Stant, both complete failures, his baby died, his wife ran away with his friend, and all this before he was twenty-five. He retired into Cornwall and lived there for some years in complete seclusion, but once again drawn back to London he did some sporting journalism and wrote what still remains his best book, Tantalus Point.

During all these years, however—and at this time when I introduced him to Cornelius—he was morose, farouche and sombre. He must have been desperately lonely and did, I think, a good deal of quiet drinking in the worst possible way, that is by himself. The War of 1914 was to liberate him; after the War he married a charming girl, Millie Trenchard, whose brother Henry Trenchard is one of the best dramatists alive in England to-day, although now he writes by far too seldom. I know that Westcott will pardon me for anything I write in this book about him. He will see, in fact, the proofs when it is finished. He was one of Cornelius' most loyal and devoted friends, and much of the detail in the second half of this Life, if you can call it that, comes from him.

But the two important things about this meeting in Carstang's room are my own first impression of Cornelius, and the instant, almost ardent relationship between Cornelius and Carstang.

Carstang was the most astonishing and unaccountable figure in the English literary world of that period. Many people, perhaps most people, said that he was mad, but madness accounts for very little of him: that he had a strain of eccentricity amounting to madness I can't deny. But if he WAS mad, it is a pity that more writers of the period were not bitten with the same insanity.

My first impression of Cornelius is important only because I remember it so very vividly. You must understand that his name meant nothing whatever to me at that moment. I had brought Westcott to call on Carstang because Carstang was one of the few people at that time whom Westcott could endure.

Carstang with his ferocious outbursts, affectations, terrific egotism, and certainty of his own genius, amused Westcott, who was now intensely cynical about the whole of the literary tribe. Besides, he thought that Carstang really HAD genius, although it was of a completely uncontrolled kind.

So there we were in Carstang's incredible room preparing to drink one of Carstang's incredible liquors, when there was a knock on the door; Aunt Hunnable came in, followed by Cornelius.

'Excuse me, Mr. Carstang,' she said. 'But this is my nephew. He writes too and would like to meet you. He's come up to London to write,' she added,

'and is lodging here, so you two ought to see plenty of one another.'

I remember this last remark because Aunt Hunnable cherished the simple notion that writers always liked one another, just because they were writers.

Carstang loathed his fellow-writers; Westcott and I were in favour at the moment but it could not be for long. (Nor was it.) So Carstang scowled and both Westcott and I were apprehensive. At first I saw nothing but a long gangly lad standing in the doorway there grinning. I noticed that he was very tall and thin, had dark untidy hair and an ill-fitting suit of clothes. From the very first, though, the impression that he made was pleasant, for he was so completely himself, entirely without pose or affectation. An honest eager-to-be-friendly country boy. That's what he was.

He came into the room and then stopped dead, looking about him with the frankest astonishment.

He well might, for Carstang's room was really extraordinary. The floor was painted red, the walls were of pale violet, the wood of the bed the yellow of fresh butter, the coverlet on the bed was scarlet, the window green; the rough toilet-table was orange, the washing-basin blue, the doors lilac. I remember

these colours because they were, as will shortly be seen, exactly the colours in the painting of Van Gogh's bedroom at Aries.

The furniture was all of wood and of the plainest and roughest description, save two very comfortable armchairs and a sofa, the materials of which were coloured a dead grey. On the walls hung three extraordinary paintings, all flagrant imitations of Van Gogh, one of the martyrdom of St. Stephen, another of Christ, entirely nude, ascending into Heaven, the third a self-

portrait. These paintings were by Carstang. In the corner of the room opposite the bed was a large ivory crucifix, and in front of it a plain wooden prie-dieu.

There was a shelf filled with books, all apparently in beautiful bindings. On a stand there was an open Missal. A shabby- looking dressing-gown hung over the back of the door.

Carstang also was peculiar in appearance. He was slim and of average height; his head was shaved German-fashion, he had pale- blue eyes and wore very thick glasses. His nose was pinched at the nostrils, his lips thin and capable of great cruelty of expression. When he smiled, however, his whole face was charming, human and benign.

He smiled now.

It is no exaggeration to say that he and Cornelius took to one another at the very first instant of meeting. It was natural enough that Cornelius should be interested, because he had read The Count of Solferino and liked it, but it is everlastingly to Carstang's credit that he saw at once the remarkable quality of Cornelius' personality.

Cornelius knew nothing as yet of Carstang's very doubtful reputation: of his mad rages, multiple feuds, amazing capacity for biting the hand that fed him, queer morals, crazy egotism, hopeless selfishness. But I doubt that, if he had known these things, it would have made the slightest difference. He detected immediately in Carstang the one thing that made him important—his creative force and energy. All the same, he was to pay for this afternoon's introduction.

The two men clasped hands and were at one. Neither of them gave any more attention to either Westcott or myself. Not that we minded. Westcott also was

struck by the naïve, honest, ingenuous enthusiasm of Johnny. Afterwards he shook his head over him. 'That poor child has a lot to go through,' he said.

'I fancy he's gone through a good deal already,' I said.

Words poured from Carstang in a flood: 'Sit down. Sit down there on the sofa. It's a strange room, isn't it? I painted it all myself—exactly from the painting Van Gogh made of his bedroom in Aries. A reproduction. I've never seen the original of course. You like Van Gogh? Never heard of him? My word, where HAVE you been? Here, try some of this wine. It's identically the same as was drunk at the marriage of Lucrezia Borgia to Alfonso d'Este.

You'll like it—it's thin and sharp like a whip. YOU like it, don't you, Westcott? ... '

I remember that Carstang stood there, the thin Venetian glass raised, while he stared through his thick spectacles at Cornelius, who sat on the edge of the sofa, rather uncomfortable, not liking the taste of the wine but beginning to be happy.

The happiness indeed was soon shining out of his eyes. Wasn't he thinking:

'Well, here I am, my heart's desire fulfilled, sitting with three real writers who have all had books published, and they have accepted me as a friend?'

Carstang, who was no respecter of persons ever, shot questions at him.

'Old Hunnable says you're a writer? Had anything published?'

'No—not yet.'

'What are you writing?'

'A book about a Walk—just finishing it.'

'A book about a Walk! Good God! People don't want books about walks....

Not that it matters what people want. To hell with them! They're all dirty bastards. But let me tell you one thing.' (Here he began to shout.) 'They may be bastards but not SUCH bastards as authors and publishers are. Publishers!

My God! Publishers! Do you know what I'd do? I'd fry the lot of them in the

fire that dieth not. By God I would. Bottoms up, with their faces frizzling, and I'd take Rose and Bertrand and Mr. Christopher Falling and little shop–

boy Roughwood and I'd shave them in two and lay on the wood and there'd be a crackling and a frizzling and a spluttering and a screeching, and His Holiness the Pope should come all the way from Rome and raise his blessed hand, and as the flesh blackened and the nostrils stared and the black mouths stretched—' Then quite mildly he'd drop his voice and, smiling his delightful smile, say: 'I'd like to see something you've written sometime. I'm glad you're here. Come in any time. You're welcome.'

Cornelius was enchanted. Very politely he had drunk his bitter wine and it had gone perhaps a little to his head. In any case he was soon telling us all about himself, his early schooldays, his ambitions—especially his ambitions.

As he went on I saw Westcott sit up and take notice, for it must have seemed queer to him, this repetition, in externals at least, of his own story, and he was touched, I don't doubt, at the naïveté and innocence of this poor country boy.

I remember years later, when he had just read The Flight of the Swans for the first time, his saying to me: 'I didn't realize it at first, of course. I thought my story and Cornelius' promised to be the same. There was this great difference.

Cornelius is a creator. I only an inventor.'

'What do you want to write?' Carstang said fiercely. 'Muck to please people or the real thing to please yourself?'

And I remember well Cornelius' answer: 'I haven't thought about it. I write what comes. All the same, I want to please people and I want to be a great writer too. I want to be with Dickens and Stevenson' (in those days before the War, Stevenson was still considered a swell) 'and Galleon and Hans Frost.'

'Oh, Hans Frost!' Carstang said contemptuously. 'That old numskull.' Then he added: 'You've got plenty of ambition.'

Cornelius flushed; he thought Carstang was laughing at him; he was always desperately sensitive. And Carstang saw it and was as kind as he could be. He went to a drawer under the washstand and returned with two heavy oblong books, their covers decorated with a rose-flower kind of wallpaper. He gave them to Cornelius.

'There!' he said with immense self-satisfaction. Cornelius opened them and uttered a little cry, as well he might. The long, lean pages were covered with the most beautiful handwriting, exquisite, as lovely as a missaled page; the writing was in bright-green ink.

Cornelius turned back to the title-page. The book, I remember, was that afterwards notorious Pageant of Bright Spirits that contained libellous and monstrous caricatures of some of those who had assisted Carstang the most.

'You write it all like this!' Cornelius cried. 'But one page must take a lifetime!'

'One phrase,' Carstang answered, raising his bristling, spectacle- flashing head proudly, 'takes a lifetime. And I—I have a million lives!'

Soon after this we left, Westcott and I. My last vision of them was of Carstang standing, his hand on Cornelius' shoulder, and Cornelius listening with his mouth open.

I think that Cornelius saw very little of Carstang during the next week or two, for he was finishing The Walk in a frenzy. This energy was partly because the excitement of the work itself drove him on, partly that he was burning to earn enough with which to pay Aunt Hunnable his board and lodging.

SHE made no complaint and said that what Charlie paid her was enough for the two rooms and that Johnny didn't eat sufficient anyway to make any difference.

According to Charlie, John paid for the value of his board over and over again by the difference that he made to the house and everyone in it. He was so exceedingly happy because here he was, a man in London, who had actually started on his literary career, had made friends with real writers, would soon have the whole world for his friend. He certainly had all that house for his friend.

They were, I imagine, a very dejected lot. It was rather as though Noah and his family had pledged themselves to remain in the Ark for a certain time, and the Flood, subsiding long before the arranged period, leaves them all high and even dry with nothing particular to do. But John, when he was happy, carried happiness with him like a lamp. It was true that the happiness could very easily be blown out, but while it was there it was warming, translucent, an innocent flame.

In any case I have never in all my experience of men known any egoist so deeply and personally interested in other people as was Johnny. His egotism came, I suppose, from an absorption in some pursuit that involved many other people as well as himself. He had also a heart like a mirror that reflected in its surface all kinds of faces besides his own. And he had two great abiding qualities: fidelity and compassion.

Lastly he found, I don't doubt, after the Merlin years, that the variety in experience of these London people was very exciting. I won't delay over them now, but I have heard often about Miss Phipps and her illegitimate child, the little Gogarths who were so passionately devoted to one another and quarrelled the whole time, Mr. Symons who was a miser, and fat Miss Parsons who constantly wrote to King Edward, warning him of the approaching Flood. Within the shortest time possible Johnny was familiar with all of them and they with him. He was so genuine and trustworthy that they told him all their secrets and he told them all of his.

He even read them chapters of The Walk.

Five months after his arrival in London—on January 22nd, 1906 (the date is written in capital letters in red at the end of the manuscript)—he finished The Walk.

The final paragraph is:

'A perfect stillness rested upon the breast of the sea as I turned up the little cobbled path into the old square of St. Ladd. Before the houses hid it I gazed at the moon which hung low, grinning above the water like a Chinese plate with an old man's face painted on it. The moonbeams shone upon the white naked walls which formed St. Ladd's only street. No human being was visible. There was no sound save the whispering murmur of the sleeping sea.

I waited for a moment, smelling the scent of the pinks and phlox in the cottage gardens, listening to the happy secure silence.

'Then I rang the bell of the house where my friend's home was.

'I had arrived.'

His discovery of old Mostyn was due to Ralph. He and Charlie spent many an evening at Ralph's Knightsbridge pub, and Ralph, in his turn, came to supper at Hunnable's. Aunt Hunnable was astonished by Ralph's manners, the most beautiful she had ever known. Johnny remembers that he himself was astonished by them because he had never before seen Ralph in the rôle of an English country gentleman come to Town for a few social engagements.

It was Charlie, however, who became Ralph's closest friend. Charlie had taken to London as a young pony to a bundle of hay. He devoured it; it quickly became his own. He was never one to show astonishment at anything, but equal to his calm survey was his inexhaustible curiosity. After he had been in London a month he knew everything about its morals, finances, food system, entertainments, sports and religions. While waiting for a bus, after a visit to Ralph's, Cornelius would stand lost in wonder at the soft waving of branches against the sky while beneath the trees there was this flow as of the sea with the hansoms, omnibuses and footsteps sounding a rhythm with a melody like the whisper of falling snow against glass. Charlie was thinking of none of these pretty things but noticing policemen's numbers, watching a girl's quick eye for the Law as she solicited a hurrier-by, or the group about the coffee-stall on the other side of the street....

He became now more a protector of Cornelius than ever. Ralph told me once that he remembered Charlie standing beside him at his bar and jerking his head toward Johnny and saying:

'He isn't like the rest of us. He don't know NOTHING about machinery for instance. You wouldn't believe it, but he doesn't know who constructed the Forth Bridge. He's always been different and so he wants looking after.... I tell you, Mr. Ralph, when I'm working away at the Polytechnic like anything I suddenly get anxious, and it's all I can do not to run home and see he's all right.'

What Ralph said I don't know, but I'm sure that he thoroughly agreed. I met Ralph myself about this time. Charlie and Cornelius took me to his place. His

face now was as round and red as the sun and he had a fine Elizabethan belly, but he was an aristocrat and, in some way or another, NOT a snob.

'You must have met Sir Wymper Harrington? No.... Strange. He goes everywhere. It was Sir Wymper who made that bet at White's about stripping himself naked in the middle of Piccadilly at three in the afternoon. He did it too, but he was INSIDE a hansom. Very clever. He drove all the way to Westminster in it. You could just see his very hairy chest through the glass.

He married Lady Lettice Potter, but they didn't get on. She was too religious for him,' and so on. Why he wasn't a snob I don't know. Snobbishness, I suppose, is the pursuit of superior people for inferior reasons. Ralph never pursued anybody. He was simply a chronicler of his time.

It was in his pub, as I have said, that Johnny met old Mr. Mostyn. Mostyn I saw only once, but I have a vivid memory of him, a little man with a back bent from rheumatism, deep piercing eyes and wearing always a black skull-

cap. He had a face yellow as parchment and bore a slight resemblance to Dr.

Nikola, who was famous at that time. There was, however, nothing diabolic about him. He lived alone in Chelsea, with a small printing-press in a shed in his garden. Ten minutes after his introduction to Cornelius he suggested that he should print something of his. Ten minutes after that the four fairy-stories were chosen—The Golden Linnet, The Three Princesses, The Wind in the Church Tower and The Old Musical-Box. Half an hour after that again an appointment was made for the following day at Mostyn's house in Fulham Road.

It was Ralph who, to his immortal literary glory, finally supplied the cost of printing The Wind in the Church Tower and Other Fairy Stories by John Cornelius. This is the description of the book in Forrester's Cornelius Bibliography:

THE WIND IN THE CHURCH TOWER, by John Cornelius. London: Privately Printed. 1906. 1 vol. Cr. 8vo. (47/8 x 71/2). Pp. iii + 65 + ii. Half-

title. Dark-green rough-edged paper, blocked in blind.

There were one hundred copies printed. It is scarcely necessary to say that it is one of the rarest books (or pamphlets if you prefer it) in modern English literature.

There is a copy in mint state—the copy that Johnny gave to Charlie— lying in front of me on my table now. Its dark-green rough-paper cover is very amateur printing, the rude little print of a church tower with rooks blown about in the wind above the title of the first story, and then the inscription in Cornelius' stubby hand:

DEAR CHARLIE WHO THINKS THESE STORIES NOT GOOD

ENOUGH FOR ROYALTY WITH LOVE FROM JOHNNY. Feb. 3, 1906.

By those last words hangs a tale—for Cornelius sent copies of The Wind in the Church Tower to His Majesty King Edward VII, to Queen Alexandra and to the Prince and Princess of Wales.

This was the letter that accompanied these copies: YOUR MAJESTY (or YOUR ROYAL HIGHNESS, as the case might be)—

With all humility I beg you to accept a copy of the first printed work of a young English writer who yields to no one in his loyalty to the Throne and his reverence for his King and his Queen.

If these stories are a little roughly printed Your Majesty will, I know, forgive the deficiency because I am a young man of very moderate means and it would surprise Your Majesty, I am sure, if you realized how costly the printing of a hundred copies of a book may be.

I trust that Your Majesty will enjoy the reading of these stories as greatly as I have enjoyed the writing of them. I am,

Your devoted and humble servant,

JOHN CORNELIUS.

In due time he received four official replies. I may add that I have been astonished but gratified to discover that all four copies are safely housed in the King's Library at

Windsor Castle. All four! None of them then was destroyed or cast away. What a miracle! It may have even been that they were read.

In any event, there they are, the four slender green-paper little books, enclosed with Cornelius' letters in a crimson leather case. They are to-day shown as among the most interesting of modern editions to curious visitors.

So time brings in its revenges!

Johnny's letter led to trouble in at least one direction. Charlie was shocked.

'You can't send a trifle like that to the King and Queen.'

'It isn't a trifle.'

'They are only bits of things.'

John remembers that he said then, fiercely:

'Don't you like them then?'

Charlie compromised.

'You know, Johnny, I'm no judge of books. What do you pay attention to ME

for?'

'Of course I pay attention to you. Aren't you my friend?'

'Aye—of course I am.'

'Well, then ... '

'Well, your stories are all about nothing at all. Fancy bothering the Queen, bless her heart, about wind blowing in a church tower.'

Perhaps Charlie was right. Johnny went to bed that night in a passion of depression. Who cared? Who wanted stories about linnets and church towers?

'And then I sat up in bed, my eyes shining, my body trembling. Let them all go to blazes, Charlie as well! I had published my first book! I had published my first book!

'I went to sleep in the big double bed, holding one of the green- paper copies

in my hand.'

CHAPTER V

How the Hero Moved Into Soho, How Charlie Enjoyed Sausages

and Mashed, What It Feels Like to See Your Book in the

Window, and Whether or No Anne Was Wise

I have constantly noticed that English readers do not take very kindly to novels that have for their theme the adventures and misadventures of men of letters. It is to be regretted only in this—that novelists have, for the most part, very little firsthand experience of life except as men of letters, and even though in their early years they have been navvies, tramps, seamen, dress-

designers or penniless members of the Peerage, after their first successful volume they become AUTHORS and are segregated thenceforth from many enlivening hazards and extravagances.

It must be admitted, too, that AUTHORS are not on the whole agreeable persons. This is universally admitted by authors regarding other authors and, as they are inside the trade, their evidence must be taken as honest.

It may be that the world of authors is no more spiteful and venomous than the world of doctors, lawyers, actors and money- lenders. The difference lies in this: that authors are able, by their own peculiar gifts, to write down on paper their feelings and then see that they are printed. This leads to a kind of perpetuation of literary scandal, backbiting and bitterness. Nor must anyone suppose that this is peculiar to our own times. Authors have from the first days detested one another and invited the world in general to share in their detestations.

Unfortunately, however, for authors, the world does not in general take them as seriously as they take themselves. It is only a very small group in any country that cares anything about authors unless they arrive in the police-

courts, as numbers of them do. An author's surest passport to immortality is to be convicted of murder. He will be read, then, it may be, even a hundred years after his hanging.

I must confess that I know a number of very agreeable authors, but that is because I am now old and am not, therefore, any longer greatly in anybody's way. But authors can be very pleasant indeed when interested in some other pursuit than writing, such as salmon- fishing, stamp-collecting or playing the saxophone. You will find them on such occasions in no way repulsive and even pleasant to be with.

They are at their worst and least interesting in their personal literary affairs, and I must apologize once again that I must give here some account of the literary London world in which John Cornelius found himself.

I promise you I will be as brief as may be.

Of the literary giants of that period, 1906-1914, I will say nothing except that Henry Galleon had died in 1899 and had left Hans Frost as the unquestioned (but by the younger generation not unchallenged) leader of contemporary English letters.

Hans Frost was the last of the great Romantic writers. When a Romantic period returns to English literature again, as beyond doubt it will, it will be a very different Romance from the Stevenson-to-Frost inspiration.

I am writing, however, of Cornelius, and the important occurrence as background to his story was that about 1906 a young publisher, Samuel Creighton, opened a modest office in the Adelphi and by a combination of good judgement, good fortune and good manners discovered half a dozen young authors of merit and presented them to the country. Between 1906 and 1909 he published the first works of H. B. Terence, P. T. Barham, Simeon Rose, Herbert Gloucester and John Glass. Only two of this group had genius

—Terence and Barham— but all were talented, and had the War of 1914 not cut short their progress, might have been more than talented.

The effect of all these new young men coming, fully armed, out of the head of a new young publisher, was considerable, and it was into their world that Cornelius, after the publication of The Walk, entered. It was a literary world of extravagant hopes and magnificent ambition. They were of course unaware, those young men, of the deepening shadow overhanging their sky....

It has been explained many times that during the second movement of the

'Eroica' one may observe the solemn funeral procession advancing, passing and vanishing into the dim distance, but for myself it presents quite another picture.

I see a high tower in the middle of which is suspended a great clock; the rhythm of this clock has the certainty, the swinging harmony, the destiny of fate. Beyond the tower there is a sun- drenched landscape on which many figures are heedlessly moving. Behind the tower deep ebon-coloured clouds are piling up, heralding a ferocious storm. This clock-rhythm seems to me, as I listen to the second movement of the 'Eroica,' to beat at the very heart of this insignificant star. At certain moments of anticipation, it is heard with especial emphasis. It may be that its tick-tack indifferent warning has now a power for us that retrospect only has provided, but on that sun-drenched landscape the figures move, and behind the tower the clouds advance and the death-

march of the 'Eroica' seems timeless....

WE had, of course, no forebodings. Rose and Gloucester wrote or began to write Trilogies as though the whole of the future was in their young fat fists. I will say something here only of the one or two fated especially to cross Cornelius' path. Among writers, his closest friends were Carstang, Westcott, myself, Rose and Bertrand. I have said something already of the first three.

Simeon Rose and Bertrand made an amusing contrast. Rose was some ten years younger than Bertrand and about my own age. He has always interested me because his exterior self represents, I imagine, the opposite of the real man. Outwardly he is plump, cherubic, rosy-faced, and with his genial smile, urbanity, and a certain mild pomposity would make an admirable Canon of any Cathedral. To meet him you would say that he was completely self-

assured and very definitely pleased with himself and his success. This self-

satisfaction can be irritating even to his friends. He is cheery and complimentary to everyone, so modest about his own works that no one believes in his modesty; he rushes from place to place, smiling, laughing, his voice booming, clapping everyone on the back. I myself have long suspected, however, that Rose is in reality a man compacted of misgivings and suspicions of his fellow- creatures. A lonely man, too, I daresay. A man loyal to his friends and passionately desirous of their affection but morbidly suspicious of those same friends and restlessly suspicious of himself. The

keynote to his character is, I think, apprehension. This makes his work, which is garrulous, long-winded, often platitudinous, sentimental and unreal (often also readable, for he has an excellent narrative gift), surprisingly interesting to me. Bertrand is Rose's exact opposite. His long bony body, the pale cadaverous countenance on top of it, does not speak for cheerfulness. He is, both in his outward self and in his books, a cynic, a pessimist, and above all (what he most wishes to be) a realist, a man who sees things exactly as they are. He is apparently a modest man who writes as he can a simple English style and tells the truth about the little bit of life that he has seen.

But within, Bertrand is, I think, self-assured, rather arrogant and deeply sentimental. He is, in fact, the man whom Rose tries to be in his writings, while Bertrand's writings have the cynicism that is in reality deeply embedded in Rose's character.

Bertrand, in his plays, his novels, his stories, his books of travel, has every gift but genius. Genius is something that is greater and more unaccountable than its possessor. It may be said to despise its possessor. But Bertrand has complete command of his gifts and can write only of what he has personally encountered. He has a fine narrative gift, humour, drama and a philosophy that is neither as original nor as true as he thinks it is. He is more delightful to read than any of his contemporaries, but he does not give joy in retrospect.

Joy and loving compassion are elements in life altogether omitted from his work.

I have delayed for a moment over these two men because they had, both of them, a real and lasting influence on Cornelius' mind and spirit. Cornelius liked Rose the better but admired Bertrand the more. That was because Rose, who was garrulous, confidential, eager to be liked, demonstrative and emotional, had characteristics that Cornelius easily understood. He could be, and was, familiar with Rose. Of Bertrand he was always a little in awe. For one thing Bertrand succeeded, beyond any man of his time, in one of the arts that for ever eluded Cornelius—the theatre. Then Bertrand's constantly expressed disbelief in men's virtues, their love, loyalty, sincerity, disturbed and distressed Cornelius, who wanted before everything to believe in his fellow-men. The key to Cornelius' life was, as I have already said, first his fidelity, second his search for the real world behind the factually visible one;

Bertrand considered (or SAID that he considered) fidelity synonymous with sterility and the spiritual life a humbug retreat for cowards. It might be, Cornelius must often have said to himself, that Bertrand was right....

And one word about the London of 1906 to 1914. How much is sentimental nostalgia, looking back now from these steel platforms and the slanting aeroplane-wing hovering over our mechanized space, to the casual charm, the quiet gossiping light of a London 1908 afternoon? All life there seems arrested or hushed; is it only fantasy again that all rooms now have shrunk to closets, all windows to peep-holes and gardens to window-boxes? Is it illusion, too, that in that other world there were other scents than petrol—the dung of horses, the parched dry sweetness of mignonette, the flame-packed gritty substance of coal-smoke and the spongy roughness of pea-green fog?

These are not phrases. Petrol has extinguished all, and men die with the fumes choking their nostrils....

No. It is not only nostalgia that brings to me, behind the clop- clop of the hoofs, the jingling of the hansom harness, the friendly call of the muffin-

man, the blaring dissonance of the German band, the echoing loneliness of the Italian's organ-grinding—a cycle of sounds rising and falling in a friendly town. Nor is it only the sentiment of a man in quest of his youth that snatches a certain lovely lazy incongruity out of that past. That world presented so odd a confusion of backgrounds; the Duchess of Wrexe's drawing-room where—

invited to tea as 'that young man whom Carrie introduced me to the other day; she says he's quite promising, a cousin of the Norfolks or something'—

you stood by the open doors and gazed across a sea of dark heavy-piled carpet to that little group by the fire, the old Duchess, her stiff-necked ancient daughter, a gentleman or two in the frock-coat and buttonhole of the 1900 courtier. That little group, the silver glittering in the firelight, the crackling of the logs, the hushed murmur of the footman, 'Yes, Your Grace,'

all that floor to cross under the gay laughing eyes of Mrs. Ellenborough in the great Romney over the marble fireplace—from that to the basement-rooms in Glebe Place, Chelsea, where for four shillings a week I prospered like the youngest of bay-trees, placing in that half-light my first few possessions, the brass coal-scuttle, the set of dumpy red-backed Waverley Novels, the copy of Lautrec's lithograph cut out of the Illustrated London News of the woman

in the black dress bending down to fill the bath-tub. Down the King's Road came the omnibuses and the hansoms and the vegetable-men and the huge dray-horses and the little carts with the ear-flicking donkey. Over the road is the Music Hall where any night you may applaud with the friendliest family feeling Marie Lloyd and Little Tich and the White-Eyed Kaffir, while somewhere near Hilldrop Crescent, Crippen is performing acts of dentistry; Bertrand is startling the world with five successes in the theatre at once, and I stand six hours outside Covent Garden that I may hear Ternina for the last time in Tannhäuser; Ellen Terry is in Alice Sit-by-the-Fire and, breathless in the pit, my hot hands clasping and unclasping, I love her so madly that afterwards in the Glebe Place basement I kiss her photograph again and again; cloppity–clop, cloppity–clop, scent of window–boxes and the line of red carpet laid in Berkeley Square for a party, a story called Stalky in a magazine with a green cover, a sudden hush at the top of St. James's Street so that the whole world seems suspended as you look down and see the pigeons circling around those squat towers; the Guards are riding through and the sun slants spear–shape from the white blanketed sky, making the silence vocal with the glitter of spear and harness and helmet.

There is all day long, it seems, in which to move, the colours are gentle and friendly: rose and violet of the Piccadilly sunsets, smoke–grey of the Green Park trees, stained Chinese–white of Westminster, cloud–dappled, moth–

winged Kensington…. Everything sails slowly to an almost sleepy rhythm, birds and trees and clouds and the comfortable bodies of unencumbered men.

Yes, certainly this is the sentimental nostalgia of the Past, for men were encumbered then as now, apprehension was no less, danger invigorating, sharp, poignant then as now. Only—yes, this for certain—London was both more casual and more dignified, the pace was slower, the claims to your attention fewer and less strident. It still had an occasional gossiping remoteness as of a country town, and the squire from his stronghold in Park Lane or Portland Place gave blankets and soup to the cottagers in the Old Kent Road, and men met on the village–green of Eros' Circus and looked at the sky and foretold the weather. Nelson looked down from his column, and the lions were still of a handsome size. This was the town that Johnny Cornelius and Charlie Christian invaded.

It was from a Soho attic that they launched their attack: in reality and truth an attic up a little street to the left of Soho Square, a little street with two plane–

trees, five restaurants and an 'animal' shop.

It happened in this way. Hunnable's, with a precipitate suddenness, completely collapsed. One morning, it seems, Aunt Hunnable knocked on Johnny's door and announced: 'Everyone is leaving.' Poor Aunt Hunnable! I saw her very seldom after this sad episode. But she stands always in my mind as the last type- figure from the Victorian novel. She could have played her part so naturally in Bleak House or Pendennis or in one of those delightful, garrulous and absurd and moving stories by Henry Kingsley. Very likely she did. I would only say here that it seems queer to me now, as I write this book, to see her as so exactly the opposite of her sister, Johnny's mother: hardworking, sober, full of rectitude, a woman of her word. No Mrs. Hoskin would have had a chance with her for a single moment. But perhaps this is often so between sisters and brothers. Aunt Hunnable may have made poor Daisy Cornelius what she was by rebellious contrast. Nevertheless everyone loved Aunt Hunnable.

Even, I gathered, the departing members of the Society. It seems that they all met one morning in a body and announced that they were not convinced any longer of the definite certainty of a Second Flood and intended to go their own ways. I was not, of course, present at the scene nor have I talked with anyone who was, but I gather that many tears were shed, that Abel was very violent, but that the Church Expectant was disbanded once and for ever.

Therefore, as Aunt Hunnable explained to Johnny and Charlie, the house must be abandoned also. It was too big and costly for a boarding-house. It seemed also that William Hunnable had been longing for years to live by the sea. His health had been poor, he had been visibly ailing, but no one had known of his desire. 'We shall go to Bournemouth,' Aunt Hunnable said, 'and if the Great Flood comes we shall be gone with the bandstands and the pine-

trees and the villas before we realize it.' I think she must have said this with a wink. Abel retired to live with a sister in Kensington and became, I believe, a Sunday preacher in some conventicle in the district. Johnny would soon hear of him again. Carstang took two rooms in Bloomsbury, painted them à la Van Gogh, bought a silver skull at an auction and hung it outside his door.

It was Ralph who found the two attic rooms for Cornelius and Charlie. Ralph, who really WAS one of the most charming souls in the world, for, unlike most of us, he always did exactly what he said he would do, and although he was busy attending to the business of his pub yet had time to perform endless kindnesses for his friends. For Johnny in especial there was nothing that he would not attempt.

The Soho attic was, in fact, precisely the thing. It must have been a very grand house once upon a time, and still had a beautiful staircase from the second to the third floor and several Adam fireplaces. On the ground floor was an Italian restaurant, Capponi's, a small quaint unambitious affair, very much liked by couples who wished to talk without being disturbed. On the first floor was Frank and Portley's Dancing School and on the second an extremely select and precious bookshop, Carlisle's.

Carlisle's was SO precious that when you entered the beautiful room with the long windows, the white-panelled walls, the Adam fireplace, the deep red Turkey carpet and the chaste busts of Joseph Addison, Adam Smith and Huxley, you saw only one glass-fronted bookcase and no sign whatever of buying or selling. Old Mr. Carlisle was a small immaculate man with a white imperial. He was said to be the greatest living authority on Peacock and a great connoisseur of wine.

One more flight and you came to the attic. This had one large room with a roof so sloping that you were for ever knocking your head, and one smaller room off it. In the smaller room Johnny and Charlie slept; in the larger everyone lived, moved and had their being. There must be many people to-

day who remember it, who can recall Yin and his cockel hat and his elephant with the cherry- coloured ear in the place of honour in the middle of the mantelpiece, and the round table and the three old armchairs with the holes in them and the plain unvarnished bookcase piled with books and the copies of the Dürers and the Altdorfers on the walls. There was a big fireplace, big considering that it was an attic.

Very soon of an evening the place would be filled with smoke and noisy conversation, for Johnny loved people, of course, and it seems that now, at this present moment, I can see him striding about, waving his arms, jerking his long loose legs, tossing his head about, radiant with happiness as long as

people liked him or pretended to. He could be taken in by anyone, believing all that was said to him for good or evil. Everyone knew that he had no money and people brought their drinks with them and often their food. From the very beginning we, his closer friends, were all in a conspiracy together not to let him have any spare money about him, for he instantly gave it all away. If anyone told him a 'hard luck' story he would at once promise them help, and then Charlie would have to go to them afterwards and tell them that Johnny WOULD help them if he could but that as he hadn't any money he couldn't! It was Charlie again, during these first months, who stretched his few pounds a week to cover expenses. Food was easy, because one meal a day seemed all that Johnny needed, and if he was talking or writing or in any way excited he forgot even about that. No one could regulate his life for him; it simply refused to be regulated. Like Cézanne he would leave abruptly in the middle of a meal to work. It was from this time of irregular living, I think, that his heart first troubled him, although we knew nothing of this for a long while after. He was a wonderful man for keeping his bodily troubles to himself, although his spiritual, mental, aesthetic troubles he would pour out to anyone.

I myself was now for the first time observing him at first hand. Two incidents, both occurring shortly after his moving into Soho, revealed him vividly to me.

He gave myself, Westcott, Carstang, copies of the rough green–paper brochure with the four fairy–stories, and I'm ashamed indeed to say that no one of us at that time found them in any way remarkable. As one of them, The Golden Linnet, was afterwards to become one of the most famous fairy–

stories in the world, was to be an opera, a ballet with music by Rapin and choreography by Lörther, it must seem very extraordinary that we experienced tea–tasters of literature, on the watch for any kind of new talent, saw, at the first reading, nothing here but a pretty little tale in simple language, like any other pretty little tale. I can't explain it. I should have supposed that the unforced pathos, beautiful selection of detail, the character–

creation of the old lady and the young watchmaker, must have excited us.

Nothing of the kind. We shook our heads and were afraid that Cornelius would never set any Thames ablaze. Only Simeon Rose was excited, but we had long ago learnt to disregard Rose's enthusiasms. He loved too many

things!

The day after Cornelius had given me the stories he appeared in my rooms.

He stood in my door and almost shouted: 'Well, what do you think of them?'

That, in the very first place, was a sign of his naïveté, for authors learn quickly NOT to ask friends what they think of their works. If a friend is enthusiastic he will say so; if he is not, better leave him alone and pass on to something else.

'Come in, Cornelius,' I cried with, I am afraid, a rather false heartiness. 'Come in and share my lunch.'

'No, no.... Thank you. No, I was only passing.... I had to ask you. You like them, don't you? They're good, aren't they?'

'Like them? Like what? Come on. Don't be a fool. Sit down.... There's plenty for both of us....'

'The stories! The four stories. What do you think of them? I hope you like them. What does Westcott say?'

Looking at him there in the doorway he seemed to me a child, almost my own child, with a trembling eagerness, an excitement, an anticipation that it would be cruel to hurt. So I said: 'Oh, they're fine. I read them last night.

They're charming.'

His face fell. His whole body seemed to droop. (I remember that he was still wearing those high pointed collars and that his tie was right up under his ear.)

'Ah ... you don't like them.... You're disappointed. Well ... '

I got up and came over to him.

'No. I'm not disappointed. Of course they're slight ... '

'What does Westcott say?'

'Peter? Oh, he liked them too. Of course he thinks as I do. They ... '

'I see.' (There were actually tears in his eyes. I was afraid, for a moment, that he would burst out crying, there in front of me.) I put my hand on his shoulder.

'Look here, Cornelius. It doesn't matter what WE think. Besides, the stories ARE charming. They are really. I like The Three Princesses especially. And anyway you mustn't take anyone's criticism so hardly. You're going to have an awful time if you do. And nobody knows about contemporary work. One's too close to it to judge. I like your style, your natural simple English. That's an excellent description of the old lady's room in The Golden Linnet. I think

—'

But he was gone.

I have found later in his Journal this fragment, written at this time, probably just after his visit to me. (He touches in this on the two great never–

abandoning fears of his life.) 'I know that it is my cursed egotism that makes me so unhappy. After all, what does it matter if some young man has had false hopes and is not to be a writer who will astonish the world? Who, after all, ever astonishes the world for more than a moment? Yes—egotism. I know that I shall only be happy when I cease to think of myself, but how CAN a writer cease to think of himself when it is out of himself that he digs everything? Am I not continually driven in on myself?

'And oh God, I pray Thee not to let me find there, deep down in myself, what is perhaps my inheritance? Is my grandfather's blood not in me? And there is my poor mother still, as it often seems, with me. I can feel her move, when I am sleepless in the early morning hours, in my own belly as though she had returned to be my child.... Yes, and now I will be quite sensible, and having had a knock I will show myself how bravely I can take it. Because I know very well that I expected Westcott and Carstang and the others to be astonished by the stories. I had dramatized it to myself again and again, and how modest I would be and how quickly I would show them that if they liked THESE stories that was nothing to what I COULD do! Well, nothing has happened at all. No one likes them, has a good word to say in their favour, except Rose, whose praise somehow makes one uncomfortable. I can see that they think them trite, trivial, quite nothing. They will think the same of The

Walk of course. Meanwhile I am living here on Charlie, not making a penny, pretending to be in good spirits, but I know that I am frightened. How I long to be praised and liked and thought wonderful! Tears rush to my eyes if anyone shows that they like me, and I despise myself for being such a child. I was as old at ten as I am now, older perhaps. And I faced Reiner for three years with more courage than I have now.

'If it were not for Charlie what should I do, where should I go? People are good to me but it isn't enough. Why should I have these feelings, these longings in me when probably I am nothing, as Reiner said I was? Can't I hear him now, when he found those verses I had been writing?

'"You haven't a spark of talent! Do you think that if you had I wouldn't notice it? I'd forgive you for being such an ass if there was anything in you, but there isn't, there isn't! If you ever do publish anything people will only laugh at you...."

'Oh Lord, how real he is to me after all this time! How real all my past is to me! And he was right. I have published something and they see nothing in it.

They are kind but they see nothing. And they KNOW. They have been trained. Why do I care so terribly what people think, about myself, my character, my work? Why am I not sure of myself? I go like a little dog fawning at people's feet. "Oh, love me, love me!" I say. "Tell me I'm a genius." It is disgusting. I am ashamed. From to-night I will take a new resolution and be proud and independent and do my work quietly, sure of myself.'

Poor Johnny! He could talk to no one at this time of these things, for he would distress Charlie, and Ralph would not understand, and there was no one else in London whom he knew sufficiently well.

And yet, within a week of this self-abnegation, I was to see the other, the triumphant side of his nature. For, looking in one afternoon at tea-time, I found him in an ecstasy of happiness.

The Walk had been accepted by Wentworth and Gibbon, the first publishing house to which he had sent it.

He had thought that I was Charlie, come back from work. He stood there in the middle of the room, looking at the door, his bright eyes shining, his long nose all eagerness, the letter in his hand. His voice trembled.

'Oh, it's you! Come in, come in. Here—I'll take your coat.'

His hands trembled too, so that, as I remember, he dropped the coat.

'What is it, Cornelius?'

'Here. Listen to this.'

He read the letter, which was pompous, indulgent, long-winded. But the effect of it was that the firm of Wentworth and Gibbon had read Mr.

Cornelius' Walk from Merlin to St. Ladd with considerable interest, thought well of its prospects, would be willing to publish it, giving the author a ten per cent royalty after the sale of fifteen hundred copies, etc.

'They don't offer you very good terms.'

'Don't they? What do I care? They'll publish it, and without my having to pay anything. They're a magnificent firm. Didn't they publish the Brontës and Thackeray?'

'Yes, they're a good firm. But they want your next two books on the same terms.'

'Perhaps I shall sell thousands of copies.'

'Perhaps you will.' Then I felt grudging and ungracious. With Cornelius I was constantly forced to be paternal. ONLY with Cornelius? Perhaps not. I am, I fear, desperately avuncular.

But his happiness was something to witness. As with his unhappiness a short while before, so now his happiness had a kind of glow, an ecstasy like a flame rising, powerful, golden, triumphant, out of the freshly-piled logs. He reminded me at moments like these of Shelley, and it was a criticism of him that, after that, it should be of Leigh Hunt one thought.

'I'm delighted,' I said, taking his hand, looking into his face and thinking, 'I believe I love this man. He is so defenceless.'

He began to dance about the room, his long legs skipping, his arms waving.

He stopped abruptly in front of me.

'Don't you see that everything is all right now? I began to doubt myself the other day when you didn't like the fairy-stories.'

'I didn't say I didn't like them.'

'Oh, well, I knew what you were thinking. And perhaps you won't like this either. The Walk, I mean. But there must be something in it. The first publishers I had sent it to taking it....'

Charlie had come in. He stood at the door, his square body firmly balanced against the situation. For he saw instantly that there was one and that Johnny was wildly happy. But Johnny was wildly happy sometimes for such strange reasons!

'Read that, Charlie.... Read that!'

He did—with his usual slow, practical cautiousness, so that Cornelius was dancing with impatience.

'So they're going to publish it! That's fine.'

'Yes, and without my paying a penny. A real book. It will be in the shops.

Anyone can go in and buy a copy.... The papers will review it.'

I could see that Charlie was as happy in his own way as Johnny was in his. I expect that he had known a good many private anxieties about his friend in the past months. He never, either then or later, saw anything very particular in Cornelius' writing. But then he was never a great reader—except of newspapers.

It was about this time that something happened to Charlie Christian of great importance. He fell in love. The story must be briefly told. Charlie's account was short.

'Oh, aye—I used to go to that Lyons in Ludgate Circus. It was handy. One day I go in and sit at my usual table and there's a new girl. I looked at her and I liked her. After a week or so we had a talk. We went to the Tivoli one night and after that we were engaged. I told her about Johnny, though—that I'd always have to sort of look after him. She didn't mind. Gwen's sensible.'

Her own account was not much more lengthy:

'Oh, well, you know how it is. I'd been working further down the Strand, near Trafalgar Square. Then I was moved and the very first day I noticed Charlie. I remember what he ordered—Sausages and Mashed. "I always have sausages and mashed on a Thursday," he said. "Oh, do you?" I said. "And why's that?"

"Because it isn't Friday," he said. Saucy, and I was a bit on my dignity for a day or two. But I liked him. I couldn't help it. He was so clean. I noticed his finger-nails and he'd got hair the colour of a young duckling. That's what I told him. "Your hair's the colour of a young duckling," I said. He asked me whether I liked it and I said not so awfully and he said he didn't care whether I did or no. I liked his being so quiet, not talking so much and having such big shoulders. Strong, silent Englishman I used to call him. Then he wasn't too tall. I'm small myself and no small woman wants a big gawky man around. Then he said he liked brunettes. "Do you?" I says. "What's that to me?" But I was pleased all the same. Then he took me to the Tivoli. Oh, it was good too! Little Tich and Harry Weldon. I remember as though it was yesterday. He said, should we keep company? I knew by that time he was beginning to be an engineer and was steady and all that. So I said yes. I hadn't anyone but myself to think of, Father and Mother being dead. Then he told me about Mr. Cornelius, how he'd leave me or the kids or anything at a moment's notice if Mr. Cornelius wanted him. "Oh, would you?" I said, thinking a woman would always be more to a man than another man could be. But it turned out right what Charlie said. He'd leave anyone for Mr.

Cornelius any time, and the funny thing is, I didn't mind. Mr. Cornelius is different somehow from anyone else, isn't he? And Charlie's a good husband.

About the best ever lived, I think.'

Thus and thus this simple familiar story. Gwen and Charlie were fine, though.

There was something very restful about both of them. No other country breeds people quite like that, quite so faithful, quite so loyal, quite so

honestly unimaginative.

Well, then. The Walk was published January 22nd, 1907. It was bound in a claret-coloured red, a handsome dignified volume for six shillings, four-and-

six net. First edition one thousand copies. Dedication: TO THE MEMORY

OF

MY MOTHER

It is, of course, extremely rare now; a copy in any bright and fine condition almost unattainable.

Westcott and I did, this time, see something in Cornelius' talent. We realized that he had a startling imagination, but the imagination of a child. He had a wonderful gift for personifying everything, 'flowers, fruits, and thorns,'

animals, children. All these things he loved and he could paint beautiful and fairy-like landscapes so long as he need not deal with anything that he disliked. Everything hostile to him in nature became like the witch or the ogre in the fairy-story. Neither then nor ever could he create a mature, saddened, disillusioned, sordid world. I saw in this book for the first time that he had great powers of creation so long as he was allowed to make his own world.

The world of War and Peace, Tom Jones, Le Rouge et le Noir, The Magic Mountain is everybody's world. No one who has had any experience of life can deny the truth and actuality in those books. But in works like The Walk or Pierre or Wuthering Heights you must bow to your author graciously, wave your hand, and say, 'Please make your own conditions and terms. If you are entertaining enough I will accept them.'

So it was with The Walk. Here, I now realized, was a new personality in English literature, but a personality that would seem absurd and unreal to many persons.

So, in a small way, now it already proved. For a week or two there was not a

single notice in the papers, save two lines somewhere saying: 'An unreal journey in an impossible Glebeshire.'

Johnny behaved well during this difficult time. An author whose first book has been accepted feels an elation and a glory. From the day of its publication, however, he learns how many other authors there are in this busy, heedless world and how many many other subjects than his talents newspapers, even very literary ones, have to consider. Then came a review in the Daily Hour, a review written by someone even more romantic than Johnny. It might have been written by Simeon Rose himself—indeed for a moment we thought that it was. 'This is a masterpiece,' the reviewer wrote. 'A masterpiece of sunshine and tears.' 'Masterpiece' was Rose's favourite word.

But he denied the accusation. As a matter of fact he had liked the four fairy-

tales better than The Walk.

Johnny showed his character when he read this review. It wasn't indiscriminate praise that he wanted. No. He made that discovery, common to all artists, that nothing causes such frightening self- suspicion as foolish praise.

Then came Stromberg. Karl Stromberg plays an important part in Cornelius'

story and, although now he is entirely forgotten, an important part in the history of English letters, 1900-1920. He was a big, fat, pot-bellied, unshaven, drunken German brought to England when a baby, deserted by mother and father, adopted by that ill-living bastard of a 'nineties poet, Crestin, dragged up into a youth of pubs, police-courts, harlots and roving journalism. He was a realist all right, Stromberg was! He revolted like hell against the whole of the viols, roses and lilies of Dowson, Pater, Lionel Johnson and Wilde. He became a critic on the Saturday, preached Stendhal and Ibsen and Havelock Ellis, was one of Crabbe's, F.A.C.'s, most ardent champions, slaughtered Romanticism whenever he saw it.

By 1907 he had become a power. In three excellent columns of concentrated abuse he slaughtered The Walk.

Cornelius, of course, as soon as he read it, thought the thing personal. Every author thinks an adverse review of his book personal. He went cold at the heart, poor Johnny, when he read it.

'I stood there, in my pyjamas. Charlie was sitting at the table eating his eggs and bacon before he went off to work. He looked at me and said: "What's up?" I read him some of the choicest bits. I don't, of course, remember the exact words now, but you know the sort of thing. I DO remember two phrases though: "Pretentious curds and whey" and "Papier-mâché moonshine."

'I had never seen Charlie so angry before. He wanted to go straight off, find Stromberg and punch his head. But of course that wasn't any use. When you're young and unsure of yourself and your whole life seems to depend on some sort of recognition, scorn and contempt like that from someone in authority cuts deep into your flesh. What I hated was the thought that anyone COULD dislike me so much. I seemed to myself so harmless, so inoffensive.

And always, on an occasion like this, I think of Mrs. Hoskin. It was as though Mrs. Hoskin had written that review....

'And then I began to wonder how I could have offended him. Had I met him anywhere? Had I turned my back on him, absent-mindedly, without knowing it? When I first read it, it had not seemed very serious. In fact I laughed at Charlie for his indignation. But at night in bed I saw the scornful sentences in letters of flame. I saw everyone in London reading them. I saw myself doomed and damned for ever....'

Very foolish. We learn wisdom through cynical and deriding experience. As a matter of truth Stromberg had no personal feeling against Cornelius, either then or later. But he sniffed, in the first five pages of The Walk, that, to him, filthy and degrading odour of romanticism, the sentiment, the water-colour scenery, the longing for the Hero, the, to him, senseless, childish division of Sheep and Goats, the appeal to God, the belief in the powers of Evil.

Knowing nothing of Cornelius he chose The Walk as his text. And so the feud began.

The Walk, in spite of Stromberg, had considerable success—not a wild success but enough to make Cornelius' name a known one in places where they read. Moreover, in 1907, the literary race was not so frantically to the swift as it is to-day. Your book was not swallowed by a flood of new books only a fortnight after publication. The lives of readers were quieter, the critics did not work under so desperate a pressure.

The Walk was in the bookshop windows. There were, in all, some sixty reviews. It sold, within the first nine months, nine hundred and fifty-six copies. It stopped then completely. Johnny, therefore, made not a penny of profit, but was rather the loser by the bill for Three pounds, twelve shillings and sixpence that he paid for his typing.

This is the full and complete history of Cornelius' Walk from Merlin to St.

Ladd.

It was about this time, I think, in the early spring of 1907, that I began to feel the drama of Cornelius' personality and history. Outwardly, so far as any of us knew at that time, there was nothing very astonishing in a young boy from the country coming up to London to try his literary fortunes. There was also nothing very extraordinary about The Walk nor about its reception. But you couldn't help but begin to be fond of Cornelius and interested in his future.

He was so frank, so generous, often so foolish. He flattered perhaps one's pride in one's own maturity.

'Dear old Johnny,' we began soon to say. 'Fancy his giving that old rip Baldwin some money. He did it before anyone could stop him.' And he hadn't any money. One of the most annoying things about him was that he would borrow a pound or two from you and then give it to some quite worthless sponger. Nor can I say that he was meticulous about repaying debts. In fact he never DID repay them. Just as he gave away any money HE had, so he took from you gladly any money YOU had. Indeed he considered money quite unimportant. 'Who steals my purse steals trash.'

He not only gave away money but also anything that he happened to possess: anything in the world, I fancy, save the photographs of Charlie and Anne—

and Yin. I gave him, I remember, that Christmas of 1906, a rather beautiful ivory carving of a mother and child and an inhumanly intelligent stork. A few weeks later Westcott and I were in his room, and Westcott, pointing to the ivory figure, said: 'That's charming.'

Johnny said: 'You can have it if you like.'

Myself: ' *I* gave it you!'

Johnny: 'Oh, I'm sorry! I'm awfully fond of it, but Westcott's such a friend of yours. If he likes it I thought you wouldn't mind his having it.'

Myself (secretly chagrined): 'Oh, not at all. Give it to anyone you like.'

Nor, if one was hurt, did he ever do anything to help the situation. If you were his friend you were his friend for life and he could not therefore believe that any of your grievances against him could be important. This little characteristic was, I think, at the root of all his trouble with Carstang.

Carstang, who was faithful to nobody, never even began to understand Cornelius' kind of fidelity.

And here comes in a scene which helped me to understand many things about Cornelius.

We—Johnny, Rose, Carstang and myself—were up in his attic room on a March afternoon when Spring made a tentative visit to London, looked around her for an hour or two, scattered some primroses and white violets, tempted some Italians into raucous song, strewed some opaque white clouds upon a gentle blue sky with ruffles of wind in it, made the sparrows a little drunk with expectation, found she was much too early and hurriedly withdrew before a dark stormy evening. This is the kind of pretty writing that belongs, I feel, rather to Rose's style than my own. When Rose begins his literary dithyrambs I can hear him cataloguing to himself: 'Item one green-

leaved tree, very old; two lambs skipping, water of pool misted as though seen through glass, two green clouds,' or possibly Albion with every word of his descriptive prose determining that it shall be part of a great English Epic

—and that urgent self-consciousness, that determination to be both fine and important is precisely what is wrong both with Rose and with Albion.

My own piece of fine writing here is, however, not self-conscious at all, for I had written it before I knew it, my gaze being entirely fixed on Cornelius.

'A good piece to cut out on revision,' any critic can say anywhere, but on further reflection I can see how rightly that hour or two of a London spring was part of Cornelius that day and part of what was to happen to him about a quarter of an hour after Carstang began to read his letter.

Johnny was sitting at the window under the slope of the roof, looking out at the absurd, agitated, bundling little clouds that sailed above the chimneys, carrying with them, I suggest, a faint odour of soot, damp laundry and wet spring primroses. Johnny sat there while Carstang baited Rose, who had just said that he wished, oh, how he wished that he were a better writer!

Carstang swore a horrible indecent oath.

'You're like a harlot who sells her body to any comer—you and your false modesty.'

Rose looked like an Archdeacon who sees a dead cat in the gutter.

'We all wish we were better writers,' he said.

'We don't care!' Carstang shouted. 'We don't bloody well care!'

'YOU care! You care horribly! You think you're a misunderstood genius!'

'I am! I AM a genius! That's better than being a snivelling hermaphrodite.

You should hear Bertrand describe you.'

'I like Bertrand.'

'Oh, God! you like everybody. And you like them all the better if they take your pants down and whip your backside. You're a masochist.'

Rose looked rather pleased at that.

'Perhaps I am. Maybe. I wonder.' He sat, his round face a little flushed with interest, staring at himself.

'Oh, God! You make me sick!' Then Carstang turned round to Cornelius, who was sitting on the window-ledge, twisting and untwisting his long thin legs, his big nose thrusting out into that spring moment, hearing the barrel-organ, smelling the lilac, seeing his Bird-Man walking the roads and scattering his seed…. And I saw, as I had seen before, Carstang's strange priest-like face with the close-cropped head, the strong shining glasses hiding eyes, take a sudden tenderness, a gentleness; for Carstang recognized that here was somebody finer in spirit and in talent than himself.

'Listen to this letter,' he said, and he took out of his pocket a paper covered with that green formal writing so especially his.

He read standing, his strong thin legs spread out, his thick glasses catching the words. (I own the letter with the majority of Carstang's manuscripts.)

'DEAR BULLIN—Your letter is exactly the kind of thing I WOULD expect from a weak, snivelling, pusillanimous cur like yourself. You're the sort of man would strip his mother bare in the market– place and rob a blind man of his last piece of toilet–paper. But if you think you can cheat a man like myself of what rightfully belongs to him and get away with it, you're mightily mistaken. I will drag you by the heels before all the courts of the world before I'm finished with you. There is a letter or two you've written in your time you wouldn't exactly like published in every English newspaper, would you? Look out then, and give me my proper dues. The kind of cur you are is afraid of public justice. But you'll be sorry before I've finished with you or I'm mightily mistaken in you.

'Your scornful contemner,

'Philip Crawford Carstang.'

'Lord!' I remember remarking. 'How you authors do love one another!'

But Cornelius had turned from the window and was standing looking at Carstang.

'Didn't Bullin help you—get you out of an awful hole—a year or two ago?'

'Oh, that's what he's saying, is he?' Carstang retorted. 'He would! As a matter of fact all he did—'

'Didn't he and his wife keep you for months, feed you, clothe you? Didn't Bullin go to Herly and get him to take those short stories? Didn't ... '

'Oh, you're a friend of Bullin's, are you?' I remember that Carstang now was looking all that the melodramatists picture the Prince of Evil, with his lip

curled, his forehead wrinkled like a snake's skin, and his dead–white glasses.

'I didn't know.'

'But,' Cornelius went on, his voice rising to that high pitch he used when he was excited, 'it's dreadful to write a letter like that to someone—'

And then the bell rang. Cornelius stopped. I went and opened the door.

Standing there was a tall, strong–looking young woman in a little round fur hat and a grey fur jacket. She walked straight into the room. Cornelius saw her and ran to her, caught her, held her, cried again and again: 'Anne! Anne!

Anne!'

I saw in that first moment that she loved him, and had long loved him. I saw that Johnny was so happy that he had forgotten Carstang and myself and all of us. Carstang saw that too, for he walked out of the room, banging the door behind him.

Anne was introduced to Rose and myself.

'Oh,' she said, staring at Rose. 'Are you the Simeon Rose who wrote Fidelity?'

'I am,' said Rose.

'Oh, I can't tell you how it's helped me. That sentence: "It's not fidelity of the spoken word that matters but of the spirit." How fine, how true!'

Johnny and I burst out laughing.

She turned to us. 'Why, what's the matter? Have I said anything?'

'Only Rose has been teased to death about that sentence. He'll hate you for mentioning it.'

'Oh, will he?' She turned wide eyes on us. 'But it's true. It HAS helped me.

You know,' she said, turning to Rose, 'I've known Johnny all his life and he's NEVER liked the books I have.'

Rose took it all very well. He is fundamentally a good creature.

Johnny said: 'But why are you here?'

He was so happy that he couldn't keep still. He danced about, he smiled and laughed and sang.

'I've come to London to stay. I'm Mr. Schleuert's secretary.'

'What! James Schleuert the picture-dealer, the—'

'James Schleuert the picture-dealer,' she interrupted.

'Whew!' Johnny whistled. 'But his reputation—'

'Yes,' Anne said quietly, 'his reputation—'

'Oh, what does it matter?' Johnny cried, going to her, putting his arms round her, dancing some steps with her.

She wasn't beautiful, I remember deciding. Too heavy, too big- boned, her face too massive. Her hair was braided and coiled on the top of her head, Scandinavian-fashion. She looked good, honest, friendly, wise. She was all these things—except wise. Or was she wise perhaps after all?

In her grey fur coat there was a small bunch of white violets. The sun and the London smoke and the faint out-of-tune note of the barrel-organ streamed in through the open window.

I thought of Carstang and Charlie and Anne. As I passed Cornelius, on my way to the door, I laid my hand for a moment lightly on his shoulder.

CHAPTER VI

Marriage

I first met Mercia Otterstone somewhere in November 1908. I have looked in my diary but cannot discover the place of our first meeting nor the exact date.

My story begins to be very difficult here because of my most earnest effort to be fair to Mercia. She is gone, poor Mercia, and will care very little about the things I say of her.

But it is essential that I should be fair to her and I did dislike her so very much. I am afraid that the word here should be something very much stronger than 'dislike.'

They say that death closes all debts, but she possessed so vivid a personality that she seems, so soon as I think of her, to be with me in the room. I can see her seated in the armchair near my table, engaged, I know, in reading the important book of the moment and, even while she is so engaged, thinking hard and fast about herself, her immediate position and the things that must be done to strengthen it.

I half turn in my chair and say: 'Well, Mercia?' and she looks quickly up at me with that bright, friendly, maternal, assured smile and in her rich deep voice answers:

'Don't disturb me, you wicked man. This is a remarkable book. No doubt of it.'

I see her lovely gold-red hair, bobbed or whatever it was called in 1921 or 1922. I see her rich opulent figure with the large firm breasts, the strong arms and legs. I see her full bright-blue eyes, her clear skin, her red lips, her freshness and strength, her vitality—and oh! how I hate and detest her!

The odd thing always was that SHE liked ME. I was the only one, I think, of

John's close friends whom she really liked. She was perfectly aware of my dislike of her. She used to say: 'He hates me, of course, but it makes no difference. I can't help liking him.' Although almost every word that she ever spoke was false, this was, I believe, really sincere. She would even fight my battles behind my back. When people said that I was garrulous and a bore and pleased with myself and couldn't write for toffee, she would answer, so I've been told: 'Yes, but he's honest. You know where you are with him. He's the only one of John's friends I trust. They are the most awful lot, you know.'

It was, of all people in the world, Peter Westcott who introduced her to John, a deed for which he never forgave himself. He met her and her old father somewhere and she had read the Merlin book. She spoke of it and said, did he know the author, and Peter, always anxious to do something for John, thought that because old Mr. Otterstone was rich he might be a help. So he brought Mercia to one of John's parties.

John and Charlie were at that time having difficult days. John was finishing his novel The Sorcerer and at the same time moving about the world taking everything in. There was so very much to absorb that he did not care whether he ate or where he slept.

Charlie managed to pay the rent. John had a theory just then that it was cheaper to be a vegetarian. He looked under this diet odder than ever, longer and thinner and uglier. He was very happy, I fancy; believed completely in himself, although he had by now learnt to speak to his closer friends only about his genius. We in return believed in HIM, and all of us—even Carstang

—were sure that The Sorcerer would be something quite wonderful. What we none of us even remotely considered was that he would marry Mercia Otterstone.

How, why did the dreadful tragic thing ever occur?

Old Mr. Otterstone was a spindly-legged, bald-headed, vague-eyed gentleman who had 'retired' from the City, where he had made a great deal of money. He was a widower and Mercia was his only daughter. He was a perfectly happy old gentleman who collected stamps, attended cricket-

matches in the summer and had a passion for Crime. He knew to the smallest detail every nerve and sinew of the Palmer, Jessie Maclachlan and other

notorious trials. When he told you about them he was interesting in his power to make them live for you. He liked his daughter so long as she left him alone and he gave her anything that she asked for.

Now WHY did Mercia marry John Cornelius? He was penniless and at the age of twenty-five anything but famous. He was ugly, absent-minded, egoistic. He had a sweet, generous, absurdly unselfish nature, but she did not especially care for those things. What did she think she was GETTING by marrying him? I asked her that question once and she answered: 'Why, what I've got, of course— Johnny.' She never, from first to last, admitted that the marriage was a failure, anything but perfect. That perhaps was not remarkable because everything that she had was perfect. Her self-

complacency was only equalled by her obtuseness, and her obtuseness by her acquisitiveness. Once she owned anything she never let it go again.

She had a passion for what she thought was the cultured world, and I expect that she had for some time before meeting Johnny been on the look-out for an author or painter or musician. She cared passionately for the cultured world but nothing at all for culture, just as she was always the 'mother' to all her friends but had really nothing maternal in her spirit. It was always astonishing to me that she was able to deceive so many people.

Women adored her and that especially because they could come and pour out to her all their troubles. She would listen to them for hours and, as she listened to them, her sense of her own importance grew and grew. Very seldom, I think, did she hear anything that they said, but no one who pours out confidences notices whether there is a response or no. She gave no real response to anybody, for she had no warmth of either curiosity or feeling. She had an egotism so colossal that nothing could penetrate it, no suffering, no need, no anger.

She was never annoyed, never lost her temper. When she disliked people, as she disliked Anne and Charlie and Carstang, they simply passed out of her ken. Because in one way or another they offended her egotism they were simply dead to her.

She saw Johnny, I think, as an artist who was exactly the figure for her scene.

He was ugly, shambling, helpless, possibly a genius. He was a perfect object

for the exhibition of her maternal care. And it was so. Soon after the marriage her friends were to say again and again: 'She mothers him; he is exactly like her child.' And later, when he was famous, one heard constantly: 'If it hadn't been for Mercia ... '

She was wonderfully clever at a sort of façade of phrases, sentences.... She was always in the movement. She was always watching for new names and new faces. She was not a lion-hunter; she never bothered herself to go out and bring anyone in, but people came to her house because she was always so bright and kind and understanding.

'Nothing ever puts Mercia Cornelius out. That's what I like about her. She's always cheerful, so understanding.'

In 1908 she was known as one of 'Meredith's women' because she was big and tall and moved gracefully. After the War she was a 'good sort; you can say anything to Mercia. She cheers you up just looking at her. She's so jolly and warm-hearted and generous.'

But she wasn't jolly or warm-hearted or generous in the least. She was as cold as an ice-box.

And why, oh, why, did Johnny marry HER? Because, I have always thought, she reminded him of his mother. She must have resembled poor Mrs.

Cornelius in build and colour. The only thing that he himself ever told me was that he felt 'at home' with her. Perhaps he saw himself back in the cottage at Merlin and Mercia's arms round him, his head on her splendid bosom. But I fancy that the true reason was that, once she had made up her mind to marry him, Johnny was lost. He was so busy at this time, as I have already said,

'taking everything in.' London, literature, music, the theatre, the skies and streets and setting suns. And then he never could resist anyone who was kind to him. It was not likely that he would understand her real nature; no, not for a long time to come. He did at last understand it fully....

Could any of us have prevented this horrible thing? Anne and Charlie disliked and distrusted her from the first moment, but it all happened so very quickly. We hadn't any idea ... We never dreamt ...

I looked in one late afternoon, a steamy sultry June day when behind the grey sky there was a red glow and all the chimney-pots seemed to have double edges and the roofs white steel linings—June 14th, 1909; I have found it in my Diary. Anne Swinnerton and Charlie were there—no Johnny. This was the day in which I was to know something about Anne, to reach some contact with her for the first time. I remember that she was in some pale-coloured dress and that I thought, as I came in at the door, 'What a kind woman that is!'

Charlie was in his shirt-sleeves, sitting at the table and drawing some kind of a bridge for Anne. Wherever Charlie was there was quiet and reassurance. I had myself been flustered and disturbed that day by some little trouble in my affairs and by the heat. The first sight of the two of them, the room, Yin on the mantelpiece— and my agitation withdrew. Charlie smiled at me and then continued: 'You see, Anne, you put a girder there ... '

'Where's Johnny?' I asked.

'He went to lunch with Mercia Otterstone.'

We looked at one another and, for the first time, publicly confessed.

'We all detest her, don't we?' I said cheerfully.

'We do that,' said Charlie.

I came over and looked at his drawing.

'I wonder why,' I said. 'She's kind, cheerful, clever....

'She's none of those things,' Anne said. 'She's a real bitch.'

In 1909 that word was considered (why I've no idea) most shocking. No lady would dream of using it. But we were, neither of us, shocked; Charlie because such things never shocked him, I because I agreed with Anne so profoundly.

'She's a bitch all right,' Charlie said, his big round head on one side considering his drawing.

I remember then that there was a flash of lightning and Yin seemed to dance on the mantelpiece. Johnny stood, most dramatically, in the doorway. He was grinning all over his face.

'I'm engaged to be married,' he said. It was characteristic of him that he never for a moment considered that to Anne and Charlie this would be a terrible piece of news. He was quite sure that because he was radiantly happy they would be radiantly happy too. Years after he said to me: 'One of the most callous, selfish things I ever did was breaking in that day and telling Charlie and Anne about my engagement to Mercia.'

Charlie was himself engaged to be married and Anne was openly mistress to one of the most notorious men in London, so they couldn't, I suppose, complain. But the point was that, for them and for myself, Johnny was something special. Even I, who had known him so brief a while as life goes, felt that.

We asked him who was the lady. He said: 'Mercia Otterstone.' He moved about the room, half dancing on his long feet, cracking his fingers. Then he turned to us, like a child, almost with his fingers in his mouth.

'The funny thing is,' he said, 'SHE proposed. Oh, I oughtn't to say that! But it doesn't matter with you three. She said—we were sitting in the Green Park

—"Why don't you marry me, Johnny?" She's so kind to me. There's nothing I wouldn't do ... ' Then he looked at us dubiously. 'People will say I'm marrying her for her money.'

What could we answer him? We had, a moment before, agreed that Mercia was a bitch. But now, with all three of us, came, I know, the same sensation: one of real overwhelming calamity. Yes, even to me—calamity. What it must have been to the other two ... for they had been together almost since they were babies. They were almost three parts of one whole. The two of them had watched over him and cared for him through every stage. Charlie had protected him always; Anne loved him as she loved no other human on earth.

It was at her that I was now looking. She made for me an inevitable antithesis to the other woman. I didn't as yet know her, but physically she was everything that Mercia was not—dark and strong in her colouring, free and honest in her movements, clear-sighted, direct, courageous. In a novel you

mustn't allow your characters to be so black and so white. Well, Anne had many faults; Mercia, I am sure, many virtues. You can see, clearly enough, how badly prejudiced I am.

But what could we do? Johnny was so sure that we were happy, because he was. He came over and put one arm around Anne and the other around Charlie.

'Wish me luck,' he said.

Anne half turned, caught his head in her hand, bent it towards her and kissed his forehead.

'Of course I do—now and always—in everything.'

But he was too wildly excited to stay still. He threw his long arms round Charlie and hugged him. Then he strode up and down the room.

'The first thing I said was: "I must tell Anne and Charlie. They're like part of me."'

'She must have loved that,' I remember Anne saying; but it was the only sarcastic word she spoke.

'She was very nice about both of you. Although of course she doesn't know you yet.'

It was then that he suddenly stopped and looked at Charlie. For the first time perhaps he considered the matter from Charlie's point of view.

'You like her, don't you, Charlie?'

But Charlie could not lie, and he was more pigheaded in his opinions than Saul.

'I don't know her,' he said, looking down at his drawing.

'Oh, you will!' A look of almost incredible sweetness came into Johnny's eyes. 'I'll give you everything you want,' he said to Charlie. 'You've kept this

place going. You've given me everything. Now it will be my turn.'

'Aye,' said Charlie. 'With her money.'

'No. With my own. I haven't been able to work so well, knowing I was such a burden to you. Now—the things I'll do—'

'You've been no burden.'

There was a silence, I remember, and Anne broke it by saying brightly: 'Well, I must be getting along.' She went up to Johnny and kissed him again, this time on the lips. 'You must be very happy. Very, very happy,' she said. He felt then, I think, that there was some kind of parting going on between himself and Anne and Charlie.

'It will make no difference, not a scrap of difference,' he said. 'You won't let it, will you? Mercia's so kind. She wants everyone to be happy.'

He kissed Anne and then went and sat down by Charlie, his hand on his shoulder.

'I'll be going along with you,' I said to Anne.

When we were in the street we could hear the thunder rolling in the distance and every once and again a fat plopping raindrop fell. She was in terrible distress.

'It's awful. It's dreadful. It's awful. That's what it is.'

'Yes,' I said.

'Oh, why, why did he do it?'

'Two reasons I can guess at,' I answered. 'One—she reminds him of his mother, whom he adored. The other—SHE wanted it.'

'But WHY did she want it? Johnny's ugly, uncouth, awkward. He's not a success. He's nobody. It's only we who love him, who see what he is.'

'He has great charm,' I answered. 'He has the maturity of some kind of genius, even though his work doesn't show it yet. At the same time he's a child. She's wanted for a long time, I'm sure, to marry some kind of artist. She'll mother him before the world.

She doesn't want to marry a rich man or an ordinary man. There's another thing—very important. She's cold sexually, I'm sure.

She doesn't want to marry anyone who will make too many demands on her in that way.'

Then I saw something that distressed me very much. Anne was crying. I put my hand on her arm.

'I'm dreadfully sorry.'

She threw up her head.

'I've loved him all my life,' she said. 'That's why, I suppose, I live as I do. It doesn't seem to matter what happens to me as long as I'm always there for Johnny if he wants me. It's as Mr. Rose said in his book: "It's not fidelity of the spoken word that matters." And Schleuert's not a bad sort. Really he isn't.

He's most awfully kind. And I give him something that he wants. I'm helping him. I don't want to be married ever. I don't feel that it's immoral to live with a man if you don't hurt anyone else. My mother ... ' She broke off. 'But now, if I lose Johnny ... '

'You won't lose him. He'll need you more than ever.'

'Oh, do you think so?'

We were at the St. James's Street turning off Piccadilly. She turned, smiled at me, gave me her hand. 'I go down here to Westminster. Thank you so much. I feel that I've made a new friend to-day.'

'Indeed you have,' I answered.

From this moment onwards we three—Anne, Charlie and myself—were involved in a most curious drama. Somehow we had to see to it that we didn't lose Johnny. I was a minor element in the situation because I was in no way as close to Johnny as they were. Nevertheless I was, at this moment, very

important because only I, of the three, could really approach Mercia. I have said already that she liked me and I think that, from the first, she looked on me as the one who would help her with Johnny. Because, to do her justice, she saw from the very beginning that she would have her difficulties with him. She wanted him to be her child before the world, but at the same time she didn't want to be SO odd and farouche that people would think him mad and herself a little mad for marrying him. So she started at once to change him, and she invited me to help her.

She lived with her father in a nice little house, 17 Errington Street, not far from Hyde Park Corner. She possessed the little house exactly; it possessed HER quality of assured niceness and up- to-dateness and soullessness.

Everything was right in it. Pictures by the right young painters of the day—

Baughan and Forster and Whiting—hung on the walls. In the quiet pastel-

shaded drawing-room were the latest works of the Great Three—Christopher Falling, Bernard Topping and Roughwood. She was marvellously up to the moment, subscribing to the support of young H. B. Terence, who declared quietly that, being a genius, he MUST be supported. She had just the right attitude to Rose and Albion, that they were popular and so not quite good enough. She marvellously sniffed in the air the coming reaction against Falling and his Bodsworth family.

She entertained most capably. Her parties were always amusing. Many people came to them, but always as though they were eager to come, not at all because she wanted them. I never knew anyone with so many admiring friends.

At once the reactions to her strange engagement could be heard abroad.

At some party, a week after its announcement, I overheard something like this:

'But surely it's the oddest thing for Mercia to do. She might have married ANYBODY!'

'Ah, but she just doesn't want to marry anybody!'

'I hear he's too strange for words—and hideously ugly. And his mother was a

washerwoman.'

'Yes. That's just like Mercia. She has to be kind to someone. She's only happy being kind. And they say he has extraordinary talent. She'll make a good job of it, you'll see.'

She was determined to. She gave the appearance of being radiantly happy and all-conquering. It might have been the Duke of Westminster she was marrying, not the ugly, awkward, penniless son of a washerwoman. And not only was Johnny these things, but a little difficult also. I happened to be present at one of the first of her difficult moments.

Mercia had given a little dinner-party at the Imperial Palace. Her guests were John, myself, the two Albions and old Myra Nettleton, the lady whom Bertrand always described as 'the virgin novelist of the 'nineties.' I must say one word about the Albions. In 1909 he was becoming very rapidly famous.

He and his sister, Mary Albion, were known by everyone as the 'Tweedles.'

For one thing they presented physically an absurd likeness. They were short, square, rosy-faced, sallow-haired. Secondly they were never apart, except, one supposes, at night. They further resembled Tweedledum and Tweedledee in their intense seriousness. Claude Albion lived a dedicated life as the novelist of England. It was his ambition in 1909 to present in novel form every aspect of English life, and now, in 1936, he may be said to have done that, several aspects a good many times over. (He has seen the paragraphs in this book that apply to himself and has no objection to them.) The Albions must of necessity be mentioned in any work concerning Cornelius because they were the earliest of all the convinced believers in his genius.

From the moment of reading the Merlin travel-book they had no doubts.

They were never close friends of Cornelius. They were sufficient to themselves always, but they were, utterly and altogether, John's champions, and their hatred, openly manifested, a little later than this, for Carstang, Karl Stromberg, Bertrand, was a fine thing to witness.

I don't like Albion's later novels nor does he like mine, but he is, still, with his sister to-day one of the finest defenders of the despised and rejected I know.

Well, we had a dreadfully dull dinner, and at last Mercia, Johnny and I agreed that we would walk some of the way home (it was a lovely June evening), said good-bye to everyone and started off along the Strand.

After a while we cut through King William Street and there, just outside the shuttered windows of Bain's bookshop, we came upon a very drunken, battered and bleeding old man.

At first we thought that he was seriously injured, possibly dying, and were about to summon a policeman. His beard was muddied, his cheek bleeding, and he could not, it seemed, move one leg. But he raised his head, fixed us with a swimming and glittering eye, and said 'Bloody hell to all of you.'

Mercia was disgusted. This was exactly the kind of incident for which she had no use. There was no point at all in being maternal to so disgusting an object as this, nor was there anyone new present to be impressed by her kindness.

She hailed a taxi-cab.

'We can't leave him like this,' I said.

But Johnny was on his knees, had his arms round the old man and was wiping the wounded cheek with his own handkerchief.

Mercia, very splendid in her white cloak and jewels in her hair, showed for once a real disgust.

'Johnny, please—not in the street.... We'll put him in this cab and send him to the hospital. As a matter of fact the Charing Cross is just across the street.'

'I won't go to a bloody hospital,' the old man said, looking at her with extreme malevolence.

'Where's your home?' Johnny asked.

'Come along with me and I'll show you,' the old man said.

As a matter of fact we did go along with him, Johnny and I, and this was Mercia Otterstone's first battle with her Johnny. A very brief one.

Mercia said: 'Surely you're not—'

But Johnny never listened to her. I stopped another passing cab and Mercia got into it. I have said that I never once saw her angry, but on this occasion, for one brief moment, as she said goodnight to me from the window of the cab, there was an expression in her large, blue eyes that made me sorry for her. For Johnny had paid no attention to her at all. He never even said good-

night. He was absorbed in the old man as though he had recovered a long-

lost friend. A very horrible old man he was. We took him into the cab and he became very jocular in spite of his wounds, singing and sneezing and pouring out a flood of filth. We found at last his dirty room somewhere near Ludgate Hill. We undressed him, washed him and put him to bed. In bed he sat up and demanded drinks, which we refused him. He cursed us heartily and then sneezed and sneezed. He said he had a bloody cold. Then Johnny astonished me by saying that he intended to stay all night. I asked him why. Well, he said, there was no one there to look after the old man and he couldn't walk on one leg and he needed some things (he did indeed!).

'And you know,' Johnny said, 'I may be this way myself one day.'

So I left him and on my road home reflected that Mercia did not know the half of what she was marrying....

I suppose that she did not, but during these first years at least there is no doubt whatever that Johnny loved her. He loved a good many people in the course of his life and it was their fault, and theirs alone, if they lost his love.

But he never loved beyond reason, as many women and some men do. If the reasons went then the love went too.

As the wedding–day (September 8th, 1909: St. George's, Hanover Square) approached, Johnny grew ever happier and happier. They were to go to Italy for the honeymoon. He had never until now left England's shores. He finished The Sorcerer in a blaze of glory. 'I think,' he said to me, 'I've brought it off this time. There are things in it that no one, NO ONE, has ever done before.'

That in fact turned out to be true. He was like a puppy in his ungainly happiness. He was never very perceptive when he was happy, so he took in very little of the things that Mercia told him.

This, beyond question, disturbed her. He was harder to change than she had supposed. So she invited Peter Westcott and myself to tea.

'It's about John.'

'Yes,' we said.

She looked at us with that warm indulgent smile of hers as though we were indeed her children and would shortly, if we were good, be allowed to play with our soldiers before going to bed.

'I want you to keep this little talk to yourselves. It's all in confidence.'

'Why, of course.'

'There's nothing disloyal to John. I'm only saying to you what I've said to him.' She wrinkled her broad smooth brow. 'There are one or two things that worry me. You are both great friends of his. Perhaps you can help me.'

'Anything we can do ... '

'Well—in the first place, one or two of his friends ... Oh, I'm not a snob. It's the very last thing that I am. But when he lives here with father and me ...

There's Mr. Christian for instance. Oh, I know John's devoted to him—'

'They've been friends from childhood,' I interrupted.

'Of course, I know. But he's so very silent. Almost sinister. I think he hates me.'

She paused. Neither of us said a word.

'He isn't comfortable in this house. He hates coming here. John doesn't realize that.'

'It's funny,' Westcott said slowly. 'When I was married—centuries ago, you know—I had the same problem. My wife had, I mean. There was a fisherman friend of mine, Stephen. He came up to London with me and my wife didn't like it—'

He stopped abruptly.

'Oh, don't think that I want to stop John having his own friends here. That's a mistake wives do make, I know. On the contrary, I want him to have his friends....' She looked at us confidingly. 'It's only that Mr. Christian dislikes me so. And then there's that other man—he keeps a public-house ... '

'Ralph,' I said. 'He was one of Johnny's best friends when he was deserted by everybody. He's a splendid fellow.'

'Oh, I'm sure he is. I'm the last person to forget old friends. He's very interesting, I believe. He was butler to all sorts of famous people, wasn't he?

And he won't come here. John's asked him but he refuses. Only now—if John goes to his public-house in the evenings it's a little awkward for me, isn't it?'

I liked her better than I ever had before. She was facing a real problem.

'Johnny's very difficult to change, I fancy,' I said. 'And he's a very loyal man.'

'Then there's that dreadful man Mr. Carstang', she went on. 'He's truly appalling. John brought him here one day and I can stand a good deal, but his indecency, and the noise he made, and the way he stamped about! He shall never enter this house again.'

'He's a bit cracked, of course,' said Westcott. 'But then there's something the matter with all of us. *I* drink, he' (nodding towards me) 'beats little girls—'

'Really, Mr. Westcott,' Mercia said, laughing. 'I'm afraid you'll think me narrow-minded and a snob. But I'm not. Really I'm not. All I want is for John to be happy. And everyone else too. Only Mr. Christian and the others—they AREN'T happy when they come here. I don't want to CHANGE John. I love him. I like him just as he is. The only thing—perhaps I should like him a little tidier. I think,' she said, looking at us both with calm protective friendliness,

'I'm extraordinarily lucky to have won the affection of a man of genius like John.'

As we walked away Westcott said: 'Why, why, why ... '

'Why what?' I asked.

'Why is Johnny doing it? It isn't physical nor mental nor spiritual ... '

'It's because,' I said, 'she puts her arms round him. He rests his head on her breast. She gives him a home; she's kind. She's his mother come to life again.

If he hadn't known Anne all his life, then perhaps the finest thing in the world might have happened to him. As it is—'

'As it is—it's awful,' Westcott agreed. 'All the same it isn't going to be nearly as simple for her as she thinks.'

'I liked her better to-day than I ever have,' I said. 'Which isn't saying much.'

The wedding was fine. The weather (the best smoky-sun early-

chrysanthemum September weather) was fine, the church was fine, the guests were fine, Lohengrin was fine. I went with Anne and Charlie. The gathering was rather-good-cum-the-Arts. Roughwood, Bertrand, Rose, Topping with his tuft, his beautiful eyes, his over- expensive clothes, Sam Creighton the publisher of young genius, the Albions, they were all there. Johnny, in full wedding attire, stood decently in front of the altar; Peter Westcott was his best man. I saw Carstang, furiously scornful, Ralph beaming, dear Aunt Hunnable and the gigantic Mr. Abel. When, at the close, the happy pair walked down the aisle, Mercia beamed, nodded to friends, was the Goddess-

mother of all the world. Johnny stumbled along and I saw that his tie was up at the back of his collar. When he saw Charlie I had a terrible fear that he was going to stop. His mouth, his very large mouth, opened as though he were about to shout 'Hullo, Charlie!' But Mercia had him firmly in hand.

The most ironical person in the whole church, I thought, was Mercia's father.

His gaze was strongly cynical.

In the pastel-coloured drawing-room they stood and shook hands with everyone. I was present when Johnny threw his arms round Aunt Hunnable and kissed her. She was older now but still as straight as a dart.

'Who is that Dickens woman?' a young friend of mine asked me.

'That is the bridegroom's aunt.'

'And that extraordinary man with her?' pointing to the gigantic Mr. Abel. 'I've never been to such an amazing wedding.'

'Amazing? ... In what way?' I asked.

'Well—Mr. Cornelius. He looks such a child.'

'Mercia is famous for her maternal instincts.'

'Oh, I know. She's SWEET. And SUCH a mixture of people. Why, there's Vanessa Herries. Isn't she a darling? And then, there's that big red-faced man who looks as though he ought to be handing the drinks round.'

'A foretaste of the future,' I said. 'One day it will be US who are handing the drinks round. In any case Johnny Cornelius' heart is large and unrestricted by class differences.'

'Oh, his heart.... I expect that's splendid. And he's supposed to be a genius, isn't he? So that makes HIM all right. But I wouldn't have thought Mercia—'

'That shows how little you know Mercia,' I answered.

'Charlie and I could endure it no longer, so after wishing Johnny luck we went with Ralph to his pub. We sat, gloomily drinking, in the little back-

room.

I remember that Charlie reminisced, his clear honest eyes recovering for me the past. He told me a number of things that I hadn't known about Johnny's childhood.

'The queer thing is,' he said, 'that he never had no doubt about his getting to the top. He was always sure of it. Yet you couldn't call him stuck-up exactly.

He was always so young about it. Tell me something. I don't know nothing about what you chaps call literature. Now do you really think he's good?

Outstanding, I mean. There's such a hell of a lot of writers about.'

'I don't know,' I answered. 'Honestly I don't know. He's so young.'

'What sort of an age,' asked Charlie, 'do writers generally show their geniuses? How young do they have to be, I mean?'

'Oh, any age.'

'So there's time.' He sighed, stood staring out of the window into the quiet sunlit street. 'What's going to happen, do you think? That's no woman for him. She'll crush the life out of him if we don't look after him. I don't know how it is,' he said, 'but I feel as though I'd just been and got wrongly married myself. It's a terrible feeling.'

CHAPTER VII

He Takes a Step Down Into Fog

I was compelled in October 1909 to pay a visit to America. While I was there, in spite of many occupations and an almost continuous talk (as it seemed, over and over again, to the same person) in a bright dry light and a trapeze-like invigorating air, I thought a great deal about Cornelius.

I have said, earlier in this book, that people do not in general seem to care to read about the lives and vicissitudes of authors. I really wonder that they do not because their vicissitudes, hairbreadth escapes, risks run, chances missed, mad accidents of good luck, rival often enough the most heart-stirring African jungle adventures or Indian fakir miracles.

I couldn't, while I was away, get out of my head the perils that Johnny Cornelius was encountering, and I wondered at the most unlikely times, when I should have been absorbed by something quite different, why I felt his story to be so dramatic. Why, indeed, I should be concerned by it at all.

No artist has any business to think of anything but himself, and when I say himself I mean the thing that he is trying to create. This nonsense about kind, chivalrous, unselfish artists always revolts me. Were Beethoven, Rembrandt, Goya, Stendhal, Cézanne, Proust, kind, chivalrous, unselfish? Of course not.

Even the noble ones—Chaucer, Cervantes, Shakespeare, Scott—were only noble and jolly when they weren't working and then only because they didn't care about anybody very much except themselves, and had good digestions.

Artists, true artists, are selfish beasts and it is right that they should be—that is, when they are working—and they ought to be working most of the time.

When they are NOT working, however, they need any amount of comforting, reassuring, defending. You may say—why bother with them? There is so much Art, and good Art, in the world already. Certainly. But they make

themselves felt. They are a disturbing element. You have to do something about them. I knew Cornelius well enough by this time to realize that he was more of a child than most artists, hungered for affection but had a terrific integrity. That is, he would never enter into any alliance with anyone if he thought it dishonourable. But I knew too that he was no good judge of people. He still, after Lady Max and Reiner and Mrs. Hoskin, believed in people if they were kind to him—a perfectly imbecile trait. So now I used to think in America, 'What will he do when he comes to know Mercia a little?' I used to ask myself too, 'HAS he any talent? Why do I and Westcott and the others think that he has? He has certainly as yet given very little evidence of it.'

So, seated in my Liverpool to London train, I opened my paper and tumbled at once upon a review of The Sorcerer, a new novel by John Cornelius. And WHAT a review! It was devastating, because, in a patronizing sort of way, it tried to be kind. 'This book,' it said, 'is a complete and utter failure, but that doesn't mean that the writer hasn't something in him. There are signs that he has.'

Reaching my flat I found a signed copy of the book waiting for me. I began it in bed that night and by the next evening I had finished it. At my club I glanced through the weekly journals and discovered some more reviews.

They were all bad and one, signed by Stromberg, was as clever as it was cruel.

Stromberg simply quoted some of the more fatuous things and made merry over them. For the book was dreadfully bad. No getting away from that.

It was absurd, but that need not of itself be disastrous. What was so awful about it was that it was exceedingly pretentious—a novel on the grand scale with a great many characters and high implications behind them. You could see that the author thought that he was writing a masterpiece. The characters talked as no human beings ever talked, but that again need not have mattered.

In those days we thought Meredith a Master, and how HIS characters talked!

But mingled with these absurd conversations were pieces of rather vulgar would-be easy jocularity that made your spine creep. I can see now that there were beauties mingled with the absurdities— descriptions of natural things, fragments of poetry, instinctive touches of reality. But then, in my

exasperation and disappointment, I threw the book across the floor. 'The boy's no good. We've been taken in by him. He knows nothing about life at all.' But mingled with my disappointment was a sense of distress and misgiving. How the boy must be feeling this, what a hurt to his pride! And Anne and Charlie. How distressed they must be for him!

A day or two later I went to a literary tea-party at Hilda Mason's on Campden Hill. Many novels contain descriptions of literary tea- parties and they are all very tiresome. I will be quick over this one. There was, however, something about those parties that Hilda Mason gave to which I now look back, so many, many years later, with a kind of nostalgia. In the summer they were in the garden and we played tennis.

On a fine summer afternoon it was very beautiful there. Soft billowy clouds loitered overhead, the thick full summer trees were brilliantly green, the pearl-coloured houses watched benevolently over the garden wall. To-day, when the world is in such a turmoil, novels and poetry and the doings of writers cannot seem of any serious matter, but then, in those halcyon days, we seemed to move in an atmosphere of drama that had real importance.

Now it was late autumn, so we were scattered about the drawing-room, its Morris-papered walls covered with drawings by Rossetti and Burne- Jones and over the fireplace a real filmy powder-blue Whistler.

I found myself next to Clare Painter, who had been writing novels for so long that it was said that George Eliot had praised her first one. Nevertheless Clare was determined to remain younger and younger. We saw Archie Bertrand in the distance. 'Oh dear!' Clare said. 'I do hope Archie won't come and say anything unkind.' But he did, for he saw us, came across to us, and in his gentle, rather sleepy voice said: 'Taking notes from the younger generation, Clare?' Then Rose most foolishly joined us and in his booming hearty way hoped that we were all well and very, very happy. Bertrand, with his long bending body, his pale countenance and half- closed eyes, had great pleasure in making Rose say a number of very foolish things.

Bertrand said:

'Your young friend Cornelius has made rather an ass of himself, I fear. Golly!

What a book!'

'I don't agree!' Rose broke out. 'There are magnificent things in it.

Magnificent things!'

'What a lot of people,' Bertrand said gently, 'you kill by kindness, Rose!' and moved on to other victims.

'I'm afraid you're for it,' I said.

'How?' asked Rose.

'You'll be in Bertrand's next novel. I always know when Bertrand is taking notes.'

'I don't care. Bertrand and I are the greatest friends.'

'That makes no difference.'

And then I saw Anne. I stood for a while watching her and I could see that she was enjoying herself immensely.

I realized that, when she was happy, she gave herself completely, generously, with no thought of caution. She was talking to Will Hampden, who was a literary critic chiefly noticeable for his indefatigable kindness and hatred of long novels. He had so many to review, poor man, that of course he preferred the short ones. A nice man. And Anne liked his niceness. She felt his generosity. If anyone was generous to her she wanted to be generous back, and I knew as I looked at her that if Hampden had been inclined to make love to her she would have made love back, not because she was sensuous but because she wanted to return happiness for happiness.

Hampden moved away and I joined her. She was delighted to see me and had quite genuinely an interest, and even excitement, in my recent doings that is so very rare. On one's return to England, after a long absence, one is lucky if there are three people who know that one has been away.

We talked about America and then I said:

'I'm afraid Johnny's book isn't very good.'

'Isn't it?' she said. 'You mean as literature? I know nothing about literature.'

'I mean any way at all. I'm afraid the reviews will hurt him.'

'They shouldn't,' Anne said quickly. 'He'll be a fool if he minds. No one, outside a little set like this, notices reviews.'

'Perhaps not.... I'm afraid, though, that he isn't a novelist.'

'How can you tell? He's only beginning.'

'What I mean is, I'm not sure whether he has much talent. He's more interesting in himself than in what he writes.'

'People ARE what they write, aren't they?'

I thought: 'I believe that they are. When you get to know them well you find that they are.'

'How is he?' I asked. 'How's the marriage doing?'

She looked at me, smiling.

'Frankly I don't know. Mercia hates me like poison. I don't go to the house.

She says I'm a grossly immoral person. But Johnny and I meet sometimes and I think he's very happy. Only I haven't seen him since the book came out.'

'You must go on looking after him,' I said. 'Now more than ever. You mustn't forsake him because Mercia doesn't like you.'

She gave me then a look which said 'What an ass you are!'

'Johnny knows that nothing's changed—on my side, I mean.'

Very shortly after this I saw Johnny; I happened to be present at rather an unagreeable little scene. I called upon Westcott for some reason or another and Carstang was there. Where Carstang was there was always an atmosphere of nervousness and apprehension. You couldn't disregard him.

There was something about his close- cropped head, his powerful glasses, his

body that was often physically still but always spiritually restless, that made you say to yourself: 'Look out! Look out!' It was not at all that Carstang was insane but that he WAS uncontrolled. He obeyed none of the rules that society has ordered for mutual good behaviour. He might behave ANYhow ANYwhere. He would stand there, his glasses shining, watching, waiting, suspicious of everyone and everything. Then you were sorry for him because you felt that he WAS having a raw deal, only not SO raw a deal as he thought he was having, for he had great talent, he was an original. He had even some genius if genius is expressing life in an entirely original way.

We had been talking for a little while when there was a knock on the door and Cornelius came in. I was surprised at my own extreme pleasure. I hadn't expected to be delighted at seeing him again. He was not at all changed.

Mercia had put him into well-fitting clothes, but his lanky shambling body, his long nose, his charming friendly eyes were beyond her power to alter. He was greatly pleased to see me. His nature was so honest and unaffected that a greeting from him WAS a greeting. He meant every word of it. I had his book on my mind, though. There is always an embarrassment when you meet, for the first time after his sending you his book (which you haven't liked), a friend. As a rule you murmur something kindly, general. But with Johnny this would not do. And, as it happened, I was spared my pains. I soon noticed that Carstang was staring at Johnny in a brooding malevolent way. I knew that stare. Johnny knew it too and after a while, in his funny high-pitched voice, he said:

'Do I want my hair cut? Or what is it?'

'A nice bloody fool you've been making of yourself,' Carstang said. When he was attacking someone he would stand very erect, his close- shaved head thrust forward.

'Why, what have I been doing?'

'Don't you KNOW when you've written muck? And if you DO know, what do you want to publish it for?'

'Oh, shut up!' Westcott broke in. 'Don't you mind him, Johnny.'

We knew, the three of us, and no one better than Carstang, what it is like when you have just published a book, the sensitiveness, the egotism, the thin-

skinned apprehension. Because you can't tell. No one can tell. If an experienced carpenter has made a table he knows whether it is good or bad.

But a book. Who knows? Who ever knows right to the end of time? Hamlet isn't so good if you're in a certain mood....

I'd often seen Carstang like this before, seized with a kind of egotistic rage, wanting to hurt because he was himself so unhappy. And then he cared passionately about literature. And he was, at that time at least, very fond of Johnny.

'What did you do it for? Why do you write a book of that length when you know nothing at all about life? The thing's hopeless, incredible, romantic sentimental nonsense. The whole of London's laughing at it.'

I watched Johnny. I knew that this book had meant everything to him, that he had been proud of it, dreadfully pleased with it. I remembered how upset he had been by my mild criticism of his fairy- stories. He got up and stood there rather like a schoolboy before a master. He LOOKED like a schoolboy.

'I'm sorry you don't like it,' he said.

'Like it! My God!' Carstang was now seized by one of his infernal rages. He was seeing himself, I suppose, the neglected, persecuted, set-upon genius who had given his friendship and encouragement to this boy from nowhere—

and now this boy had betrayed this encouragement before the world. 'Like it!

That's a joke! Why, you can't write! You don't know the first thing about writing! Look at the way your people talk, with all their bloody fine sentiments—'

It was about now, as I remember it, that Westcott interrupted. He was as angry, in his own way, as Carstang was, but of course very quiet.

'You're a bit of a brute, aren't you, Carstang? Who cares what YOU think anyway? You haven't been such a success yourself that—'

But then Johnny interrupted him.

'Carstang's right, I expect, from his point of view. People DO seem to think it silly. Perhaps I shouldn't have published it. But you don't really write for other people. What I mean is that as soon as you begin to consider other people you're lost.'

Johnny's growing up, I thought. As I watched him I saw that his underlip was trembling a little and his eyes were bright, but he was standing up to it, and Carstang in a rage was something to stand up to. I thought in fact that Carstang was going to spit in Johnny's face. When he stood, his cropped head thrust forward, it seemed that he must do something melodramatic, absurd.

His body had a sort of electric energy of anger about it as though it were about to be shot into space.

'You've disgraced us all—everyone who's had some sort of belief in you.

However, you don't need to worry, I suppose. You've married a rich wife.

You can go on producing rotten books. She'll pay for them.'

Johnny smiled.

'I don't see what that's got to do with it,' he said quietly. 'I'd have written just the same whether I'd married or no. All the same I think you're wrong about the novel. It's fine, some of it. And some of it isn't so good. But there's nothing for you to get angry over, I don't like YOU because I like your books.

I'm glad I do like them of course. But you can't say they're real life either. At least not life as it's lived every day. But does that matter? They're true as you see them, and mine are true as I see them. That's all we've got to bother about

—that we're not false to ourselves, I mean.' Then he laughed. 'Do you remember the bit about the Unicorn in your last book? That wasn't like real life, was it?'

Carstang glared at him. Then he turned away.

'Oh, get out!' he said. 'I'm sick of the sight of you.'

This was very like Carstang. Any place where he was seemed to be his. It didn't seem so to Westcott of course.

'I'm afraid it's you that's got to go, Carstang. It's YOU that I'm sick of!'

And Carstang went.

All Johnny said then was:

'Tell me about America. Is New York marvellous? Don't you walk in the streets as though they were canyons?'

Only, with a sigh, he said a little later:

'You'd think I'd murdered someone the way everyone goes for me.'

'Oh, Carstang's mad,' Westcott said.

'He writes jolly well,' Johnny said. 'Perhaps it's a help being mad.' And then he was silent for a little and looked unhappy. Later, when he told me about his grandfather, I remembered this, and knew the reason.

But after this I thought of Johnny continually. The times were propitious for that because from 1911 to the outbreak of the War I was a rather lonely person. Cornelius was, in fact, my chief interest during that time.

I called on Mercia and found her alone, massively embroidering a small square of purple silk with green flowers, smiling, patting her beautiful golden hair, a very exact representation of Britannia, having laid her sceptre aside, enjoying domesticity. Johnny would be back in a minute. Oh yes, and how had I enjoyed America? She talked to me, her eyes on her work but raising them once and again to beam on me. You knew, though, that she was thinking hard all the time of herself, not of you and America at all, of her position, whether it would be advantageous to move in this or that direction, who would help and who would hinder.

We talked of Johnny.

'His novel's been a great failure, I'm afraid,' she said, placidly hunting among her strands of silk. I saw that she was glad that it had been. She said: 'John would have been dreadfully cast down, I'm afraid, if I hadn't been there to console him. Dear Johnny ... he's only a child, the merest child.' Then, quite sharply: 'All the same I wish he wouldn't give his money away as he does.'

'Give his money away?'

'Yes. That horrible Mr. Carstang, I'm sure he simply bleeds him. And his aunt. And a man called Abel. And others too. Anyone who asks him. And after all, although I wouldn't dream of saying so to him, it's MY money.'

I saw her point.

'I wish you'd say something to him. There's another thing. I like to make you my confidant, you know.' She beamed at me. 'He lives too much in the past.

He's known such dreadful people. Two old women in his village when he was a child, and that awful old woman who looked after him in London, and a dreadful schoolmaster.... And he talks sometimes about a man who keeps birds.... I don't mind a bit for myself,' she went on brightly. 'That's what I'm here for—to look after him. It seems to be my job in life, to look after people

... but it's bad for him, brooding on all his dreadful childhood when he hadn't enough to eat....' (She implied: 'Thanks to me, he has plenty to eat NOW.')

'Anyway they are putting on a play he's written.'

I was astonished.

'A play Johnny's written?'

She nodded her head.

'Yes. The Ragamuffin. It's that old Mr. Hills who has the Penny Lane Theatre. Of course he's eccentric. But never mind that. He has plenty of money. Johnny's play's eccentric too.' She laughed. 'But you never can tell in the theatre, can you?'

'But I didn't know Johnny had written a play.'

'Oh yes. Two years ago. Before he began The Sorcerer.'

The door opened and Johnny came in. We had a nice talk. Oh yes, it was true about the play. Wasn't it grand? Old Hills was a bit queer but he intended to spare no expense. They would have the best possible cast....

I had to go. Johnny also would be out for half an hour. But Mercia thought

not.

'I want you. Never mind what for.' She pulled his head down, kissed his forehead just as though he were her beloved long lanky eldest boy. He submitted without a word. He went downstairs with me, though, his hand pressed on my arm, stumbling once or twice at a step.

'Look here. Which way are you going home?'

'By Hyde Park Corner,' I said.

'Would you mind doing something for me? Look in on Ralph. Tell him I can't come after all. I'd telephone—only—you know how it is. There's always someone listening in a house this size.'

I did step in and tell Ralph. He was pretty stout now and had a face like a rising sun.

'She wouldn't let him out.'

'Oh, I wouldn't say that.'

'You can't kid me.' He shrugged his enormous shoulders. 'Come and have a drink on the house.... He's been captured, that poor boy. Captured. That's what he is. One day we'll have to do a bit of rescuing.'

The approaching production of The Ragamuffin attracted a great deal of attention. Anything to do with the theatre has a much greater and wider publicity than book-publishing. It was now for the first time, I think, that Cornelius became generally known. Anything that the eccentric old Mr. Hills did was news. He was a millionaire who kept a private zoo in Epping. Just now he was dabbling in the theatre.

I became, myself, obsessed with The Ragamuffin. I had an odd feeling that the climax of Johnny's career would arrive with the fate of this play—silly, because he was as yet only a boy. If it failed, as The Sorcerer had failed, no one would believe in him any more. He would himself lose heart, would be swallowed up by Mercia. Finis to Johnny Cornelius.

The first night was fixed for January 18th, 1910. There was to be a supper-

party in their home afterwards.

'Do you think that's wise?' I asked Mercia. 'Suppose the play's a failure? The party will be pretty grim.' I had attended in my time so many grim parties after first-night failures.

'If it's a failure,' she said, 'Johnny will need cheering up all the more,' and I perceived at once that that would be a fine sight— Mercia, the maternal, cheering up her poor ass of a husband before all the world!

Well, the night came and I dressed for the event with a nervousness that might have been preparatory to my own hanging. Everything, I remember, was against cheerfulness. There was a fog, not a briny- smelling wall of darkness but a melancholy half-fog with lights burning with shudders of movement and the walls of houses trembling as though blown with wind.

First nights are in any case horrible things, but if a friend is concerned in them they are nightmares. I arrived in good time but to find the pit and the gallery restless and ready for anything. Although the stalls and the boxes were still almost empty there was an air of savage expectation in the theatre.

You could almost hear the murmurs: 'We have waited outside on this beastly night for hours and we'll have our sensation one way or another. If it isn't to be the excitement of a thundering success then we'll satisfy our feelings with a gigantic failure.'

People began to come in. There was then as now that nightmarish assembly of accustomed first-nighters, proud, polite, bored and ready to be savage.

A famous actress entered slowly; I remember to this day her piled- up pale hair, her heavy white dress. The pit and gallery applauded. She turned and gave a slight bow with a studied indifference which said: 'I'm very used to this and it's a fearful bore.'

Conversation buzzed; everyone was eagerly greeting everyone else as though everyone had been in Northern China and had unexpectedly returned. Critics appeared, mournful, apathetic, beaten into sullen resignation by the harshness of their lives. Anne came with Schleuert. I detected at once her almost intolerable nervousness. I looked up and saw, in the front row of the dress–

circle, Charlie and his young woman. Charlie was, of course, imperturbable; he looked quietly and critically about him as though he were wondering which of the distinguished gathering he would decide to arrest.

I realized then that Anne and Charlie and myself were drawn together as though we were alone in the theatre. We were all three of us part of Johnny that night; what happened to Johnny would happen to us also. I remember I was shivering as though with a fever; I could not keep my hands still. Yet I don't doubt that my friends, as they greeted me, thought me completely unmoved. The place seemed to me infernally hot. I heard a woman behind me say: 'Who's the thing by? John Cornelius. Who's he? Silly title anyway.'

Old Hills, dressed up with a gardenia and white tie, showed his brown monkey–face in a box, was applauded, and bowed.

In the opposite box appeared Mercia, very massive and bejewelled. Her father was with her.

She had brought, I saw, Archie Bertrand as her guest and he stood behind her, bending forward, his pale impassive face suddenly assuring me, I don't know why, that the play would be a failure. I saw Rose, red–faced, clerical, extremely friendly. There were the little Albions, and Westcott and the great Roughwood. We were all there.

When the orchestra stopped and the lights went down I sat forward, gripping my hands. You must remember that I knew nothing about the play at all. I had asked Johnny no questions; indeed, during these last weeks I had seen nothing of him. He had been absorbed by rehearsals, at which, I learnt afterwards, he had been an infernal nuisance, jumping about, interrupting, wanting to act parts himself ... There were many scenes, I believe, between Redfern, the producer, and Johnny. He was finally put out of the theatre until the dress-rehearsal. I knew nothing of this at the time.

When the curtain rose on the interior of a cottage with the sound of the sea beating upon the shore offstage, I was excited; this was Johnny's own childhood. For a while, everyone was held. All through the first Act there was suspension of judgement. When, at last, we all packed out into the foyer and pressed together, began to throw little careless indifferent judgements

into the air, you could feel that the general opinion was kindly—yes, kindly but puzzled.

I myself was surprised that Johnny had shown so much stage-craft. I remembered then that he had told me that he had been crazy from babyhood about the theatre. I didn't know at that time about Ada Montgomery and the rest. What this play really was it was hard to define. A realistic study of the life of the drunken down-at-heels poor? A fairy-story? Who was the long thin man in the bright red hat who looked spitefully in through the window?

And was the young girl awake when she saw the merman or merely dreaming? I realized, at any rate, that old Hills had either been mad or wonderfully courageous to put the play on. I heard the little Albions shrilling their appreciation and Rose pontificating. I exchanged one word with Charlie.

All he said, in his measured cautious tones, was: 'You know, that window in that cottage wasn't fixed right. One storm of rain and the whole thing would blow away.'

I met Gwen, his young woman, for the first time that evening, and liked her.

Through the first part of the second Act attention still held. Then quite suddenly there arrived that awful First Night warning. It was as though the temperature changed and a chilling wind blew through the theatre. It was as though a slow solemn voice said in everyone's ear: 'The seats are hard. You are far from home. Your left ear is itching. In a week or two's time you will have to pay that account. Your baby is probably catching pneumonia at this very moment.'

Concentration broke. There was a cough or two. The young girl who had been kneeling in front of the window, gazing out at the sunset, longing for her lover, turned back into the room and stumbled against a chair.

Then that awful fool Rose sneezed. He was sitting only two rows in front of me and the whole of his big frame heaved and then out it came. Rose was famous for his sneezing. There was a story that once, in Vienna, he had held up the Opera by his sneeze. In any case it did dreadful damage now. He turned round grinning, the idiot. It wasn't the first time in my life that I had wanted to slaughter Rose. Somebody in the pit laughed. There were titters.

People said, 'Hush.' Someone near me said, 'It's a damned shame.'

There was never, after that, the same concentration again. People suffered the play in decent patience until the Second Act curtain fell. There was perfunctory applause. Montrose, the critic of The View, got up and was, I realized, about to go home.

I went up to pay my compliments in Mercia's box. There were several gushing ladies there.

'Marvellous, dear…. Better than Maeterlinck.'

'Yes, he IS a clever boy, my Johnny,' I heard Mercia say.

Bertrand had gone for a drink. I knew just what he would be saying.

As I walked back down to the stalls Charlie's little girl caught my arm. 'It WILL be all right, won't it?'

'It all depends on the last act,' I said.

And so, indeed, it did.

It was at the beginning of the Third Act that I received, curiously enough, my first intimation that Cornelius had something strangely like genius; this impact of something new, beautiful and moving from a scene that did not play for more than five minutes. I do not know how the scene would read to–

day. Anyone may test this for himself. The Ragamuffin is printed first in the first of his two volumes of Plays. [3]

The Third Act is in two scenes, the first exceedingly brief. This is the seashore under moonlight; you see the long stretch of moonlit sand, black cliff, the sea with its opalescent path of light. The heroine comes here to meet her lover who, unknown to her, has deserted her. She waits, the only sound in the world the rhythmic purl and slither of the tide. Somewhere a distant church– clock strikes the hour. The moon is gradually darkened and in the half–light the unhappy girl fancies that she sees the merman who, whether real or no, has loved her throughout the play, rise from the water and approach her. He tries to console her; he is very diffident and shows his adoration of her by lying at her feet.

But she cries out and runs away; the moon emerges, and the only figure on the scene is the merman on a rock, looking after her, above swirling waters.

I do not know now what there was in his few broken words to her, but I was suddenly sure of Cornelius. I was never to doubt him again. I realized that this simple, poetic, fairy but ACTUAL world was his kingdom, and that he could make one believe in it and be part of it as no one had done since Hans Andersen. Unfortunately mermen are dangerous 'cattle' on the modern stage and this merman's silvery tail amused the gallery. The rest of the play was disastrous. Cornelius had not learnt how to bind his interests together into one cumulative effect; his Ragamuffin, the gentleman in the red hat, had a long speech to make about God and Charity and Heaven–knows–what that stirred the audience to an infernal restlessness. At the end the tide comes up as it does in Götterdämmerung and everyone who has been to The Ring a time or two knows how difficult swirling waters are to stage with conviction. The heroine leaps out of the cottage window and swims after her merman. Part of her skirt caught in the woodwork and, as Charlie had prophesied, the scenery began to totter. The curtain came down to peals of ironic laughter.

What followed was horrible. Great men have suffered it, Henry Galleon amongst them, and he, I think, never quite recovered from the shock. The curtain went up, the actors stood there bowing, the stalls politely applauded.

At the second rising, when the heroine, the Ragamuffin and the merman, minus his tail, appeared together, someone in the gallery called out, 'Where's your tail, old cock?' Things might, I think, have ended there had not, most unfortunately, the curtain risen to reveal Johnny, alone, apparently about to make a speech. This habit of the author's appearance is, in any case, an abomination. Authors are not decorative and should never be illuminated. But Johnny's appearance was especially unfortunate. His hair was untidy, his white waistcoat, rucked up over the shirt, was divided widely from his trousers, his white tie was, of course, climbing his collar. He was, I could see, quite fearfully excited.

He began to speak. 'I must thank you—' he began. Then the noise broke out: yelling, cat-calls, abuse like, 'It's a rotten play,' 'Where's your merman?' The stalls rebuked the gallery, crying, 'Shame! shame!' and some gentleman shouted, 'Pull down the curtain! Pull down the curtain!'

I caught sight of Bertrand staring with sombre gravity at the stage. He had been through too many theatrical moments for this to seem to him funny or food for his satiric muse.

Then the worst thing happened. Johnny had taken the noisy storm with amazement. He stared up at the gallery as though he couldn't believe his ears.

He looked around him as though for help. I feared for a moment that he would burst into tears. But no. He was swung into a regal tempest of anger.

He actually stamped with his foot and cried out:

'It's a good play! I tell you it's a good play!'

How the gallery laughed! The stalls began quickly to steal away. The curtain came down. The band played 'God save the King.' We all stood at attention.

That was the end of that. The last thing I heard was the voice of little Albion saying, 'It's always the way. You are persecuted for years. I didn't sell anything—not what you could CALL selling—for ever so long....'

Yes, the party was horrible. The little drawing-room was crowded and women were saying to Johnny over and over: 'But so BEAUTIFUL! And so COURAGEOUS ... ' then hurrying to the little buffet for a drink and murmuring, 'A disaster, my dear. Well, what could you expect? Oh, but Norma was far too old for one thing for the part— and then— I ask you!

Mermen!'

It was all entirely hateful but Mercia enjoyed it. Strange woman! I think that on this night she felt that she HAD Johnny, safe in her grasp, now and for ever. She was such a terrible liar that you never could tell, but I fancy that she spoke the truth when later on she said to me: 'The first night of The Ragamuffin I really loved Johnny, I think; felt stirred and moved by him for the first time, that night. He seemed at last to belong to me.'

He certainly behaved beautifully. As I watched him I greatly admired him.

He went about handing drinks and sandwiches, smiling most charmingly, stumbling over people's feet and saying, 'Oh, I beg your pardon'; murmuring again and again, 'Thank you, very much. I'm glad you liked it. I don't think anyone else did, much, except you and me!'

At the back of everyone's consciousness must have been the excited horror at his crying out before the whole theatre. No one had ever done that, not even Oscar Wilde or Austin Crabbe—and Johnny was certainly neither a Wilde nor a Crabbe!

What a scandal! Wouldn't the papers be full of it in the morning! Good publicity, but the boy was simply making a general ass of himself. He would be the joke of London for a day and then forgotten. Only Roughwood, who, being a genial, friendly human creature to whom world-fame had made no sort of difference, caught my arm, and said in his squeaky little voice: 'All the same there was something there.'

'I thought so too,' I said. 'The child's a poet. When he's first- hand he's good.

When he's second-hand he's terrible.'

I was just thinking that I couldn't endure the horror of this awful party any longer when I found that Johnny was holding my arm.

'Charlie's downstairs,' he whispered. 'Let's go.'

In the grimy stale-tobaccoed little room where Mr. Otterstone considered his stamps, Charlie was seated. Why he was put in there I do not know, but he did not seem to mind. There he sat, his stout legs planted wide, his fair hair untidy over his forehead, his calm blue eyes meditative.

'Hullo,' he said. 'I came to see you were all right.' Then he added: 'I don't want to butt in on your party.'

'Let's go out,' Johnny said.

I remember that then I suggested leaving them. They might wish to be alone.

They insisted, however, that I should stay with them.

Charlie never said a word about the play. It was the kind of poetic thing that he wouldn't care for. We let ourselves out of the house and fell into the fog. I don't know where we went. A long way, I think. All the time Johnny talked.

Words poured out of him. Like this:

'I know you think I shouldn't have said a word, Charlie. My speaking like that

—it would sound very bad like that. But I seem to have been badgered all my life; never let alone. Why's it wrong to write a play? It isn't a crime, is it?

What do they want to shout for? If you don't like a sofa in a furniture-shop you don't hit the manager. First the novel. Then the play. What's the matter?

They're good. They're beautiful. Or they have beautiful things in them—my own things. What have I ever done to anyone? It's Mrs. Hoskin. You don't know Mrs. Hoskin, do you? Charlie does. But no. She doesn't matter—Mrs.

Hoskin doesn't matter. Perhaps I've been wrong about myself all this time.

You know, Charlie, don't you, my grandfather was crazy. He used to sit there thinking he was King Solomon. Perhaps I'm crazy, too, thinking I'm writing about real things. And they aren't real. How are you to know? But my grandfather was happy and I'm not. That's where he scored. Those people to-

night and Stromberg tearing my novel to pieces! I haven't done them any harm. I'm not asking to be treated kindly, mind you. I don't mind. I'm not asking to be pitied. But if I've been wrong all this time? Reiner said so; Lady Max said so. And there's Mercia—she doesn't really believe ... '

At some point or other he pulled himself up abruptly. He stopped in his tracks. 'Oh, God, I'm tired. I've been trying so hard for years—'

I remember his saying that, and I can see now, all these years after, just what the scene was. The fog was thin but acrid like chimney-smoke. There was a pub near by and a church.

Johnny said: 'Oh, look here; I feel ill. Wait a minute.' He would have collapsed if Charlie hadn't held him.

'It's my heart. It's bad, sometimes. It will go in a minute.'

Charlie held him as though he were his mother. He said to me huskily: 'Look here, can't you get a taxi?'

But Johnny stood up straight. 'No, I'm all right. It was only a moment.'

He stared about him. He sniffed the fog. He looked up at the dimly seen church-tower as though he were listening.

'Let's not go back,' he said.

'Back? Where?' I asked.

'We'll get hold of Anne and we'll all go off somewhere—another country.

Now—without a word to anyone.' He looked at Charlie, and I will never forget the loneliness and isolation of that look. 'Oh no—you've got Gwen.'

Turning to me: 'And you've got ... That's right. Let's find a taxi and go home.'

[3] The Ragamuffin and Other Plays (Roger and Winchester), 1919.

CHAPTER VIII

Anne--'the Bright-green Shoes'--wild Party--vision of Man

Through Chimney-pots

This is the story of John Cornelius' life, not mine. And yet, at this point, I feel it necessary to say that somewhere early in 1911 I fell in love with Anne Swinnerton. I knew that it was hopeless; for a long time I didn't speak to her of it. Whether she knew it I can't tell, but I suppose that she did. A woman is always aware if a man's in love with her. At first it was exceedingly difficult for me. It was a kind of obsession, and these years, 1911–1914, were the most difficult of my life. Anne and John Cornelius, although neither was conscious of it, pulled me through to safety. They were very difficult years for Anne and Johnny also.

The moment when I first realized that I loved Anne was created by a fellow called Minniken. He is altogether forgotten now, but he played a certain part in that pre–War London. He was an art critic, social butterfly, knew everyone's business. He was an arrant mischief-maker. His favourite line was:

'By Jove, W—, I had to stand up for you at Smith's the other night! You don't know what they weren't saying! But I let them have it.'

'WHAT were they saying?'

'Oh, nothing that mattered. General talk—'

Or another opening:

'I know you think X— is a friend of yours. I wouldn't be too sure.'

And another:

'Y— is a friend of yours, isn't he? You might drop him a hint some time

about what everyone's saying. I don't know him well enough myself. If I did

—'

And so, one day, Minniken said: 'You know Schleuert, don't you?'

I said I did.

'Shortly he'll be passing on to pastures new. That nice Miss Swinnerton—

you've met her, haven't you?—she'll have to be looking for a fresh job.'

I told Minniken to go to hell and realized that Anne meant everything in the world to me. Yes. Literally everything.

I went to see her. I had met her at some party and she invited me to tea. She had been living quite openly with Schleuert for some time, and it was to his house that I went. It was in Barren Street, I remember. He was, as I have said elsewhere, one of the most famous art-dealers in Europe and the little house had some lovely pictures. Schleuert was one of the first men in London to deal consistently in Manet, Monet, Sisley, Van Gogh, Gauguin, Cézanne. I remember a lovely Sisley all soft silver and blue, a Manet still-life of a crystal vase and some pale-pink carnations. He was there himself and he showed me a Cézanne water-colour, the first I had ever seen. It was a miracle of painting, so it seemed to me; a hill, some trees, a lake, and in it there were no statements, only indications—blue, green, rose, purple—and the empty parts of the canvas were as eloquent as those that were covered. Schleuert was quiet, courteous, restrained while he talked to me about Cézanne, showing me how these little marks of brilliant colour were in reality only notes, but that every note was really a definite sequence from one plane to another. They were rhythmic phrases, as in a piece of music. I remember that my spirit was dazzled by the brilliant, pure, sun-filled quality of the colour.

But when the painting was put aside and we had tea, Schleuert became the gross common man that his reputation suggested. He was heavy of figure, bull-necked, thick-coloured, his mouth loose and discontented. Some three years after this meeting he shot himself in Paris.

As I sat there I wondered how Anne could have been his intimate companion for so long. I realized very quickly that they were now uneasy in one

another's company and I was certain that the baleful Minniken's information was correct. I remember that at first I wondered whether, if Anne was going to leave Schleuert, I might not persuade her to marry me, but I soon realized that neither of us mattered to her very greatly. She was charming. She had become by now a delightful woman of the world. She made no pretence about the Arts, for which she never greatly cared, but her long association with Schleuert had taught her a good deal about pictures. She had just been with Schleuert to Paris and she gave a lively, most humorous account of their evening with Ambrose Vollard. Schleuert watched her from under his heavy black eyebrows and I realized that there was something desperately restless in his spirit that drove him, never satisfied, on and on; that he knew that he was leaving her; and that he knew, too, that he would never care for anyone so much again.

Anne herself made all clear, for after Schleuert left us she said at once, very quietly:

'He's got to go to New York next week and I must find new quarters.'

I said something or other. I remember that she stood up, balancing herself on her toes, raising her arms, like a child.

'I'm a bird of passage. It doesn't matter much where I alight.'

Then, looking down at me from her height, she said:

'Life isn't very important, is it? One's own life, I mean. There are only a few lives that are important—like Johnny's.'

'YOUR life seems important to me,' I said foolishly.

'Oh, we're friends. I like you awfully and a real friend IS important. That isn't what I mean. I mean GENERALLY important.'

'Do you really feel Johnny to be that?'

'Oh, of course. People will realize it ... '

'They're all laughing at him at present, I'm afraid.'

'Oh, what does THAT matter? And perhaps they always WILL laugh at him.

They laughed at Cézanne. I wish I could do more for him, though.'

I asked her in what way.

'He's terribly unhappy. That marriage is going all wrong. It's done one good thing, though. It's changed him from a boy into a man.' She grinned. 'Do you know what I did the other night? I climbed in at the basement window.

Johnny and I had a meal in the kitchen. We were there till about two in the morning.'

'That looks as though he were afraid of Mercia.'

'He is. That's the worst of it. He's always been afraid of people who threaten his liberty. She's grown very fond of him in some odd way—I'm sure she wasn't at first—or fond of her power over him. She's bending all her powers now to subduing him. She's marvellous. She's got the strength of an army. If she'd only put all that force into some public cause, like slums or votes for women. But poor little Johnny ... '

She came and sat beside me.

'But I'll be free soon. I'll be on my own and then I'll do something about Johnny. We'll all do something, won't we?'

When she spoke of him her voice changed. It had a lovely, soft, protective note. I remember that I thought that I would give all the world if she would only speak like that about me....

I was in London for a while after this and realized with a shock of discomfort the completeness with which Johnny had 'ditched' himself.

He really seemed to be the 'fool' of literary and artistic London. It says something for his personality that he should have impressed London at all.

But every once and again quite unimportant people assume a kind of symbolic weight. I can remember several—Taggert, Frinton and Meables, for example. But Johnny was really despised. Sometimes a kind of a general

antagonism grows up against someone. There is always a reason for this. The hated figure is arrogant or self-advertising or says stupid things in the Press.

It means, of course, a real force of personality and character. Someone like poor Elstry, who died only the other day, went his life long being helped and applauded because he was a nice good man and so hopeless a novelist that he never made anyone jealous.

'Oh, we must do something for poor Elstry,' you used to hear people saying.

'He's such a nice fellow and has three children and his wife has to do all the housework.'

But Johnny had made a public ass of himself and married a rich woman.

There had been something dreadfully un-English about his outbreak in the theatre; he was so ugly and dishevelled and, in spite of the failure of everything that he had done, he thought apparently a tremendous lot of himself.

Rose didn't help him by his loyalty, nor the little Albions; whether Westcott and I did him any good I can't say. He did himself all the possible harm by going about the clubs and parties and behaving with perfect and very naïf naturalness. That is, if anyone, simply to pass the time, asked whether he was working at anything, he would launch out into a long excited account of the novel on which he was engaged, and then, as likely as not, would defend all his other work and say that The Sorcerer had been misunderstood and The Ragamuffin maligned. He afforded Archie Bertrand much quiet amusement.

I heard, too, a great deal about the wonderful tolerance, kindness and wisdom of Mercia. How she could put up with the fool! But she did. She looked after him and mothered him and restrained him from grosser follies. 'And he spends her money like water,' I overheard Milliken remarking.

When, one evening, I went to a dinner-party there, I was able to realize, with more poignancy than was pleasant, how rapidly the drama was progressing.

It was a real pre-War dinner-party of the kind that scarcely exists in England any more. There were a dozen of us and we were packed pretty tightly into the little dining-room. I realized, as I looked at my fellow-guests, that Mercia really HAD got where she wanted to be through marrying Johnny.

Through Johnny she had known Westcott, Bertrand, Owen Roughwood, myself and many more, and out of these she had created for herself exactly the world that suited her.

She was not herself clever enough for the very clever. Archie Bertrand found her out in half a second. But there are always so many distinguished people in London who are not clever at all; that was precisely Mercia's world. She had as guests on this occasion, I remember, the director of an Art Gallery and his wife, a bachelor Bishop, Rose and the Albions, Lady Doris Plumley, old Mrs.

Falk, and the beautiful brainless Rachel Anthony.

How strange to see Johnny sitting at the head of this table (Mr. Otterstone never appeared at his daughter's dinner-parties); strange, and uncomfortable.

He was very polite and very talkative. He paid Mercia the greatest attention and seemed to reverence her. He was charming to everyone in a rather timid way.

I am sure that there were many sentences like: 'But the point, I think, is that someone should put his foot down. How the Liberals are ever going to ... ' or

'Of course, if you're talking of Botticelli ... 'or 'Well, Maple's does very well for us. We've never had to complain....'

I do remember, after the ladies had gone upstairs, that the bachelor Bishop made a lot of me, was very friendly and genial, but thought that I was an actor.

Later on I was alone for a minute or two with Johnny in a very small, rather stuffy room that he called his study. He was nervous and, I could see, unhappy.

'We mustn't stay a minute. Mercia won't like it.'

'How's the novel getting on?'

'There it is. Piles of it.' He patted the manuscript affectionately. 'I'm afraid it will be very long.' (This was The Three Beggar-Men, and LONG it was!)

'But I'm quite sure it's my best. Far and away. This is the book that's going to show everybody. It will and it MUST.' He looked at me in that determined,

rather piteous way of authors who spend their days and nights in hoping for the best. What a hell of a life an author's is, I thought, and why, oh, why ... ?

'It's GOT to succeed,' Johnny said. 'Because the other books have hardly made a penny. I MUST make money.'

He saw that I was looking at him inquisitively, so he went on: 'Oh, Mercia's very kind. She lets me have anything I want. But I oughtn't to take anything from her. I see that now. I didn't at first.' He put his hand on my arm and looked at me pleadingly. 'I wish you came here more often. Why don't you?

And Charlie's on a job in Newcastle. And Anne—'

'Anne's left Schleuert.'

'Yes, I know. She came here one night and we sat in the kitchen. Mercia doesn't like her, you know.'

'I know she doesn't.'

'There are some things Mercia doesn't quite understand—that Anne and Charlie have been my friends all my life, for instance.' Then he felt, I suppose, that he was being disloyal, for he pulled himself up. 'We must be getting back.... I say, aren't these people boring? Or is it my fault? When I was a kid I never found anyone boring. All the men to-night have such deep voices.'

I touched a thin manuscript on his table.

'What's this?'

'Oh, that's nothing. It's a fairy-story I wrote the other night when I couldn't sleep. Not serious like the novel.'

'May I look at it?'

'Certainly. But you don't like my fairy-stories.'

'Yes, I do.'

'Well, I don't like them myself. They're too easy.'

So I took the manuscript home and was the first person in the whole world to read The Bright-Green Shoes.

This is now a world-famous story. Branson's play has made it famous if nothing else has. And now, in these last years, there has been an opera and a film. But, very briefly, I must recapitulate the little fable: of how there was a Prince, the only son of his father, the king of the richest kingdom in the world; of how this Prince was ugly and lonely and unhappy, and would sit in the gardens of the palace looking out to the glassy sea, wondering whether there was any happiness ever in store for him. Then, walking one day by the seashore, he meets a pedlar. In the pedlar's basket is a pair of green leather shoes. The pedlar offers these to him and says that they have wonderful properties. Whoever wears them will be able to have any wish granted. But, the pedlar warns him, the wish granted to the wearer will always do harm to someone else. The Prince purchases the shoes.

Then the Princess, the beautiful lovely Princess, comes from the neighbouring kingdom. Her father, who is poor, wishes her to marry the Prince because he will be, one day, the richest man in the world. But alas! the Prince is so ugly that when the Princess sees him she almost swoons with disgust. The poor Prince falls madly, madly in love with her. They are betrothed. There are great public rejoicings, but as the days pass the Princess finds it more and more impossible to overcome her distaste for the Prince's ugliness, and the Prince, perceiving everything, is breaking his heart.

He knows that if he wears the green shoes and wishes, he will instantly become very beautiful, but he fears that at the same moment something terrible will happen to his Princess. He makes, when he is alone, some private experiments with the shoes, wishing only for little things. He finds the pedlar spoke truth—his wishes are granted, but little misfortunes occur. His younger sister cuts her finger, his pet dwarf breaks a glass and is whipped, his father has the colic.

The marriage is celebrated magnificently. At last the Prince and Princess are alone together. She breaks down, weeps her heart out, tells him that she likes him so much but cannot love him because he is so ugly. It is, she says, the

dearest wish of her heart that he should be beautiful. Then—oh, then!—how devotedly she would love him!

He sees at once what he must do. He tells her to put on the green shoes and wish that he should be beautiful. As he tells her this, his face is very pale, his heart has almost stopped; he knows that, if she obeys him, his doom is sealed.

She hesitates, looking doubtfully at the shoes that lie there in front of her.

Their room is high up in the Castle overlooking the sea, above whose silver silence dawn is now breaking. A sea-gull circles through the sky and beats with its wings against the window.

The Princess bends down, picks up the shoes and puts them on. Then she looks up at the Prince and his beauty dazzles her. She is blinded by it, hiding her eyes with her hand, knowing that she loves him now with all her heart and soul for ever. With a cry of joy she runs to him; he clasps her to his heart and as their lips meet he dies.

The sea-gull beats and beats again against the window as the sunlight floods the sea and the room.

A very commonplace little fable perhaps! And yet most certainly not commonplace as Cornelius tells it. What I realized as I read it alone in my rooms that night was that THIS at last was Cornelius' own world. He belongs, I suppose, to the little group of unique amateurs of literature—Goldsmith, Beddoes, FitzGerald, Peacock, Lewis Carroll, Kenneth Grahame—men who, learning no rules, acquiring no professional efficiency, discover kingdoms that are theirs and theirs alone for ever. Cornelius' true ancestor was Hans Andersen. Andersen was undoubtedly a greater master. He belonged to a simpler time, but even he had not quite the power of creating a world that was Cornelius's. And that only in his fairy- stories.

I realized this at once as I devoured The Bright-Green Shoes. The detail was exquisitely chosen. The king was alive as no king in any fairy-story before.

The oddities, that were also beauties, of the Castle—the long glass-topped table on whose surface clouds and the reflections of green trees and the wings of strange birds could be seen, the three Dwarfs who sang so melodiously, the garden above the sea at whose heart the warning bell from the Black Rock out to sea gave rhythm to the fountains, the courtiers—marvellously

described, each in a line or two. Best of all, he gave a wonderful colour to the Prince and Princess, making them alive and individual and deeply touching.

Yet there was no whimsy nor pretty phrasing nor artificial delicacy. The prose was simple, direct; any child could (and every child soon did) understand it. What was so curious to me was that all the crudity and falseness of his play and novels was absent here. He was moving in a world of which he knew every turn, every sound, every scent. What a child could not detect in these fairy-stories was the deep pathos and the gentle irony.

Later, in the post-War world, when Freud was to become so popular, much Freudian psychology would be discovered behind these simple stories. They were made to stand for all the trials and sorrows of the post-War world, as Maeterlinck's plays were once acclaimed as symbols of an earlier one.

But Cornelius was saved, in his work and in himself, I think, because he was never self-conscious about anything. He never knew what he was doing. In so far as he DID know, his heart was set on his BAD work, not on his good.

Well, I knew, as I finished The Bright-Green Shoes that night, that here was a wonderful story. Had there been the same qualities in those four earlier stories? If so, I had been a grievous ass. I took them out and re-read them.

Although The Bright-Green Shoes seemed to me maturer, yet I detected qualities in the first tales that surely I had been a fool to miss. Or was I, because my affection for Cornelius had grown so strongly, imagining virtues?

No, I was certain that I was not. I remember that I placed the manuscript of The Bright-Green Shoes beside my bed, and woke up once and again during the night to make certain that the precious thing was safe.

When next day I told him my opinion, he laughed at me. He, who was so obstinately proud of his plays and novels, could see nothing in these fairy-

stories at all. He had been proud of that little green, rough-backed first volume because it WAS his first.

'I'm glad you like it,' he said as I gave him the manuscript (but he wasn't very glad; he was thinking of something else). 'You wait till you read this novel.

I've learnt a lot lately, about life. About REAL life. They won't be able to say THIS book is unreal.' (But they did.)

And so I come to an adventurous evening which, afterwards, seemed to me to have closed the whole of this period, not only for myself and Cornelius and Anne, but for everybody, for everything, for the whole world.

We all of us look back now and see those years, 1911 to 1914, as the end of a world-period, and so, I suppose, they were. A commonplace. A platitude.

How many novels since then have pictured the tranquillity, tea on the lawn, wonderful summer weather, and then a voice, indifferent, absent-minded: 'I see an Archduke has been assassinated ... ' The poor devils—novelists, I mean—if they write of the past they have to bring it in. Yes, they have to, and they don't like it. They try to be as casual as they can....

But we hadn't got to Sarajevo yet on the night of Johnny's party. It isn't, I think, on looking back, all imagination to see those years as sinister, a little fantastic, wild a little. We are inclined now to envy those years, but I don't know that they were very enviable. Men and women were troubled, alarmed, wildly gay, broken-hearted, exactly as they are now. Life and death came then as they do now, although since then some of us have realized both the fears and the triumph of physical horror—and also the deep, deep experience of spiritual reality. I think that that is in the main what I feel about those years before the War—that they were unreal in their texture, something flimsy in their structure, as though with a push of the finger you could knock them over. I can see myself watching, for the first time, Chaliapin as he rode his white horse in Boris, and laughing at a sun-drenched Henley Regatta as a white-flannelled man missed his step and fell out of his boat into the river, and the fishing-boats stealing out in the saffron-coloured light from the little Polperro harbour, and a girl saying, as we walked down the red-carpeted steps into the hot summer Square one evening at a Hill Street dance: 'Nothing ever happens now, does it? And it's the beginning of a century. They say things always happen at the beginning of a century, don't they?' and some theatricals in Devonshire House, thinking of Dickens and Wilkie Collins and THEIR theatricals, and the flowers at Kew, a light dusty rain falling, someone murmuring: 'I'm bored. I want to do something wild. Let's have a party,' and that last summer of all, going with the Polperro choir to Newquay, then at the very end of July, and answering questions about Ireland, bathing in a sticky sea, having pilchards for tea—all unreal, phantasmal, something out of one of Johnny's fairy-stories. But Johnny's party was real enough. I can remember every sound, every word, as though it were happening now at

this actual minute. As perhaps indeed it is.

Mercia went away on a visit and her father with her. It was seldom that she did this, but one of her many woman friends was to be married in the country

—a very splendid wedding, I suppose. For once Johnny was allowed his freedom. He told me what he intended to do. He would have a party for all his old friends, for all those (although he didn't say so) disliked by Mercia.

He would invite Anne, Charlie and Charlie's wife (Charlie was back from Newcastle and married now), Aunt Hunnable, Mr. Abel, Carstang, Westcott, Rose and myself. We would have a splendid party and we would all do exactly as we pleased. He seemed the old careless, excited, happy Johnny as he told me. I thought it a splendid idea: for one thing, Anne would be there.

We were almost like conspirators when first we entered that night. We had, all of us except Westcott and myself, learned that this place was not for us. A simple little house with clean stone steps, a blue door, a brass knocker—but a place we were forbidden.

We crept upstairs and then the fun began. There was first, I think, a glorious sense of reassurance. We had been afraid, perhaps, that we would never see Johnny again, or we had been afraid that he would be sadly changed by this life that he was living—that, in that sense at least, we would never see our Johnny again. But from the moment that we were all gathered together in the drawing-room—that room so chaste with 'young' modern pictures, its big Russian ikon, twisted-silver old French candlesticks, books in leather bindings—we knew that we were safe, back in our old life, and that Johnny was back too. Indeed we nearly shook hands in congratulation with one another. The strangest of us in appearance was undoubtedly Mr. Abel. There was his great height for one thing, and then he was dressed in a long frock-

coat with rather shabby shiny silk lapels, and he wore, of all things, side-

whiskers. He looked not as though he were out of Dickens but something still more fantastic, Theodore Hook or Frank Smedley. He had a big booming voice like a bell-buoy at sea. He was a humbug, I suppose—I have never been quite sure—but he was an amiable, kindly one. Carstang, in a blood-red stock, was in a mood of sweet generosity. That was the last occasion on which I was to see him thus. Aunt Hunnable, now an elderly woman but still straight from Bleak House—she was just that much more real than Mr. Abel

—was very quietly happy at having Johnny restored to her. She whispered to me in the course of the evening that she thought she had lost him. 'Not that I've a thing against his wife, you understand, except that I don't think she understands Johnny in the least—not in the very least. He's not only a child as she'd like to keep him. He's something very much more than that. My poor sister, weak though she was, she always maintained that he was different.

That's what Johnny is—he's different.'

Charlie, very hushed and clean, was excellently proud of his wife and, at the same time, anxious that she should not take that pride too thoroughly for granted. A happier woman than his Gwen I had never seen. But Ralph, very red and large, was, I think, of us all the one who was happiest at getting Johnny back again. I have said elsewhere that Johnny was, I fancy, the only human being whom, since his youth, he had really loved. He was thinking to-

night, he told me, of the first time he'd ever seen Johnny, standing there in Mr. Schaaf's hall: 'Such an ugly little boy, wearing very odd clothes indeed.'

'"He has a letter for Mr. Schaaf," the footman says.

'"Oh, I MUST give it to him myself," Johnny says, looking up at me— and from that very moment we was friends, as you might say.' Ralph pinched his fat cheek reflectively. 'Not that I'd have let him see Mr. Schaaf in the ordinary way. Schaaf's reputation concerning boys was something shocking. But one look at him and I knew he was safe, seeing how ugly he was!' Ralph drew a deep breath. 'Queer tastes some people have. Anyway you could have knocked me down with a feather when I see the child, later on, coming down the stairs with that old termagant Lady Max. She carried him off in her carriage and I don't wonder if that hadn't something to do with my going into her service later on— Johnny being in her house, I mean. I kind of felt responsible, having introduced him to Schaaf in the first place. Anyway I had to leave Schaaf. What people do's their own affair, but the way they do it—

that's anybody's.'

And, last of all, I remember Rose, exuberant and sensitive both at the same time, like an elephant who would be riotously happy were it not for the mockery that is going on, he is sure, in the monkey- cage. He never, I think, learnt the invaluable lesson that monkeys are, except for swift moments of naughty mischief, intensely preoccupied with themselves.

We certainly had a splendid time. After a while we went downstairs and had a glorious supper. How blissfully happy, happily blissful was Johnny! Charlie and Anne and Ralph, who had all known him in the earlier days, all realized that they had the old real Johnny back again. He placed Aunt Hunnable on his right and Anne on his left. I had the good luck to sit on Anne's other side.

I noticed that the servants—an old stout woman and a pale-faced serious-

looking young girl—seemed also to enjoy the festivities as though they too were suddenly free. The food was excellent and there was plenty to drink. I had always noticed that Mercia was careful with her cellar and I fancy that there was a glint in Johnny's eye. We soon became, all of us, very gay indeed.

Johnny himself was almost a teetotaller, but another kind of excitement stirred and moved him. His eyes shone; he was here, there and everywhere.

'Come on, Aunt. You MUST have a bit more!' 'Carstang, you're drinking nothing!' 'Anne, darling, no? Of COURSE you must!' He rushed about from place to place, tripping and stumbling. He was especially charming to Charlie's wife and to Ralph. He came back to Ralph again and again, putting his hand on his shoulder. He got up to make a speech. 'Friends, I can't tell you how happy I am! You're all my life, my past life and my present one. As I look round the table I see how lucky I am. Perhaps I worry about all the wrong things, writing and nonsense like that. I ought to remember always that I'm the luckiest man alive to have such friends. I ought never to worry again as long as you're all round me. You know what I'm thinking and wishing you.'

Then Rose stood up and made a speech. He had a rich fruity voice and the gift of meaning everything he said, however foolish, and that's why he was a successful lecturer. Then we all stood up and sang 'For he's a jolly good fellow.' We were very gay and jolly indeed by this time. I wonder whether now, on looking back, I am right in thinking that there was a strong, almost sinister, note of urgency underneath our gaiety—as though this were the very last, last time that we would be all together, as though we mustn't lose a scrap of this great moment of comradeship and trust.

I know that I did my own share of the drinking and by the end of the supper the thing of which I was most strongly conscious was Anne's love for Johnny.

We had all of us thrown off some restraint, and Anne (she too clutching at

one of her few trustworthy moments) touched his arm with her hand and watched, watched him with her eyes, going back, I suppose, to the days in Port Merlin, to that first moment when she encountered her....

I myself developed a kind of benevolence, thinking nobly of myself and her.

' Tis better to have loved and lost ... '

Upstairs we sat about and talked. There was a little literary conversation but not much.

I have some sentences, Bertrand-fashion, down in my Diary.

Rose, very flushed and earnest, saying: 'I have novels in my head— enough to last me until my seventieth birthday.'

Westcott said: 'Good God! I hope you don't live till then.'

'I shan't,' said Rose. 'I may die any minute. Two fortune-tellers have told me I shan't live beyond fifty.'

'Alas! that's a long way off,' said Peter Westcott.

'Novel-writing!' cried Rose. 'There's nothing like it. I can write and write and write.'

'On the contrary,' said Westcott. 'It's a cursed business. You must be on tenterhooks all the time. You don't know what awful blunders you're making.

You strain and strain and bring forth a mouse. Oh, God! I'd rather be a coal-

heaver.'

Charlie was sitting beside me and, dropping his voice, said:

'Why are all these writers important?'

'They aren't important,' I answered.

'No; what I mean is, ANY writer ANY time. Johnny's always talking about a man called Keats. He wrote poetry.'

'Yes,' I said.

'Well, what's poetry ever done for anybody? Writers and actors and men like that, they're just like anyone else. You pay them the money and they supply the goods. What's the reason for all the fuss?'

'I suppose it's because a good writer or painter or musician does something no one else can do.'

'So does someone who invents a new car,' said Charlie. 'And a blessed sight more useful it is. I hope you're not offended,' he suddenly said, looking at me rather anxiously.

'Of course not. But writers can't help writing any more than another man can help building bridges.'

'No,' said Charlie, wrinkling his brow. 'But if a man makes bad bridges he stops making them. If a man writes what you might call a bad book he doesn't stop writing, does he?'

'No. But a bad bridge is dangerous. Nobody need read a bad book.'

'Plenty do, from what I hear,' said Charlie.

We gathered closer together and Johnny told us stories.

Now he was enchanting. I can see him sitting forward in a high- backed chair, one long leg cocked over the other, his hair ruffled over his forehead.

His bright eyes stared beyond us. He was looking into the past, which was, for him, always the present. And he was safe with us. He had no fears—the first time, perhaps, for many months. He loved us, all of us. He had the gift, that every real friend has, of making us part of him. He went back, back, telling us even of the awful afternoon when Old Laces had died at his feet.

Then of his first meeting with Anne and Charlie. 'Do you remember, Anne?'

'Do you remember, Charlie?' Old Mrs. Hoskin, not so terrible now, and Ada Montgomery. Then the London time and Aunt Hunnable at the station, the visit to Mr. Schaaf, Reiner's ... Here he suddenly stopped.

'Well, that's enough. You'll all be bored. Now let's have a game.'

We played games and by this time we were all a little tipsy—with wine, with pleasure, comfortable in our security. Carstang sang a song and we joined in the chorus. I hadn't known, until then, that he could look so amiable. He was hot and took off his glasses and looked like an overgrown boy.

Then we played charades. Johnny went down into the hall and brought up hats and coats and a Spanish shawl and (I was alarmed a little when I saw it) two of Mercia's hats. The charades were marvellous. Johnny could act all right. He was a female fortune-teller and was murdered by Carstang with a paper-knife. And then, suddenly, acting alone, he was a man who whistled and called birds round him. We could see them, there in Mercia's drawing-room, coming in their dozens about us. He made us, in some wonderful way, hear the whirr of their wings.

Then he and Anne were a King and Queen condemning Rose and Charlie to death. But Rose refused to die and Charlie arrested the King and Queen and tied them up in a cellar.

Everything became a little riotous. There were one or two unimportant accidents. A vase was knocked over and broken, and some of Mercia's beautiful leather books fell to the floor.

Aunt Hunnable, Westcott, Johnny and I came on as music-hall artistes. Aunt Hunnable was an acrobat with Johnny. I was a magician....

I was a magician. I stopped in the middle of my patter and stared at the door.

I don't know how it was, but I was certain that there was someone on the other side of it. In a kind of panic, looking about me and seeing Aunt Hunnable in the Spanish shawl, Johnny trying to stand on his head, Westcott crying, 'Walk up! Walk up! Come and see the next performance!' it was all I could do not to cry out, 'Look out! Look out!'

And I was right. The door opened and Mercia stood there. This was no new situation. The immediate picture in my mind was of Mansfield Park—the return of Sir Thomas ...

I stared, like a perfect fool, with my mouth open.

Mercia was nobly wrapped in furs and on her coiled golden hair was a fur cap, Russian-fashion. She looked very grand indeed. She smiled upon everybody.

'Well, indeed ... ' she said.

The noise we were making must have been tremendous. I can imagine her standing in the hall, listening, amazed. She had then time to prepare herself.

We looked ridiculously foolish, I in one of Johnny's overcoats, Aunt Hunnable in a Spanish shawl, Rose in a kind of nightshirt.

'Why, Johnny!' she said. 'You're having a party ... how jolly!' She came, beaming, and said 'how do you do' to each of us. 'Dear Mrs. Hunnable, how are you? ... Ah, Mr. Abel, how nice to see you! Mr. Lambert, how do you do?' (Lambert was Ralph's other name.) Before Charlie's wife she stopped.

'I'm afraid I don't—' she began.

'This is my wife,' Charlie said, stiff as a poker.

Only to Anne she was not quite cordial. For the briefest moment her round friendly face froze. She kissed Johnny and said: 'Well, isn't this delightful!

Charades, is it? How charming! Do go on!' and then, with a little gasp: 'Oh, my poor vase!' She bent down to pick up the pieces, her furs falling a little askew.

'Ah! and my books!' she said.

And then didn't we go! Carstang had already left. Mercia, rising flushed from picking up the books, said: 'Oh no, don't go! Please don't go! I'm afraid I've broken up the party! It's quite early.'

Yes, how we went! Only Charlie showed no discomposure at all. He shook her hand, looking in her face very sternly.

'Pleasant evening,' he said. 'Thanks.'

Johnny, who had hitherto said not a single word, went down to the door with his guests.

Mercia and I were left alone. She gave me rather a grim little smile and said:

'Well, well.'

She held a piece of the vase in her hand.

'I'll buy you another,' I said.

'Oh, it isn't that. Didn't Johnny get my telegram?'

'I don't suppose so. Or there wouldn't have been the party.'

She stood there, hating, as I well knew, the disorder of her room.

'It won't do. It WON'T do,' I heard her murmur under her breath.

'No, I don't think it will,' I answered and left.

On the stairs I met Johnny. Everyone had gone, hadn't wasted a minute.

'Good night, Johnny,' I said, putting my hand on his arm. 'It's been a lovely party.'

But he never said a word, went straight on up the stairs.

Out in the street I drew a deep breath. It was a grand night, the air sharp, the sky cold, the stars like fragments of ice.

I was a little drunk, but as I looked up I saw a concourse of chimneys—

cheeky chimneys, learned chimneys, abnormal chimneys, haughty conventional chimneys, ragamuffin chimneys, poetical chimneys, overfed chimneys, starving chimneys—and out of every one of them I saw, so drunk was I, figures flying, bodies naked and clad, long cadaverous bodies, cheering, waving their arms, their heads under their shoulders, bodies like spears and bodies like balloons—all escaping, all fleeing skywards, all rejoicing (although there was no sound) in their freedom.

And then, out of the sedate chimney of Mercia's proper little house, came Johnny—Johnny with his long legs and arms, his head high, his arms extended, Johnny flying into the stars.

I was delighted that he had escaped.

I cried out: 'Bravo, Johnny!' and went, rejoicing, home.

PART III: FLYING GULLS

CHAPTER I

For This Reality is No Reality

Early in August 1914 I was sent to Russia as roving correspondent for one of the London newspapers. I afterwards entered the Ninth Russian Army as stretcher-bearer, and it was not until the spring of 1916 that I returned to England. I did not, therefore, see anything of Cornelius during the first two years of the War.

I must here recapitulate, very briefly, my purpose in writing this book.

It has been my intention to select, out of a great mass of notes, recollected conversations, letters, journals, and reports of friends, the scenes and adventures that illuminate most eloquently Cornelius' growth and development.

I think that this is the FORM of book that Johnny would, himself, have liked to write about himself—a romantic, truthful history, romantic in its colour, truthful in its realism. I myself like a novel to be both romantic AND

realistic, and Johnny was the right figure for such a book. So that everything in this book hangs round him—and everybody in it too.

But when I come to these two first years of the War there are great difficulties. To the great adventure of his life at Baupon (he always considered it the great adventure of his life) I give a chapter by itself. Of the important things that happened to him BEFORE this adventure I have had to select and arrange, as well as I could. The things in this chapter are brought together from many different talks that I had with him; the main episode here

—the episode of the little French soldier—is exactly as he told me.

When the War broke out he was being unhappy. One of the causes of his unhappiness was his inability to earn his own living. I have before me now a letter that he wrote to his publisher at this time.

DEAR MR. WENTWORTH—I went to your office yesterday but you were unable to see me. I would like very much to have a little more money. I have received nothing for a year now—but perhaps there is nothing owing to me?

Would you kindly tell me? Would it also be impertinent of me if I asked you to send me a few books from your list of publications? I enclose a list and I hope you won't find my request unreasonable. Of course I don't want them all and will let you choose the ones you like to send me. I'm afraid that you are disappointed in my work so far although you haven't said so. Possibly I am late in maturing. My childhood went by without my learning a thing. When I finally went to school I was treated so harshly that it was a wonder I wasn't crushed completely. I am not complaining and I never talk nor write like this to anybody. But I want to explain things to you and I know you won't show this letter to anyone. I am thirty years of age and have published a number of books, but just now I feel very despondent, as though I had dropped back instead of moving forward. My wife has means, but it is the dearest wish of my life to be independent. You will not think me vain if I say that I am sure that I shall make my name one day and then everyone will claim that they have always understood me and praised me. Perhaps every unsuccessful writer believes this in his heart, but if one did not believe it one could not go on. When I was young, I was, in spite of hardships, very happy because my soul was filled with beautiful dreams—but now my soul is filled with reality.

It is all there, but the problem is how to bring it out in writing. I know that I shall do so. My three novels, The Sorcerer, The Three Beggar-Men, Anton Guld, have all been laughed at by the critics and yet they have in them certain things of which I am not ashamed. One critic said about Anton, 'Mr.

Cornelius wastes his time in this kind of writing.' Another said, 'Once he promised something but that hope is gone.' You told me yourself last time I saw you not to worry about critics and that nobody can please everybody, but it is because I think that YOU may be influenced that I am distressed. When the critics are bad and the books don't sell, then of course the publisher has a right to be discouraged. That is why I write like this to you. Please let no one else see this letter.

Yours very sincerely,

JOHN CORNELIUS.

The War came to him almost as a personal rescue. He forgot all his own troubles in his passionate desire to help his country. That sort of patriotism is rather suspect now when it seems to lead so easily to despotic tyranny. We are inclined to look back to those August days and smile contemptuously at those who thought that 'patriotism was enough.' And we see very clearly now that it isn't enough. But the emotions and beliefs of those young patriots of 1914 were genuine, ardent, and altogether self-sacrificing. Cornelius was in a fever to serve his country. 'I rushed at once to join up but my health wasn't good enough.' (We none of us knew then, as HE knew, without one word spoken to us, what his health WAS like!) 'I was C Three at once. Then I waited in London. That was hell. Everyone was hurrying to do something.

Mercia was in some sort of uniform almost before you could open your eyes.

Anne went into some Government office, you to Russia, Charlie to sea, Westcott and Rose to some training-camp. I was left alone. No one wanted me. The London streets were ghastly. Everyone went about saying it would be over in six months, but then

Black Sunday came, and I knew, somehow, in my heart, that it was going to be long and horrible.

'Then I got the offer of a job at a hospital in Paris. Some friend of Mercia's got it for me.' (I must repeat that this account of Johnny's time in Paris came to me always in bits and pieces. I would say, when we were walking or quietly smoking together after dinner, 'Tell me about the time in Paris,' and he would answer perhaps, 'Oh, we don't want to think of the War now' or he would begin:) 'Oh, Paris! ... yes, that was a muddled little hospital, you know. Old fat Mrs. Crosthwaite started it with her money, but that was at the beginning in 1914, when everyone was feeling their way. I got there when the Germans were in a stone's-throw. Before the taxi-cabs went out and rescued us. You could hear the guns all day. And the hospital was packed, filled to screaming-point. I was quite inexperienced, knew nothing at all. The hospital was in a suburb somewhere and I remember standing in the hall not knowing where to go and smelling carnations, roses, iodine and ether. They brought men on stretchers through the hall while I was waiting, one of them screaming, and I remember thinking with that double sense that all writers have, detached altogether and yet in the middle of it too (I felt it first that first day at Reiner's when the boys kicked me), I thought to myself—"Now I'm going to know what reality is at last." Because, you see, after what they had said about my novels never being real I wanted to bury myself, yes, right up

to the nose, in reality. "Now I'll know what reality is!"

'But that was the writing part of me. The other part wanted, above everything else, to help, to be of use.

'But I was stopped at the very outset by Miss Fennimore. Miss Fennimore hated me at sight. She was very tall, thin and frightfully efficient. She had a voice as clear and cold and peremptory as a dinner-bell. She wore her uniform as though it were made of white crisp iron and she liked it to be made of iron. She was upset, I suppose, in any case, by the confusion of the little hospital and the tiresome interfering fussiness of Mrs. Carey-Field. She knew her job and no one else there did. Then when she saw me, a writer (she heartily despised all artists) put in there by favour, knowing nothing, sycophantic (I was so desperately anxious to please) and always untidy—

well, she loathed the sight of me.

'I was greatly depressed by that. I have never liked being disliked—it always makes me nervous—and with her cold eye upon me I was even more clumsy than usual. I think I would have been dreadfully unhappy and even given it up had it not been for the episode of Miss Britten.' (He told me this little incident of Miss Britten several times. It was one of the really influencing things that happened to him.)

'Miss Britten was a little old English lady, something over sixty. One of those ladies that only England in all the world produces, quite a GRAND lady, absolutely virginal, Victorian, slender, charmingly neat, very reserved. She had come out to Paris, at the very beginning, to try and "do her bit." Some friend got her into this hospital. Miss Fennimore disliked her even more than she disliked me. Miss Britten had a voice like egg-shell china. She was religious and wore a gold crucifix on a chain. On my second or third day I was ordered into the operating-room and there I stood, holding things. Miss Fennimore was there and I saw that she had brought Miss Britten in and commanded her to a very unpleasant job. A young French soldier was being operated on. He had had both testicles shot away, and what remained of his private parts Miss Britten, by Miss Fennimore's orders, was holding. I doubt whether the old lady had ever seen a naked man in her life before. The young soldier wasn't a pretty sight. I thought that she would faint. But nothing of the kind. She was filled with a kind of glory and looked quite beautiful. I think of

Miss Britten quite often still. Is she alive, I wonder? What was the world like to her after her war experiences? Did she go back to the same Victorian reticence and decorum again? Very probably, because I imagine that none of the things that she did in that hospital were real to her. It was her own Victorian life that was real.

'I spent a lot of time at the beginning trying to placate Miss Fennimore. I wish now that I hadn't. It is of no use at all placating people. Not to hate them is the thing, hate being so ruinous to oneself.

'Then there was Mrs. Carey-Field. She was a well-meaning idiot, very rich—

before the War she was what you call "a young leader of the smart set," one of those women you see in the illustrated weeklies walking through the Park with one leg in the air. She was TERRIBLY silly, had a face like a good-

natured pig, and in a shrill piping voice would say, "But it's extraordinary!

Amazin'.... What can Miss Fennimore be thinkin' of?" and what Miss Fennimore WAS thinking would burn the air if spoken aloud.

'After a while I settled down very fairly. The Germans had retreated. We heard the guns no longer. The trees turned to gold and amber; the delicate lattice-work grille of the balconies of the houses on the little street seemed still to hold the heat of the baking summer days. The air had the soft powdery look of Paris skies. And I did what I could, bandaging, washing bodies, carrying meals. All my other life was dead. Mercia wrote to me. Otherwise I lived in expectation of letters from Charlie and Anne. They'd always written to me, you see, all my life when we'd been separated. Anne wrote regularly from her Government office in London. At long intervals I got strange laconic epistles, rather like police-reports, from Charlie, who was with the Fleet somewhere. For the rest I was in a vacuum, suspended in mid-air. My writing was no longer real to me. Nothing was real. The poor French soldiers were operated on, were washed, shrieked in delirium, were incredibly patient, and died. Those that didn't die sat about in chairs, hopped about on crutches, were charmingly polite, smiled, or stayed silent, their eyes gazing into space.

In spite of Miss Fennimore our little hospital was always in a muddle.

'Mrs. Carey-Field and her friends were the trouble, I suppose. As the War lengthened, ladies of her type were eradicated but they were dreadfully prevalent in that first autumn of 1914. They saw it all either as a screaming joke or as a melodrama. They had no touch with reality at all. But I had none either. I became to them all, except Miss Fennimore, a funny little oddity. I overheard one of Mrs. Carey-Field's friends one day saying something like

"Oh yes, my dear, he writes—but, darling, the most dreadful books. No one has ever been able to read them." That didn't matter; but Lord, how lonely I was! How I ached and ached for a sight of Charlie or Anne or you or Westcott! I kept thinking of my mother, as though she were with me in the hospital, wringing her damp hands and saying, "Oh, deary deary me! What ARE we going to do!" And my dear little father, he seemed to appear too, working at his shell-boxes, and old Mrs. Hoskin as I bundled her out of our cottage. They were all very much more real to me than anyone else. For I'd failed altogether to touch reality. Although death and suffering and courage and good humour were round me on every side I couldn't believe in any of it.

The soldiers liked me, I think, although I was a joke to them as I was to everyone else. They'd smile when they saw me coming. They gave me some kind of a nickname. They realized that Miss Fennimore was down on me, and, as they didn't like her, that put them on my side. Poor Miss Fennimore!

She did her very utmost to get some order and discipline into that place. She left at Christmas for some larger and more satisfactory job. Before she left she suddenly smiled at me and said: "You know, Mr. Cornelius, it's a great pity God didn't make a complete human being out of the two of us. I'm a drum-major and you're a—"

'"Clown, Miss Fennimore," I said.

'"Oh, well. That's too severe. I expect you're a genius. If I've been unfair to you please forgive me."

'"I haven't meant to irritate you," I said, "as much as I have done." At that she laughed very heartily.

'"If you had," she said, "I would have murdered you long ago."

'But it didn't matter very much, because she was no more real than the rest of them. Miss Britten had been real for one brief moment, but in private life she was desperately dull and uninteresting. Reality was nowhere and that was why I was so terribly lonely. And then (the whole point of all that I'm telling you) the little French soldier came— Pierre Rabelais. Yes, that was honestly

his name, and it was because of his name that I first noticed him. Rabelais, I thought—is there someone really to remind me of that enchanting, wall-

bursting, sky-tearing genius in here?

'"Is his name really Rabelais?" I asked one of the nurses, a dense plain-faced hockey-playing unluminous girl from Lancashire.

'"Of course," she said, looking at me severely. "Why shouldn't it be?"

'He was a short, plump, chubby little man with jet-black hair, sparkling black eyes, red-brown cheeks and only one leg. He had already had two operations and he had no left leg now below the thigh. He had suffered a great deal but still had his wonderful high colour and he was always smiling. Dressed in the uniform of the hospital, a blue jacket, a white shirt open at the neck, bright-

blue trousers, he pushed himself about in a chair. You could see on his brown chest the wiry black hairs. He must have been very strong before the piece of shell stopped him. I chatted to him and he was amiable and friendly to me as he was to everyone. He had a wife and two children at Villefranche down in the South and his thought was of them all the time. His reason for his superabundant happiness was that now that he had lost his leg ("définitivement," as he said) he wouldn't have to go back to the War any longer. His business was a little haberdasher's which he managed with his elder brother. "My leg, monsieur, what is it? It is here to-day. It is gone to-

morrow. Certainly it aches a little. They say that it is for the moment. I can sell my ties and my collars quite as well with one leg as two. And Armand my brother he is a good fellow, très bon garçon. He is serious-minded—very serious. And I—I am gay! So we suit one another handsomely. And my wife

—my small girl. Now I shall be always with them. We shall never part again.

She is the best woman—perhaps she is the very best woman in the whole of France."

'He was so extravagantly happy at the thought of going home "in one week, two weeks—at most three" that he couldn't keep quiet, was always flirting with the nurses, joking with the other wounded who were well enough to joke back, comforting those in pain. He was for ever pushing his wheel-chair up and down the passages.

'All this is commonplace enough—there are hundreds and hundreds of

anecdotes about the War just like it. What made it different for ME was his strong attachment to myself. He was, I think, the one and only creature in the whole of that little hospital who didn't think me comic or, at least, an oddity.

He took me, from the first, with the utmost seriousness. For one thing, he had the greatest reverence for anyone who had published a book. It didn't matter what sort of book—ANY book. There was a Monsieur Didier in Villefranche of whom I used to hear a great deal. He wrote poetry and, once and again, his poems were published at his own expense. "You ought to know him, monsieur. He buys his collars and his ties from us. He is a big tall gentleman with a long black beard and he is very indignant sometimes, there in our shop, at the bad writing that is published and often successful."

"'I've known other poets like that," I would say.

"'You have, monsieur?" Pierre would answer gravely. "I don't doubt it. One strange thing about Monsieur Didier," he would go on, "is that he will take very especial trouble in choosing his ties. And that is unnecessary because his magnificent beard always hides his tie. It would be charming—oh, very charming—if you and Monsieur Didier were to meet."

'One of Pierre's sorrows was that he could neither read nor speak English. So he could not read my books.

'"And none of them are translated into French, monsieur?"

'I feared they were not—as yet.

'"Why is that, do you think?"

'"You have so many excellent writers in your own language already."

'"Monsieur Didier does not think so," he answered.

'I discovered soon that I had a very great attraction for him. He was the hospital's favourite and I was HIS favourite—this really did something to raise me in my own esteem. I have wondered very often since what it was that made him fond of me. I think that, in the beginning, his protective feelings were roused. He saw that I was laughed at, that I was incompetent,

and that Miss Fennimore, especially, was hard on me. He thought this all very unfair, when I was, in his estimation, by far the cleverest person in the hospital because I had written books and nobody else had.

'I overheard him, on several occasions, hotly in my defence. The French seem to us in many ways hard, material, grasping. That is partly because they have, often, a clearer view of actual values than we have. Money and property are money and property to them, while we, who have been called a nation of shopkeepers, so often translate our money into sentimental enthusiasms. But the Frenchman is capable of intense personal feeling and affection. He can be exceedingly romantic and faithful as a dog.

'Some of my interest in him sprang undoubtedly from my anxiety about Charlie. They seemed, different though they were in temperament and character, to be one person. When, first thing in the morning, I arrived at Pierre's bed and saw his black eyes sparkling, and then with an arm about his tough shoulders helped him out of bed and into his chair so that he could go to the toilet, I seemed to feel a reassurance that because Pierre was "all right"

Charlie was "all right" too.

'He told me one afternoon of his affection for me. I was reminded of that day when I had sat with Charlie by the sea and we swore friendship. Pierre asked me whether I were married. I said yes. Then he asked whether I had any children. I said no. Ah, he said, shaking his head, that was a pity—children were a great blessing. Well, then, had I friends in England? Yes, I said, several, and especially two, one a man, one a woman.

'At that he shook his head again. He had never had close men friends. Of course he loved his brother Armand, and he had many good friends in Villefranche with whom he would drink and play dominoes. But a man close to your heart—no…. Women, yes! Many of them. He loved pretty women just as much now as he had done before his marriage even though he adored his wife. "A pretty woman is a pretty woman—always, until you die!" Then he became very serious. He put his hand on my knee. "But I love you, monsieur. You are the first man I have ever loved. I would do anything for you."

'I asked him why.

'"Why? Why? How does one know why?" He paused. Then he said: "I think it is because you have to be looked after. I feel for you a little as though you were my child. But then at the same time you are intelligent and have written books that have been printed. And then you are interested in my life, my little unimportant life. You listen when I tell you things…. But then, at the last, how does one know why one loves anybody if it is not of the opposite sex? If it is a woman—why, then of course it is because one wants to go to bed with her. But a man—a brother, a friend, a companion … " Then he laughed, catching my hand and holding it. "But it doesn't matter. Soon I go home and then, later, when this filthy war is finished, you come to visit me and meet my wife and children. That will be real happiness…. I will take you … " and he began to tell me of all the things we would do when I came to Villefranche.

'After that talk (which would have been ridiculous had it not been so honest) I was very much happier in the hospital. A great intimacy grew up between us.

I told him many things that I have told to you only—except Charlie and Anne of course.

'Then the weeks passed and still he did not go home. There was a slight wound in the thigh that did not heal. His bright black eyes were sometimes dimmed with a certain anxiety. We were approaching Christmas and it was all very melancholy. There seemed now to be no movement either on the Western Front or in our little suburb. A kind of icy frozen stillness filmed the world. Although everyone persisted in a determined brightness, melancholy dominated our hospital. Pierre was greatly distressed because it might be now that he would not be at home for Christmas. He had certainly counted on that, and his wife and little girl had counted on it too. "The boy's too young to understand. I imagine that he forgets me, but the others … And my brother.

He needs me in the shop. There is much business at Christmas-time."

'But they wouldn't let him go. The wound would not heal. I had been in the hospital now for more than four months without any leave and a kind of fantastic unreal curtain dropped down and intervened between oneself and the real world. No, certainly—reality was not here. We were all tired, overstrained, nervous. I slept badly and dreamt constantly of Pierre and Charlie as one person. Ah, how well, how exactly I remember it! I pursued

them through the tangled labyrinths of sleep, and at every turn, missing him, I was in a torture lest I should never see him again. If anything happened to Pierre then something would happen to Charlie too.

'Poor Pierre! Something DID happen! I had been out for a walk and, returning, chilled and windblown, heard that Pierre must have another operation—his third. "They must cut some more of the bone away." I went to see him. It was he who was now the child and I the protector. He held my hand and his eyes never left my face. It seemed that it was I in whom he had all the confidence, not doctors nor nurses. I could make it all right. He was dreadfully distressed that he would not go home for Christmas. He was also in great pain. Tears filled his eyes, but not because of the pain; because of his wife and children alone at Christmas-time.

'One grey drizzling morning there was the operation. I sat beside his bed afterwards, waiting for him to come round. At last he recognized me but did not speak, only held my hand.

'Next day he was worse and his wife was sent for. He was sometimes under opiates, sometimes asleep, but in his lucid hours he said again and again:

"You can do it, monsieur. You can make me well. It rests with you."

'In nightmarish fashion I felt that it did. I wrestled, I struggled, I prayed to God. I sat there and fought for his life and knew, beyond words to express, that I had not the reality in my own life to force my desires upon God.

'I had, in my own way, suffered, struggled, but it seemed like the ashes of a dying fire against the need of a moment like this. I realized then what the Saints, the Holy Ones can do. I was not real enough. My soul was not strong enough to give Pierre strength. He knew that his wife had been sent for, and now, in his conscious moments, he thought only of her arriving. He muttered her name and that of his little girl again and again: "Madeleine! ...

Madeleine! ... Lucille! ... Madeleine!"

'His eyes retained their brightness as though they must not lose sight of those he loved. Once, very weak but quite conscious, he smiled at me and said:

"Ah, monsieur, if I could but read one of your books," and then, with piteous anxiety, "Do you think she will arrive? Why is she not here?"

'I concentrated all that I had, all that I thought I was, on helping him. It was not enough.

'He died in the evening. His wife and child arrived half an hour later.'

CHAPTER II

The chÂteau at Baupon

This chapter is by far the most difficult and most dangerous in this book. I have watched with fear its approach from the very beginning.

In the first place, it was not my own experience: I must tell it at second hand.

Then it is the statement of someone's experience of a world which for a great many persons simply does not exist. Further, the very statement of it may shake my readers' belief in Cornelius' existence. Exist of course he did. There are the books; there are the eye-witnesses. But if he believed his experiences at Baupon to be true, then he must be both so foolish and so readily credulous of absurdities as to be uninteresting. But he DID believe them! They were the corner-stone of his life- experience. He found in them what he had, all his days, been expecting. He confided, I think, this adventure to no one but myself. He recounted the whole affair to me at one unbroken stretch, and it is a thousand pities that you must have it at second hand only.

I cannot be sure that I myself believed as I listened. I believed that JOHNNY

believed, but there had been things in his life, like the Bird-Man, that no one could prove.

There are perhaps in all our lives such things. We keep them as a rule to ourselves, because in the open air they dim, dissolve, offer opportunity for derision. Johnny had been derided often enough—THAT wouldn't disturb him. But it was nobody's business— nobody's but his.

Nevertheless any true account of his life must include it, because it was a most important factor in his development. And it gave him happiness as nothing else in his life did. So I translate it into my own unsatisfactory terms.

In the spring of 1916 he was sent to a hospital at Baupon, a small town south of Neuve-Chapelle. Storm had passed over it and gone, leaving it a ghost of a

place, a place of tranquillity that comes to those who have suffered so deeply that no more pain is possible.

It is described, as it happens, very eloquently in John Llewellyn's Spirit of War, the best perhaps of all the English War books. Strangely enough, both Llewellyn and Johnny emphasized the same two or three things—or is that strange? Both men were poets, dreamers, kindly-simple and yet NOT so simple.

Llewellyn describes the great farmhouse with its sandbags and splendid woodwork, the poplar colonnades, the windows of the houses sandbagged ...

Especially the church; Llewellyn writes of it: 'The large church, and the almost rococo churchyard, astonished everybody; they had been bombarded into that state of demi-ruin which discovers the strongest fascination. At the foot of the monolith-like steeple stood a fine and great bell, and against that a rusty shell of almost the same size; the body and blood of Christ, in effigy of ochred wood, remained on the wall of the church....' He ends (and I know he will forgive me for stealing these words from his pages) thus beautifully: '...

the spell which made us haunt there; the cajoling ghostliness of the many painted papers and manuscript sermons which littered the floor of the priest's house and drifted into his garden; the sunny terror which dwelt in every dust-grain on the road, in every leaf on the currant-bushes near that churchyard; the clatter of guns, the co-existent extraordinary silence, the summer ripeness, the futility of it, the absence of farmyard and cottage-doorway voices which yet you could hear.'

And here is the echo of Cornelius' voice as I tried to catch it: '...The War had passed the place over. There was the church, the priest's house, the graveyard, some of the graves open and pools of dirty green water there, the street with the poplars, best of all the great old farmhouse where they were beginning to live again in a kind of a way. It was all very peaceful with an awful sense of rape about it; shameful indignity ... in its eyes a beaten, disgraced look as though it had never conceived of the things that could be done to it.'

Their hospital was in a kind of large manor-house at the end of the street.

This house had escaped even partial destruction by a sort of miracle, although it was bare and gaunt and shame-faced. The hospital had always a temporary,

impermanent feeling, but it was efficient. Johnny too was efficient now. It was during this war- time that he lost for ever his more obvious clumsiness.

He would always be apt to forget where in fact he was, and he would at any time pass into states of contemplation and wonder that would make him blind to his more obvious company, but he learnt during these years a technique which helped him to cover up, for the outside world, his abstractions. He could listen and yet not listen, busy himself about practical things and yet pursue his imaginative journeys.

He had learnt by now a considerable amount of Red Cross routine. He would never be VERY useful, but he was useful enough.... After the experience with Rabelais he forced himself into what he hoped would turn out to be reality.

They all, apparently, liked him at this hospital. He never, after Rabelais'

death, seemed such a clown to anyone again. It was as though Rabelais, out of love for him, had taken some of that oddity away.

Mercia, Anne, myself, Westcott still wrote to him with fairly constant regularity, but he heard only at long intervals from Charlie, and this worried him terribly. It was, naturally, no fault of Charlie's. From his naval mysteries communication was never easy. Charlie was, I think, his only anxiety. 'No place in my memory, except Merlin, is so deeply interpenetrated with Charlie as Baupon. It seemed to me again and again that he was there with me, walking beside me down the ward, or standing at the end of the street waiting for me, serious-eyed, protective, his one business in the world to see that I was all right.

'Otherwise I was, I think, hypnotized by this place, as so many of us were by one place or another during the War. As though it would go on for ever and ever just like that. And I don't know that I wouldn't have been glad. For one thing I was useful. For another I was liked. Do you remember Rose telling us once how unhappy and lonely and unpopular he was in his schooldays? And then, his first night in Hall at Cambridge, he looked about him at the other freshmen round him, discovered that they were friendly, didn't know a thing about his awkward childhood and didn't care. His life began anew that night.

So it was with me at Baupon.'

It is here that I begin Cornelius' own account of his experience. He told me it without a break, in my flat in Jermyn Street on the evening of June 3rd, 1921.

He had dined with me there and we had intended to go to the theatre, but it was a close and stuffy evening, thunder threatening. All the windows were open, the sky was black above the roofs, and a sort of lazy indifference seized both of us, so that we sat, drinking our coffee, not wishing to move.

Johnny sat there staring at a small Cézanne water-colour on the opposite wall, my dearest possession. It showed Mt. St. Victoire and some fields, fragments of green, purple, brown.

'That's like Baupon,' he said suddenly, 'without the mountain, of course. I'll tell you about Baupon. My adventure there. Do you mind?'

'No, of course not. Go ahead.'

'Well—I've never told anybody. You won't believe it, but never mind. It's true. I'll try and give it you word for word just as it was. I've mentioned the place often enough. You must have known that something happened to me there.'

'Yes, I've always wondered.'

'I've never told anyone because they'd laugh. But you're fond of me and you're used to my fairy-stories. Not the ones that are published, but the others.... I'll try and make it as actual as I can. It seems to go on with me—

still to be happening, and it's the most real experience I've ever had. So, believe it or not as you please, but don't mock me.'

'Of course not.'

He continued, from beginning to end, without stopping, walking up and down part of the time, carried away into his experience, forgetting very soon my existence. The thunderstorm came and went. Then the rain came pelting down. After that there was a great hush over the world, only the weaving, slumbering murmur of the Piccadilly traffic.

Next day I wrote every word of it down. I forgot, I think, very little, but the

very fact of its being only second-hand loses it some of its vraisemblance.

Besides, if you never knew Cornelius you can't feel so certain of his honesty.

'Baupon was funny in some ways. Although it had been swept by war much of it had been spared. There were the poplars and the building where we had our hospital. It was never quite a REAL place—many others felt that besides myself. I remember a hospital orderly telling me that every morning he woke up he half expected to find the place gone. The hospital work was real enough for most of them, but never quite for me. Only the past seemed real to me. I felt like a ghost myself sometimes, and I used to think: "No wonder people say your books aren't real when life seems so unreal to you." You know how devoted I had been, since childhood, to Herman Melville. I had Pierre out there with me, one of the most unreal books ever written and one of the most real too. You've never read such unreal dialogue as there is in that book. How masters of actual dialogue like Bertrand would laugh at it! And yet behind the unreality it tells of the truest, most poignant experiences!

Melville was always with me, and when I went for my solitary walks we used to talk together. I expect I walked along talking aloud, and I'm glad no one caught me at it. If they had I might have been shut up for a madman! In the hospital I did my work all right; I was quiet and in nobody's way. I think they quite liked me. I was happy in a sort of fashion. The only thing that worried me was Charlie. I bothered about him terribly. I always bothered a bit when he wasn't with me, even in London. But now he was in constant danger and I knew that he was the kind of man who would be always quietly where danger was, because the authorities would trust him as a man who would never lose his head and would be first-rate in a crisis. I wrote practically nothing all this time. A poem or two and, I think, three fairy-stories. Nothing serious or important.

'Well—it was in the early part of June and beautiful summer weather, I remember. At this time I used to take a walk every day about four in the afternoon. I was on night duty just then. There were not very many walks you COULD take, but there was one road of which I was very fond. I liked it because of its scent. You could hear the very distant rumble of the guns like someone snoring through thick walls, but in spite of that this was an area of peace, on this road, and there was the scent of flowers and the dry richness of corn.

'I walked along this road every day and I used to imagine to myself that I could summon for my company anyone I pleased. Very incongruous company too—my old mad grandfather, my father and mother, Charlie and Anne, Ralph, Melville, Hans Andersen, Dickens. We had a grand time, though, understanding one another so perfectly. Why do you NEVER get that in real life—JUST the people who belong to one another and no one else? No spite then, nor jealousy, nor artificial talk, nor misunderstanding. We had it once, do you remember, that evening at my house when Mercia came back from the wedding in the country?

'Anyway it was like that in my road. I shambled along, kicking up the dust, smelling roses and carnations and corn, forgetting the War and those poor men in the hospital, really hearing the roll of the sea on the shore at Merlin, seeing Charlie seated at the cottage table taking a watch to pieces, which he did miraculously, hearing old Rose's voice booming, being almost TOO jolly, you know, with that nervous look in his eye, and Melville's handsome black beard, and Dickens very noisy, restless, impatient; my little father, my dear darling little father, taking my arm, smiling up at me to make sure that I didn't mind....

'I tell you all this because, to the sceptical, it may explain something of what happened afterwards. Certainly during these walks I lived in the past, present and future, all of them together— for me, at that period at least, there WAS

no time and, if Charlie had been with me, it would have been, I think, as happy as any phase of my life. Never QUITE happy, you know, for more than a moment. Is anyone, do you think, except a saint?

'Now to facts. It was a flat summer country that I saw, treeless, rolling a little in the distance to higher slopes. It was full summer. Against that distant roll of guns was the murmur of flies, of bees, and scents so strong that they seemed to HUM in one's ear....

'I noticed on a day that at the turn of the road there was a clump of poplar trees and a stream that ran by the roadside. I had never seen the trees until this day and I was surprised because I was certain-sure that I had passed beyond that point on many walks. Then another day and another I could not find them and began to believe that I must have been sleeping, then suddenly once again I came on them and the stream running beneath them. But on

THIS occasion three old men were seated under them, three beggarly-

looking old men, one of them in such rags and tatters that it would have been indecent had I had a lady with me. I stopped and spoke to them. They were, all three, brown-skinned and strong. One of them, naked to the waist, was washing his shirt in the little stream. His skin was almost blackened by the sun. I spoke to them but they did not answer. They looked through me as though I were not there. One of them was crunching a crust of bread; that was the only sound, his jaws munching. One of them got up to relieve himself and did so exactly as though I were not there. So, thinking them uncivil and ill-

mannered, I walked on.

'Now comes the day of which I want to tell you. I will try and remember every detail of it so that anyway you will believe that there WAS such a day, whatever may have really happened on it. In the earlier part of the afternoon I had assisted at the operation on a very fat middle-aged man whose leg must be amputated. It hadn't been easy, because the man was so fat, with very heavy thighs, and his leg was severed above the knee. I remember that, afterwards, some patient wanted me to stay and play chess with him and I had to struggle with my conscience because I longed for the fresh air and my own company so badly. Selfishness won, and when I reached my road I sighed with satisfaction as though I had escaped imprisonment.

'I remember that I wondered whether the trees and the stream would be there to-day. But of course they must be! If I had seen them once in actuality, then they MUST be there, whether I personally saw them or no—a blunder, perhaps, that we all of us make!

It was a glorious afternoon, fresh, with a breeze and utterly peaceful. No sound of the guns.

'"This is the sort of day we like, isn't it, Charlie?" I said. Yes. There were my trees and my stream and, most astonishingly, my three old men. Did they live there, then? They were eating something out of greasy bits of paper and one of them had his shaggy head tilted back and was drinking from a long rough–

looking green–coloured bottle. It struck me then that neither on the other day nor on this had I heard them speak a word, but, as I came up to them, one, an old white-bearded fellow, crumpled his piece of paper and threw it into the stream. It landed in the water at a little distance, was impeded by some stones and whirled round and round in the sparkling eddy. As on the other occasion,

they looked at me as though I weren't there, and now this exasperated me, so I spoke to them, wishing them good–day. It was quite clear that they didn't hear me and I had a quick thought that they might be deaf–and–dumb vagrants. I had encountered such once and again in France.

'But what I saw then took all my attention away from them—for there, on the right of the poplar trees, was a little road! I stared and rubbed my eyes. This exactly resembled one of my own fairy–stories! A road—and day after day I had wandered along here and not seen it! To reach it you had to cross the little stream, and I remember that I hesitated, as though to cross that stream would be something very eventful in my life. The sun was shining, the leaves of the trees moving ever so slightly in the breeze, the old man had the green bottle raised in the air, the white paper whirled in the stream....

'I stepped over and started down the little road. Almost at once I had turned a corner and saw to my astonishment ahead of me a beautiful scrolled gate with white pillars on which carved lions' heads were set, a high stone wall and the grey chimneys, bell–tower and rose–covered roof of a small château.

'I stopped and stared. What struck me at once was that I was in a new world.

Not only was I somewhere that had altogether been untouched by war. That was in itself remarkable enough. I quoted Llewellyn just now. I can give you the whole of his description of Baupon without misplacing a word: "the sunny terror which dwelt in every dust–grain on the road." Well, that "sunny terror" was for the first time since I had come to Baupon altogether absent.

Peace was victorious here, so strongly victorious that nothing, no sudden irruption of violence into the world's history could break it. I felt this as though it were a new experience in my life's knowledge. "Then there IS

peace," I thought. "One layer down. Dig only a little way and you will find it

—at any time, in any place, whatever is happening on the upper crust. Why haven't I always known this?"

'I didn't want to move forward. I felt as though one step of mine would break it, and I stood there staring at the old lions' heads gleaming in the sun, and the quiet roofs of the château and the trees thickly clustered beyond the stone wall.

'But of course I moved forward at last. Curiosity impelled me. I thought: "I'll

just look through the gates and see what there is inside." When I came to them I saw that they were double gates of exquisitely wrought iron and plainly of a great age. I saw another thing too: that they were open—and without any hesitation I walked through them. I was now in a curving drive lined with heavy old trees. The only sound was the very faint musical rustle of the leaves. I turned the corner and there was the house in my full view.

'It was a little château the like of which you will see often in France. Oddly enough, all the details around it are very clear to me but the house itself is vague. The bell-tower, the strong thick chimneys, a smooth green lawn, flower-beds, box-hedges clipped into shapes of animals, a ship, I remember, and the silence, the rich warm air, the thick clotted fragrance of roses and carnations— these things will never again leave me.

'Broad stone steps led to the door, which was ajar. I pushed it back and stood in an old panelled hall from whose shadowed afternoon somnolence a staircase led upwards. I went on. Nothing could have stopped me. It was as though I were led by a friendly hand.

'A heavy oak door faced me, and again as though obeying an order, I turned the handle, pushed with some force and then stayed, staring, amazed. What I saw was a large hall, high-roofed, black-beamed, a vast stone fireplace, some heraldic arms stamped on the stone, bare walls, a high window with plain glass, a long oak table, and at it, seated on trestles, some forty or fifty persons. What I felt instantly, as though someone had placed a finger on my lips, was the silence. These figures, old, middle-aged, young, were sitting there, looking quietly and absorbedly in front of them, but speaking no word.

The sun was shining in great shafts of light through the window and yet there was a cool fresh air in the great room.

'Then I looked and saw that at the far end of the table a man with white hair was seated. At once I knew him; I had seen him somewhere before. Every detail of his face and person was familiar to me. His head was massive, his hair of a brilliant snowy whiteness; he was deep-chested, broad-shouldered, thick-armed, but I recognized at once my old earlier knowledge that his white hair, his blue eyes, his ruddy cheeks, and above all, his large friendly intelligent mouth, in fact the strong firm greatness of his head, made one forget the rest of his body. He was wearing a loose easy suit of French

workmen's corduroys, almost a dull faded purple in colour, a very white, fresh crisp shirt open at his thick, corded, brown neck. I knew his clothes, I knew everything about him. I recalled at once the pressure of his brown strong hand—a working- man's hand, a little rough, the skin padded on the palms. And although he was now gazing very quietly in front of him I knew well his smile, which was as warm as cherry-blossom and as friendly as a dog resting his head on your knee.'

(I remember very well the exact moment when Cornelius said these words.

The thunder had passed but there was an angry slash of the after-rain against the panes. Cornelius was standing staring at the Cézanne water-colour, which, however, he did not see. I remember that I was telling myself: I don't believe a word of this. He's making it up as he goes along. Or perhaps he fell asleep after that long stretch at the hospital there, in the hedge by the side of the road.... And then I knew that I didn't want him to stop—that, whether this tale were dream or invention or whatever, two things were certain. First that the conviction of its reality had changed the whole tone and colour of Cornelius' inner life, and that secondly I was myself getting something from it, a sense of peace, of comradeship, of reassurance—and I smiled as I thought of Carstang's indignant outcry 'Bloody nonsense!' or of Bertrand's quiet weary cynicism, or even dear old Westcott's murmur: 'Let's skip this chapter, old man.' The rain fell more gently and Cornelius, who had been silent as though caught right back into that place, went on again.)

'...The strange thing is that I can't talk about this, can't THINK about it, without being transported back there. It's as though it's always going on; eternal that opening of the door, that high black-beamed hall, that silent, absorbed gathering and my friend at the table head. I have only to look, to gaze, and the actual scene strips away as with your hand you tear tissue-

paper. I can recapture his company at any moment. Well, that is fancy, of course, simply a trick that imagination plays. But this day of which I'm telling you was no trick. How am I to convince you? How? How? It can't be done.

But take that Cézanne down from the wall and hold it in your hands. Stare into it and see the little thick JABS of paint that Cézanne always makes—

thick, angry, so that you can see the man behind them angry, rebellious because he will ALWAYS fail; although he tries night and day all his life long he will never get what he wants on to his canvas. Isn't Cézanne real to

you then, MORE real than ninety out of a hundred you meet? So is my host to me, and this hall and the men and women round the table.

'One odd thing, by the way, was the YOUNG men. I hadn't seen a young man in France, save marching or wounded in the hospital, for months. But they were there—healthy, brown, with all their limbs. Old men and women too.

Peasants for the most part.

'I saw that there was an empty chair and I sat down at the table. Then I FELT

the silence. I've often thought that with August 1914 the whole earth began to rumble and with every month of every year that rumbling has increased. You know how it is with a live volcano—the movement, the muttering, the growing savagery, the fire and smoke, the explosion. So with the world since

'Fourteen. The noise, the unsteadiness of the ground under our feet, grows ever greater, and so it will perhaps for what seems to us a long time; a period, though, that is very brief in history. At last the explosion comes. The whole surface of the world is changed. A new ground appears for men to work on.

'As the earth trembles every sound is accentuated—the walls shake, the rivers murmur, the trees quiver, men shout to make themselves heard, and behind their shouts you can hear their hearts beating. But I said ON THE SURFACE.

One layer down there is the same peace there has always been. Yes, although your body dies. I don't know what terrors are in store for us—the whole world in conflict perhaps—but beneath the surface this peace that I realized in Baupon is always to be found.

'As we sat there, no one speaking or moving, peace increased with every beat of time. It was like the silent flooding–in of waters. You remember last year when we were at Roundstone in County Galway? We drove to some beach to bathe and, coming back, we watched the tide flood in through every creek and flat. The colour held us entranced, the blood–red seaweed, the white cottages, the deep blackness of the peat, the green of the turf so bright one shaded one's eyes. And I stayed there lost, while all the waters flooded in without a sound, and the wild geese flew, as strong and still and certain of their course as fate, across the sky.

'You said: "It's peaceful here, isn't it?" and I didn't reply because, once again, I had recovered the peace of Baupon and was plunged into it, the whole depth

of my being. That's what it was like. While one sat there peace rose higher and higher and one waited at last, in a kind of ecstasy, for the moment to come when one would be submerged by it....

'We all bowed our heads. Our host lifted his hands to bless us.

'When I raised my head again it seemed to me that he was smiling directly into my eyes, and I smiled back to him. Oh! how happy I was! This at last was reality. I felt too that it was eternal and, whatever outward things happened to me, I would never again be without this friendship. I can't convey to you how SAFE I felt. That friendship would always be there for me, and I knew that, in the days to come, I could always now, by an effort of will, move into this peace and stay there.

'Everyone rose and we all, like a cloud dissolving, passed from the room. I walked with head erect as though I had been given a prize, but in the garden, once again, I found I was alone. Where all my friends had gone I couldn't tell.

'I passed out of the beautiful gates, down the road, and there were the trees, the stream, the three old men. I crossed the stream. Here was a strange thing!

Looking about me I saw that the shaggy–haired man was still drinking out of the green bottle, and in the stream the crumpled paper was whirling against the stones.

'That's all,' Cornelius said.

He didn't, I remember, look sheepish as a man does when he has finished a story without point. For his story WAS without point. Had I been less fond of him, less tender to his naïvetés, I might have known that embarrassment one feels when a friend has, unwittingly, betrayed himself. But I felt no embarrassment, nor did he.

'Now you know why I think so often of Baupon,' he said.

CHAPTER III

Charlie

In the late spring of 1917 I returned to England on leave from Russia, and Cornelius was given some kind of job as a temporary supernumerary in the Foreign Office.

When I met him again after our long parting he seemed to me greatly changed. I knew nothing at that time about Baupon; if I had, I might have accounted to myself for a new maturity that I found in him. He was still often irresponsible, forgetful, untidy, and foolishly generous and extravagantly trustful, but his old boastfulness was altogether gone. He told none of us any more of the wonderful writer he was going to be. Naturally, by this time no one thought or talked very much about literature. It seemed, even the best of it, of small importance, and I fancy that from that year to this one—from 1917 to 1936—English Letters have never recovered the quiet happiness and friendliness that they had before 1914. Fretful, restless, irritable, innovating for innovation's sake, so it has been, much of it, since then.

But, in any case, this was the year when Cornelius published his fourth novel, The Wagon and the Horses, which was, alas, his saddest failure of them all.

Once again he attempted a large canvas with many figures, once again he aimed at a grandiose symbolism and perpetrated some very naïf moralizing.

The book received short indifferent notices. There was an exception to this brevity. Once again Stromberg poured out his scorn in two full columns of sarcastic derision. He could not let Cornelius alone. Something in the colour of poor Johnny's work irritated him to a frenzy—and, I must sorrowfully admit, once again the extracts that he quoted were ridiculous—too sentimental and naïf to be borne. The book was a complete failure. It was the last in Wentworth and Gibbon's contract and they informed Johnny that they did not think they could make another.

I noticed, too, with a good deal of uneasiness, that the other critics seemed to

dislike Johnny very much indeed; not only his work but himself also.

Some writers are disliked, as I've said, because they are bombastic, self-

advertising, always pushing their noses into other people's affairs, arrogant and so forth. But Cornelius had been none of these. He had never written letters to the papers, or publicly praised other writers (thereby exasperating the writers he DIDN'T praise), or joined committees, or lectured in America.

He had been as quiet as a little lamb, except among his friends, where his self-applause had been so innocent and young that no one could have been offended by it. Moreover, he had never had any success, and writers in general like unsuccessful writers and seek to do them a kindness whenever they can. No, the general opinion conveyed to me was that Cornelius was an ass who had married a rich woman for her money. He was also praised by the WRONG people, like Rose, who need only to speak well of something for everyone to turn their heads away from it.

It would certainly have seemed to me (as it seemed to Westcott and Carstang) that Johnny had failed altogether as a writer had I not read The Bright-Green Shoes.

I ventured to say something about it. 'Publish a real volume of your fairy-

stories. That's where your talent lies, Johnny.'

He didn't say very much at the time, but a week or so later, when I was visiting my people in Scotland, I got this letter from him.

'...One of the great things that the War has done for me, old man, is that I have been for two years now financially independent of Mercia. I am earning more in good hard cash than I ever have in my life before. I'm happier and Mercia is happier too. In fact Mercia is very happy indeed, because in the Trenton Street Hospital she is in daily contact with Lady Pauley-Walker and sees, twice every week, the Countess of Moles. Is that unkind of me? You know us all anyway and I can't hurt Mercia by anything that I say. In fact I can't hurt anybody! That's the truth. No one in the world save Charlie, Gwen, Anne and yourself, takes me seriously at all. I'm a sort of Toy Clown—first to Mercia and then to everyone else. In the F.O. they pay me generously but treat me with a contemptuous kindness. I'm useful, it seems, in helping to entertain unimportant foreigners, arranging meetings, writing little articles.

I'm an odd handy man whom everyone at heart despises. What is it in me, old man, that has made everyone from childhood onwards—Mrs. Hoskin and Mrs. Garriman, Mr. Lipper, Lady Max, Reiner and so on and on—find me so inconsiderable? Shall I reassert some of my old arrogance and say that I don't find myself inconsiderable at all? I'm a serious person like everyone else born of man and woman. I love my fellow-man and wish him well. I've seen things in France that all the ancient stars in all their sparkling arrogance can't equal for courage and fortitude and humour in the very eyes of death. They are considerable, my fellow- men, of a grand pattern, and often they move and act like gods. But am I not considerable too? They won't have me so.

Which brings me to this creative business. The Wagon has failed, I understand, as completely as a book can fail. And this man Stromberg—why does he hate me so? You would think I had raped his daughter or stolen his fortune by the way he writes of me. It isn't even as though he had my reputation to destroy, for I have none. There is something in the very smell of me that makes him sick. We have met only twice, I think—once at Bertrand's, once at the Crossbow Club. Both times it was difficult not to laugh, for he is so broad and fat and red-faced, so confident and deep-voiced, and I so lanky and shambly and apt to say such foolish things if in the wrong company. And how Bertrand watched us! Not unkindly. It is rather that in his own deep suspicion of himself there is something that welcomes the reassurance that he is not alone in his discomfort.... Anyway it is not, of course, Stromberg only. They all think the same, don't they? All except kindly creatures like Rose and Albion. It's strange by the way, isn't it, that while Bertrand denies the virtues because he at heart believes in them, Rose accepts them for the same reason? But I believe that DENIAL is going to be

"The Thing" for the next thirty years at least. Here we are. I'm no novelist, I'm no writer at all. All the same, who knows what a creator is? Does he perhaps not exist before his audience have discovered him, or, at any rate, is he never really created UNTIL then? Meanwhile the fun is in the creating, and I suppose that in any case that's no crime. I spend a year in writing a book and every day of that year it's as though I were digging for treasure. I loathe the sweat of it. I curse and abuse my fellows and behave like a swine.

But at last my mattock hits the wood of the chest, with eager cries we haul it up out of the dust, and then—if it seems authentic treasure to oneself isn't that reward enough? Who has ever cared for Melville's Pierre or Redburn save one or two, and aren't THEY treasure, I ask you?

'But it's a lonely business. I'd like to be acclaimed. Of course. Of course. Who wouldn't? Yes, I'd like men to say I was a grand fellow. I've wanted it all my life. Once like hay to a starving donkey. Now less. Perhaps less and less as life moves on.... I'm a failure then and perhaps shall always be one and there's this filthy war that maybe will never end, and my few friends scattered. And against these bad things what? A child's fairy-story of six thousand words, you'd say. You want me to make a book of them. I've got now— how many? A dozen perhaps. And how foolish they'd seem, poor little things. THERE'D be food for Stromberg indeed! I do those stones too easily, my friend. They are so childish that I'd blush for the world to see them. No, I'll at another novel, say what you like. I'm CONVINCED I can do it. And I know now, after Baupon, what reality is. You don't know about Baupon, do you? I'll tell you one day. OF COURSE my novels are real. I've a right to make my own world, haven't I? Charlie is coming home on leave, Gwen tells me. He's been somewhere off Galway. Isn't that grand? You and Charlie and Anne, all of us in town together, in the middle of this beastly war. We'll have a dinner....'

We did.

But first I had some interesting contact with Mercia. If Johnny had matured since my last meeting with him, so had she.

It is true—half-true at least—as Bernard Topping used to say: 'The moment you're born you're done for!' That is, the qualities with which you start the race you have still with you at the defeated conclusion. All the same, some of these same qualities, defects, are starved, some fed to repletion. Like animals in the Zoo they thrive, or sink into a decline—monkeys, snakes, hyenas, birds of paradise and the time-ancient crocodile— what a collection! And believe me, my friends, the preaching friar will tell you, it is your own affair, this starving and fattening. Blame neither God nor Fate for it.

The War, then, had fostered the wrong qualities in Mercia. She was an egoist and a snob. People forget in these days how good a time some patriotic workers had in the War. Mercia was among these. It was, I am sure, the happiest period of her life.

She moved now, with the assistance of Lady Pauley-Walker and the

Countess of Moles. They were honest women, doing, I don't doubt, their best for their country and considering Mercia very little, if at all. But they saw her every day, she was efficient and obedient; she was at their houses. There were Charity Concerts, Committee Meetings and the rest.

The effect of all this upon Mercia was intolerable. When I saw her she was in an official blue uniform with stiff cuffs and collar and looked, with her magnificent hair, resplendent. I have said before that she liked me although she knew that I detested her. She stood, ready to go out, in the middle of the little drawing-room where, once upon a time, we had played charades, and greeted me like a queen.

'You've come to see Johnny, of course, not me. All the same, I'm glad to see you. How well you look! Russian Revolutions seem to agree with you! What do you think of Johnny? Poor boy ... the critics do go for him, don't they? It's lucky he married me or I don't know WHERE he'd be! Yes, I've got to go.

You must forgive me, but we're working night and day. Mildred Moles is calling for me in half a minute. She's late as it is. Not like her. Sit down a minute. Johnny's at the F.O. Just the same. As feckless and helpless as ever.

DEAR Johnny. Now tell me about Russia. Rather an illusion the steam-roller business, wasn't it? Ah, there's Mildred! ... '

And that was all that I got this time out of Mercia. Nevertheless something of importance. For I detected, I fancied, a different timbre in her allusions to Johnny. It was something very faint, as when, moving a familiar clock from the mantelpiece where it has always stood, you place it on a table by the window. That familiar tick-tick, always associated by its silvery note with the bowl of roses near the fire, the flicker of the flames, the stupid faces of the two nodding Chinese mandarins, is now more distant, and has part in the sudden opening of the window, the rushing-in of air, the billowing curtain, the creaking of a swaying bough.

Mercia, I reflected, as I walked slowly homewards, would possibly be beginning now to repent of her bargain. When she had married Johnny she had got just what she wanted with him, people like myself, Westcott ...

people more interesting (God help us!) than those she had hitherto known.

But now we were of little value to her in comparison with Mildred, Countess of Moles. And Johnny too had changed. Then he had been a child, helpless,

dependent on her, to whom she could play the Divine Goddess. But NOW—

to play Divine Goddess to a hopeless, foolish failure whose social tastes were irretrievably bad! Besides, although she had not wished for Johnny such success as would make him independent of her, she certainly had not wanted that he should be independent of her WITHOUT the success!

Worst of all, Johnny's sweetness and unselfishness must have been a bad thing for her egotism. Johnny would not be harmed by Charlie's unselfishness because Charlie loved him and he loved Charlie. But, where no love is, selfishness if fed by unselfishness becomes a devouring flame. Mercia, I could see, would take all now that Johnny could give her and despise him the more for giving it. I was sorry for her, very sorry, but oh! didn't I dislike her!

We had our dinner—Johnny, Gwen, Charlie, Anne and I. We dined at Paolo's in Covent Garden. I have mentioned before that this book has nothing to do with my feelings for Anne, so I will only say here that for many and many a month I had been anticipating this meeting.

Anne was living now, quite openly, with Lieutenant-Colonel Henry Batten, D.S.O., a distinguished officer who had lost a leg in France, who was no chicken, no beauty, no intellectual, who loved Anne with all the passion of a good, stupid Englishman. Anne was as usual moved by being desperately sorry for him. His wife, maddened by his five-minute bouts of raucous coughing first thing in every morning, had left him and lived comfortably at Cannes. Yes, Anne was desperately sorry for him and there is nothing more to be said.

She was looking wonderful that evening, radiantly happy because she was with Johnny again. The three of them sat together on the faded plush settee at Paolo's while Gwen and I, on chairs, faced them. They sat, Johnny in the middle, as though they were one person. But Gwen and I were happy too, Gwen because she knew that she had something of Charlie's that no one else had, I because my feelings about Anne were my own and no one could take them away from me.

We had, too, that night, something of the melodrama that was, in that year, possessing the whole of London. Like thousands and thousands of others at that same moment, we were fostering a hectic feverish happiness because we

had our warrior home from the wars— and because a week from that festivity, he might be trailing his guts in the dust.

I doubt whether Charlie was conscious of this. He possessed more common sense than any human being I have ever known, and he always took the immediate situation for exactly what it was. Here he was in London, safe and sound, in London with Johnny, Anne and his wife close beside him. What else mattered? Nevertheless the War had done something to him, too. It had given him a new responsibility, a fresh certainty of his powers. He was just one of the best engineers alive in England to-day. You could never call Charlie conceited. If he THOUGHT himself one of the best engineers in England he WAS one, that was all. Also he knew now what he hadn't known before—he could command men. On the ships where he had served he had been given more and more authority because men obeyed him without question. He never said anything of this. He was the least boastful of men.

But it could be detected. Gwen, who was a mousy, round, soft little woman, allowed herself to be entirely ordered by him. She may have rebelled a little at first, for she had, outside her relation with Charlie, much independence of spirit, but where the uninstructed observer might see only a broad-

shouldered, blue-eyed, uneloquent, pig-headed English mechanic, she discerned one of the most remarkable men in the world—and I'm not sure that she wasn't right.

But the wonderful thing about these three was that they had, when they were together, an increased vitality and intelligence. Anne lent jollity, gay exuberance, confidence in life, Charlie common sense and sobriety, while Johnny was so happy when he was with them that he was the very spirit of almost unearthly joy.

His complete life indeed no one has ever seen who has not known him with his two friends.

To-night we had all the best that Paolo's could offer. Johnny had brought a bottle of champagne with him. We had the famous Trout and the still more famous Paolo Chicken à la King. Gwen had never seen chicken served under glass before, nor had she ever tasted a Bombe surprise. Although these were rationed days we had an excellent meal.

Johnny looked after everybody and Charlie looked after Johnny. 'Now you must all drink MY health. I'm the host and it's wrong for me to ask it, I know.

But I tell you why. It's because I want you to drink to the greatest literary failure in Europe. Does that throw a damper on the proceedings? No, it doesn't. Because I don't care a damn. It's something to be the greatest anything. So here goes.'

Charlie, putting his hand on Johnny's arm: 'Don't you care what those men say in the paper. They wouldn't be writing about your books at all if they could write books themselves.'

'I'm not so sure about that,' said Johnny, laughing. 'It's the excuse that every bad author makes.'

'What are books anyway?' said Charlie. 'Writers aren't important. Who cares what they do or say? No man who IS a man reads a book unless he's tired and wants to sleep.' He looked up affectionately into Johnny's face. 'You're a lot more than a writer, Johnny.'

'I hope I am,' said Johnny, laughing, 'or where WOULD I be?'

Here occurred a strange little incident. At the very moment when Johnny was making his first public confession of failure, the meeting occurred that was to give the lie to his every sentence.

I had already noticed that, seated at a little table near to us, were Will Hampden, the critic, and his guest, Luke Smith, the artist. Luke Smith, a young, cherubic, pink-faced fellow, was a very fine artist indeed, deriving, in his serious drawings, from William Blake, but extremely talented also in his humorous drawings. His illustrations to The Book of Common Beasts were very famous.

They got up to go. Hampden nodded to us and said:

'Cornelius, one moment ... '

Johnny rose and they stood talking close beside us. I heard what they said. I was made indignant at once by the veiled patronage in Hampden's voice

when he spoke to Johnny, but I was pleased to see that Luke Smith was far from patronizing. He was indeed eager, enthusiastic, and his large, round, rather baby eyes gazed on Johnny with admiration. The two men had not met before.

'The fact is, Mr. Cornelius,' Smith said, 'only this week someone lent me your fairy-stories.'

'My fairy-stories?'

'Yes, the four stories in the green cover. A very rare book, I believe. The truth is I'm crazy about them and they're designed by Heaven for me to illustrate. I hope you don't think it cheek, but I couldn't let the chance slip. I've thought of nothing else since I read them. Have you considered republishing them—an illustrated edition perhaps?'

Johnny, as always when his fairy-stories were mentioned, was very unenthusiastic.

'Could we meet one day? Would you let me show you a drawing or two?'

Johnny, liking Smith at sight, most amiably agreed.

When he sat down again Charlie said: 'What's all that about?' He showed at once all his old alarm lest Johnny should commit himself to something foolish.

'Oh, nothing,' said Johnny. 'That's an artist fellow.'

We decided to walk to my flat, so lovely a moonlit night. 'What a night for a raid!' we heard someone say as we left the restaurant. We started down the hill towards the Strand, Anne, Charlie and Johnny in front, Gwen and myself behind.

Gwen, elated perhaps a little by the drink, talked to me in her soft, slightly Cockney, shy-friendly voice.

'It's nice having Charlie back. I wish he hadn't got to go away again.'

'So do we all, Gwen.'

'You know, I have to say it. I've been wanting to a long time. You're all so awfully good to me, I mean you and Miss Swinnerton and Mr. Cornelius, of course—I mean HE'S good to everybody, isn't he?'

'And the rest of us only to some people?' I teased her, laughing.

'Oh no, I don't mean that. You know I don't. But I do love Charlie so and really he belongs to all of you, doesn't he?'

'Of course he doesn't. He belongs to you.'

'To Mr. Cornelius most. And I don't mind a bit. What I mean is that Mr.

Cornelius needs him more than any of us. He's so alone in the world. If it weren't for Miss Swinnerton and Charlie he wouldn't have anybody.'

'Well, aren't you alone, Gwen, except for Charlie?'

'Oh, I'm used to being alone. I always was. I can get along. Besides Charlie's my husband and that gives you a kind of special relationship, doesn't it? But Mr. Cornelius is one of those gentlemen who wants affection and kind treatment. At least that's what I think. If anything ever happened to Charlie, Mr. Cornelius would be more lonely than I should, if you understand what I mean. Although I don't know what I'D do without Charlie. I really don't. He's such a splendid man, isn't he?'

'Splendid,' I said.

'He doesn't say much, of course, but he's cautious. He says words are dangerous. I think he's right, don't you?' Then she added, giving me a shy, quick look:

'I don't like Mrs. Cornelius, do you?'

'No, I don't,' I said.

'I think it's hard on Mr. Cornelius being married like that and not having success with his books. And yet he's often in high spirits, isn't he? Like to–

night. I DO like him! Oh, I do! He isn't like other people, is he? I wish they could feed him up a bit. He's so very thin.'

The Strand, under the moon, was like running water, and swimming in its crystal flood was all that war population, the strange figures belonging to this unusual world, soldiers with their girls, women hysterical with the unreal closeness of sudden death, and, outside the moonlight, where the shadows fell, such darkness and silence and a breathless waiting for events.

For myself, who had but just come from a whole world in Revolution, who had seen, in the space of one short half–hour, a familiar town with its cabs and shops and canals changed into an unknown landscape where life was unimportant and human nature threw away all its laws of self–protection, it was not difficult to imagine this street deserted and a rifle behind every window....

One ... two ... three ... A shout, the waving of a rag, a rifle–shot, a rush of men ...

We were standing outside Charing Cross Station, had paused there.

'We must finish up in my flat,' I said. 'I'll like to remember ... '

The raid-warning sounded. At that sound and at the immediate awareness that the sky was slashed with searchlights, I was plunged back into that world of terror and panic that I had so lately left. It was as though I had been sitting in a warm room and someone, lifting me bodily, had flung me out of window into an ice-cold world.

Moreover on every side of me my fellow-beings were hastening into shelter.

They disappeared, men, women and children, with an astonishing celerity into the bowels of Charing Cross and down the steep side-street into the security of the Underground. Men on motor-bicycles tore along the Strand sounding their orders for us to take shelter.

The Strand was, in that instant of time, cleared of all human beings and slept now in a new lovely tranquillity, streaming its silver waters under the banks of the dark houses. The only activity now was in the moonlit sky, where long

shining smoke-bands of light quivered with a sort of triumphant happiness while in the distance very faintly could be heard the whisper of aeroplanes.

'What about it?' said Johnny, smiling.

'Oh, let's go on to his flat,' said Anne. 'Let's walk. Nothing will happen.'

'Yes. Let's walk. Let's walk,' said Gwen, taking Charlie's arm.

So we started forward, our hearts beating a little perhaps, but feeling, I am sure, that imminent closeness to actuality that was one of the War's best gifts.

So many things in our lives had been sham and artificial and disappointingly without bottom that we might have fancied, had it continued like that, we had been born, like torn litter, in a waste-paper basket. Charlie's indifference to the situation would have reassured anybody. He had Gwen on one side of him and Johnny on the other; his supercilious disdain of anything the Germans could do would have been foolish had it not been so unconscious.

We came to the edge of Trafalgar Square and hesitated.

I hesitated, I remember, simply because it looked so very vast. I recalled very vividly the Nevski Prospect when there had been no soul in sight and it had seemed the most dangerous length of ground I had ever experienced. A delightful writer of my youth, Mr. Guy Boothby, used in every one of his fifty novels this phrase—'One step forward meant death'—and I can only explain Trafalgar Square by saying that life had quite suddenly become Guy Boothby. The lions, which had always seemed to me very silly animals and much too true to be good, appeared to have eyes full of apprehension, to have sprung, for once, to agitated life, and Nelson, at the height he was, was preparing, I thought, to jump at any moment. It was Charlie again who gave us reassurance.

'I was just thinking,' he said (and it was what he WAS thinking— there was no pose about it), 'of a new pump they're trying on the Damocles. It's so blinkin' simple that—'

And so we walked across, picking our way rather carefully as though we were trying not to crush the buttercups....

But at the very moment when we reached the further pavement there was an explosion that seemed to come from the very ground under our feet. As a matter of history it didn't. We learned the next morning that a bomb fell on some newspaper offices near the Lyceum Theatre in the Strand, killing a number of persons.

But, for that instant, it was as though our whole world blew up. We looked, expecting to see the lions tumble and Nelson fall from the sky. Charlie (I can see him still) had one arm round Cornelius, one round Anne, but what he said as the roar died away was, 'All right, Gwen?'

The impulse of all of us was, I know, to run for our lives. There might, at any moment, be another directly where we stood. But the most eerie thing, as I remember it, was a dog's howl, the only sound now, but so grievous and eloquent that it seemed to come from the very heart of living things.

Then, recovering a little, and feeling in some unexplained way a bit of a fool, I had a momentary but at the same time eternal sensation that it was the complete old familiar London that has blown up. I say 'eternal' because it has, in a way, been 'eternal' to me. I shall never lose it as long as I live. I look back, all these years after, to that explosion, as the end of the London of Chaucer, Shakespeare, Fielding, Dickens—the London of romantic grime and obscurity, of Quilp and Jonas Chuzzlewit and Mrs. Gamp, of twisted chimneys and dark alleys, and the beef-and-beer hostelries and the low music-halls and gin-palaces, and drunken women and skulking beggars—a world over which the sky pressed, dark and lowering, when, as though under ground, the gas-jets flared to the distant rattle of the cloppetty cabs and there was a wild lawless gaiety of poverty and battle and fecund drinking conviviality, smoke and fog, gaslight and jollity, muddled, disregarded birth and death....

London from that night became another world to me—better or worse I don't know. An explosion doesn't change the world. Only the slow progress of knowledge in the hearts and minds of men. The scene-shifters had crossed the stage. That's all.

We reached my flat and were very happy there. It was the last evening we were ever to have all together.

Three months later—early in October 1917—my telephone rang. It was about seven in the evening and I was dressing for dinner. I was, as a matter of fact, drying myself after my bath and I stood at the telephone, a towel around my middle, water dripping on to the carpet.

'Hallo! hallo!' I remember that I was impatient because I was wet and naked.

It was Johnny's voice. I said at once, very anxiously:

'What's the matter?'

'I've just had a telegram. There's been an explosion on Charlie's ship. He's in hospital in Portsmouth. Badly hurt.' Johnny's voice had a childlike, beseeching quality, as though he were saying: 'Please don't believe this. I don't believe it myself. I shall wake up in a minute.'

The voice began again:

'Would you be a brick and come down to Portsmouth with Gwen and me?'

'Yes. Of course. I'll meet you. What train are you going by?'

He told me.

I put down the telephone, finished drying and dressed. I remember very clearly that I did what I seldom do. I talked aloud to myself. I said something like this: 'Charlie will be all right. Charlie's so strong and independent.

Nothing can touch him. No explosion. Nothing. It can't. It can't.'

I realized with a start of surprise how extremely fond of Charlie I myself was and how often, without knowing it, I had gone to him for advice. Many people did. If he liked you there was nothing he wouldn't do. If he disliked you (and he was often irrational in his judgement of people) you always disliked him, thought him pig- headed, unmannerly, obstinate, conceited. But if he liked you— what a friend!

However, I was, very soon, thinking only of Cornelius. If anything happened to Charlie what WOULD Cornelius do? Lonely enough as he was, but now, at the moment of his complete failure, this other, more desperate blow would

END him surely, put finis to his whole story ... ?

In the dark and gloomy station (stations in the War had a fearful air of doom and damnation about them) we met, Cornelius, Gwen and I. Gwen had, since she heard the news, mustered every scrap of courage, endurance and wisdom that belonged to her. Like all fine women when someone loved is threatened with danger, she achieved at once a kind of selfless heroism that is beyond any man's attainment. She was thinking only now of Charlie. Small, mousy (her eyes bright and watchful like those of a bird who is suspicious of harm to its young), wrapped in some rather cheap furs, she only said:

'Charlie will be all right, don't you fear ... and he'll be home for a bit, thank heaven. That's the first thing I thought of, Mr. Cornelius. Charlie will be home for a bit now, I said.'

I asked Johnny exactly what his message had been.

'Only that ... only the usual one. "Seriously injured." They sent it to Gwen and she rang me up.'

'Yes. I had to tell Mr. Cornelius at once. He was so kind. He said at once he'd go down with me.'

Go down with her? Did she realize that this would be worse? Oh yes, infinitely worse for Johnny than for her.

But presently she said something that moved Johnny very deeply.

'You know, I've something to tell Charlie. I was going to write him, but now I shall be telling him. We're going to have a baby.'

Johnny turned and stared at her.

'Are you really?'

'Yes, we are. I'm ever so glad. We'd thought we wouldn't for a bit yet, but it was that night of the air-raid. He said if anything DID happen, why, I'd have somebody ... '

Here there was a catch in her throat. She struggled for a moment, then said:

'I hope it's a boy. I like boys.'

The only thing Johnny said about Charlie was once, when I thought he was asleep, he muttered:

'Do you think he's bad?'

'You can't tell. You can't tell anything from a telegram like that.'

'No. You can't, can you? I expect he'll pull through. He's awfully strong. You think he'll pull through, don't you?'

'He's wonderfully fit,' I said. 'He always has been.'

When we reached Portsmouth we went at once to the hospital. We were received into that world of order, discipline, cleanliness. Waiting in a little room, an old doctor with a kind mouth and white bushy eyebrows came in to see us. He addressed himself chiefly to Gwen.

'I'm afraid your husband is pretty bad. We have had to amputate the right leg.'

Gwen, staring into his eyes, only said: 'Then he'll never go into the War again?'

'No. He'll never go into the War again.'

But Charlie, Charlie, the strongest human being we had ever known! As the doctor spoke I saw Charlie swimming as I had seen him once when I had been for a day or two with him and Johnny at Eastbourne— out and out and out on that glittering sun-water-spangled summer day when the air quivered in the heat and there was no cloud. But you can swim with your arms, can't you?

'Can I see him, doctor?'

'Yes. I think so. He's quite conscious. It's collapse from the shock we're afraid of. He was terribly scalded and now the leg ... '

He went away and Johnny went up to Gwen and, smiling, put his arm round her.

'Here, you sit down. You must be tired.'

They sat down, side by side, holding hands and looking like two helpless children.

'I'm glad,' Gwen said, 'Charlie's the sort of man he is. Some men would find it difficult without a leg, but he won't. He's so adaptable. He can do anything with his hands. You should see him take a watch to pieces and put it together again. He's happy for hours with things like that. And they make very good artificial legs now, don't they? Much better than they used to.'

'Much better,' said Johnny.

I don't know how I knew it, but I was aware that the whole of Johnny's imaginative mind was fixed on the pain that Charlie must have suffered.

Physical pain had always been to Johnny the real nightmare of life. He had always said that he could endure anything but long-continued physical pain

—anything, anything but that. And now scalding—days and nights, days and nights of it.... Charlie, to whom so often in their childhood he had gone because of a headache, a cut finger. And Charlie had always made light of pain, always made light of anything that happened to himself....

A severe-faced sister entered and said Mrs. Christian could go to her husband.

'These are two of his great friends,' Gwen said.

'Is one of you Mr. Cornelius?'

'I am,' said Johnny.

'Oh yes—he's been asking for you. You mustn't stay for more than a moment.'

It was in the lower part of his body that Charlie had been scalded. His blue eyes were half closed as though he were sleepy, but he opened them and

looked at us. He had always been one of the cleanest-looking men, but now he appeared bleached, shadowed, almost the phantom of washed reality. But that reality returned with his voice, a husky whisper, but in it that obstinacy, that determined bull-dog hold on his object....

'Hullo, Gwen.... Hullo, Johnny.... This is a blinkin' nuisance, isn't it?' He struggled for his voice and meanwhile all the time his eyes gazed into ours as though searching for something. He was holding Gwen's hand on one side of the bed, Johnny's on the other.

'It was young Padget passed with a candle close to an air-breather— air-

breather of the oil-sump ... damn' silly thing ... '

He smiled faintly.

'Cheer up, Gwen, old girl. I'll be all right.' Very slowly he turned his head toward Johnny, stared at him. 'You're a pal, Johnny, to come down....'

How intently he stared at him, as though, wherever he was to go, whatever he would be called on to do, he would take Johnny with him, never part from him!

'You'd better go now,' whispered the nurse. 'He ought to sleep.'

Indeed his eyes were closed. His head was back on the pillow.

Gwen remained at the hospital. We went to an hotel.

We didn't see him again. He died at five-thirty in the morning.

Afterwards Johnny only spoke once. In the hotel, a pale morning sunshine washing the room, he said as though to himself: 'I don't know how I'll manage now. I don't know how on earth I'll manage.'

CHAPTER IV

Carstang--fame--mercia and Anne

On the morning of Armistice Day, November 11th, 1918, I was writing very quietly in my flat in St. James's when the sirens blew and everyone came pouring out of their doors into the street. I looked from my window down into Duke Street and saw how the russia leather and pigskin tobacco-

pouches, and portraits of eighteenth-century ladies, and the Tang purple lions that I was so friendly with, and the rows of silver, porcelain and gold clocks, and the palms in pots outside No. 2 Ryder Street, and the whispers from the men in green-baize aprons who lift the heavy furniture in Christie's, and the urbane kindly ghost of George Alexander, and the little Manet still-life of two roses in Lefevre's window, and the two girl chambermaids from the gentlemen's apartments at No. 8—all these plus the ghosts of Mr. Gibbon, young Thackeray, Mr. Boswell, Mr. Ackerman, Mr. Rowlandson and Lady Mary Wortley Montagu, yes, they one and all mingled under the grey-blue, snow-dappled sky, in and out and through the smoke-white, pearl-shadowed walls, the milk-green surfaces of St. James's Park, all, with snuff-box, tobacco- pouch, diamond-buckled, powdered, pigtailed, top-hatted exuberance, danced to what they hoped would be, now and for ever, a free and disencumbered London.

Only Mr. Gibbon, I could see, refused the general optimism. With his paunchy, strutting, short-legged wisdom he murmured 'Decline and Fall,' and vanished into smoke.

Shaking off these visions and wondering why it was that I didn't feel more gay, I turned round to find Johnny and Anne standing in the doorway. Johnny had in his hand a parcel. He came forward to the table and undid it with his long clumsy fingers. I was afraid, with every moment, that he would let it fall. It was Yin, cockle- shaped hat, pink-eared elephant and all.

'Why—whatever have you brought him here for?'

'I want you to look after him for me.'

'Of course I will. But I thought you would never be parted from him.'

'Your looking after him isn't parting from him. I don't want anything to happen to him.'

He smiled his gentle, shy, half–deprecating smile. He had taken off his bowler hat, which didn't suit him, and ran his hands through his long black hair.

He seemed thinner than ever, his nose longer, his eyes brighter. He sat down, kicking out his legs, smiling in front of him.

'So it's Armistice. Let's go out and look at everything.' He suggested that, as he always did any excitement, with the eagerness of a child. He went on: 'Do you know what I overheard just now as we were coming out of the Tube?

One woman said to another: "God, isn't that an ugly devil?" Yes, I did. Anne heard it too. Anne's Colonel's left her. His wife's taken him back. A villa in Cannes and no freedom.... Oh yes, and Roger and Winchester are bringing out my fairy–stories. The Bright–Green Shoes and Other Stories. With Illustrations by Luke Smith. That's what it's going to be called. The pictures are wonderful. They are really. Ever so much better than the stories. They're just what I'd have done myself if I could draw. Really extraordinary. Oh yes, and what else is there? ... Anyway you ought to be pleased, you old tyrant, because it's what you wanted—for the fairy–stories to be printed. If anyone buys them it will be because of Luke's pictures. He's a nice chap, Luke is.

And so is Sir Donald Winchester. He's my publisher, he is! And he's the grandest old man I've ever known. He looks you straight in the eye and says what he thinks. But he's kind with it and a swell with his riding in the Park every morning and his square top-hats and his black stock and pearl pin.

'"How are you, Cornelius?" he says, like they said it in the eighteenth century.

But yesterday he said, "How are you, Johnny? They're the best fairy–stories since Hans Andersen," he said. And he's Scotch and never says a word he doesn't mean, but so clean and handsome sitting in his chair in his oak-

panelled room. Complexion as fresh as a baby's. Strong as a lion every way.

"Best fairy- stories since Hans Andersen." I had to laugh. "Why, Sir Donald,"

I said. "It's only because I was pushed into it that I'm publishing them.

They're nothing. Now my novels—"

'"To tell you the truth, Cornelius," he says, "I've never been able to finish one of your novels." Then, lest he should have hurt me by his honesty, he gets up and pats me on the shoulder, as though I was his son.

'"There's fifty new novels published a week in the season," he says, "but not stories like these of yours. No, indeed. We're going to give them all we can."

And so they will. They're the best publishing house in the world, aren't they?

Of course they are. Why, any time I'm a bit low I think to myself of Sir Donald, aged eighty, sitting there in his shining white collar and black stock and white pin, and his voice with just a bit of Scotch in it and his eye as clear and sharp as a bird's.'

He stopped. He was kicking his legs about and laughing. He didn't care for his fairy-stories, but this was the first time in all his life that any publisher had praised him. When someone whom he admired was kind to him he was all sweetness and light and modesty. Opposition made him proud and obstinate. Praise, kindliness, warmed him like a fire. He got up and stood looking out of the window at the crowds now filling the street.

'So it's all over,' I heard him say to himself—and I knew that he was thinking of Charlie.

I went up to Anne, whose cheeks were bright with excitement, her tall slender body strung to an intentness of emotion.

'Anne,' I said. 'Marry me. We're such good friends. We understand one another. I love you and I know you care for me.'

She took my hand in her gloved one. She looked at Johnny.

'Now that Charlie's gone, he needs me.' She caught her breath in a way she had. 'At last he needs me. I've waited for such years.' Then she leant over and very lightly kissed my cheek.

We went out into the streets. Johnny was a little ahead of us down the stairs.

'What did he bring Yin to me for?' I asked her.

'Mercia's been kicking up a row.'

'What about?'

'I wasn't there, of course. All Johnny said to me when I met him at the South Kensington Tube was: "Mercia thinks I stuff the pockets of my coats with things. I ought to keep them tidy, she says. I say I buy my own clothes. SHE says she's got a scarecrow for a husband. I may be a scarecrow, I say, but I'm clean. Scarecrows always are. The wind and the rain see to that." Then he laughed and took my arm and said, "Yin shan't be hurt anyway."'

I can't say that we any of us felt very jolly in the Armistice crowd. We were all thinking too much about Charlie. It would turn to rain later, I said, and in Trafalgar Square we were pushed about and shouted at. Everyone was glad the war was over, but nobody believed it quite—and, by God, they've turned out to be correct!

Johnny said to me: 'I suppose my job's over now. I shall have to be fed by Mercia again.'

'They'll give you something for the fairy-stories, I suppose,' I said.

'Well, not much of an advance, you know. They can't. I don't suppose they'll sell many copies. What do people want with fairy- stories and the world like this?'

'Perhaps it's just what they DO want,' I said.

The crowd now was terrific. Motor-cars, loaded with cheering, screaming boys and girls, were moving slowly along, dozens of people holding on to them. It was a kind of Mafeking, I suppose, without the Mafeking innocence.

We knew too much now for light- heartedness. The sky was heavy, bearing down on us as though it said, 'Look around you, above you, beneath you, and whisper—don't shout.' Leaden drops of rain fell once and again. A wild-eyed man, bare-headed, caught my arm and said, 'What's the good of all this? It doesn't bring Tom back.'

But, of course, there were many millions in the world that day who simply lifted up their hearts and thanked God that the thing had stopped. 'Cease Fire!'

'Cease Fire!' That was what they heard. And so they all burst out singing....

We had two strange little encounters that morning, both with significance for Johnny.

The first was that, just beyond Charing Cross Station, a little way down the hill and standing on the steps of a public-house, was Mr. Abel preaching.

'Why, there's Mr. Abel!' said Anne, and there he was, looking gigantic and most impressive.

He had grown stouter since I had last seen him and, in some mysterious way, much more commanding. He had a voice like a dinner- gong and many people were standing listening to him, listening in a sort of hypnotized state, having, I don't doubt, their pockets picked. I caught phrases like 'Except it be in your hearts of what avail is Peace?' 'The night cometh when it shall be demanded of you ... ' and then, quite familiarly: 'You know, friends, you aren't safe yet. Don't you think it. Nobody's safe unless they trust in God. And what do I mean by God? G-O-D. Three simple little letters, and I don't suppose one of you has ever given a moment's thought to what those little letters really ... ' and so on. I don't know whether he saw us. I fancy that he did, but he made no pause, only his large staring eyes (he had the kind of eye you see in a doctor's diagram when he's testing your sight—larger than life and improperly naked) rested for a moment on Johnny.

'He looks very prosperous,' Johnny said, as we were carried on.

The other friend whom we encountered could NOT be called prosperous. It was Carstang. We had been borne by the crowd into Aldwych and there under the arches of Drury Lane Theatre we found Carstang. He was standing quite alone, hatless, holding over his head an umbrella with a hole in it. Here the crowd had thinned and Carstang saw us at once. He pulled the umbrella lower over his head, but Cornelius was not to be denied. He caught Carstang's arm.

'Why—where have you been? I haven't seen you for months....'

The man glared at all three of us. His heavy glasses had no life behind them.

His face was drawn, he wore a shabby untidy waterproof, and on his hands were a dirty pair of grey gloves. He pulled down the umbrella and stood staring at us with the utmost hostility. At last he spoke to Cornelius. (He ignored Anne and myself completely.)

'You've got some impudence—speaking to me,' he said.

Johnny, bewildered, drew back from the step.

'What is it?' he said. 'What's the matter?'

Carstang lifted his umbrella, looked at it, then put two fingers through the hole in it.

'Ask Hampden,' he said.

'Hampden?' Johnny asked.

Carstang put his umbrella up again and then, walking through the three of us as though we did not exist, started up the street.

'Hampden? Hampden?' Johnny repeated to himself. 'What on earth does he mean?'

'He's crazy,' I said. 'He's always quarrelling with somebody.' I had, myself, very little use for Carstang.

'He looks awful—half starved. I must go and see him.'

A long while after, when we were almost home again, he repeated: 'It's dreadful, isn't it? Writing, I mean. Carstang's got genius. He has really. He looked as though he hadn't eaten anything for weeks.'

I shivered. The day was turning raw and a drizzle had begun. Abel and Carstang ... a kind of craziness in the world. 'If we all begin to be a little mad now ... What had the War been fought about?' I was so tired that I really couldn't remember.

I received a letter from Anne next morning, and this is the place for it, I think.

DEAR H—,

That was very sweet of you yesterday. The only nice thing in what was to me a perfectly horrible day. I couldn't get away from Charlie, waiting for me, a rather stocky little boy with very bright blue eyes, outside school at Merlin, to see me home. Then Johnny would join us and we'd all began talking at once

—or rather Johnny and I would. There must have been thousands of people seeing the same kind of pictures yesterday. And then Abel and Carstang. I was frightened. Were you? But what I really wanted to say was to thank you.

You are the best friend I have in the world after Johnny, and the way you've stuck to me and my shocking reputation has made me marvel and feel terribly proud of you.

But my 'promiscuous' days are over now. I've wanted to make people happy and I've wanted a good time for myself. I've never thought that what happened to me mattered a damn. But from now on Johnny's my business. I told you yesterday he needs me at last. Not physically of course. While Charlie was there he had some sort of barrier against the world, but now he's married to a woman who hates him, he's a failure, he doesn't know why things have gone wrong. What I'd give to hear him say now as he used to do:

'You just wait. I'll show them.' Wouldn't you? I feel somehow that it's going to be a dangerous world from now on, and I'm sorry for all of us although I know that pity's a rather poor quality and I hate being pitied myself. The problem seems to me to love people without being sentimental, being weak and making them weak. Not that either of us will ever make Johnny weak.

Isn't it strange that inside he should be so strong and independent, although outwardly he seems so often helpless? But strong though he is I think he's beginning to wonder why he's a failure and he feels people's unkindness more than he did. He's afraid too of the insanity of his grandfather. I believe he thinks of it continually ... Anyway we've got to look after him as much as he allows us to.

I've got a very good job at Roscoe and Morris. I meant to have told you yesterday. Wouldn't it be nice if you and Johnny and I lunched together once a week, made a regular thing of it? What about Thursday at Paolo's? Again, thank you.

Your loving friend,

ANNE.

Also Johnny next day brought me a letter from Carstang. This is it. It is on my table now, written in Carstang's beautiful sculptured hand, in bright-red ink.

You would think when you read his letters that they would be written in a frenzied hand, so crazily angry were they. But no. He wrote the filthiest, maddest, foulest things always in this lovely elaborate script and in green, purple or crimson ink.

The letter began at once:

You've got a nerve asking me before your dear friends what the matter was.

But that's the kind of man you are—a hypocrite if ever there was one.

But don't you think you can carry out your dirty lying plans without being found out. I suppose you think because you sent me some money six months ago that I should be on my bended knees to you, licking your shoes. That's for people like Rose, with their pink episcopal cheeks and fat hams and chins like door-knockers. They'd lick anyone's shoes and be happy, but not me. I despise your dirty money. At the same time allow me to observe that even Rose wouldn't sink so low as to hurry round to one of the most chattering gossips in London who earns ten bob a week at criticism because he hasn't the brain for anything else, and tell him all about his noble charities and ...

'Poor Carstang! I had to help him out, you know, or he'd be on the streets!'—

that's the act of a real friend, isn't it? But why should I ever have expected anything else of you? Funny! I can remember the day when once I thought you had some talent. I was prettily deceived, wasn't I! You had all the airs of intelligent interest in those days, the kind of hero Rose would choose for one of his nine-hundred-page novels and call 'Purity' or 'Fidelity' or something—

one of those Cinderella-heroes who are so charming because they have long noses, large mouths and are completely helpless. Well, you can keep your dirty money and yourself away from my door. Any time you want to laugh at me because I have an umbrella with a hole in it, bring your friends.

CARSTANG.

Johnny stood, looking at it over my shoulder, while I read it. He laughed.

'He's got me pretty accurately, hasn't he? As a matter of fact I WOULD make a good hero for one of Rose's novels. I'll suggest it to him.' Then, walking away from me, shaking his head. 'What have I done? I wouldn't have hurt him for worlds.'

'Did you lend him money?'

'Oh yes, I suppose so. Twenty pounds about six months ago.'

'Did you tell anyone about it?'

'As a matter of fact I WAS talking about Carstang one day to Hampden. All I said was that he was very proud and hard to help.'

'That was it. Hampden's the town-crier in petticoats. He likes making mischief too in the kindest possible way.'

'Yes, perhaps that's it.'

Johnny went round to see Carstang, who stood there in a purple dressing-gown shouting to him to get out. It was a fitting room in a fitting house, Johnny said.

And then there followed an incident and a conversation that I'm never likely to forget. It was on the night before the publication of the fairy-stories—

November 28th, 1918—and it was a Christmas party given by Nina Roslynn at her big house in Eaton Place. Nina Roslynn had been a very good pianist, but on marrying Sir Percival Roslynn, who was exceedingly rich, had surrendered the piano for ever. I used to watch her with interest, speculating whether she had lost or gained by abandoning beauty and creative splendour for a large warm bed, a large warm man and a large warm income. The good books will all tell you that such a woman is frustrated, can never forgive herself and so on. It wasn't true of Nina. She flourished on her surrender and was now as stout as her husband. Also very happy indeed!

She gave artistic parties on a very big scale; this was one of them. The house, full of sheet glass, steel, silver, and white curtains, swam with people like an aquarium with fish.

I came upon little Tickell who, short and stumpy, with a long solemn face like a door-knocker and a Scottish accent as melancholy as a funeral, was perhaps the stupidest and at the same time the best-satisfied of all the London critics. He reviewed everything, plays, books, films, and all with the same dreary, pompous, blind- eyed mediocrity. So it gave me pleasure when he caught me by the arm and said: 'That's a re-markable book of fairy-stories by your friend Cornelius. Just reviewed it for The Sitting Hen. Very remarkable indeed.' It was as though he were standing, clad in decent black, holding out the collection plate. So I put in my sixpence.

'Praise from you is praise indeed, Mr. Tickell.'

He didn't know whether I was laughing at him or no, which was one reason why he disliked me very much.

But I was pleased because I knew that Tickell, having no judgement at all of his own, had been nosing around and had sniffed that the pronouncement on the fairy-stories would be favourable. Yes, I was greatly pleased.

And then something occurred. There was a great crowd of people standing about the drawing-room under the rather crooked eyes of a big 'blue' Picasso (it was advanced to admire Picasso then) and a gay portrait of Nina by Peter Augustus. The noise was deafening. I saw Anne, and then, a moment later, Mercia. Mercia's little father had died a month or so before and she was in black. Black didn't suit either her yellow hair or her opulent milkmaid person.

She was being grand to the little Albions, who, one on either side of her, looked like birds pecking at the bark of a large tree. Anne, who was, I thought, so much lovelier than anyone else in the room, came over to me, saw Mercia, held out her hand.

'How do you do, Mrs. Cornelius?'

Mercia looked straight through her. Anne's hand dropped and she turned to talk to the Albions, who realized at once that something had occurred and

were especially kind to Anne because they never liked anyone's feelings to be hurt. I was so furious that, for a moment, I saw men as trees walking.

Someone was speaking to me but I heard nothing. A long while later, as it seemed, I realized that Mercia was saying something.

'Please ... I must talk to you ... Is there somewhere we can go?'

'No, thank you, Mercia. I'd rather not.'

'But you must.... I won't keep you more than a moment.'

Well, I thought, if you want a little plain speaking you shall have it. We found a little writing-room with sets and sets of Victorian novels glazed and stiff like jellied tongues. We sat on a sofa together.

'You're furious, I suppose?' Mercia said. 'I know she's a great pet of yours. All the same I wonder how YOU'D behave, if you came face to face with the man who'd ruined your wife.'

She sat, staring in front of her, looking common and mean and vindictive, while a rope of pearls rose and fell on her massive black bosom.

'That's wicked, malicious nonsense. Anne is the only good thing Johnny's got in his life.'

She looked at me with curiosity.

'How you hate me!' she said. 'You always have. No one has ever disliked me as you have.'

'Shall I tell you why?'

'Yes, do.'

'You took Johnny in the first place because you wanted his circle of friends.

Then you moved up socially and found him a nuisance and a failure. Now you're bored to death with him. You've always thought of yourself.'

'I don't know where he'd have been if it hadn't been for me.'

'He'd be happy and maybe a success. You've tried to crush the life out of him.'

'Why are you so fond of him?' She looked at me with real curiosity. 'I admit that I can't now see anything in him at all. He's shiftless and careless and irresponsible about money, and a bad writer. And the worst of all, he's so damned virtuous. He's always wanting to do things for everybody, never loses his temper with me—and yet he never does anything I really want him to.'

'All these things,' I said, 'would be virtues to you if he'd been a success. You liked at first his being dependent on you, but you soon tired of it. Now, with your grand friends, he's nothing but a ludicrous encumbrance. You never think, you have never thought, for a single moment in all your life, but of yourself.'

'Perhaps that's true. It's true of almost everybody. If you don't fight for yourself nobody else will fight for you.'

'What are you going to do about it?' I asked her.

'Do about what?'

'About Johnny. Why don't you let him go?'

'Let him go! To that woman?'

'Anne's been his friend all his life, and now that Charlie's dead—'

'Charlie! Charlie!' she broke in. 'Charlie! Think of his friends! Butlers and beggars and street-preachers and prostitutes—'

'Let him go, Mercia! Let him go!'

She got up. She stood there like a massive figure in butter at an Agricultural Show.

'No, I don't believe in that. He's a failure, he'll always be one now, but no one's going to run away from me—right in front of everyone's eyes. He

would make me absurd.'

'Perhaps he'll take it into his own head and go, whether you like it or not.'

'No.' She looked at me with sombre concentration. 'He's the strangest creature. He's had my money and although he's given it away, when he could get it, to anyone he happened to meet, yet he feels he's under an obligation.

He has a rectitude that's maddening. And yet,' she repeated, 'with all that he won't do anything I want. There's something inside him as hard as iron. But that's what I wanted to say to you. You're his friend. Can't you get him to give up this writing nonsense now? He's tried again and again and always failed. I could get him into some business. Make him settle down. He wanders about like a lunatic. Can't you persuade him?'

'He may be a success yet,' I said. 'His fairy-stories come out to- morrow.'

'Fairy-stories!' she repeated scornfully. 'Who wants to read fairy- stories?'

'Give him a chance! Give him a chance! Let him go away a bit by himself.

You're on one another's nerves. You know you are.'

'No. He shall stick to me and do what I want. I've never failed in anything yet

—'

'Never failed in anything!' I cried. 'Why, you've failed in everything.'

'Do you think so?' She grinned and for a moment I rather liked her. 'What a funny notion you have of failure! That's why your novels are always so unreal.' Then she did a ridiculous thing. She kissed me very lightly on the forehead and patted me on the shoulder. 'A lot of people think you're an awful bore, but I like you. I've always told you so. Now if YOU were my husband instead of poor Johnny—'

'God forbid!' I answered, shuddering. 'And let me tell you one thing. If you're rude to Anne Swinnerton in front of me again I shan't stop at only words.'

'You're in love with her, aren't you?' she said. 'It's all right. She'll never speak to me again in public.'

The very next morning—November 29th, 1918—saw the publication of—

THE BRIGHT-GREEN SHOES

AND

OTHER STORIES

by

JOHN CORNELIUS

Roger & Winchester. 7s. 6d. net.

The book's appearance had the dignity and handsome beauty for which this firm's publications are justly famous. Even if a book published by Roger and Winchester doesn't live very long, it always looks as though it ought to! The colour was a brilliant claret and the cover both on spine and side was stamped in gold with a reproduction of Luke Smith's illustration 'The Fish Family on their Way to Church'—destined to become a very famous drawing indeed, because of Luke Smith's uncanny anticipation of the features of a later-

notorious despot in the beetling brows and hammer-chin of Mr. Fish.

(And by the way the point that now marks the First Issue of the First Edition for collectors is, oddly enough, in this same 'Fish' picture. In the first issue Mrs. Fish has a feather in her bonnet. In the second issue the feather is omitted. This point makes, I believe, some hundred pounds difference in the book's value.)

There was no sign between the covers that Cornelius had ever written anything but this. By his own wish. It was as though he felt that here was a different (and in his own opinion inferior) writer from the novelist and dramatist.

The stories in The Bright-Green Shoes are as follows: The Bright-Green Shoes.

The Three Princesses—Fat, Thin and Inbetween.

The Golden Linnet.

The Little Nutmeg-Grater.

The Bells under the Sea.

Mr. Fish and Family.

The Witch with the Feather.

The Prince and his Friend, the Hedgehog.

The Great Sea Wave that had Such a Tumble.

The Reindeer with One Eye.

The Big Seal and the Little Seal.

The Showman and his Puppets.

The Snowdrops.

How the Sea Lost a Breaker.

The Little Cart with Red Wheels.

"I Don't Want to Sell my Pig."

The Princess's Button-Hook.

The Moon's Good-Night.

The Wind in the Church Tower.

The Old Musical-Box.

Two more volumes of fairy-stories. In 1920 The Flight of the Wild Swans and Other Tales. And, posthumously, in 1929, The Red Moon's Shadow.

There is now an omnibus volume of Cornelius' Fairy-Tales with all the Luke Smith illustrations. It contains in all fifty- six stories.

I remember that I bought all the morning newspapers on November 29th, and was delighted to find no less than four reviews. To be reviewed on the day of publication is, of course, a sign of real and absolute 'arrival.' Johnny had never been reviewed on the day of publication before.

All four reviews were enthusiastic, but rather because of Luke Smith's pictures than because of the stories. One paper indeed talked about nothing but the pictures. It was plain that the stories had not been read. With the Sunday papers, however, and the Literary Weeklies, there was a difference.

That Temple of Modern Intellectualism, The New World, yielded a column and a half of superlatives. As I read it I realized, with a shock, that Johnny was destined to be adopted by the young moderns, and, reading this review

again, I was aware, for the first time, that there was a note, not of cynicism, but of satire in these stories— a note entirely absent from the novels and the plays. The young man in The New World, in fact, called them 'Freudian' and then I did for the first time thoroughly grasp the idea of the astounding possibility that these stories might sweep the world. For the reason, the great supreme reason, that these stories were for everybody. You got out of them exactly what you put into them. They were the stories of a child talking to children, but a child who knew, as some children do, the basic, unchanging elements in human nature. How many children had I met who had looked at me with a glance so penetrating and cynical that I had turned away in sheer embarrassment. And who will forget Robert Mather's A Ship in a Storm?

But Cornelius was not only a child; he was a story-teller of a marvellous kind. There had been signs of this gift in the novels, but again and again he had been betrayed by his passion for clotted and very jejune philosophy.

There was no expressed philosophy here at all. He simply tells his little stories as though he had no other business BUT that.

In the very smallest of the stories you catch your breath in your eagerness to know 'what happens next,' that great gift in the writer's art that most of the post–War English novelists have altogether lost. Bertrand, of course, has this gift supremely.

In addition to these things he was, of course (he had always been), a poet.

That had been clear enough in all his books from The Walk onward, but now, because he was working unconsciously and was only recording what his imagination saw in the simplest of words, he created, through his poetry, a completely real world. The unreality of his novels and plays had been caused by the fact that his realistic world—realistic in the sense of all the great novelists from Stendhal and Tolstoi to Hardy—was not the real world at all.

He endeavoured to create living human beings in a world that was true to him but untrue to everyone else.

But once he could work freely in his fairy-tale world everything became real for everybody—the country fields with the dark furrowed soil, the villages with the grey roofs, the village spire, the clouds sweeping up over the avenue of swaying trees, the green mud of the stagnant pond, the giant oak with the cows sheltering beneath it, the approach to the long pale stretch of sand over

the dunes with their sea-pinks and rough tufted grass, the sea- breakers, as they hung, crystal green, before crashing on to the froth-scattered welter that gleamed against the grey sand, the sea– horizon, dark line of plum–purple with the milk–white cloud resting there and throwing its ghostly shadow over the pale–green water. Into all this reality he was able to throw his fairy world of Kings and Princesses, Mermaids and Witches, and mingle them with old farmers, dogs, swans, fish, hedgehogs, foxes, swallows and wrens and robins, mingle them fearlessly together because in HIS world they were all true.

'"Oh, that is dreadful," said the swallow–mother. "I have such a tender heart. I really can't bear to hear any more of it. Tell me, though. What happened next?"

'"Well, you see," said the little Princess. "It wasn't really so terrible because

... "'

Nothing was REALLY so terrible because Cornelius, like the swallow-

mother, had a tender heart and loved all created things.

Last of all one must remember the miracle of that collaboration. The only thing to be compared with it perhaps is its Tenniel– Carroll predecessor. In the eighteen years that have passed since that first publication other illustrators have attempted the Cornelius fairy–stories, but they have failed one and all. Luke Smith had been right when he had seen, in a flash of revelation, that here was his work, and his alone in all the world. Not only had his 'line' the lovely simplicity of Flaxman and Blake, but he was also a creator. His Fish Family, his 'King Samuel in a Temper because he has lost a Stocking,' his 'Dog Rufus is proud after winning his New Collar,' his

'Chancellor of the Royal Exchequer going out to Bathe,' his 'The Turbots entertaining the Whitings to Supper,' his 'The May Tree listens to the Moon,'

his 'The Sea is tired after an Exhausting Day'—but why continue? They are the most famous illustrations of any book in the modern world. Everybody has them by heart.

For the rest, the book, as I have said, was published on November 29th.

Within three weeks it was being sold for Christmas as soap and tooth-paste are sold. A new Cornelius had been created. It was as though, in the eyes of the world, November 29th, 1918, was his first birthday.

CHAPTER V

Home Sweet Home Again

On the first anniversary of the publication of the fairy-tales— November 29th, 1919— Peter Westcott and I gave a little party to celebrate the event.

There was nothing especial to record about this, except that Johnny himself wasn't present. At the very last moment I received this note: DEAR OLD BOY—I suppose this is as shabby and disgraceful a thing as I've ever done. I can't come to your party because I'm just catching a train to—I don't know where. Mercia will represent me. Just when you're all drinking my health, I shall be pulling on my pyjamas and creeping into bed in some little pub—well off the main line. I can't help it. I fully meant to come and I greatly appreciated yours and Peter's kindness. But the truth is the success of the fairy-stories hasn't given me any pleasure whatever— quite the contrary.

I think somehow this is very vain of me: not to be pleased, I mean. But I'm not really vain—at least vain only of the things that nobody praises. I CAN'T

face your party. I tried to. I summoned up all the courage I had, but it wasn't enough. Forgive me. Make my excuses to Peter.

Affectionately,

JOHNNY.

I must admit that I was exceedingly annoyed. Sir Donald was coming and Luke Smith and many friends of mine and Peter's. We had wanted it to be a sort of demonstration to the world of Johnny's wonderful success. As it was, the reputation that Cornelius was beginning now to make for himself was greatly increased by his non- appearance. For the humorous thing was that, now that Johnny was famous, everything in him that had made him unpopular before made him popular now.

His physical appearance—untidy black hair, big nose, large mouth, long

lanky bending body, loose shapeless clothes—was now considered extremely interesting and unusual. Someone made a drawing of him, walking across the floor, his shoulders bent, his long body at an incredible angle, a lock of hair tumbling into his eye, his nose sticking out like a signpost, he eagerly gesticulating. Two years earlier it would have been a mockery. Now it showed genius, lovable eccentricity, humorous vitality.

The fantastic success of the book was not so strange—apart altogether from the merits of the stories and Luke Smith's pictures, there were several instances in these years of the almost insane success of childlike and simple narratives—the immense sales, just at this time, for example, of Charles Richards' Spring is Round the Corner and K. Bellow's Peter Moffatt's Farmyard (which, by the way, also owed a great deal to its illustrator).

But I had not, I must confess, expected that Johnny's personality was now to be so exactly right for the legend that formed round him— it had been so exactly wrong for everything before!

All his earlier defects were now virtues. He had married a wealthy woman, but never did any man care less about money! He probably did not know that his wife WAS wealthy! His novels had, it was true, been queer, rather clumsy, oratorical, romantic, but one could see now, looking at them in the light of the fairy-stories, how full of originality and strange power they were!

He was himself eccentric, they said he wandered about at night giving half-

crowns to beggars asleep in doorways, but how exactly right it was that he should be eccentric! Look at novelists like Albion and Rose and Westcott!

How conventional and ordinary they were, but then how conventional and ordinary their books! But Cornelius— with his lankiness and untidiness and impulsiveness and absentmindedness—how RIGHT for a teller of fairy-

tales!

Then how romantic his origins! His mother, they said, had taken in washing down in Glebeshire somewhere. His father on the other hand was a member of one of England's oldest families and had had a family estate. And so Port Merlin came into the picture. The little simple fishing town, so beautiful, so remote; and it was here that all Cornelius' stories were born! He, a ragged neglected urchin wandering about the seashore, listening to the roar of the sea and the shrill cry of the gulls!

It looked as though Port Merlin would not be simple and remote very much longer!

As to the party, it might indeed have been Hamlet without the Prince, save for the presence of Mercia.

She entered, radiant, transcendently happy! I simply could not believe that this was the same woman who, in Nina's house, had urged me to persuade Johnny to abandon writing! A miracle had occurred. Once, in very early days, she had liked Johnny to be a failure because she was his protector; but oh!

how long ago that had been! Now his amazing, his almost FAIRY-TALE

success gave her exactly what she needed! She could indeed at last hold up her head among her splendid friends! She was the wife of the most famous literary man in London—and, more than that, oh! far, far more, it was she who had made him! Where would Johnny be but for her? In those years when he had been a starving ragamuffin she had come and fed him, clothed him, watched over him, guided him. Had it not been for her he would have died of starvation. Yes, and more than that, through all those later years when book after book had been a failure she had never lost faith in him, had reassured and comforted and encouraged him. SHE knew he had it in him. SHE knew that he was a genius. When all the world derided him she kept her faith.

The wonderful thing was that she really and most sincerely believed all this.

Her eyes sparkling, her opulent person carried to its full height, she whispered in my ear:

'Well, my dear? What did I say? Didn't I always know that Johnny had it in him?'

To which I answered:

'What about the business you were to find for him? Now's the time to announce to everybody that Johnny's got a job in a bank.'

She laughed good-naturedly.

'I was teasing you, just to see what you would say.'

Will Hampden, the critic, who thought success bad for people, murmured in my ear, 'Have you seen Stromberg's review?'

Of course I had. Stromberg, alone, had not capitulated. In his review he had praised Luke Smith but had been even more bitter than usual about Johnny.

People would be taken in by these stories, he supposed. They were just the things that the undiscerning would love, but anyone with taste would perceive very quickly how cheap, how imitative, how second-rate these stories were. For himself he preferred the novels, bad though they had been.

They at least had been sincere in their very clumsiness.

I had to confess that I admired Stromberg. I thought that Johnny would cordially agree with this article.

One thing I remember Peter Westcott saying at our party:

'Funny thing, isn't it? It seems to us important, this success of Johnny's. And so it is. It's a solemn thought all the same that out of all the thirty million—or is it forty?—population of Great Britain, there are a few thousand only who, even now, know that Johnny has written a book. My landlady, a nice intelligent woman, gets three novels a week from the library. That is, she reads about a hundred and fifty novels a year. She tells me that she never looks at the name of the author. She often reads the same novel twice without realizing it. The only people in England who are really interested in writers are other writers. Not that they ever read one another's books.'

'Who do read new books?' someone asked.

'I don't know. Upon my word I don't know.'

'If you enjoy writing them,' Rose said, 'it doesn't matter who reads them.'

'The fact is,' someone said, 'authors' lives are terribly uninteresting. Nobody wants to hear about them.'

'I don't know,' Westcott said. 'Anyone's life is interesting if you only know the truth about it. Crippen, for instance. He wasn't interesting because he murdered Belle Elmore. It was the detail of that Hilldrop Crescent existence,

with Belle's flash clothing and the theatrical suppers and the dentist's parlour, that have made it so fascinating. Writers are just as interesting as anyone else

—no more and no less.'

Then they attacked Mercia.

'Come, Mrs. Cornelius. Tell us the truth about Johnny. We none of us REALLY know him.'

And Mercia, delighted and triumphant, unrolled a fascinating and most romantic story....

Very soon, however, Peter, Anne and I began to be greatly worried about Johnny. He seemed to be hiding himself—not his physical but his real self—

from us all. It was as though we were in a play with Johnny who was acting a part that convinced nobody. And then followed a very grim incident.

In the early summer of 1919—at the beginning of May I think—I found among my morning letters a large envelope addressed in green ink and Carstang's unmistakable hand. I had not seen Carstang since Armistice Day.

Opening the envelope I discovered inside several pages of typewritten matter.

Here and there were corrections in the same green ink. It was headed 'The Case of John Cornelius.'

I read this precious affair with increasing dismay and disgust. I will not bother anyone with details of its contents. In general it was an insane, hysterical, and often pitiful attack on Johnny. It began by saying that this document was being sent to some fifty persons, including the Commissioner of Police, the editors of the more important daily and weekly newspapers, many of Johnny's friends and acquaintances. It went on to accuse Johnny of every known vice and misdemeanour. It said that his mother had been a penniless washerwoman whom Johnny had basely deserted, that, when still a boy, he had beaten and nearly killed a helpless old woman in Merlin, that, in fear of the police, he had run away to London, been picked up by Schaaf, a notorious pederast of the period, been sent to school where he had perverted the boys' morals, that, coming again to London, he had stolen, sold his body to anybody who wanted it, married a woman for her money and then derided her, stolen two of Carstang's works, a play and a novel, and produced them as

his own, lived with a notorious woman who came from his own town, and had at last achieved success by publishing a volume of fairy-stories that were the most obvious 'cribs' of Grimm and Andersen.

There was a great deal more than this and when I finished it I laid it down on the breakfast-table and said to myself aloud:

'Mrs. Hoskin!'

Yes (for by now Johnny had told me much about his childhood), it was that crazy old witch who was still alive in the world, who would always be alive in the world. The impersonal, persistent creator of evil thinking, malicious falsehood, motiveless cruelty— the evil companion, not only of Johnny himself, but of MYself, Peter, Rose, Anne—how many, many more?

'Poor Carstang,' was the next thing I said, because this was touching, pitiful in its crazy insane irresponsibility.

It was TOO crazy, in fact, to do any harm in the general world; but to Johnny himself what might it not do?

He appeared shortly afterwards and the very first thing that he said was:

'Mrs. Hoskin isn't dead, you see.'

I saw at once that he was thinking only of Carstang. If he was unhappy it was because he thought that, in some way, he had done Carstang a hurt. But what could it have been? After the incident on Armistice Day he should have gone again and again to Carstang, insisted on seeing him, helping him, doing something for him. He had heard, as I had, that he had been for a long time in the direst poverty. Some people had said that he had gone to live abroad; on the other hand someone thought that he had seen him skulking furtively in ragged clothes.

We rang up a number of people and at last discovered a man who had visited Carstang only a fortnight before. He gave us the address and said that it was a horrible room in a miserable street and that Carstang, who looked very ill and was in bed, had fiercely refused any assistance.

We set off in the direction of the Old Kent Road. It was, I remember, the right kind of day for such an expedition—not a proper day for May at all, but dim and gritty, with a teasing exasperating little wind that blew dust and fragments of paper mournfully into our faces. On such a day London is truly obscene: she has no glory, no past history, no beauty of coloured smoke, opalescent street, bloomy cloud. I thought of the bomb in the air- raid. Well, this London to-day had escaped that—men crawled like worms, houses leered, filthy meat hung on the butchers' hooks, and the windows of the sweetshops were thick with creeping flies.

In a shabby street off the Old Kent Road we found the place; 35 Sebastian Road, it was, I think. The house was led up to by some dirty steps and on these a cat and a filthy-faced child were very happily playing. Outside a window at the very top was a bird-cage and in it a canary or something sang like mad. Curious on this grim, smoke-clouded day! The dirty-faced child was pressing the middle of the cat's back into the stone step and the cat seemed to like it, for it was purring and looked at us with a winking gaze of quite idiotic pleasure.

A woman with gigantic breasts suddenly appeared at the top of the steps and screamed:

'M'rier!' The child paid not the least attention, but with its black-grimed hand pressed the cat the harder.

We asked the woman whether Mr. Carstang lived here. Yes, he did— top floor but one…. But she hadn't set eyes on him for days. How was that, we asked her.

Well, she began, her arms akimbo. She was one of the nicest women, kindly, humorous, and thoroughly contented with her lot. She told us so, and her eyes beamed good-nature on all the world. She had ten children and her husband was a strong man on the music-halls. We asked her again about Carstang.

Her smile thinned. She scratched her bosom. Oh, yes, poor gentleman. He hadn't paid his rent for ten weeks, but as her two elder boys were earning and her husband getting jobs

(' E can lie with 'orse and cart and two men on 'is chest. 'E can, straight'). Then she added, laughing heartily: 'No wonder I got ten kids. Although they do say these strong men ain't much as lovers. I could

tell different.' She informed us that they should have moved to a better neighbourhood by now. They could afford to. But there it was. They'd sort o'

got used to the house. Been there fifteen years and you wouldn't believe 'ow large it was. They could take in a dozen lodgers including their own family and ...

Once again we enquired about Carstang. Ah, poor gentleman, he was a bit odd in the head. No doubt of it. Latterly he wouldn't have anyone in the room. Cooked his own food on the gas-stove, but it was her conviction that there wasn't nothing to cook. Hadn't a bean in the world, she believed. They'd HAVE to ask him to go if he didn't pay up—or a bit of it anyway. But she'd be sorry. Sort of class he was, and kind to the children ... wonderful kind to the children and they took to him, ugly though he was. And that reminded her

—she hadn't set eyes on Mr. Carstang for three days or more. When was the last time? Was it Sunday he came down in his pyjamas to borrow a paper?

And real bad he looked too—yellow, and his glasses shining and the top of his head naked. She must ask 'Enery. So at last we all moved into the house.

Henry appeared in a singlet and an old pair of trousers. He looked a very nice strong man indeed, with a great chest, arms like pillars, and thighs like the towers of Ilion. He had a most good-natured grinning countenance and all the hair on his head stood up interrogatively.

We all waited at the bottom of the stairs, listening.

'Three days, is it, or four?'

The strong man scratched his arm.

'Aye—it'll be more than that.'

We all stood listening. A little man, a flight up, appeared and stood listening too. He was apparently a lodger.

We listened some more, then the strong man said: 'Well, we'd better go up and 'ave a look.'

As we went up the stairs we could hear the canary singing like mad. The cat, freed of the child, was following us. I could see now that it had only one eye.

On the second floor a lady joined us. She was wearing a dressing-gown and very soiled white slippers that flapped on the stair.

On the third floor was Carstang's room. The strong man went to it and knocked.

'Mr. Carstang! Mr. Carstang!'

We all listened. There was no answer—only the canary singing.

' E may 'ave 'ooked it,' said the lodger.

'Doesn't seem like it,' said the strong man, and now he banged on the door, making a terrific noise through the silent house. The cat rubbed its back against the door, arching its tail and seeming terribly pleased about something!

'Mr. Carstang! Mr. Carstang!'

'Better break the lock,' said the strong man, and, with a huge heave and thrust, he did. The cat led the way. There was a foul smell. In the half-light I saw Carstang hanging from a short rope tied to a hook in the wall. His body ever so slightly swayed. His tongue stuck out from between his teeth. His head was a little on one side and his naked toes were rigid and a little crooked like question-marks. He was in pyjamas, but what I saw at once was that he was not wearing his glasses. His eyes stared at us—they were rather small, very innocent, childish; stared at me as though they said: 'You've never seen me until now. This is what I am. Take a good look.'

I describe these details not for any morbidity but because this was what Cornelius saw and never again forgot.

The strong man cut the body down with his pocket-knife, carried it reverently to the dirty bed and laid it down there. Then he covered the face with a torn and tattered towel. There was scarcely anything in the room; only, very pathetically to me, the little chest of drawers and a small table by the bed were painted a bright blue. They had been painted quite recently.

On the table was a note and, surprisingly, it was addressed to Johnny. He opened it, read it, and handed it to me.

DEAR JOHNNY—Forgive me. Mad with hunger, disappointment, the evil falseness of this bloody world. Glad of your success really.

'Excuse me, sir,' the strong man said. 'The police will have to see that.'

'Yes,' said Johnny.

Then he spoke to the lady of the house, addressing her as though he had known her all his life.

'He was a genius. He was really. Only nothing went right for him. It was my fault. I ought to have helped him.'

'Poor gentleman,' said the lady, crying. 'He was that kind to the children although 'e 'ad a temper when 'e was roused. We'd have given 'im something if we'd known. Most certingly we would, only I'm that busy ... '

We all went out because the smell in the room was so bad. The lady went for the police, and the strong man stood on guard.

I have said already that I do not think that poor Carstang's indictment damaged Johnny. The Police Commissioner and his like threw it, in all probability, immediately into any waste-paper- basket, never having heard of Johnny. Editors and such had little time for it. Johnny's friends and acquaintances found it at once too mad for seriousness.

And yet it helped to build up that atmosphere of queer 'difference' that hangs now, at this time, about Cornelius. After all, it is not only three volumes of short stories that make him, these many years after his death, in a world so sadly convulsed and perilous, the figure of strange interest that he is. I doubt whether a copy of the Carstang thing, other than my own, exists anywhere to-day. Certainly no one dreams of accusing him of desertion of his mother, or pederasty or robbery. Yet every word written about him in these last fifteen years has made him a figure out of one of his own fairy-stories.

Perhaps this book too....

He said to me only one thing about Carstang's death.

'It was my success, or what he thought was success. He couldn't stand it.

Success is more dangerous than failure, you see. The one thing I thought was that I could begin to do some good now— people and things I could help. But Carstang kills himself.'

All the same, in the autumn of this year 1920, there was one joyful affair: the adventure of Port Merlin. And I, by a lucky chance, shared in it.

He was receiving, of course, every kind of invitation, to lecture, to read his fairy-stories, to be a guest at this and that public dinner. He was a dreadfully bad lecturer. I would have thought that the element of the actor in him would have helped him. It did not. He stammered and stuttered, shifted his long legs, giggled from nervousness, stopped and looked helplessly about him. He read one of his fairy-stories, though, excellently, and no one could be happier or more charming than he when he was in the company, intimately and easily, of people whom he trusted. Then he would talk, and tell stories and throw his head back, laughing, and grow excited and unself-conscious—

simply because he thought he was among friends. But if, on an occasion, someone accidentally aroused his suspicions or angered him by what he thought was an impertinence, then he shut up like one of his father's shell-

boxes. Lady Max, Mr. Schaaf, Reiner—those were the recurring types that frightened him. To nobody did he tell stories so admirably as to old Ralph, who was now bed-ridden with arthritis in a little flat near the British Museum. He was always going to see Ralph in these days. I fancy that Ralph seemed to him a closer resemblance than anyone else now alive to Charlie.

The one other place where I found him at his best and happiest was at Gwen's. Gwen Christian now ran a boarding-house in South Kensington, and Johnny would go in there and have a meal with the boarders and chaff them and tell them tales and be one of them, as though he had no other life in the world. But the great attraction was young Charlie, Gwen's baby— always known as Young Charlie and promising to be just like his father. He was a thick-set square baby with hair 'like a young duckling's' and there he would sit, sucking his thumb, not uttering a word. But he adored Johnny.

Then this invitation came to go to Port Merlin and open the new Public Library there. Johnny was simply delighted. I think that, secretly, he had been

waiting for some sign from his old town. The last time he had been there was during the War—in 1915 or 1916. Oddly enough, Mr. Abel had been visiting there and Carstang had come up from some place in Cornwall. I have mentioned the photograph of the three of them bathing together. He'd been nobody then. Now, for once, he was glad that he was somebody—not because he wanted to show off, but because—because of everything that had ever happened to him in his youth.

Fortunately Mercia had gone on a cruise with some very grand people to the Greek Islands. Otherwise she would have come too. He invited Anne.

'No,' she said.

'Why in heaven not?'

'I'd rather not; besides, I am very busy at the office.'

I knew why she wouldn't go. She was right.

So it was Johnny and myself.

'There's one good thing about being a novelist,' I said. 'You can go anywhere you want to, any time you want to.'

'Can you?' he said, looking at me wistfully.

At the Merlin station there was a small gathering of people to meet us.

Johnny was dressed with neatness on this occasion—in a dark- blue suit and a dark-blue tie. There was never a hat that didn't look absurd on him, but he always took it off as soon as he got out of anything, a train or a car. Often he threw it on to a bench or left it in a room or dropped it (sometimes, I think, purposely).

I've forgotten the names of the people at the station, but there was a very stout man with a red face and a chin so deeply cleft that his countenance seemed to be in constant danger of splitting in half. I remember that, because Johnny's eyes constantly wandered to this oddity. I remember, too, that on the way to the car he said a number of times, 'You know, I never read books—no

time, no time at all.' 'I'm no reader. No. Haven't a minute to spare,' and seemed immensely proud of the fact.

There was also a very important lady who was dressed in a costume so rich and rare that she SMELT of newness. I have never known anyone so grand, and as she was tall with a very fine bust it was surprising to hear her speak in a little thin languid voice as though she were a young lady serving (because times were difficult) in a tea-shop. She looked at me with great scorn and I don't think that she thought VERY highly of Johnny. She was, we discovered, a Miss West-Darling (they had been once the grand people here but were now reduced rather).

On our way to the car a little anxious man who, like the Ancient Mariner, must at one time or another have shot an albatross (or at least a seagull), so nervous and apprehensive was he, confided to me that it had been very good indeed of Miss West-Darling to give up her time to come on this Committee.

'Why,' I asked, 'is she so very busy?'

'Oh yes, indeed. She's President of the Glebeshire Archaeologist Society.'

'She doesn't LOOK like an archaeologist,' I said.

'Well, of course, the West-Darlings are among the very best families in the South of England.' He confided also to me that she had come on this Committee with some reluctance because she didn't really believe in fairy-

tales. 'She says that she's going to tell Mr. Cornelius so.'

'That's all right,' I said. 'He doesn't believe in them either. What DOES she believe in?' I asked him.

'She thinks novels ought to deal in facts—real life, you know. We had a very interesting conversation about it.'

'Do you agree with her?'

'Oh, I do, I do. As long as it's not indecent, you know.'

'Ah,' I said gravely. 'That's the problem.'

All the ceremonies of the day seemed to myself to have this slightly absurd inconsequence. But then I was bewitched perhaps by the extraordinary beauty of the weather. I caught Port Merlin, too, before it had been finally swamped by the waters of modern improvement. Under this warm September sun everything sparkled and shone. The little town seemed to be linked so closely to its sea- waters that you could hear the boom and surge and scutter in the very heart of the High Street. Constant vistas of their deep blue and sunny glitter broke between walls of houses and at the end of its little streets. There was a constant whiff of sea-salt and you felt as though beneath your boots there was the crunch of sea-sand.

And in what an ecstasy was Johnny! I had not seen him so happy since the party in Mercia's house. When he was happy he was charming and everyone felt his charm.

Up through the High Street we drove and at one point Johnny touched Miss West-Darling's arm.

'Do you know, Miss West-Darling, that it was just here the funniest thing happened to me when I was a child? I was walking with my father and your mother was driving—'

'It was my grandmother, I think.'

'Oh, your grandmother. Well, I had run out into the street and your grandmother's horses came charging right down on me, and when your grandmother saw that I wasn't hurt she gave me half a crown.'

'Did she really, Mr. Cornelius.'

'Yes, but father was angry and threw it into the road.'

'Did he indeed?'

'Yes. You see, he was very independent.... Oh, there's the Town Hall—and it's still got the clock with the brass figures playing the drum and the fife!'

'Yes, we have tea in the Town Hall after the Ceremony,' said the red-faced

man with the cleft chin. 'The new Library is quite close at hand. There'll be a goodly gathering for the Ceremony, I don't doubt. Our town knows its duty

—'

I was aware, in fact, that the Committee considered itself of far greater importance than Johnny, and I a little resented it. But Johnny wasn't aware of it. He was aware of nothing but that he was home again, and so happy was he that he would have embraced Miss West-Darling had she wished him to do so. That was far from her desire, however. I could see that she thought Johnny very odd-looking and just the kind of person to write fairy-stories.

She also probably remembered that his mother had been a washerwoman.

It was all very different when we arrived at the Ceremony. Here Johnny had a true welcome.

In the space outside the new Public Library a large crowd had formed. There were all classes of people, many children too: some had their hands over their eyes because the sun was shining so brightly, a number had their mouths open, and most of the women were smiling. When Johnny stepped on to the rather rickety wooden platform with the Mayor and the Headmaster of Rush's Day School (where Johnny himself had once been) everyone clapped like anything and some of them cheered. For Merlin had not possessed a real celebrity for hundreds of years, not, maybe, since John Curley, the Demon Sailor, and there was something in Johnny's simplicity and unpretentiousness that they took to at once.

Then the young Headmaster of Rush's made a speech about him. They said that they must all be very proud indeed to have Mr. Cornelius here to-day.

He was a writer who, in a remarkably short time, had become world-famous.

Indeed he understood from the newspapers that his book of fairy-stories The Bright-Green Shoes was now sweeping America and had already been translated into a number of foreign languages. They all knew what a beautiful book it was, the kind of book that was especially needed in these days because it appealed to the best in human nature, and everyone, whatever his or her age, could enjoy it. They had, too, especial reasons for being proud because so much of it had sprung from Mr. Cornelius' childhood days in Port Merlin. That had already made their town interesting to a great many people and it would increasingly do so to a great many more people. They were

extremely proud that Mr. Cornelius was a citizen of their town. He said something about the Library and added that the Mayor would kindly say a few words. So the Mayor, who was pursy and scant of breath, stepped forward and said that he was proud that he was Mayor of Port Merlin and that he hoped to continue to be proud so long as he was Mayor.

Then Johnny came forward and was himself surprised at the really tremendous outburst of applause. He stood there grinning, and shifting from one foot to another and swinging his arms a little. Then he made one of the shortest speeches ever recorded. He said that he was jolly glad to be there and very glad to open a new Library because he thought there weren't enough Libraries, but for the most part he was thinking of some of his friends who had helped him when he was young; and he wished that Mr. Bartholomew and Mr. Darlington and Mrs. Winchester and Mr. Sam Beakin and Miss Ada Montgomery were here with him now. And he thanked them all very much.

Of course no one present knew anything of the names he mentioned (even little Mr. Bartholomew was forgotten), so that part of his speech meant very little, but everyone was very glad that nobody had spoken at great length and therefore the applause was very hearty.

After that Johnny moved across to the Library, followed by the Mayor and the Committee, unlocked a door with a new key, and declared the Library open. Then they all walked inside and inspected the Library.

Next there was tea in the Town Hall, and Johnny grew very uncomfortable while a succession of persons told him how wonderful his fairy-stories were.

As with every other author, so Johnny found it very difficult to answer these congratulations, because if he said: 'Yes, they are very fine,' he was considered conceited; if he said: 'They're very poor really,' he was said to be mock- modest; if he said: 'Thank you very much,' it was considered stupid, and if he said nothing at all he was held to be very rude.

As soon as we decently could we escaped, said good–bye to our friends, refused several invitations; Johnny also was photographed a number of times in the company of the Mayor and the Committee.

Then came a wonderful moment when, free of everyone, we wandered down

the hill towards the sea.

'If we're quick,' Johnny said, 'we'll have time to see my mother's cottage and then, before the light goes, the Tower.'

'The Tower?'

'Yes. The Tower, where I taught the boys. Where I knew my mother was dying.'

The late autumn afternoon lay in a gold–crushed peace and splendour upon the earth. There was the hush in the air that often comes before real autumn sets in. The light was bronze, although the sea was so still a blue, and every house and tree and the very stones in the road had the ringing reflection of bronze–shielded cool strong light in their outline. When we came to his cottage the stillness was broken by the near rhythm of the sea, and a gull circled over our heads, making itself no sound, but, as it swooped, we heard the strong indifferently–contemptuous beat of its wings.

The cottages were still standing (there are redbrick workmen's houses there now). We couldn't go in, of course.

'So here I was born,' Johnny said. 'May the Twelfth, Eighteen Eighty–four.

Not that it matters except that it doesn't seem long ago. Up that little path my father would carry me and put me in that sheltered corner of the sea–wall and I'd look out to the Lion Rock.... Our cottage had calico window–curtains of red roses and green leaves. Mother was very proud of them.'

We stood there in silence, and the only thing he said was:

'My mother and father were awfully good people.'

We spoke scarcely at all as we walked by the sea, through some fields and then climbed the gentle rise of Sale Head. The Tower stood away from the house where the school had been, in a field by itself. The sun, sinking over the sea, flooded the fields with light, but the Tower itself was quite black. It was a little bent, as though it were listening, and when you were close to it, you saw that its colour was pearl–grey but in its shadows orange–tinted.

Johnny went to it and pressed his hands against the stones. He stood with his face touching the ivy that embraced it.

At last he turned round to me and said rather wistfully: 'I do wish Charlie had been here to–day—don't you?'

I knew that he had been thinking of him all the day long.

CHAPTER VI

Anne

In the spring of 1921 Cornelius published another novel, The Three Beggar-

Men, and in the autumn of the same year another volume of fairy-stories, The Flight of the Wild Swans.

The Three Beggar-Men received very much more attention than had any other novel by him. It was reviewed everywhere on the day of publication and at length. The reviewers (again with the exception of Stromberg) were kind and even reverential. Nevertheless it was clear that they did not want the book, nor did the General Public. All that they wanted from Johnny were fairy-stories, and when The Flight of the Wild Swans appeared with, once again, pictures by Luke Smith, the excitement was wonderful. Luke Smith's pictures were even better than before, and two or three of Johnny's stories—

'The King and the Two Shoemakers,' 'The Crab with the Broken Claw,'—at once were ranked with the very best in the first volume.

I think that this failure of the novel (because, in spite of amiable reviews and announcement of huge 'printings' by the publisher, it always becomes quickly clear whether a novel is a failure or no), this second rapturous greeting of the fairy-tales sickened Johnny almost to craziness. He caught now that most fatal of all author-diseases, the conviction that he was unjustly treated.

He had not had it—or at most light-heartedly—in the early days of his failures; now, although he said very little, we could detect a kind of cynicism quite new in his character. And, in a way, he was justified, for The Three Beggar-Men was, in all respects, his best novel. His best and most disregarded! The character of Campion in this book—a portrait quite obviously drawn from his beloved Herman Melville—was a magnificent thing. There is, perhaps, something of Carstang also in Campion, and I can see now, very clearly, what for some reason I did not see at the time, that The Three Beggar-Men is a kind of romantic plea for all the misjudged, unhappy,

deformed, lonely artists of the world—and it may be that the three principal figures in the story, Campion, Hazard and Rockage, stand for Melville, George Gissing and himself....

It must not be supposed that Johnny showed us any self-pity. He did not pity himself in the least. He began to be much more like someone entangled in a host of perplexities from which he was always struggling to free himself.

In the first place he seemed to be quite unable to deal with his position as a public man. He hated and loathed any kind of public appearance, but again and again, if someone caught him alone or wrote an especially tactful letter, he would be moved and feel that the cause was a good one and want to help, and then, at some later date, there he would be, entrapped into some public function, uneasy, bewildered, halting. I used to think sometimes of that long, lanky, bright-eyed boy he had once been, standing up to sing or recite or act, intensely determined 'to win people over.' But now he was continually winning people over by his shyness, his modesty, his eagerness to be kind, and then running away in terror from the success that he had himself created.

He LOATHED his success. He hated the way in which what he said was wrongly reported, the hideous photographs of him that appeared in the papers, the foolish false things that people said to him, the way in which everyone took it for granted that he must be LOVING his success, the inevitable jealousy that less apparently-successful people felt for him, the general acceptance that he must himself think his work 'wonderful,' whereas, in fact, he thought nothing of his fairy-stories.

All this absurd noise and fuss seemed to him to stand in the way of everything that he wanted to do and to be. He longed—oh, how he longed—

for the old days when he had lived (hoping passionately for the very thing that now he had) with Charlie in Soho.

He began to retire—gently and sweetly, but quite firmly—from all of us. I think that he saw less of Gwen's baby and of Anne. I fancy that Sir Donald, with his clear common sense, absence of all melodrama, loyal good heart and wise experience of life, was of greater use to him just now than any other man. The older writing- men gave him nothing any more. He knew every shape and colour of Bertrand's would-be cynical and realistic narrative, Rose's romanticism, my own sentiment, Albion's English landscape.

One new acquaintance he had whom he intensely admired—B. J. Ward, the author of, perhaps, the best poem, the best book of criticism, the best poetic drama in our post-War literature. Johnny was one of the earliest in his enthusiasm for Iron Country which was published about this time. And, as much as the work, he admired the man's character—his modesty, allowance for others' weakness, rectitude, gentleness of heart.

He went, once and again, to have a meal with Ward in the City, for Ward was at this time, of all things in the world, on the Stock Exchange.

Otherwise he made no new friends. I began, I will admit, to be deeply worried concerning him, not only because I felt that our friendship was less honest and frank than it had been, but because I was afraid for him. I had heard from him by now the story of Baupon which I have earlier related, and I knew of course about his grandfather.

So, as Anne could not, or would not, tell me anything, I went to see Mercia. I had tea alone with her and found her radiant.

'Well, how's Johnny?' I said at last.

'Johnny? He's splendid! Haven't you seen him?'

'Not so much as I did.' (I could see that she was pleased with this.)

'Well, he's so much in demand now. Although I've never known anyone so loyal to his friends as Johnny is.'

'Do you think he likes all this hullabaloo?'

'Naturally he does. It's what he's wanted all his life long. It's brought him out.'

She beamed at me benevolently. 'I have an apology to make,' she said.

'Yes, you have. For hundreds of things.'

'Oh, you stupid man! As though we didn't understand one another perfectly.

No, what I mean is that you were quite right and I was wrong. About Johnny, I mean. I never properly understood him before. Johnny is a darling. There's no doubt about it.'

'What's made you change your opinion?'

'Johnny himself, I imagine. Of course I always believed in him. I knew he had genius, but I was disappointed, I suppose, because he couldn't find his right medium. And success has brought out only the best in him. He's so sweet, so gentle and so nice to everybody. We went down for a weekend to Clare Longworthy's the other day and you wouldn't believe how charming he was to everybody. And he doesn't see all those terrible people any more. I know some of them were friends of yours, but you must admit … '

'Did he really enjoy Clare Longworthy's?'

'Loved it! Positively loved it. They all made a tremendous fuss of him.'

'Splendid!'

'There's only one thing.' She leant a little towards me. 'He will go out walking at night.'

'Walking.'

'Yes. He says he can't sleep unless he does. He walks up and down the streets by himself. Of course it's all right, but several people have seen him—and it looks odd. That's the only thing—he says he sleeps badly. What I want is for him to go on a cruise. Clara and Beaty Murray, and Cuckoo Beaminster—one or two more—are thinking of making up a party.'

'So you're happy now, Mercia?'

'Oh, well, it's not good form to say you're happy, but why not confess it?

Johnny and I are the happiest pair in the world.'

'Grand. I'm so glad.'

I had heard something about these walks of Johnny's. Anne had said something. Ralph too. Ralph, lying now on his back all day, did a good deal of thinking, and most of it, I fancy, was about Johnny.

'I don't like it,' he said. 'He was in here the other day and I don't think he's happy. He's been out several times with that man Abel, whom I don't like and never have liked.'

'Abel?' I said, startled. That was the last name I had expected.

'Yes, he goes round with him sometimes when he's preaching. He collects crowds, you know, and it's been my experience that anyone who collects street crowds for his own personal vanity isn't much good. You may think it's to the glory of God, but really it's to the glory of yourself. Anyway, what's our Johnny doing with all that riff-raff?'

He turned over in bed and went on with his crosswords. Crosswords, detective stories and his friends were now Ralph's principal occupations.

And then one night I myself saw Johnny.

I was walking through Covent Garden on my way home. It would be, I think, about ten o'clock at night, and it was a wild windy evening. There were very few people about and the clouds were racing overhead, plaguing a pale watery moon that seemed to be imploring them to let her alone. The houses seemed small and mean under those clouds and sometimes there were heavy sulky spots of rain. On the other side of the street, walking slowly along, was Johnny. I recognized him at once. I thought at first that I would go and speak to him, then I decided to follow him.

He came to the end of the street and stopped. He turned and bent down and I saw that there was some huddled figure in a doorway. I saw him leaning over, saw a white face under a dingy ragged bonnet, saw him give her something and then go on.

I followed him across the market and there, under an arch, were three or four more figures. Here also he stopped. Then we continued a long weary way. At last I caught up with him. He was delighted to see me.

'Why, what are YOU doing here?'

'I was going home, and then when I saw you I had to speak to you.'

'Why, of course! Dear old chap! I AM so glad!'

'But what are YOU doing, Johnny?'

'Oh, I don't know.... I can't bear to think of these poor devils....'

We walked along, his arm in mine.

'But what ARE you to do? They tell me it's all wrong to give them money.

That they only drink it away and it's worse than before. But why shouldn't they have a drink if they want one? They say one ought to help the Charities.

There are splendid ones. I know there are. But that isn't any use to me, somehow. I don't seem any good at anything that's organized.'

We were walking slowly along. The rain was beginning to fall.

'Shall we get a taxi?'

'No. Let's walk a little bit. You don't mind getting wet, do you? I AM so glad to see you. Where have you been lately?'

'Mercia tells me you're very busy now—house-parties and all sorts.'

'Oh, Mercia! ... She's awfully good. There's ONE person I've made happy by my success anyway. And I owe her a lot, you know.'

Then he suddenly said:

'I walk at night often. It's the only way I have of being alone.'

'Why don't you go away for a time?' I asked.

'Yes, I'd like to.... Perhaps I will one day. Only,' he added, laughing, 'Mercia would want to come too.'

'Well, she mustn't,' I said sternly. 'It would do you good to be away from Mercia for a bit. You mustn't be weak about Mercia, Johnny.'

'No. Perhaps you're right. Only,' he looked up at me rather timidly, 'she's the

one person I seem to be of much use to now.'

'There's myself and Anne and Gwen and Ralph and—'

'You're all my friends. That's different. Of course I like being with you, but Mercia's my job—the only one I seem to have really.'

The rain had stopped, the moon was shining fully, and Leicester Square was empty and glittering like a pool in a forest. It was a short while before the theatres came out.

'Soon this will be filled with people again,' he said. 'Aren't there a lot of people in London?'

'A terrible lot,' I said.

'Yes, it's rather terrible, isn't it?'

'If you went somewhere quiet for a bit—like Connemara or Skye....'

'Yes, that would be lovely,' he sighed. 'But I have the tiresome feeling that I ought to be helping in some way—that it isn't right to be doing nothing. And yet I don't know what exactly to do. Everyone has all sorts of suggestions, of course. I have a silly idea that what I OUGHT to do is hidden just round the corner. But perhaps it isn't.'

'How are you now?' I asked him. 'Does your heart ever worry you?'

'Oh, a bit, sometimes. But it's nothing. Don't tell Mercia about it, will you?'

We reached my flat and I asked him to come in, but he wouldn't. As he got into his taxi he gave me an affectionate, merry, almost mischievous look.

'By Jove, it HAS been good seeing you,' he said.

I realized that it was not only the fairy-stories that made and increased his fame, but his personality also. There's nothing more interesting, as you go on through life, than to watch the way in which certain persons are picked out for fame and others of equal merit altogether neglected. This has nothing to

do with history or even a star-dust fragment of immortality. But once and again someone appears who stirs curiosity with his every movement. Robert Louis Stevenson was an example of this, and after his death there was a wide decrying of his talents because his books were seen for the first time without the glittering colour of his living figure.

Something of this kind was now happening to Cornelius. Papers constantly had paragraphs about him. He was caricatured and drawn, and the drawings looked like caricatures! There was his odd history and perhaps something from Carstang's indictment. But most of all there were the millions of people who, the world over, felt from the fairytales that they knew him personally and that he was their friend. It is this crowd-contact—this feeling of affection and individual possession—that has led, in these later days, to the mad worship of the stars of the cinematograph—a thing so ephemeral and transitory that the stars themselves must often feel mocked by it. With Cornelius it was not so ephemeral, for into these fairy-stories he had put, without knowing it, his real self. Because he hadn't known it or sought for it, his real self was there. But in his novels, where he had striven to be himself, there was unreality.

How he hated this public contact and applause I did not realize wholly until I had the strange and moving scene with Anne which I am now going to describe as fully as I can....

It was some fortnight after the occasion of my meeting Johnny in Covent Garden and I was working in my flat about ten-thirty in the evening. The manservant knocked on my door and came in.

'Well, what is it?' I asked sharply, because I hate to be disturbed when I am working.

'There is a lady in the hall, sir, and she says she must see you.'

I thought at once of Anne—and she was indeed, at this time, never out of my mind. I went into the hall and there she was, in her day clothes and looking greatly disturbed.

'Come in, Anne. What is it? You look tired. Sit down there. Have a drink.'

She sat down, took off her hat.

'Yes, I will. Thank you. I've disturbed you. You're working. But I won't even apologize. I had to see you. It's about Johnny.'

I sat very close to her and longed to put my arms around her, as I had so often longed to do. But her distress was far away from me in her mind. I was her friend, though. She had come to me before anyone else in the world and I was thankful for that.

'What about Johnny? He isn't ill or anything, is he?'

'No. Not ill. Except that there's always his heart. But he's been with me just now and in the most awful state.'

'Tell me about it.'

She drank her whisky and soda, and some colour came into her cheeks.

However old she grew and however many experiences she had, there was always a great deal of the child in her, and that especially when she talked of Johnny.

'It was like this. I had just come back from work and was going to change. I was going to a Prom concert with Hilda Baynes. There was a ring at the bell and I called out to old Mrs. Holly, who was fussing about in the kitchen, that I wasn't in to anybody. She opened the flat-door and said something, but a moment later Johnny had brushed past her and come in.

'"Can I speak to you, Anne?" he called out, and I answered back cheerfully,

"Of course. I'm changing. I'll be with you in a minute." But I didn't change. I don't know why. There was something in Johnny's voice that frightened me. I went straight in and there he was, looking as though he had run a hundred miles; he was walking about the room. It's a wretched little room, you know.

No place for anyone to move. He looked at me and said: "Anne, will you come away with me—now, to-night?"

'"Come away?" I said. "Where?"

'"Anywhere—miles and miles—to the other end of the earth."'

Anne turned to me and held out her glass for another whisky.

'I'm trying to tell you exactly how it was,' she said. 'Perhaps I'll forget something, but it's mostly correct.

'Now you know—all my life long I've wanted him to say just those words to me. I've waited and waited. But I tried to behave decently, so I said: "Sit down, Johnny, and tell me what you mean. Of course we can't go away together."

'But he wouldn't sit down.

'"Why can't we? Why can't we? Of course we can."

'Then he beat his hands together. He came to the sofa, sat down and put his arms round me and I could feel that his whole body was trembling.

'"You're part of me and I'm part of you. We were like that always, you, I and Charlie, and now that Charlie's gone there's only you and me. I can't stand this, Anne. I can't stand it! I can't really. It's all wrong and I'm all wrong. I can't hear a thing for the noise and I can't be myself anywhere—they make me false, they are killing me, Anne—killing all the reality in me. If I don't get away I'll die." He went on like that, holding on to me, shaking....

'"Of course I'll go, Johnny. I'll do anything you ask. It's always been the same."

'Then he began incoherently to pour out his thoughts. I can't tell you how mixed up it all was. I didn't understand it all and I don't remember it all now.

He talked a lot about some soldier who had died when he was in a hospital in France, and he hadn't been able to help him as he ought, and then there was an extraordinary story about some place in France where he'd sat with some people—'

'Baupon,' I said.

'Yes. Baupon. Where he was at a hospital. An extraordinary story like a

dream—'

'It WAS a dream, I think.'

'And then there was a lot about Carstang—how he'd been responsible for his death. Then more about that Abel man, the preacher. How he'd listened to him and talked to him and that wasn't real either. Then he began again about our going away—at once, at once—to the uttermost parts of the earth, he said.'

'Poor Johnny,' I said.

'Well, he quieted a little then and I got him a drink and some fruit. He sat there, just as he used to sit in Merlin, his eyes staring out of his head, eating fruit off the plate....'

She stopped there, I remember. She turned her head away. I could see that she was trying very hard not to cry. I saw her shoulders heave. Oh! how I longed to comfort her!

'And now comes the rest of the story,' she went on. 'I behaved like a fool. I always do. I always have. I suppose it was seeing him sitting there eating like a little boy. And I've loved him always, remember—all my life long. And I'd waited a damned long time. Anyway I couldn't help it. I put my arms round him, I drew him close to me, I stroked his hair, I kissed him. And I knew at once, as any woman in the world would know, that he didn't love me. I was his friend and, now that Charlie was gone, his closest friend, but he didn't love me as I thought of love, and he never had…. That didn't make any difference, you know, about my doing what he wanted, anything he wanted.

But I didn't cheat myself. To go away with him would be hell for me always

—always, and he wouldn't be happy either. He said, "Dear Anne. Dear Anne."'

She waited a long time before she said another word. There was a silence that seemed endless. Then she said:

'The rest of it was this. I got up and put the plate on a table. Then I said:

"What about Mercia, Johnny? How will she feel?"

'He stayed there looking down at the carpet, and at last he said:

'"Yes, Anne. She's been good to me, hasn't she?"

'I said that I didn't like her and that she'd never understood him, but all the same she'd done her best by him, I thought.

'"So it's like that, Anne," he said at last. "Either way—whether I go or stay it's pretty bad."

'He was ever so much quieter now, but he looked terribly tired.

'"I suppose running away's pretty cowardly?" he said, as though he were asking a question.

'"I'll do whatever you want," I said. "Now and ever."

'"Yes, I know you will," he said. "And so would I for you, Anne." He got up and kissed me of his own free will, a brotherly kind of kiss.

'"Yes, I mustn't do anything to hurt Mercia," he said, as though he were considering. Then he thanked me and kissed me again and went away. He left me in a state of terrible distress, you can understand. He looked so tired and lonely and troubled. I had to come straight to you because you're the best friend I have, after Johnny of course.'

I find it very difficult to describe with any reality the anxiety that I now felt about Cornelius. For one thing it is all a long time ago. For another if you did not know him you may say with justice that he was not the first to feel that the world was not made exactly to his design, that indeed he should have been pleased with the luck that had come his way and settled into it. Indeed he felt very acutely all that criticism himself as I will soon show.

There was, however, something real and general in his trouble, something that is as old as the mastodon, and older, but something that has increasingly attacked our post-war world. It is the disease of HOMELESSNESS. Very many of us seem today to belong to no place, no purpose, scarcely to ourselves. We look at ourselves in a mirror as though we were reflections of

ourselves. There IS the reality somewhere to give us that reflection, but WHERE is the reality?—and as we are, all of us, posturing before mirrors at one and the same time, we destroy one another's chances—for reality can be found only when we are completely and in isolation ourselves. In our anger and disappointment we break the glass of our mirror and are surprised that even the reflection is gone.

But my fear for Johnny was much more active and personal. He was very unhappy and bewildered and, with his ancestry and in his loneliness, might do something desperate.

Charlie would have been the man for him here, but Charlie was gone. I loved Cornelius as I have never loved another man. I can't say why, except that he was very kind and generous, impractical and easily taken in and exceedingly honest and quite ridiculously faithful. These opposite things made him very dear to me and to several others, but he had not many friends at any time in his life. And I would like to make very clear that there was none of the whimsical oddity, or charming infantilism, that you will find in characters in novels by Rose or plays by Sir Richard Hanson. He was awkward, angular, suddenly abrupt, often anything but charming. He was a very lonely man; the whimsical heroes of the romantic novelist always secretly delight in their own company.

In any case I began now to be very nervous and frightened for him, and London, in that gloomy and sun-forsaken winter, became a sinister place to me. I dreamt of him constantly. One dream in especial I remember, when I was walking along the shore in Merlin on a dull grey day, the sea booming with that hateful, self- satisfied indifference that the sea can have. A gull flying seawards appeared suddenly perplexed. Although it had the whole sky for its province it beat now here, now there. I saw its eyes and they were terrified.

I thought it would sink into the sea from very exhaustion. Then, quite suddenly, its doubt and confusion were gone. It rose and, with steady and confident drive, bore out to sea. I was intensely happy at its release and woke full of relief and joy.

I saw Johnny once or twice. We had no serious talk. I puzzled my brains as to

what I could do for him and for Anne.

The solution came, but it was through no thought or action of mine.

CHAPTER VII

...with That I Awoke

On the morning of December 5th of this year 1921 I received the longest and most personal letter that I have ever had from Cornelius.

I think, perhaps (although I have not known it until now), that the whole of this book has been written TOWARDS this letter. And nevertheless it may appear to some readers that the letter is of little importance. I am myself too close to judge.

The letter has neither date nor address. It is as follows: DEAR H—,

I am quite alone in the house to-night or at any rate I feel quite alone. Mercia is away with the Rowlandsons in Kent. I had meant to sit down and read, and in fact I have been reading a little, Fitzgerald's Letters—and then I came to this bit: 'And three nights ago I looked out at about ten o'clock at night, before going to bed. It seemed perfectly still; frosty, and the stars shining bright. I heard a continuous moaning sound, which I knew to be, not that of an infant exposed, or female ravished, but of the sea, more than ten miles off!

What little wind there was carried to us the murmurs of the waves circulating round these coasts so far over a flat country. But people here think that this sound so heard is not from the waves that break, but a kind of prophetic voice from the body of the sea itself announcing great gales.'

I had got so far when I laid the book down (it is page 184 of the first volume of the Eversley edition, if you want to look it up). I think you should, just to make your obeisance to Fitz, who is the real father of this letter to you. I laid the book down and thought of Merlin and Charlie and then of you. And I looked to where Yin USED to be (I think I'm going to ask you to give him back. You've had him for three years. It's a healthy sign for me to think it's

safe to have him here, isn't it?), and I said to Yin (for Yin is all-pervasive; there's no place where Yin isn't), 'I think I'll write to the man.' Can't you see Fitz sitting in that stuffy room of his, the curtains (dingy old things I bet) not drawn, and he looking at the starry sky, going to the window and opening it, sniffing the frost and then hearing that faint long- drawn moan of the sea across the flats? Anyway I wanted to tell you to read the Letters and that's why, under Yin's command, I moved to the writing-table. But now that I have begun and have got the Introduction over, I want to go on.

You remember, that night we met in Covent Garden, you hinted that I'd been deserting you a little, not only you but all my old friends? I knew that you were unhappy about me—that all of you were—and that I had been withdrawing from you. I would like to try and explain a little. This letter is a kind of apology really— Lord knows what it will end in! You've been a little unhappy; well, I've been unhappy too!

Now I think there are two unforgivable things (there are probably many more, but here at least are two!). One is to think that you are unique when you are unhappy, the other is to burden other people with that same unhappiness. Well, one of my excuses is that you're my friend—my real true life-long friend and nothing can touch our friendship. The other excuse is that I think from now on I'm going to be able to remove my unhappiness.

Perhaps unhappiness isn't the right word, though—it's more bewilderedness, a sense of entanglement, a kind of imprisonment almost. Mind you, I'm young yet, I'm not forty, although sometimes I feel ever so old, but that, I expect, is because I began life so young.

It's because I don't think my case unique that I dare to tell you about it. You know a lot about my youth now; you've been awfully good in being interested because Charlie and Anne knew it anyway, and there was no one but you I cared to talk about it to. Of course I was the most awful sentimental, idealistic, ingenuous kid, H—. I was sure I was a genius when I wasn't. I believed in everyone I met till they stepped on me. BUT THAT ISN'T THE

POINT. The point really is that I was always certain that there was a miraculous state of being just round the corner if I could only find it. When I was a child in Merlin, when I was with Lady Max and then with Reiner, when I was in Soho with Charlie, I was always sure that this wonderful

PLACE was about to appear. I was always in this excitement of expectation, just as Aunt Hunnable expected the Second Flood. And, mixed with that, was my love for, and confidence in my fellow human beings. There are two things I've found that you can't, in these days, talk to others about without making a fool of yourself—love of God and love of Man. You could once. Chaucer and Donne and Bunyan and Wesley and Wordsworth and Dickens didn't have any fear of it, and weren't fools either.

But right up to the War I was sure that God was good and that my companions on this earth were nobly to be loved. The trouble is, H—, that I'm still sure I'm as certain of both things as that Fitz heard the sea moan across the Suffolk flats. But I'm lost now. I'm confused. There is so much noise around me. I can't hear myself speak. I don't know the way to the place where, quietly and without any fuss, I can stand and listen and know those two things to be true.

You know that I've failed altogether in what I meant to do. Nobody wants my REAL work. I expect it's bad and Stromberg has always been right, but even though it IS bad the good thing is inside it— and I might go on and learn to bring the good thing out, so that everyone would see it, but I'm discouraged now. I've lost heart. For ten years I've done the best I can and it's no good—

even YOU know, loyal though you are, that it's worth nothing. Then on top of that I bring this success about my head with little stories that any child could write. I'm ashamed, bewildered. I HATE this success. I must run away from it or I'll die. I see myself in public—I stand outside myself, watching myself—

and I see the false smile and I hear the false voice. 'Thank you so much,' I say. 'Oh, thank you so VERY much!'

Oh, H—, old man, I MUST be quiet in a real place. Because, near me, so little a distance away, IS reality. Baupon—I told you that story in your flat that night. I know you think I dreamed it all— perhaps I did—but don't you see that that makes no difference? Whether real or a dream, in that happy moment I shared in the real life. He blessed me at that table. My friends sat about me. There was a silence in which everything that is true and lovely and of good report could be told. I know that to so many men and women this seems so foolish that the very mention of it is exasperating to them. Donald Winchester, who is the best old man I have ever known or ever will know,—

honest, kind, loyal, noble—has no place for such imaginations. 'If there is nothing after death,' he tells me, 'I shall be at peace. And if there IS

something it will be time enough then....' Well for him and for all good people who think like him, but don't you see that we, each one of us, have our own personal experience to deal with? And that I, having once known what that is, must somehow somewhere find it again. It may be logical enough.

They say that nothing is past and over, and I may have broken through into a real Feast that He once held in such a place, and is for ever holding. They talk about 'Above the Battle,' but I think that it is really 'Below the Battle'—that just below all this noise and confusion and hatred the real life is continuous, always there waiting for us to find it.

I have told no one of this but you and Anne—and I would have told Charlie if he had lived. Dismiss all this as nonsense if you like. Just take it that my problem is how to find peace somewhere. Everywhere the noise is increasing.

I think the world of men is entering on a long stage of anarchy and cruelty and confusion, while they learn to condition themselves to the new shapes and sounds and devices that have come on them so suddenly.

But as I am writing to you so privately and you are my friend, it is perhaps not selfish to put my personal case. I want to help; I want to be of good in the world, but I am stopped on every side. I won't say anything about Mercia, although that marriage was the greatest mistake I ever made. You know well it was. Why did I do it? I suppose because I was already, by then, afraid of what I might become. I thought that through her (and she seemed good and kind and friendly), I might be a useful citizen and do my part normally—yes, and write my great books in the peace she would give me (that's ironical, isn't it?). And now it has so happened that she is the only human being I've made happy. If I leave her I'm false to the only person I can do good to. Did Anne tell you that, half crazy one night, I went to her and begged her to go away with me to some far-distant place where no one would know me and want me to say thank-you? And then she kissed me and I knew and she knew that it would be no good. And I can't leave Mercia anyway. So here I am—and for many past months I've thought that I was going mad like my grandfather before me. But it isn't so bad after all. Now, in these last days, something has told me to be patient. There's some solution coming. Everyone is given their conditions within which they live—and THOSE are the conditions they are

given— none other. All my life seems to have led me to this point. I have been always so fussy, so eager to make my OWN terms, so rebellious if they haven't been what I wanted. I see now that it must be the other way round.

I've always thought fidelity was the thing—fidelity to work, to people, to ideals. But only now at last I understand the greater fidelity—to life itself which is, I believe, given to me to use in such a shape—yes, in just this shape and no other. It may be that with death only I will find reality, and my friend sitting at the table head.

But, by God, H—, I won't write any more fairy-stories. I won't really. And I won't read them to people at house-parties and I won't be a public person. I'll have to tell Mercia, won't I, that we must compromise. I'll take up fishing, perhaps, and at night while they're playing bridge or backgammon I'll go in for astronomy. I'll have a telescope a mile high and sit in the very lap of Sirius.

Have I preached to you? Well, if I have I don't care because you're a good soul and can remember Charlie showing Anne how to build a bridge and you know that once I sang 'Weep no more, sad Fountains' in red tights in Merlin.

So I can't be a prig, can I? We'll see each other often, won't we? Perhaps you'll learn to fish too. And I'm happier than I've been for many a day. When I'm eighty like Sir Donald, I'll be the wisest, cheeriest, soberest old man in the world—if there's any world left by then.

Your loving

JOHN.

After reading the letter my impulse was to go at once to him: he would be home, I was sure. But certain things kept me. There was a piece of work that I wanted to finish, and maybe Mercia would be at home, and perhaps Johnny would be shy of his letter, now 'the morning after,' and in any case I would be seeing him very soon— and so—and so—I didn't see him. How often, how deeply I have regretted it!

Three days later was December 8th. I saw in my engagement-book 'Lady Lettice Craven, 62 Grosvenor Street.' Then I remembered. This was an invitation to a function, the sort of function that I most greatly disliked. It was

a Charity Party for some Children's Hospital, and Lady Lettice, who was a good woman (and incidentally a friend of Mercia's), had thought that it would be charming for the children of the wealthy to help the children of the poor.

Tickets were a guinea apiece, and purchased, of course, by the wealthy mothers of the wealthy children. There was to be a conjurer. And—now I remembered—Mr. John Cornelius himself would read one of his fairy-

stories.

I thought rather ruefully of Johnny's letter. He had been caught, I supposed, by Lady Lettice in one of his impulsive affectionate moments—or more probably Mercia had driven him into it. I knew well enough with what agony he must at this moment be regretting it.

And so I thought I would go. I had already answered his letter but now I might have a word with him. And perhaps the presence of a friend might help him through. It was a dark December day with a threatening of snow in the heavy brown air, but the

Grosvenor Street house was warm as a tea-cosy and so brilliantly lit that we seemed to move in the very heart of the great glass lustre candelabra that hung from the drawing-room ceiling. There were a great many elegant children, numbers of nurses, ladies and a few gentlemen.

Among these last to my puzzled amazement I saw Stromberg!

What on earth could he be doing there? And then I remembered that, behind his gruffness and pugnacity, he was said to have an especial interest in Children's Hospitals. He was an old man now and I had not seen him for a year or more. But he seemed to me very much finer than he had ever been.

He had lost the old semi-shaven, ragged-collar carelessness. He was, it is true, wearing rough brown country clothes, but they suited him with his brown cheeks and snow-white hair.

Then I saw Johnny, looking nervous and unhappy, a book in his hand. I went up to him and at the same time Stromberg joined us. He greeted me and held out his hand to Johnny.

'How do you do, Mr. Cornelius? We haven't met for a long time. And I hope you bear me no malice.'

Johnny took his hand and looked with smiling friendliness in his face. They

made a strange contrast, I thought—Johnny so thin and delicate, Stromberg so vigorous, thick-set, self-confident.

'Why, no, of course not, Mr. Stromberg. But I'm sorry you've got to hear me read one of the stories you so much dislike. But perhaps you won't. Go away and smoke a cigarette till it's over.'

'No, I won't.' Stromberg smiled and put his hand on Johnny's shoulder. 'I expected you to cut me. But there's nothing personal in my dislike of your books. You're an incurable romantic, you know, and I've been fighting romanticism all my life.'

'Yes,' Johnny said. 'Such a lot of energy on your part and with so little result.'

Stromberg laughed, and I could see how much Johnny liked him—his oldest enemy, unless you count Mrs. Hoskin.

Then it was time for Johnny to begin. The children were all arranged on the little gilt chairs facing the magnificent Gainsborough over the fireplace, their elders grouped behind them. Johnny stood on a little improvised platform that would be used afterwards also by the conjurer. He opened the book and began to read 'The Crab with the Broken Claw.' I looked across and gave Mercia a smiling greeting. I had never seen her more happy and confident.

Her cup of joy was full.

And then, from the very start, everything went wrong. For one thing Johnny was odd to look at from a child's point of view. The brilliant lustred light shone on his long nose, the Gainsborough lady stared down at him disdainfully. Then, at a function of this kind, he was never at ease. If there had been half a dozen of us in a little room he would have read it beautifully, but the theatrical gifts of his childhood seemed, in his later years, to have turned on him and mocked him.

Then these were sophisticated modern children who were developing under the good modern theory that a child must not be inhibited. So these were NOT inhibited, and what they wanted they asked for, and the way that they wanted to behave they DID behave. Alone, with a governess or nurse, when listening to a story was an alternative to going to bed, they might have listened and even enjoyed. But now, in this brilliant lighted room, they

wanted to show themselves off and be noisy; in any case they preferred tea and a conjurer to this nervous ugly man who read so fast and so clumsily that they couldn't hear what he said.

Disorder broke out. A little boy laughed. Then a stout little girl, whom I had already noticed, pushed another little girl until she fell with a scream off her chair, began to cry, was rescued by a nurse. Johnny stopped. Everyone was greatly distressed.

Lady Lettice in her soft muffin–voice said: 'Oh, I AM so sorry, Mr.

Cornelius.'

Order was restored, it seemed. Johnny (his eyes, I fancied, now maliciously humorous) began again. Alas! there was mischief in the air. A boy giggled aloud, a little girl was whimpering, and then two children began actually to struggle together, pushing their chairs and snatching at one another's ribbons.

It was very strange; I had been at many children's parties but never at one like this.

Johnny closed his book, grinning broadly upon everyone.

Lady Lettice came forward. She was dreadfully upset and her pretty boneless face was flushed with dismay.

'Really, Mr. Cornelius, I can't tell you—'

'Oh, but I sympathize so truly with the children. They don't want a fairy–story at a time like this. Why should they?'

The children seemed to like him when they were close about him. They began to press round him, and he, now entirely happy and at his ease, to laugh with them.

Nevertheless, the affair had been disgraceful and ladies began to crowd around him and tell him how they loved his books and they heard that Dimitrieff was making a ballet from The Bright–Green Shoes and ...

But Lady Lettice rescued him from this.

'Mr. Cornelius, while the children are going in to tea I wish you'd come and see our Giorgione. At least,' she went on, laughing, 'we are sure it IS a Giorgione. But you know what the experts are.... It's in the Library.'

He was looking tired, I thought. As we moved out of the room he leaned for a moment on my arm.

'It's not in there.'

'Those children ... ' I began indignantly.

He laughed. He seemed strangely happy as though he'd heard a piece of good news.

'Why, no. They're perfectly right. You can't take children in. They know those stories are all bunkum.'

He pressed my arm affectionately.

'Thank you for your letter. Everything's fine.' Then lower: 'You bet—this is my last public appearance—my VERY last.'

The Library was a fine room with deep long windows. Over the stone fireplace was a picture of great loveliness, a Madonna and a Child seated under a tree with a gentle tender landscape in the background.

Johnny said to Stromberg, who was with us:

'You know, Stromberg—now I look at you—you're just like a man in a dream I had once—a dream I had in France in the War.'

Stromberg laughed and said:

'Why didn't we meet before? I'd have understood you.'

'We HAVE met,' Johnny said.

'But I mean really—a long evening over a pipe—when we could have argued our heads off.'

We three moved to the window. Outside it was very beautiful, for the lamp from the street threw up an arc of light like a fan of shining metal. Against this, as we watched, the snow began to fall, flakes of dead whiteness against the dark trees, descending into the arc of light as into a cup to be absorbed and disappear there.

Johnny watched, his lips parted in wonder.

'Oh, how beautiful!' he said.

His face at that moment was radiantly happy. I have liked to think since then that in that instant he had a vision of all the beautiful things that he had ever known, the froth of the sea breaking on the Merlin shore, the Lion Rock that he watched from his corner in the sunny wall, his father at the little table making his shell-boxes, the gaslit smell of the footlights as he sang 'Weep you no more, sad Fountains,' the first ride with Aunt Hunnable through the London streets, the sunlit Downs as he approached Reiner's, Charlie's face as he learned that the book was taken, little Rabelais the soldier telling him his story, the gates of the château at Baupon—all forming in that arc of light against the dark....

He turned into the room again, the happiness still shining in his face. Then, as I watched him, it changed. His brows puckered. He gave a little cry.

Stromberg moved to him, saying, 'What is it?'

Johnny's hand was at his breast. I saw a spasm of sharp agonizing pain strike him.

Stromberg caught him and held him. Johnny sank on his knees.

'My heart!' he said. 'Hold me! ... Hold me!

And he died in Stromberg's arms.

Later, they wanted to put up a tablet to him in the Merlin Church. The affair was in my charge, and I chose a sentence from Galleon's essay on Herman Melville.

On the tablet were the words:

JOHN CORNELIUS

BORN MAY 12, 1884

DIED DECEMBER 8, 1921

'It may be said of him truly that he loved his fellow-men, but with equal truth that he was always a stranger in the world that they had made'

Anne Swinnerton died of pneumonia in Madrid in 1923. Gwen Christian died in 1929, and Mercia Cornelius was killed in a motor- accident in 1932. It happens therefore that I am the only person alive now who knew John Cornelius intimately.

That is my excuse and my defence for having written this book.

Many people thought that Cornelius' death was cruelly sudden and that he was cut off at the very beginning of his real career. I myself feel that he had given the world, in his fairy-stories, the work that he was intended to do. He would never have gone beyond these, I think.

In his personal life he was, I am sure, after his experience at Baupon, Charlie's death, and his awareness of the complete failure of his marriage, a restless stranger on this earth. His experience at Baupon was real to himself and that is all that here need concern us—and, after it, all his earlier realities, his personal ambitions, his anxiety for his material happiness (which was never very strong) faded ...

I have been occupied here with no purpose other than to try and make my friend alive for those who never knew him.

I like to think that, in a world of new experiences, he is working creatively—

happy, faithful and busy. He is, I hope, in company that he enjoys, and is amused a little, ironic, perhaps, and eagerly expecting the next adventure.

Made in the USA
Las Vegas, NV
23 September 2024